The American Campaign ★

Second Edition

The ★ American Campaign

Second Edition

U.S. Presidential Campaigns and the National Vote

JAMES E. CAMPBELL

Texas A&M University Press
COLLEGE STATION

This paper meets the requirements of
ANSI/NISO Z39.48-1992 (Permanence of Paper).
∞ ♻

*For a list of available books in this
series, see the back of the book.*

Library of Congress Cataloging-in-Publication
Data

Campbell, James E., 1952–
  The American campaign : U.S. presidential
campaigns and the national vote / James E.
Campbell.—2nd ed.
      p. cm.
  Includes bibliographical references and index.
  ISBN-13: 978-1-58544-644-5 (cloth : alk. paper)
  ISBN-10: 1-58544-644-0 (cloth : alk. paper)
  ISBN-13: 978-1-58544-628-5 (pbk. : alk. paper)
  ISBN-10: 1-58544-628-9 (pbk. : alk. paper)
  1. Presidents—United States—Election.
2. Political campaigns—United States. 3. Voting—
United States. 4. Election forecasting—United
States. 5. Political science—United States. I. Title.
  JK528.C36 2007
  324.70973—dc22
                            2007012869

To my mom,
Mary Campbell,
to my brothers,
John, Bob, Dick, and Stephen,
and
to the memory of my dad,
Wallace J. Campbell Jr.

Contents

Figures

Tables

Preface

This book came out of a life-long fascination with presidential campaigns and an enduring ambition to find some order out of what appeared to be chaos. One of my earliest memories is of an editorial cartoon about the 1956 Eisenhower-Stevenson campaign. Many years later I studied with Tom Patterson and Bob McClure at Syracuse University and worked on their media and elections project for the 1972 campaign, a project that culminated in *The Unseeing Eye* and Patterson's follow-up study of the 1976 campaign, which he reported in *The Mass Media Election*. My thinking about campaigns was certainly shaped by these and other experiences, as well as many observations along the way.

More concretely, this project evolved over about a decade. It began with a pair of papers I wrote on convention bumps and election forecasting (J. Campbell, Cherry, and Wink 1992; J. Campbell and Wink 1990). The presidential election forecasting project was stimulated by other forecasting research, particularly that of Michael Lewis-Beck and Tom Rice. At about the same time, in reaction to news media comments about the effects of political conventions on the poll standings of the candidates, I decided to examine the history of convention bumps more systematically. The project sought to determine not only whether conventions bumped up their presidential nominees' poll numbers but also what affected the size of these bumps and whether the effects of conventions survived to election day or were merely temporary bursts of enthusiasm that quickly faded. In chapter 7 of this book I have reanalyzed the convention bump phenomenon.

I also began thinking seriously about the relation of election forecasting to campaigns after considering some reactions of several prominent political scientists to the growing field of election forecasting. Several scholars voiced the opinion that election forecasting was not the business of political science. In their view, political science is the business of explaining and not predicting politics. This view seemed both overly narrow to me and dismissive of the potential value of forecasting for the explanation of elections and campaigns. In this regard, I was heartened and intrigued by the research of Andrew Gelman and

Gary King, who attempted to explain why presidential elections could be forecast so accurately while the pre-election polls remained so volatile.

Tom Holbrook's book *Do Campaigns Matter?*, the first comprehensive and rigorous examination of presidential campaign effects in decades, heightened my interest in extending my research on election forecasting and convention effects. Holbrook's book and his equilibrium theory of elections quite directly connected the forecasting research to campaign effects. The book inspired me both by what it accomplished and by what I regarded as its missteps. Based on my reactions to Holbrook's book and my thinking stimulated by the criticisms of election forecasting research, Tom Mann and I wrote a piece for *The Brookings Review* prior to the 1996 election on the lessons learned from recent experiences with election forecasting models. I refined and elaborated a bit more on some of these lessons in a presidential election forecasting article, which was published in *American Politics Quarterly* before the 1996 election. That article and a chapter on the scientific implications of election forecasting are included in *Before the Vote*, co-edited with Jim Garand (1999).

Along the way, I realized that I also had pedagogical reasons for writing this book. Since 1980 I have taught courses on elections, campaigns, and voting behavior. During this time I wanted to use a book in these courses that systematically examined presidential campaigns in a way that was well integrated with voting behavior research, that offered a plausible theory of macro-level campaigns compatible with theories of micro-level vote choice, and that provided a systematic and hard-nosed analysis of campaign effects but also offered perspectives on the rich history of political campaigns. I wanted a study that combined the scientific rigor and theory of voting behavior with the historical richness of traditional campaign research. There have been many excellent books written about presidential campaigns, but none accomplished what I envisioned, and so this is the book that I have tried to write.

Since the first edition of this book was written before the 2000 election, there have been two more presidential elections and a considerable amount of additional research on presidential campaigns, including a good deal of my own research that followed up on points raised in the first edition. Virtually every chapter of this edition reflects these new data and additional analyses. The core of the book, the theory of the predictable campaign, however, remains unchanged.

I began writing the first edition of this book at Louisiana State University in the fall of 1996 and completed it and the revisions for the second edition after I joined the faculty of the University at Buffalo, SUNY (still known to many outside Erie County as SUNY–Buffalo). I appreciate the research support that I received at both of these institutions, as well as the support I received in the work leading up to this project while at the National Science Foundation. I want to express my gratitude for the support and advice of my former colleagues at LSU, Jim Garand and the late Gene Wittkopf. I also particularly want to acknowledge the good work of Frank Zagare, Franco Mattei, Chuck Finocchiaro, as well as my other colleagues at UB. It has certainly been a pleasure to work on this book in such a hospitable, professional, and supportive environment.

A number of people helped in one way or another in this project, and I would like to thank them. First, there are many political scientists whose work on voting behavior and presidential campaigns influenced me. The names of many of these scholars can be found among the references at the back of the book, but several deserve particular mention. Among these are Alan Abramowitz, Paul Abramson, John Aldrich, Herbert Asher, Larry Bartels, Louis Bean, Bill Crotty, Bob Erikson, Ray Fair, Steve Finkel, Mo Fiorina, Tom Holbrook, Bill Jacoby, Gary King, Mike Lewis-Beck, Tom Mann, Bill Mayer, Bob McClure, Helmut Norpoth, Ben Page, Tom Patterson, Nelson Polsby, David Rohde, Daron Shaw, Stephen Wayne, Christopher Wlezien, Gerry Wright, and Bruce Keith and his collaborators on *The Myth of the Independent Voter*. Like anyone working in the field of elections research, I also owe a debt to the researchers responsible for several of the classics in the voting behavior field. These scholars include Paul Lazarsfeld, Bernard Berelson, and their collaborators; V. O. Key Jr.; and Angus Campbell, Philip Converse, Warren Miller, and Donald Stokes (forever known more simply to psephologists everywhere by their "Tinker-to-Evers-to-Chance" string of last names).

It was my good fortune to have mentioned this project to Professor George Edwards of Texas A&M University, who put me in touch with Professor Jim Pfiffner of George Mason University, the general editor of this series, and Mary Lenn Dixon, the editor-in-chief at Texas A&M University Press. Jim, Mary Lenn, George, everyone associated with this series at Texas A&M Press, and the reviewers have been a real pleasure to work with in turning my manuscript into a book. They have all helped to make it better, and I greatly appreciate their efforts and advice.

Over the course of working on this book I have been fortunate to have had the assistance of several very able and diligent graduate students. Ken Wink and Lynna Cherry at LSU coauthored with me some of the early research that eventually led to this study. While I was working on this project at LSU, I was also fortunate to have had the generous assistance of Phil Ardoin, Bill Blair, and Chad Long. Mike Mahar at UB was especially helpful in the later stages of preparing the first edition.

Several other institutions responsible for the original collection of the data used in this study deserve particular thanks. Gallup along with *USA Today* and CNN in recent years collected the trial-heat polls that are used here extensively. The Survey Research Center and the Center for Political Studies of the Institute for Social Research at the University of Michigan have been responsible for conducting the National Election Studies since 1952 with funding from the National Science Foundation since 1977. The NES and the Inter-university Consortium for Political and Social Research collaborated on the distribution of the data.

My wife, Susan Porter, exhibited great patience, provided much-appreciated support, and made many terrific pasta dinners while I worked away at this project. Ralph, Alice, and Iggy and now Rufus also are due gratitude for their welcome camaraderie. They all share in whatever credit this book receives.

Introduction

This book is about the effects of general election campaigns on the popular vote for the major-party presidential candidates in presidential elections. It makes two central points: that presidential campaigns typically have significant net effects on the division of the presidential vote and that these effects are to a large extent systematic or predictable. The systematic nature of campaign effects are the result of the fundamental conditions of political competition, presidential incumbency, and election-year economic conditions. These fundamentals are in place before a campaign begins and usually play themselves out or are incorporated into the vote during the campaign in expected ways.

The study tells us several things about presidential campaigns that we did not know before. First, while the finding that campaigns significantly affect the vote may not be surprising to some, it may be unexpected by others. Even for those who had no doubt about the efficacy of presidential campaigns, the study provides some specifics regarding just how great these effects have been in past elections. In fact, they have been generally greater than often supposed.

The systematic nature or predictability of campaign effects is perhaps less generally appreciated. Campaigns are often thought of as a collection of events emerging from candidate strategies that cannot be anticipated. Like a chess match, some moves in a campaign suggest countermoves, but how the game develops generally cannot be foreseen beyond a few moves. However, while this study finds that there are significant unpredictable aspects of campaigns, the effects of presidential campaigns are predictable to a greater degree than generally understood. There are four reasons for this predictability, and together these reasons compose the theory of the predictable campaign. First, the effects of campaigns are predictable because the effects of campaigns, though significant, are also constrained. They are constrained because many voters have decided how they will vote before the campaign begins. There are several factors leading to early decisions, the most important of which is partisanship. Most voters are partisans and most partisans find it easy to decide quite early on that they will remain loyal to their party. Second, if there is an incumbent president in the race, the campaign affects the vote with a tilt toward the incumbent because of the many advantages available to incumbent presidents as candidates. Third, reactions to the election-year economy become incorporated into voter decisions during the campaign and establish the general mood of the public toward the in-party candidate. As a result, the campaign tends to have more favorable effects for the in-party candidate if the election-year economy is healthy and fewer favorable effects if it is weak. Finally, every presidential campaign is highly competitive, and this intense competition tends to narrow the lead of the candidate who is ahead in the polls at the outset. Campaigns usually narrow the leads of frontrunners.

These findings address two common misunderstandings about presidential campaigns. These could be labeled "the journalistic misperception" and "the political science misperception," though there are certainly a wide variety of views about campaigns among both journalists and political scientists. A common view of campaigns among journalists seems to be that campaigns frequently decide the outcome of presidential elections and that the critical impact of campaigns depends on the highly unpredictable twists and turns of candidate strategies and unforeseeable events arising during the campaign. By this view, elections often turn on the inspirational speech, the regrettable gaffe, the brilliant maneuver, the key endorsement, or the bungled strategic move. Immersed in the day-to-day events of campaigns, close to the personalities involved, and particularly attentive to new developments and strategies, journalists naturally come to vest great importance in the particulars or idiosyncrasies of campaigns, perhaps more than is warranted.

Political scientists, on the other hand, have come to view presidential campaigns almost as rituals or spectacles having minimal effects on the actual results. They may inform voters, cause potential voters to turn out, or even disillusion potential voters when they grow irritated by negative campaigning, but campaigns have very little impact on the vote division between the candidates. There are several good reasons why political scientists have often come to this conclusion. The preeminence of partisanship guides voters to an early choice. Moreover, the propensity of voters to rationalize what they see in a campaign, along with the superficiality of campaigns and the way they are covered, means that campaigns transmit precious little information that would shake voters from their pre-campaign inclinations.

The theory of the predictable campaign provides a corrective to both the journalistic and political science misconceptions about campaigns. The theory of the predictable campaign, supported by the evidence in the following chapters, claims that the effects of presidential campaigns are smaller and much more systematic than the journalistic view would have it, yet larger than supposed by the conventional wisdom of political science. The major difference between the conventional view of political science about campaign effects and that which I propose is that the theory of the predictable campaign recognizes that a number of fundamentals in place before the campaign begins, such as the state of the election-year economy and presidential incumbency, affect or shape the course of the campaign and its impact on the vote. Previous examinations of campaigns have viewed these fundamentals as having effects on the vote that were essentially independent of what happened during the campaign. As such, campaign effects were underestimated by examining only those campaign effects that were not shaped by their pre-campaign context.

The book is organized around the theory of the predictable campaign. The theory is a macro-level theory grounded in the micro-level voting behavior model that draws heavily from *The American Voter* (A. Campbell et al. 1960) and work that has followed in its tradition. I have drawn on a variety of data and sources. I have used Gallup poll data collected since 1948, American National Election Studies surveys since 1952, Commerce Department economic data since 1948, and actual election returns going back as far as the presidential election of 1868. I have also drawn on a wide range of sources. These include a large number of journalistic accounts of campaigns in the tradition of Theodore White's *The Making of the President* series as well as first-hand accounts (such as James Farley's reflections on Franklin Roosevelt's 1932 and 1936 campaigns) and more general historical accounts, from Paul Boller's lively compendium of campaign anecdotes (1985) to Gil Troy's thorough history of campaigning by presidential candidates (1996). The study also draws on the several series of political science analyses of elections (from the *American Political Science Review* articles by *The American Voter* authors and their successors, the volumes by the Pomper group, the Nelson volumes, and Abramson, Aldrich, and Rohde's election books) as well as a wide body of related political science research, from research on partisanship to research on the effects of presidential debates.

As mentioned above, this book is in part a reaction to Tom Holbrook's book *Do Campaigns Matter?* Professor Holbrook and I deal with essentially the same question: to what extent do general election campaigns have an impact on the national vote? While the focus of the following chapters is on this question and related issues about the campaigns, the differences between Holbrook's analysis and that presented here may be of interest, particularly to those already acquainted with Holbrook's influential study.

In general, Holbrook and I reach similar conclusions about the impact of campaigns: campaigns do matter. However, we also differ in a number of important respects—in why elections can be forecast accurately, in our definitions of campaigns, in our theories of campaign effects, and in the measurement of campaign effects. Although the differences between my analysis and Holbrook's and their implications are discussed in chapters 2 and 3, four principal differences can be summarized as follows. First, the theories differ in their treatment of the pre-campaign fundamentals (the election-year economy, etc.). For Holbrook, they create an "equilibrium" that affects the election. For my theory, they affect the election directly but also affect the course of the campaign and voter reactions to it. Second, the theories differ in their definition of the campaign. In Holbrook's analysis, campaigns are a series of events. I regard the campaign as a time period encompassing events but other activities as well, such as any communication that might sway a potential voter's decision. Third, the analyses differ in their use of data. Holbrook examines time-series of polls. I examine the relation of polls at various times to the actual vote. The importance of this methodological difference is discussed in chapter 3. Fourth, the theories claim different general public opinion dynamics. Holbrook claims that momentum is at work in campaigns, poll gains beget more gains, and poll declines lead to further declines.[1] I claim, on the other hand, that competition narrows the frontrunners' leads in campaigns. The leads of frontrunners tend to dwindle even if they had recently registered poll gains. In addition, the analyses also differ in their evaluations of partisan dealignment, convention bumps, debate effects, and the media's impact on the campaign, as well as in the time span of elections examined. Tom Holbrook concentrates his study on the 1984, 1988, and 1992 election campaigns while this study examines campaigns from 1948 to 1996 and extends as far back as the campaign of 1868 in portions of the analysis (chapters 5 and 8).

The American Campaign ★

Second Edition

★ *Chapter 1*

The Impact of Presidential Campaigns

THE PRESIDENTIAL CAMPAIGN is the focal point of American politics. No other political event attracts nearly as much attention. It is the Super Bowl, the World Series, and, some might say, center ring of American politics. The centrality of presidential electoral politics in American political life is demonstrated by the turnout in presidential elections. Voter turnout in presidential elections routinely surpasses by a wide margin any other form of political participation by Americans.

Interest in presidential campaigns, moreover, does not end on election day. Presidential elections occur every four years, but their campaigns in some form are perpetually in progress.[1] Even before an election is over, speculation begins about who might make the run in the next election or even the one after that. Every major policy decision, every triumph or misstep by a national politician is read in the context of its implications for the next presidential election, and every act of every prominent politician is interpreted as politically calculated to achieve the upper hand in the next campaign. Despite the broad dispersal of governmental powers well beyond the presidency, presidential campaign politics permeate nearly every aspect of American national politics.

One reason that presidential election campaigns stimulate such interest is that they are dramatic events of epic proportions. There is conflict, from personality differences to fundamental clashes of world views. There are interesting characters, issues, strategies, and intrigue and all on a grand scale. There is also resolution, with definite winners and losers. Presidential campaigns can at times be great theater or, at least, great spectacle. None of these are good reasons for public attention, but better reasons exist as well. Certainly no office in

American government is as powerful as the presidency, and the election determines who will hold that office and what might be done with its powers. The presidential election also affects election to other offices, through something like presidential coattails (J. Campbell 1997b). It affects the course that the government will take over the next several years, and the policies put in place may profoundly affect future generations around the world.

Questions about Presidential Campaigns

Although often the subject of derision, with many Americans finding them to be "too lengthy, too costly, too nasty, and too silly" (Troy 1996, 4), presidential campaigns are nevertheless important. As such, there are many questions to ask about them and their role in representative government.[2] Do they help citizens effectively control the direction of the government? Do they educate the public about the great and vital public policy issues of the day or do they distract voters? Does the public learn about the important character traits, issue positions, and public philosophies of the candidates through campaigns? Do campaigns provide accurate and important information to voters or are they mechanisms for manipulating voters to think and act the way the candidates and their advisors want them to? Do campaigns mobilize citizens to get involved in politics or do they overwhelm and "turn off" voters? Do candidates learn much of value from voters as they crisscross the country seeking votes or are they simply going through the motions of mechanically repeating canned speeches for photo-ops and television sound bites? Do the rigors of campaigns discourage potentially great leaders from seeking the presidency or do they help to separate the truly committed leaders from the half-hearted?

All of these questions are important, but perhaps the most basic question of all about presidential campaigns is as Thomas Holbrook (1996a) quite simply and directly put it: do campaigns matter? This is also the central question of this book. Do presidential campaigns ultimately affect election results, who wins and who loses and by how much? Closely related to this central question is another: why or in what ways do presidential campaigns affect election results?

Given the great attention that presidential elections receive and the tremendous resources and energy poured into presidential campaigns, it would seem obvious that presidential campaigns must have substantial, perhaps even decisive effects on elections. However, this is not so clear. Ironically, as important as presidential elections are and as closely followed as presidential campaigns are, the impact of these campaigns remains in question.

Doubts about the Impact of Presidential Campaigns

Doubts about the effects of presidential campaigns on the vote in presidential elections arise from several sources. These doubts are embodied in "Farley's Law," an observation attributed to Franklin Roosevelt's campaign manager James A. Farley by historian Gil Troy. Farley's Law held that "most elections were decided before the campaign began" (Troy 1996, 191; see also Faber 1965, 186). From a more systematic perspective, some of the earliest scientific studies of voting also raised questions about the impact of presidential campaigns. These studies found that the net change in vote intentions during the campaign was small and that most voters made their voting decisions quite early in the election year. Paul Lazarsfeld effectively concurred with Farley when he wrote that "in an important sense, modern Presidential campaigns are over before they begin" (1944, 317). Later research emphasized that most voters enter the campaign with strong partisan attachments that usually guide their vote decisions. Accompanying this research was a theoretical explanation for why campaigns should have minimal effects on voters. Other research on issue voting in elections effectively relegated the campaign to a minor role by emphasizing the voters' retrospective evaluations of the previous administration. Most recently, doubts about the overall impact of campaigns have been fueled by presidential election forecasting models that have accurately predicted election results before the start of the campaign.[3]

Individual Vote Choice Stability

Early studies of presidential voting suggested that campaigns may only marginally affect the vote. The first of these was the landmark sociological study of voting, *The People's Choice* (Lazarsfeld, Berelson, and Gaudet, 1968, first published in 1944), a study based on a panel survey in Erie County, Ohio, during the 1940 presidential campaign between Democratic president Franklin Roosevelt and his Republican opponent Wendell Willkie. The main panel of survey respondents was questioned seven times over the course of the election year, every month from May to November.

The People's Choice found that the principal effect of the campaign was to reinforce or stabilize preferences, rather than change them. Most vote intentions of individual survey respondents in November were the same or about the same as they had been six months earlier in May. About half of those surveyed (49 percent) did not change their vote intention in any way between May and election day.[4] Of the remaining respondents who in some way changed their preferences, most did so only marginally, being undecided at some point or flirting with changing their vote choice.[5] Only 8 percent definitively changed their minds. These "party changers" initially indicated a vote intention for one party's presidential candidate and later favored the opposing candidate.

Although about half of the electorate changed their vote intentions in some way between May and November (using a seemingly generous definition of change), this overstates the amount of significant preference change during the general election campaign. Since respondents were first questioned in May, well before the first party convention and the start-up of the general election campaign, the lack of an early preference by some is quite understandable and might not even be counted as a real change attributable to the campaign. Those who apparently wavered in their vote choice also may not be strictly counted as changing. Even without considering the contribution of measurement error to this total, wavering preferences might be better considered as reflecting uncertainty about preferences rather than campaign-induced change. Only the so-called party changers (those who first indicated that they would vote one way and then decided later to vote another way) appear to be likely cases of the campaign affecting the decisions of voters.[6] Moreover, since the study used a very early start date for examining change in vote intentions—before many voters would have been certain about who the two major-party presidential candidates were—even the 8 percent of changers probably exaggerates the true amount of campaign-induced change.

The aggregate or net effect of campaign-related change is even smaller than the amount of individual or gross effects of the campaign. With fairly liberal assumptions—accepting May as a very early starting point for the campaign, taking the change in reported vote intentions from May to November at face value, and attributing all of the vote change occurring during the campaign to the campaign itself (as opposed to survey error or simply a reconsideration of preferences)—the campaign shifted only about four percentage points of the vote from Roosevelt to Willkie.[7]

Small campaign effects are also evident in recent elections. Table 1.1 demonstrates the vote intention stability for the 2004 presidential election. The table cross-tabulates the pre-election intention of voters with their reported vote as they indicated it in the post-election survey. Stable vote intentions are those on the table's northwest to southeast diagonal. The figures are the percentage of all respondents who indicated that they would vote for president and who then reported that they did vote. Adding up three groups of voters whose vote choice was unchanged from their earlier vote intention, nearly 94 percent of voters in 2004 had stable vote intentions through the campaign. Among the small minority of voters who changed or made up their minds between the pre-election and post-election surveys, Kerry gained .8 of one percentage point (picking up 3.0 but losing 2.2 of those who had intended to vote for him),

Table 1.1. The Pre-Election Vote Intention and the Post-Election Reported Presidential Vote, 2004

| | | The Post-Election Reported Presidential Vote | | |
		Bush	*Kerry*	*Other*
The Pre-Election				
Intended	Bush	47.9	1.6	.5
Presidential	Kerry	2.2	45.3	.0
Vote	Other	.6	1.4	.5

Note: Each number is the percentage of all respondents with the indicated vote intention and reported vote choice. The table includes only those reported voting. The data are from the NES 2004 survey and have been weighted to correct for the difference between the national reported and actual vote percentages for the candidates.

Bush gained .7 of one percentage point (gaining 2.8 but losing 2.1 of his intended vote), and minor candidates lost 1.5 percentage points of the total presidential vote. The net impact of the 2004 presidential campaign was to leave Bush's 2.5 percentage points of the vote lead over Kerry virtually unchanged.

Early Vote Decisions

Both *The People's Choice* as well as the follow-up study *Voting* (Berelson, Lazarsfeld, and McPhee 1954), which examined the 1948 election, found that nearly four out of five voters say that they made up their minds by August of the election year, after the second nominating convention and just before the traditional kickoff of the general election campaign.[8] *The American Voter* (A. Campbell, Converse, Miller, and Stokes 1960, 41), in examining the 1952 and 1956 elections, also found that a majority of voters claimed to have reached an early decision.[9] Subsequent studies (Asher 1992; Holbrook 1996a) have confirmed the prevalence of early vote decisions.

Table 1.2 presents the distribution of self-reported times of the vote decision for voters in the American National Election Studies (NES) surveys since 1952. These data indicate that most voters make up their minds quite early in the election year. Anywhere from half to four-fifths of the electorate report that they decided who they would vote for before or during the parties' conventions.[10] In most years, roughly another fifth indicate that they decided after the conventions. As few as one in ten and no more than one in four voters said that they made their vote decisions in the last weeks of the campaign or on election day.

While the data indicate the prevalence of early vote decisions, there are reasons to suspect that even this understates how early most vote decisions are usually made. First, of the five elections in which more than a fifth of the

Table 1.2. Reported Time Voters Decided Their Presidential Vote Choice, 1952–2004

Reported Time of the Vote Decision	Percentage of Voters in Presidential Election														Mean
	1952	1956	1960	1964	1968	1972	1976	1980	1984	1988	1992	1996	2000	2004	
Knew all along	32	45	25	18	21	33	20	20	30	15	19	28	12	34	25.1
Before conventions	4	15	6	23	14	11	14	20	22	17	21	23	32	22	17.4
During conventions	32	19	31	25	24	18	21	18	18	29	14	13	10	15	20.5
After conventions	21	12	26	21	19	24	22	15	17	22	22	17	23	15	19.7
Last two weeks	9	7	9	9	14	8	17	17	10	12	17	12	18	13	12.3
Election day	2	2	3	4	7	5	7	9	4	5	8	7	5	2	5.0
Total	100	100	100	100	100	100	100	100	100	100	101	100	100	101	100.0

Source: The American National Election Study's website and calculated by the author.

electorate decided in the last weeks of the campaign (1968, 1976, 1980, 1992, and 2000), four involved the complication of a major third-party candidate (the exception being 1976). Many of these very late deciders may not have been deciding whether to vote for the Democratic or Republican presidential candidate, but whether to vote for the third-party alternative. Second, there may be a difference between the reported and the actual time of decision. Given the social norm of giving all sides a complete hearing before reaching a firm decision, some voters may say that they decided later in the election year than they actually did. In short, usually a substantial majority of those voting reached their decision about how they would vote early in the election year.

The report of predominantly early decision-making by voters, along with the observed small amount of vote intention change taking place during the campaign, raises serious doubts about the influence of campaigns. Campaigns may reinforce and stabilize many existing preferences, they may manifest some latent views and move others to act on their intentions, they may even on rare occasions cause a few to shift their vote intentions, but they apparently do not cause voters as a group to shift their support appreciably from one candidate to another.

A Stable Partisan Electorate

Doubts about campaign effects on election results were heightened by *The American Voter* (A. Campbell et al. 1960) study's findings of the pervasiveness, stability, and impact of party identification on partisan attitudes and vote choices. An electorate that is highly partisan, that holds firmly to its party identifications through many presidential campaigns, and that views and evaluates political events, policy issues, and political candidates in partisan terms does not leave much room for the effects of a particular campaign. The fundamental stability of partisanship is at odds with the fluidity inherent in the ups and downs of a campaign.

The path-breaking collection of studies in *Elections and the Political Order* (A. Campbell et al. 1966) provided additional grounds for skepticism about campaign effects. Philip Converse's concept of the normal vote, an aggregate baseline measure of partisanship's effect on the national vote, suggested a stability in political judgments that minimized the likely impact of short-term campaign effects.

Complementing the evidence of long-term partisan effects on the vote was evidence that short-term forces in elections made only marginal effects. Angus Campbell (1966) laid out the conceptual framework by using the normal vote to classify elections, identifying those in which the minority party won without a realignment changing the normal vote as "deviating" elections. Donald

Stokes (1966) then examined the variation in the national vote around the normal vote to determine the likelihood of a deviating presidential election. His analysis determined that the minority party had only about one chance in four (27 percent) of winning a two-party popular vote majority. Moreover, since pre-campaign factors, such as initial assessments of the presidential candidates or economic circumstances before the campaign season, probably contributed to the chances of a deviating election, the likelihood of the campaign itself swaying voters from their partisan predisposition seemed rather remote.

The Minimal Effects Conundrum

Another study in *Elections and the Political Order* also provided an individual-level theory of political information processing that supplied yet additional reasons to suspect that campaigns have minimal effects. Philip Converse (in A. Campbell et al. 1966) developed a theory to explain why partisan attitudes remained stable despite the heavy flow of political information during campaigns, much of which is intended to disturb or change preexisting attitudes and vote intentions.[11]

The theory of minimal effects is built on four interrelated and eminently reasonable premises. The first two of these involve the effects of an individual's interest in politics. The first premise is that a person's political involvement or innate interest in politics positively affects how much he or she knows about politics. People naturally tend to know more about what they find interesting. Second, a person's level of interest in politics positively affects how much new politically relevant information the person picks up and digests. People naturally follow more closely subjects in which they are interested, and they are likely to acquire and understand more new information about those subjects.

The third and fourth premises of the minimal effects theory concern the impact of prior political knowledge and newly acquired campaign information on the likelihood of someone changing their opinions. The third premise is that the more someone's opinions are grounded in a great deal of prior information, the less likely he or she is to change those opinions. If a person knows a great deal about something and has formed a view about it, that view is likely to be more definite and fixed. On the other hand, views that are not anchored in a great deal of prior information may be more easily changed. Some opinions of this sort may be so lightly held that they barely qualify as opinions at all.[12]

The final premise of the minimal effects theory is that acquiring new information increases the likelihood of attitude change. The more new information that a person learns, the more likely that some of that new information will challenge preexisting views. Conversely, if a person learns nothing new about a subject, there is no reason to change any opinions.

Figure 1.1. The Minimal Effects Theory of Political Campaigns

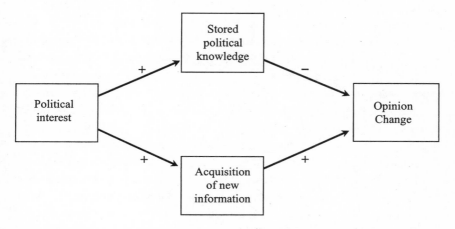

Source: Constructed by the author from Converse 1966a. For a more complete version of the model see Campbell 1997b.

While the third and fourth premises of the theory apply to all sorts of political opinions, the opinion of central interest is the intended vote choice. The more knowledgeable someone is, the less likely that person is to change his or her vote decision (by the third premise). The more new information a person comes into contact with, the more likely that person is to change his or her vote decision (by the fourth premise). The effects of campaigns are minimal because both the *positive* effects of new information on vote intention change and the *negative* effects of prior knowledge on vote intention change spring from a common cause: the voter's political interest.

Figure 1.1 casts the four premises in a simple causal model. The extent of a person's political interest is suspected of having a positive effect on both the amount of knowledge about politics that the person has already accumulated and the amount of new politically relevant information that the person has acquired recently. The suspected effects of preexisting knowledge and new information on opinion change, however, are opposite one another. While more political knowledge makes opinion change less likely, more new information makes opinion change more likely.

First, how are campaigns likely to affect those most interested in politics? On the one hand, the politically interested should be more open to campaign influence and thus more likely to change their minds because they absorb more of the new information transmitted by the campaign. However, precisely because they are more interested in politics, they are also likely to have accumulated a great deal of knowledge and to have formed firm and lasting views not easily disrupted by the new information of a single campaign. Campaigns are no match for the rich political histories of these voters.

At the other end of the interest spectrum, how are campaigns likely to affect those voters least interested in politics? On the one hand, the least politically interested are prime targets for campaigns and attitude change because their opinions are not anchored in a deep knowledge base. However, precisely because of their lack of interest in politics, these voters are less likely to come into contact with and pay attention to the new information offered by the campaign and, therefore, the campaign is likely to have little impact on them.[13] Campaigns are no match for the deep-seated apathy of these voters. Thus, the minimal effects conundrum: *those who are most attentive to campaign information are the least open to persuasion by it and those who are the most open to persuasion by campaign information are the least likely to be attentive to it.*[14]

The finding of substantial stability in vote intentions and minimal campaign effects in changing those intentions has most recently been reconfirmed by Steven Finkel (1993). Finkel found that individual voters in 1980 rarely changed their intended vote during the campaign (only about 3 or 4 percent) and, after taking into account countervailing shifts, that the aggregate vote shift from one candidate to another was even smaller (about 0.3 to 1.0 percentage points). Although he estimated a shift of more than 3 percentage points in the 1984 campaign between Reagan and Mondale, none of the three campaigns he studied (1980, 1984, and 1988) came close to changing the outcomes of these elections.

Issues that Draw on the Past
Although the American electorate has been and is still very partisan, identifying in overwhelming numbers with one of the two major political parties and voting with a great deal of regularity for that party's candidates, there is also substantial research to show that many voters decide to vote for the candidate who most nearly reflects their issue preferences (Key 1966). If a voter favors more government spending on education, for instance, then he or she would most likely vote for the candidate believed to also hold that policy view, all things being equal. Issue voting would seem to suggest that campaigns would make a great deal of difference to the decision-making of voters. After all, much of the candidates' campaigns are devoted to the discussion of issues. Even the much maligned negative campaigning usually involves a good deal of issue content, usually associating the opposition with a patently unpopular position or suggesting that the opposition's claim to support a popular issue position is insincere or duplicitous.

That the voters' evaluations of the candidates' issue positions substantially shape their presidential vote decisions, however, does not necessarily mean that presidential campaigns significantly affect the election outcomes. A good deal of the information on which voters base their own issue preferences as well as their beliefs about where the candidates stand on the issues is accumulated before the campaign gets under way.

Partisanship and experience supply a significant amount of the information needed to evaluate which candidate might better serve the voter's issue interests. Although often labeled as a "short-term force" in an election, most policy areas have a fairly clear political history in which the parties have staked out distinct positions—or at least clear general perspectives. It is not too difficult to tell, well before the candidates are ever named, which party's candidate will be pro-choice or pro-life, more or less sympathetic to environmental regulations, more or less sympathetic to reducing regulations on business, more or less committed to tax cuts, and so on. Much of issue voting then is retrospective and highly partisan in nature and not dependent on what is said or promised by candidates during the campaign.[15]

Predictable Election Results

The impact of presidential campaigns has also been called into question by the success of forecasting models that predict the results with a good deal of accuracy well before the general election campaign gets under way. If election results can be accurately forecast without knowledge of what the candidates will do or say during the campaign, it suggests that campaigns may not make much of a difference to the results.

The success of presidential election forecasting models is not limited to a single model or even to the same measurement of predictor variables for a single model. If it were so limited one might be tempted simply to regard the forecasting success as a fluke. However, several pre-campaign presidential election forecasting models have proven to be both accurate and robust (Campbell and Garand 1999).[16]

One of the these models, developed by Alan Abramowitz (1988 and 2005), predicts the presidential two-party popular vote for the current presidential party's candidate based on three factors: (1) the president's job approval rating in July of the election year, (2) the growth rate in the economy in the first half of the election year as measured by the real gross domestic product (GDP), and (3) whether the president's party was seeking more than a second consecutive term in the White House.[17] The model supposes that a significant portion of the electorate feels that it is "time for a change" after one party has served at least eight years in the presidency.[18] As specified here, the model is

Table 1.3. Forecasting the Presidential Vote Based on Presidential Approval, the Economy, and the Number of Consecutive Presidential Terms, 1948–2004

Dependent Variable: The Two-party Popular Vote for the In-party's Presidential Candidate

Predictor Variables	Coefficients
Mid-July Gallup Poll approval ratings for the president	.19 (3.32)
First-half year growth rate for the real Gross Domestic Product (GDP) (annualized)	.65 (2.68)
In-party seeking more than a second consecutive term	−4.53 (3.23)
Constant	43.12
N	15
R^2	.86
Adjusted R^2	.82
Standard error	2.40
Durbin-Watson	1.67
Mean absolute error	1.62
Median absolute error	1.29
Largest absolute error	3.59

Source: Updated by the author from Abramowitz 1988 and 1996, though the economic variable has been adjusted to provide half credit or blame to successor candidates (non-incumbents) of the in-party. This uses the conventional approval rating rather than the revised measure now used by Abramowitz 2004.

Note: The coefficients in parentheses are t-ratios. A null model expecting an in-party vote of 50 percent has a mean absolute error of 4.55 percentage points and a median absolute error of 3.90 percentage points, and its largest absolute error is 11.79 percentage points.

amended slightly by giving non-incumbents partial credit or blame for the state of the economy.

This popularity-economy-term model, estimated with data from the fifteen presidential elections from 1948 to 2004, is presented in table 1.3. The model closely corresponds to the actual vote, accounting for an 82 percent of the variance in the national vote and with an average error of plus or minus 1.6 percentage points. This compares quite favorably to the errors of a baseline or null model predicting an even vote split. The mean absolute error of the null model was more than 4.6 percentage points. The median absolute error of the amended Abramowitz model is only 1.3 percentage points. The model is robust in that it performs about as well when slightly earlier polls or slightly different economic indicators or time spans are used.

The coefficients of this model indicate that the presidential candidate of the in-party can expect to gain 0.2 percentage point of the two-party popular voter for every additional percentage point of presidential approval, and incumbents can expect about two-thirds of a percentage point of the vote for every percentage point improvement in the GDP. The presidential candidate of the in-party can expect to be set back by about 4.5 percentage points if the candidate's party is seeking more than a second consecutive term. Over the last fifty years, this variable suggests that in-party candidates Harry Truman in 1948, Richard Nixon in 1960, Hubert Humphrey in 1968, Gerald Ford in 1976, George Bush in 1988 and 1992, and Al Gore in 2000 were at a 4.5 percentage point disadvantage relative to in-party candidates Dwight Eisenhower in 1956, Lyndon Johnson in 1964, Richard Nixon in 1972, Jimmy Carter in 1980, Ronald Reagan in 1984, Bill Clinton in 1996, and George W. Bush in 2004 because the former candidates were attempting the difficult task of extending their party's string of presidential victories beyond two in a row.

A second successful presidential election forecasting model, introduced in J. Campbell and Wink 1990, and one that guides much of the subsequent analysis in this book, predicts the presidential two-party popular vote for the current presidential party's candidate based on two predictor variables: the precampaign preference polls on the contest and the growth rate in the economy. The preference polls (also known as trial-heat polls) examined are Gallup polls in which survey respondents are asked who they would vote for if the presidential election were held that day. The indicator of economic growth is the growth rate in the GDP in the second quarter of the election year (April to June). Because there is an element of personal (as well as party) accountability for incumbents, economic growth rates are halved for non-incumbents or successor candidates of the in-party. This awards partial credit or blame for candidates not personally at the helm of the economy over the period in question and full credit or blame to incumbents seeking reelection.

A rough indicator of the success of trial-heat polls in predicting the vote is the frequency with which the candidate leading in the polls went on to win the election. Table 1.4 presents the number of times Gallup poll leaders at seven different points in the election year won or lost the election for the fifteen presidential elections since 1948. Although early poll leaders, at least those leading after the June polls, more often won than lost the election, their election was certainly not a foregone conclusion.

Figure 1.2 depicts how well the polls at the seven points during the election years have predicted the eventual vote percentages for the candidates as opposed to simply who would win or lose. The top line of the figure, labeled raw trial-heat polls, indicates the average difference between the preference

Correct Forecast of Winner?	Timing of Trial-Heat Poll						
	June	Late July	Post-convention	Early September	Late September	October	November
Candidate ahead won election	8	10	12	13	14	12	12
Candidate ahead lost election	7	5	3	2	1	3	3

Note: The winning candidate is defined here as the candidate receiving the majority of the two-party popular vote. Each timing of the trial-heat poll incorrectly predicted the winner of the 1948 election. With the exception of the post-convention poll and the September polls, each timing also incorrectly predicted the 2000 election. In addition to these errors, the June poll missed in 1968, 1980, 1988, 1992, and 2004. The late July poll missed in 1960, 1988, and 2004. The post-convention poll missed in 1960 and 1980. The early September poll missed in 1960. The October poll missed in 2004. The November poll missed in 1976.

poll results at different points in the election year and the actual November vote percentage. The first poll examined every year was in June, prior to either party's national nominating conventions. As their won-loss record in table 1.1 would suggest, June polls have been very inaccurate. Their average error has been nearly seven percentage points. Guessing an even division of the November vote is actually much more accurate than relying on the June poll results. July polls do not fare much better. However, preference polls become substantially more accurate after both parties have held their conventions in August and, as one would expect, their accuracy grows as they are taken closer to election day.

The second line in figure 1.2, the trial-heat-only regression, is based on a series of bivariate regression analyses using the preference poll alone to predict the vote. Rather than accepting the poll results at face value, as we did above in examining the raw trial-heat polls as literal forecasts of the election results, the bivariate regressions take into account common patterns observed over the years in the relationship between the polls and the vote. Using the trial-heat polls as literal forecasts assumes that, in a plot of the polls against the vote, the slope is one, and the line summarizing the relationship passes through the point where the poll is 50 percent and the vote is 50 percent. Of course, unless you assume that the poll perfectly captures the vote preferences of the electorate and that nothing systematically shifts vote intentions between the time of the poll and election day, there is no reason to insist on a one-to-one relationship between the poll results and the vote. Rather than predetermine the relationship of the polls to the vote, bivariate regression analysis empirically determines that historical relationship.

Figure 1.3 shows the plot of early September poll percentages for the in-party candidate against the subsequent vote and includes the regression line that summarizes this relationship. The slope of the regression line is about .55, indicating that early September poll percentages should be heavily discounted in interpreting them as precursors of the vote. A poll lead in September is about half real and half ephemeral.

Returning to figure 1.2, there is a consistent and considerable reduction in the difference or error in interpreting trial-heat results through bivariate regression and accepting them at face value as literal forecasts of the vote. The poll results are more in line with the vote after they have been discounted by

Figure 1.2. The Mean Absolute Error of Trial-Heat "Forecasts" at Seven Points in the Campaign. 1948–2004

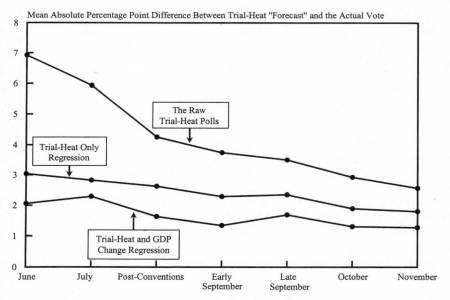

Time of Trial-Heat Poll in the Campaign

Note: The actual vote is the percentage of the two-party popular vote for the incumbent party's presidential candidate. The bivariate regressions include only the trial-heat poll standing of the incumbent party's presidential candidate. The multivariate regressions also include the second-quarter change in the real GDP (halved for non-incumbent candidates of the in-party).

Figure 1.3. Trial-Heat Poll Support in Early September for the Incumbent Party's Presidential Candidate and the Incumbent Party's Two-Party Presidential Vote, 1948–2004

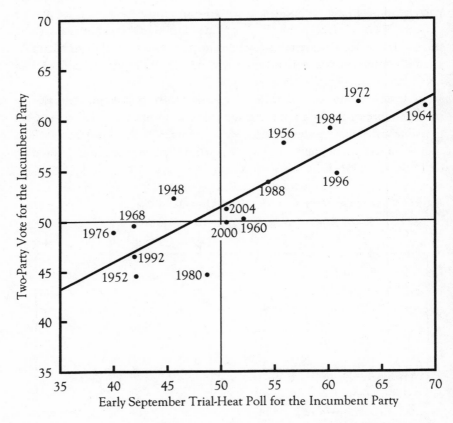

Note: *Both the popular vote for the incumbent party and the division of the early September trial-heat poll are divisions of major two-party preferences. The trial-heat poll is the division of registered voters. The estimated regression equation is: incumbent party vote = 24.00 + (.55 × trial-heat poll for the incumbent party candidate). The adjusted R-square is .73. The t-ratio of the poll coefficient is 6.19. The standard error of the equation is 2.92.*

some proportion. The regressions indicate that the proportion of discounting, as one might expect, is greatest for polls early in the election year and least for polls closer to election day.

While the polls are more useful when their historical relationship is taken into account through regression analysis, there is considerable room for improving polls as forecasting instruments of the vote. Besides taking the historical context of the poll results into account, the forecasting value of the polls can be enhanced by taking the contemporary context of the poll into account. The best general indication of the contemporary context of an election is the state of the economy.

The economy, as measured by the (annualized) growth rate in real or inflation-adjusted GDP for the second quarter of the election year (from April to June, and halved for successor candidates), is included with the presidential trial-heat polls in a series of multiple regressions. The bottom line in figure 1.2 plots the mean absolute difference between the actual and the expected vote for the incumbent party based on the trial-heat and economy regression for each of the seven periods during the election years from 1948 to 2004. The mean absolute differences were greatest using the June polls (a mean difference of 2.06) and were not appreciably more accurate after early September (1.34). Just as the bivariate regressions improved upon the raw trial-heat forecasts, the trial-heat and economy regression results consistently improve upon the bivariate trial-heat-only regressions. In short, the state of the economy supplies us with important additional information—beyond that of the trial-heat polls—about which political party's presidential candidate the electorate may favor.

Table 1.5 presents the trial-heat and economy forecasting model for early September trial-heat polls. As already noted, the early September version of the trial-heat and economy model is more accurate than those using earlier preference polls and, quite interestingly, about as accurate as those using much later polls. It accounts for an impressive 89 percent of the variance in the national vote and has an average error of about plus or minus 1.3 percentage points. The median error is less than plus or minus .9 of one percentage point.

As in the bivariate case, the regression indicates that typically about half of early September preference poll margins are maintained to the election and half evaporate. The results also indicate that the in-party candidate can expect about a .6 of a percentage point boost from every percentage point of economic growth during the second quarter of the election year.

Both the accuracy and the robustness of the early September trial-heat and economy forecasting model can be better assessed by examining out-of-sample errors. Out-of-sample errors are calculated by first estimating coefficients for the equation without data from one of the election years and then inserting the data for the excluded year into the estimated equation to produce a pseudo-forecast for that year. For instance, in order to generate a pseudo-forecast for the 1948 election, the equation is estimated using data for all years except 1948. Using the coefficients from this estimation and the trial-heat poll and economic growth numbers for 1948, the expected vote for the in-party in 1948 is then calculated and compared to the actual in-party vote that year. This technique of examining out-of-sample errors is preferable to examining in-sample

Table 1.5. Forecasting the Presidential Vote with Preference Polls and Economic Growth, 1948–2004

Dependent Variable: The Two-party Popular Vote for the In-party's Presidential Candidate

Predictor Variables	Coefficients
Early September preference poll two-party percentage for the in-party candidate	.47 (7.85)
Second-quarter growth rate for the real Gross Domestic Product (GDP annualized) (halved for successor candidates)	.61 (4.48)
Constant	26.89
N	15
R²	.91
Adjusted R²	.89
Standard error	1.86
Durbin-Watson	1.79
Mean absolute error	1.34
Median absolute error	.89
Largest absolute error	3.22

Source: Updated from J. Campbell and Wink 1990 and J. Campbell 2004.
Note: The coefficients in parentheses are t-ratios. See the note to table 1.3 for error comparisons to a null model.

errors since it more closely approximates a real forecast. As in a real forecast, none of the information on the election being forecast enters into the estimation of the coefficients in the forecast equation.

The mean out-of-sample error for the model is only 1.7 percentage points. The out-of-sample errors were without exception less than 3.6 percentage points, less than three percentage points in most cases, and less than one percentage point in about half of the elections.

The accuracy of the early September trial-heat and economy model can perhaps be best illustrated by comparing its out-of-sample errors to the errors in the November trial-heat polls taken just days before the election. While the September model's average out-of-sample error was plus or minus 1.7 percentage points of the vote, the average error of the November poll was about 2.6 percentage points. The forecasting model, based on information obtained fully two months before the election, is a generally better predictor of the election results than the national surveys conducted within a few days of the election.

Restrained and Systematic Campaign Effects

The accuracy of these and other presidential election forecasting models is but the latest reason to doubt the impact of the presidential campaign. How important can the presidential campaigns be if the results of the election can be quite accurately predicted before the campaigns have begun?

The purpose of this book is to provide an answer to this basic question: do presidential campaigns make a difference to the election results? My answer is that they do matter, though certainly not nearly as much as many believe, and that presidential elections are so predictable because of the muted net effects of the campaigns and because the net effects of the campaigns are themselves quite predictable. The effects of campaigns are muted or restrained for reasons already noted—stability in the individual vote choice, many early vote decisions, the prevalence of stable partisanship, the minimal effects conundrum, and retrospective issue voting.

Campaign effects are not only limited; they are also systematic and generally quite predictable in advance of the campaign. Although some campaign effects are significant, especially those resulting from unpredictable idiosyncratic events such as unusual candidate activities or gaffes, the fact remains that most of the effects of campaigns are systematic and thus can be anticipated.

The general effects of campaigns are predictable because the fundamental factors establishing the campaign context, which shapes the course of the campaign, are in place before the campaign gets under way. The most fundamental of these contextual factors is the rough balance between the major political parties and their candidates. American presidential politics are very competitive. Usually the two major-party candidates are relatively well known. Both are relatively well financed. Both receive a good deal of media coverage. Both are taken as serious options by the voters. Both campaigns have their good and bad days. Through the course of several months of campaigning, this rough parity has a leveling effect. Further contributing to this leveling effect are the closer scrutiny of the frontrunning candidates and the more cautious campaign strategies that candidates with large poll leads are likely to adopt. Taken together these forces suggest that presidential campaigns should generally have the effect of narrowing the vote difference between the candidates.

Two other fundamental factors are in place before the campaign—the state of the economy that sets the public's mood and the advantages of presidential incumbency. Economic conditions are important in and of themselves. The public is likely to keep the president's party in office during periods of prosperity but may be reluctant to do so if the economy has been weak. The voters' evaluations of how the administration has affected their economic well-being undoubtedly affects vote decision-making during the campaign, but economic conditions may have broader implications as well. During good economic times voters may be predisposed to believe the best about the in-party candidate—on noneconomic matters as well as on strictly economic issues. In contrast, a weak economy may sour the public on the president's party. Voters may not only hold the in-party responsible for the nation's economic woes but may also be inclined to believe that the in-party is deficient on other scores.

Although congressional incumbency is commonly regarded as a major asset in congressional elections, there is remarkably little attention paid to the value of presidential incumbency. In fact, not so long ago presidential incumbency was considered an electoral liability. After President Carter's defeat in the 1980 election, some analysts speculated that American government was so plagued with chronic, unsolvable problems that the system was ungovernable, that presidents would bear the blame, and that they would be defeated for reelection as a result. The future, from this perspective, was to be strewn with one-term presidential failures (Hargrove and Nelson 1981, 48–50).

While there can be little doubt about the difficulty of the president's job, it is a serious mistake to regard presidential incumbency as an electoral disadvantage. On the contrary, it has been and continues to be an asset that, along with competitiveness factors and the economy, shapes the course of the campaign. The prerogatives of the presidency, the fact that the president has already been elected by a national popular vote plurality, and the role of the president as the national head of state provide the president with an electoral boost.

We have actually already seen some evidence of the effects of the three pre-campaign fundamentals—competitive campaigns, presidential incumbency, and the economy. First, the narrowing effect of the campaign is demonstrated by the shallow slope in figure 1.3's plot of the early September preference polls against the actual vote. Winning candidates generally won by less than their early September poll lead, and the showing of losing candidates was generally better than their early September poll deficit. Second, the advantage of presidential incumbency was also evident in figure 1.3. If both candidates were dead-even in the early September polls and if history is a guide, the incumbent would likely win a popular vote plurality in November. This is demonstrated graphically by the regression line in the figure cutting above the fifty-fifty point of the plot. The impact of presidential incumbency is also suggested by the vote distribution. In the fifteen presidential elections since 1948, four in-party candidates (Eisenhower in 1956, Johnson in 1964, Nixon in 1972, and Reagan in 1984) have received more than 56 percent of the two-party vote. None of the fifteen out-party candidates in this period received a vote of this magnitude. Finally, the impact of the economy on the course of the campaign is evident in both of the forecasting equations we examined. Adding economic conditions to the forecasting equations made a significant contribution to the accuracy of both forecasting equations.[19]

An Overview

The central purpose of this book is to provide an answer to the question of whether and how presidential campaigns affect presidential elections. The effect of presidential campaigns on election results may best be understood by the theory of the predictable campaign, discussed in chapter 2. The course of presidential campaigns are predictable because they begin with an established base of pre-campaign voter decisions, and later decisions made during the campaign are largely shaped by the pre-campaign context as well as factors common to all modern presidential elections (such as the competitiveness of the parties).

Several conceptual and methodological issues are the subjects of chapter 3. This chapter prepares the groundwork for the later empirical analysis, by defining some central concepts and discussing the data that will be used to examine the theory of the predictable campaign. The chapter addresses what constitutes the general election campaign, when the general election campaign begins, and the differences between systematic and unsystematic campaign effects and between real and transitory campaign effects. Additionally, since much of the analysis draws on data from the fifteen presidential elections from 1948 to 2004, some background is provided on these elections.

In the closing section of chapter 3, I use data from these fifteen elections to estimate how much campaigns have affected the vote, their total effect, and the portion of their impact that is systematic or unsystematic. The analysis suggests that campaigns have a significant impact on the vote, larger than previously estimated, and that most of the effect of campaigns is systematic. This analysis answers in preliminary form the basic questions of the analysis but also paves the way for a closer examination of what makes campaign effects largely predictable.

Chapter 4 examines one important reason that campaigns are predictable: the stable pre-campaign base of voter commitments. Many voters have made up their minds before the campaign begins, and there is virtually nothing that could shake their commitment. A number of considerations may cause voters to reach an early decision and forestall any possible influence by the campaign — approval of the incumbent's performance, economic conditions, policy successes or failures. However, the core reason for pre-campaign decisions is partisanship. There are die-hard Democrats and die-hard Republicans who cannot under any conceivable circumstances be shaken. One fact suggests the importance of these two partisan bases for candidates: even in the worst of times for a major party, it seldom receives less than 40 percent of the national two-party presidential popular vote; in the best of times, it rarely receives much more than 60 percent.[20] Large partisan bases constrain the size of both campaign effects and vote majorities.

Chapter 4 also explores the puzzle of how partisanship affects election outcomes. Despite alarms about partisan dealignment, the vast majority of American voters are partisan, and the overwhelming majority of partisans loyally vote for their party's presidential candidate. This is documented in appendix A's detailed analysis of partisanship and how it has changed since the 1950s. As important as partisanship is to explaining how individuals vote, its role in explaining or predicting presidential election outcomes is less clear. For instance, in the era from 1950 to 1980, in which Democrats greatly outnumbered Republicans in the electorate, Republicans won five of the eight presidential elections. It is also notable that none of the major presidential election forecasting models include partisanship as a predictor variable. Moreover, aggregate partisanship changes very little from election to election, but the party that wins presidential elections changes quite often. Is partisanship unimportant to explaining election outcomes? To the extent that partisanship in the aggregate is not vital to presidential election results, why not? Have the political parties been so perfectly competitive that they effectively cancel each other out? If not, how has partisanship affected presidential election outcomes and why can election results be accurately predicted without consulting the partisanship of the electorate?

The next two chapters turn to the variable context of the campaign. The two most important aspects of the variable context are presidential incumbency (chapter 5) and national economic conditions (chapter 6). The party holding the White House has many advantages and opportunities going into an election. If the current president is seeking reelection, there is the advantage of staking out popular positions, framing the national policy debate, and using the considerable trappings of the office to one's own benefit—the "Rose Garden strategy."[21] It also appears that the advantages of presidential incumbency are significantly greater for a party seeking a second consecutive term in the White House than they are for a party seeking to extend its control beyond two terms.

Chapter 6 turns to an examination of the election-year economy. Political observers have long appreciated how important economic conditions are to presidential elections. To some extent economic conditions prior to the campaign direct voters toward one candidate or the other, but just as voters do not constantly monitor politics, neither do they constantly monitor the economy and translate its ups and downs into political rewards and punishments for candidates. Much of this translation takes place during the campaign when the need to reach a decision is approaching. Moreover, the economy has an impact on the course of the campaign beyond the dollars and cents. That is, the economy conditions the public mood toward the incumbent presidential party. A strong economy puts the electorate in a good mood and tilts it toward overlooking in-party shortcomings. A weak economy puts the electorate in a surly mood toward the in-party.

The analysis turns to the normal narrowing effect of the campaign in chapter 7. From the time that a significant segment of opinion regarding the election begins to gel around the end of the nomination process until election day, there are a variety of campaign conditions that should reduce the lead of the frontrunning candidate. Among the reasons for the frontrunner's lead to narrow as a result of the campaign are the relatively evenly matched, high-intensity campaign efforts by both parties' candidates, the normally greater initial divisions within the trailing candidate's party, the logic of a cautious frontrunner-strategy, the tendency of increased media scrutiny of frontrunners, and the even pull that the candidates have on the votes of late-deciding voters.

Chapter 8 turns to a more historical analysis of presidential elections to gauge the likelihood that nonsystematic campaign effects made a difference to the election's outcome. The competitiveness of the thirty-five presidential elections from 1868 to 2004 is examined to determine whether even slight nonsystematic campaign effects may have decided who was elected and who was defeated. While the effects of nonsystematic campaign events—candidate gaffes or triumphs—are for many reasons small in absolute size and even small in relation to the systematic effects of campaigns, they may take on a great importance in very close elections. The analysis suggests that the idiosyncrasies of campaigns, the dramatic events that all campaign watchers live for, may have been decisive in five or six of these elections (14 to 17 percent of the examined elections).

The closing chapter of the book steps back to summarize and to put the elements of the predictable campaign in perspective. It assesses the extent of overall campaign effects and the extent of the various systematic components of campaign effects. It also reviews what we know about the localized effects of presidential campaigns. The final section of the chapter explores some of the implications of the findings regarding the extent and predictability of campaign effects: how they might affect the candidates' campaigns, the media's coverage and the voters' attention to the politics and substance of campaigns and how campaigns affect elections as instruments for democratic governance.

★ *Chapter 2*

The Theory of the Predictable Campaign

DO PRESIDENTIAL CAMPAIGNS affect the results of presidential elections? The answer is that they do. That this is not altogether obvious, particularly in light of the predictability of election results, is because most effects of presidential campaigns are themselves systematic and predictable. This chapter presents the theory of the predictable campaign, the reasons why most of the effects of presidential campaigns are systematic.

From some perspectives, the idea that presidential campaigns have largely systematic effects on election results may be hard to believe. Presidential campaigns are chaotic. Each involves different candidates with different backgrounds, capabilities, strengths, and flaws. Each takes place under different circumstances and addresses different issues. Candidate strategies and media interests evolve and shift through the course of campaigns with new developments that arise and in reaction to the opponent's campaign. With all of these differences and with all of the flux during campaigns, how can most campaign effects be systematic and predictable?

The theory of the predictable presidential campaign offers an explanation. There are three components to this theory. The first is that the effects of campaigns are, in fact, limited. Because partisanship in the electorate is pervasive, potent, and stable and because retrospective evaluations of the candidates and issues allow many additional voters to decide before the campaign how they will vote, the candidates have a stable base of support in place before the campaign begins. Beyond this stable base, the minimal effects conundrum and the high level of competition in presidential campaigns further narrow the range of potential campaign effects.

The theory's second component is that several of the most important circumstances setting the contexts for campaigns are in place and known prior to the campaign. Two regular but variable contexts for presidential campaigns are the incumbency status of the candidates and the state of the national economy. Both of these factors essentially play themselves out in fairly predictable ways over the course of the campaign, becoming incorporated into voter decisions.

The third component of the theory is that vigorous presidential campaigns narrow the gap between candidates leading and trailing in the polls. Competition produces some convergence. Before the campaign gets under way, one side or the other may have built a sizable lead. This poll lead often is the result of the public hearing predominantly one side of things. The 1996 election offers a good example. While the eventual Republican presidential nominee Bob Dole was attempting to secure his party's nomination from several opponents, the Democratic Party was already running a massive national media campaign extolling the achievements of the first Clinton administration. One side effectively started the general election campaign long before the other, and for several weeks voters heard only one side of the story. As a result, Clinton built a large poll lead over Dole.

When general election campaigns begin for both candidates, both sides are heard. Both candidates' campaigns are credible, well financed, highly visible, and have access to the media for their messages. The effect of this competition is to put both candidates on more nearly equal footing and to narrow the vote gap between the candidates. For these reasons and several others, the regular course of the presidential campaign is for the trailing candidate to gain support and close the gap on the frontrunner.

Figure 2.1 is a causal model presenting the general elements of the theory of the predictable campaign. The starting point in the model is the grouping of the pre-campaign fundamentals. The fundamentals are all of the politically relevant conditions in place before the campaign begins, including the long-standing partisan attachments of voters and their ideological perspectives as well as the state of the economy and all other social conditions that voters might care about in deciding how to vote. Many of these fundamentals have already affected voters and are the basis for voters arriving at early decisions. This establishes the stable context for the campaign, the direct link from the fundamentals to the election results. Some portion of the impact of the fundamentals, however, affects the developments of the campaign and how the campaign is interpreted by voters.[1] In particular, economic developments not yet fully incorporated into the political assessments of voters and the advantages of presidential incumbency systematically affect the campaign and the impressions it leaves with the voters. These campaign-processed fundamentals and

Figure 2.1. The Theory of the Predictable Campaign

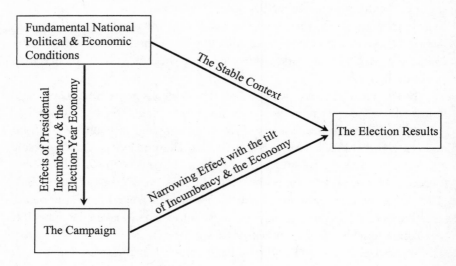

the competitive or narrowing effects of campaigns are the important systematic influences of the campaign on election results.

The purpose of this chapter is to present the argument of the theory of the predictable presidential campaign and to establish the plausibility of each of the three components of the theory.

Limits to Campaign Effects

The effects of presidential campaigns are to some extent predictable because they are limited in magnitude. In effect, you cannot go too far wrong in predicting how the campaign will develop. There are several reasons for this. A large number of voters have made up their minds before the campaign begins. Barring some cataclysmic event, nothing in the campaign can change the vote intentions of these voters. Some may waver a bit over the course of the campaign, but their votes are all but cast before the campaign begins.

Early deciders provide a baseline vote that establishes outside boundaries for the potential effects of the campaign. In any election year, a substantial number of voters are effectively committed to vote for a candidate before the campaign begins. These voters are out of play for the campaign. The campaign can only realistically hope to change the preferences of the subset of voters who lack a pre-campaign commitment or whose commitment is so tenuous that they might be persuaded to change by the right campaign message.

The record of previous elections provides an idea about the constraints on potential campaign effects. One clue to the upper bound placed on campaign effects by pre-campaign decisions comes from the number of people indicating that they had reached an early vote decision. At least half and often nearly two-thirds of voters say that they have decided their votes prior to the campaign (during or before the conventions). This places a hypothetical upper bound of a 50 percent campaign-induced vote shift in some elections and, more often, a hypothetical upper bound on campaign effects of about a third of the vote.

These hypothetical limits on campaign effects are quite generous because they are based on the implausible assumption that all voters influenced by the campaign will uniformly move from one candidate to the other. Some of these voters, however, will already be inclined toward the candidate for whom they will eventually vote. In addition, campaigns normally have cross-currents. The same campaign may move some to vote for the Democrat and others to vote for the Republican. So the net effect of a campaign, because of these cross-currents and nonuniform movements, is almost always less than its gross effects.

How much less? If we assume that voters deciding during the campaign split two to one in favor of one candidate, the upper bound of effects on even a campaign with half of the electorate up for grabs is about a seventeen-percentage-point vote shift.[2] A change of seventeen percentage points, by the way, happens to be the biggest change from July polls to the November vote in the fifteen presidential elections since 1948.[3] In the more typical case of a third of the electorate open to influence by the campaign, the upper bound of campaign effects would be less than twelve percentage points of the vote. Of course, actual campaign effects are smaller than these upper bounds.

While the effects of campaigns are substantially constrained, this does not necessarily diminish their importance in deciding election outcomes. As the election of 2000 dramatically illustrated, a shift of as little as a fraction of one percentage point of the vote can decide an election. The 2000 election is not unique in this respect. Other narrowly decided presidential elections in which small vote shifts would have elected a different candidate are identified in chapter 8. Nevertheless, it is still important to acknowledge that campaign effects are limited because of decisions made beforehand and that this makes campaign effects more predictable. For example, if one candidate has a large lead over his opponent going into the campaign, we could accept the possibility of that lead shrinking but, because of the limits of campaign effects, we could rule out the possibility of the frontrunner losing the election by a wide margin. That kind of massive movement simply does not occur in American presidential campaigns because the raw materials for it—large numbers of late deciders—are not available.

Easy Decisions Can Be Early Decisions

Why are so many votes set before the campaign begins and why is the campaign unable to change these pre-determined votes? The simple answer to these questions is that, for many voters, choosing a candidate is an easy decision. Thus, for voters who find the choice to be easy, there is no reason to delay; the choice can be made early.

Why is the vote choice so obvious for so many voters? The vote choice is essentially determined by the evaluation of two candidate characteristics: their values and their performance (or likely performance) in office. These evaluations are often clear to voters well before the campaign begins.

The values of voters and candidates are long-term characteristics embodied in partisanship and ideology. Though the median voter is a moderate independent who must face a tough choice between a fairly liberal Democrat and a fairly conservative Republican, most American voters are neither moderates nor independents. They are, to one degree or another, liberals or conservatives and Democrats or Republicans. This has become even more the case in recent years (Abramowitz 2007, J. Campbell 2007b). These voting cues or information shortcuts, as Samuel Popkin (1991, 13) terms them, greatly simplify the vote choice. The clear preference for candidates and parties based on agreements or disagreements about values lead many voters to easy and early decisions.

Distinct from partisan politics, though related to it, are the public's well-formed views of the performance of the administration. After four years or more of living with an administration, most voters have definite ideas about the incumbent president and party. Many regard the record as either commendable or condemnable. To these voters, the choice of whether to reward or punish past performance is obvious.

A note about the information or political knowledge of voters is perhaps appropriate here. Many political observers have decried how ignorant voters are about political issues, and many American voters are, in fact, amazingly ill-informed (Berelson, Lazarsfeld, and McPhee 1954; Delli Carpini and Keeter 1996; Bennett and Bennett 1993; Neuman 1986; Smith 1989).[4] However, from the standpoint of democratic theory, the standard that should be used to evaluate voters is whether they are informed enough to cast a ballot that reflects their views and whether any additional information would have caused them to vote differently.

By these standards, rather than some absolute knowledge standards, most voters may not be so ill-equipped to perform their political roles.[5] If you are a conservative, how much do you really need to know to be sure that a Republican vote best reflects your point of view? If you see things from a liberal perspective, there is probably nothing you would learn during the campaign that could dissuade you from a Democratic vote. Similarly, if you are convinced that the in-party has done an excellent job in office, that the economy is humming along, and that all is basically right with the world, the campaign is not going to prevent you from returning that party to office. On the other hand, if you think that the in-party has fouled up the nation, nothing that is said during the campaign will prevent you from trying to "throw the bums out."

For these voters, voting is easy, and additional information from the campaign is unnecessary. They may or may not know much, but they know enough. They know enough to arrive at a vote choice that they feel comfortable about, a decision that they doubt they will regret. An effective or reasoned vote need not be an especially well-informed vote. In his classic voting behavior study, *The Responsible Electorate*, V. O. Key forwarded the simple argument that the "voters are not fools" (1966, 7). It may also be argued that most voters are not going to be mistaken for political geniuses either, but they do not need to be. Voting is, after all, not brain surgery.[6]

Partisanship and Ideology

Partisanship is one voting cue that makes the act of voting simple. Despite much hand-wringing about the weakening of partisanship and partisan dealignment, the great majority of American voters are partisan, and the overwhelming majority of them vote for their political party's presidential candidate. Based on parental influences, values, issue positions, evaluations of past candidates, and observations about the parties' performance over time, most voters identify to some degree with one of the two major political parties. They have a "standing decision" to vote for a party's presidential candidate. Moreover, party identifications, though changeable, are generally quite stable over time.

The distribution of party identifications among voters is presented in table 2.1. The partisan distributions are of those NES survey respondents who reported having voted. The data have been corrected to reflect the actual popular national presidential vote percentages for the presidential candidates.[7] Based on findings by Keith et al. (1992) that independents who lean toward one of the parties resemble partisans in attitudes and voting behavior, the so-called "leaning independents" are grouped with their associated partisans. A detailed examination of partisanship and its trends is presented in appendix A.

As the table demonstrates, partisanship in the electorate is pervasive and has not changed much in the aggregate from one election to the next.[8] Until 1984, a majority of voters were Democrats and about 40 percent were Republicans. Beginning in 1984, the gap between Democrats and Republicans closed, with an increase in the number of Republicans and a decline in the number of Democrats. Most importantly, however, the data demonstrate that the voting

Table 2.1. The Partisanship of American Voters, 1952–2004

Presidential Election Year	Party Identification			Loyal Party Presidential Votes of All Votes		Loyal Party Presidential Votes of Major-Party Votes	
	Democrats	Independents	Republicans	Democrats	Republicans	Democrats	Republicans
1952	57.4	5.2	37.4	72.3	95.2	72.7	95.2
1956	52.0	8.9	39.1	74.2	95.4	75.2	95.4
1960	52.4	8.1	39.5	81.6	91.6	82.4	91.9
1964	56.6	5.3	38.1	86.5	77.1	86.5	78.1
1968	56.3	8.5	35.2	67.9	83.7	79.7	92.6
1972	52.0	8.8	39.2	60.4	90.0	61.1	90.9
1976	51.2	10.4	38.3	78.8	84.6	80.7	86.2
1980	52.9	8.7	38.5	68.6	85.6	74.7	92.4
1984	46.7	8.1	45.2	77.5	94.4	78.0	95.1
1988	46.6	6.9	46.5	83.3	90.1	84.4	90.2
1992	48.0	8.8	43.2	75.7	71.8	89.5	90.0
1996	49.8	5.7	44.6	79.5	80.0	93.5	86.6
2000	48.0	7.4	44.6	86.6	88.7	89.3	91.4
2004	47.7	5.7	46.6	88.8	91.8	89.7	93.3
Mean	51.3	7.6	41.1	77.6	87.1	81.2	90.7

Note: The figures are percentages of reported voters. They are calculated from the American National Election Studies. Independent leaners are grouped with the party they lean toward (Keith et al. 1992). The loyal party vote percentages are the percentage of all voters identifying with a political party who voted for their party's presidential candidate. In the "all votes" categories, votes cast for third-party candidates are counted as disloyal votes. Non-major-party candidates are not counted in loyalty rates in the "major-party votes" categories. The data have been corrected to accurately reflect the known division of the national popular vote. The corrections involved weighting data by a factor equal to the actual percentage of the vote for a party's candidate divided by the percentage of the vote for a party's candidate reported in the NES surveys. Further details regarding this reweighting are presented in chapter 3 and appendix A.

public is overwhelmingly partisan. In all but one election (1976), fewer than 10 percent of voters were "purely" independent of partisan attachment.

Table 2.1 also presents the percentage of partisans who report voting for their party's presidential candidate in elections since 1952. The loyalty of partisans is reported in two ways: the percentage of all voting partisans who voted for their party's presidential candidate and the percentage voting loyally among those who voted for one of the two major-party candidates (their two-party vote). The first measure counts third-party votes by partisans as disloyal votes and the second measure ignores third-party votes. Although the percentage of loyal party voting for president is not perfect, in most elections it is quite high and has never dropped below 60 percent. The loyalty of Republicans has been especially impressive, averaging 87 percent and nearly 91 percent by the two-party measure. Historically, Democratic Party loyalty, though high in absolute terms, lagged behind that of Republicans. This probably reflected the considerable internal divisions within the Democratic Party's large coalition. In recent elections, as the size and diversity of the Democratic Party's coalition diminished, their loyalty rates increased to levels just about on par with the Republicans.

As both the party identification and party loyalty rates presented in table 2.1 suggest, most voters enter the election year already strongly predisposed to vote for one party. Contrary to exaggerated claims of partisan dealignment, American voters have been and remain quite partisan and routinely vote their partisanship in presidential elections. More than 90 percent of voters are to some degree partisan and about 90 percent of partisans vote loyally for their party's standard-bearer. For many partisan voters, the presidential vote decision is an easy decision.

Adding further to the ease with which many voters reach a vote decision are the consistent and distinct issue positions and values of the political parties and their presidential candidates. Although many voters lack a sophisticated understanding of ideological terminology and are unclear about exactly what being a liberal or conservative entails, most have gut-level values that they apply to politics and generally find one party to reflect these general views better than the other. Voters coming from the more liberal end of the political spectrum are nearly automatic Democratic votes. Conservative voters, likewise, may see no real alternative to voting Republican.

The Known Record
While long-term partisan commitments may lock up the votes of many voters prior to the campaign, others may reach a pre-campaign vote decision based on their evaluations of the preceding presidential administration. The votes of

both independents and some partisans may be swayed by reactions to particularly successful or unsuccessful administrations. The experience of these voters with the in-party's administration is a tangible basis for reaching a verdict of whether to vote to keep that party in office or turn it out.

Information that might be introduced during the campaign stands little chance of reversing preexisting views grounded in personal experience. Since voters have lived through an administration and may have felt the consequences of administration policies directly or indirectly, they may feel that the campaign can tell them little that they do not already know or that the campaigns would only serve to distort what they know to one or the other candidate's political advantage. Voters find hard information and information learned through observing the actions of a party in office to be more reliable than the relatively soft information of charges, countercharges, claims, and promises made during a campaign. As the old saying goes, actions speak louder than words.

Voters have every reason to be skeptical of campaign promises and charges. Candidates may say many things, some with only a tether to the truth, in the hope of attracting votes. Some knowledge of the record may further limit campaign effects beyond normal skepticism. Voters may dismiss campaign promises and charges that do not jibe with what they already know from experience. If voters think that a candidate has acted dishonestly while in office, campaign protestations to the contrary or a slick repackaging of the candidate will not change impressions. Similarly, if a candidate raised taxes while in office and then pledges in the next campaign to cut taxes, voters may well think that the candidate is trying to play them as fools. Past performance establishes the credibility of campaign promises. In short, the record counts. The most important parts of the record of the parties and candidates are largely known to most voters before the campaign begins, and this provides the basis for early vote decisions.

Evaluations of an administration's record are most relevant to vote decisions when an incumbent president is seeking reelection. In this case, what the candidate has done in the past should provide voters with a pretty good idea about what to expect in the future.

Matters are not quite so simple when the incumbent is not seeking reelection. Some presidential candidates run as the heir-apparent or natural successor to their party's president (e.g., George H. W. Bush in 1992). In other cases the candidate may run at arm's length from the incumbent (e.g., Al Gore in 2000), but whatever the strategy, there are generally strong grounds for associating the in-party's presidential candidate with the administration.

Moreover, though not as well known as a sitting president, non-incumbent presidential candidates have records of their own. The most important parts of these records also may have come to light and received a good amount of publicity during the contest for the party's nomination. Although these records may not be so directly or widely known and may not be as relevant to the potential presidential performance of these candidates, this information may nonetheless be very useful to voters and may convince some voters to reach an early vote decision.

How do voters acquire this information about the record of the administration and the history of the candidates? If there is one thing we know for certain in American politics, it is that the political interest of the typical voter is marginal. Most are motivated or can be stimulated to vote in presidential elections, perhaps in midterm elections, and not much more. So they are not going to expend much energy to study the candidates, to search out information in order to reach a fully informed vote decision. And they do not have to. Voters can pick up enough general information about the records of the administration and the candidates without any real effort during the course of everyday life and with marginal attention to politics. As Samuel Popkin suggests, "most of the information that voters use when they vote is acquired as a byproduct of activities they pursue as part of their daily lives. In that sense, political uses of this information are free" (1991, 23).

The key to reconciling the apparent low level of voter information with reasoned vote choices is that while generally voters do not know a great deal, most know enough. Voters do not need to know or to recall the record of the administration in great depth to use the record in arriving at a reasoned vote choice. Voters prepare to make a vote choice, not to take an information quiz. They only need to have known enough about the record that it has left them with a definite general impression of the acceptability of the administration's performance. Since the vote choice only asks voters to decide between two (or at most three) serious presidential candidates, they only need to know how the administration performed on matters most important to the voter, not on everything, and whether that performance was likely better or worse than the alternative. For many, the records are clear enough that the vote choice is easy and nothing said or done in a campaign could make a difference.

The Known Candidates

Mixed in with partisanship, ideology, and impressions about the records of the candidates and their parties are evaluations of the candidates themselves. Voters are not asked to elect a party or a record to the presidency, but a person. Inevitably some assessment by the voters of the candidates as people and potential leaders—their abilities and shortcomings, the strengths and weaknesses of their personalities and character—enter the vote decision.

Voter evaluations of candidate qualities are affected by two facts: presidential candidates are well known and presidential candidates are also unknowable. That is, by the time that each of the major-party candidates receives the party's presidential nomination voters know who they are. They recognize the name, have some background information, have heard the candidates speak, and have probably seen them on television. They are familiar with the candidates and have probably formed some opinion about what kind of people they are and perhaps their suitability as leaders. In this broad sense, candidates are well known. However, the candidates will never be known very deeply by voters. There is a distance between presidential candidates and voters that is insurmountable. Presidential candidates are managed, and it is not just "handlers" who manage them. They are in a role as candidates, potential presidents. Voters do not have access to the candid, unguarded candidate.

Adding to the difficulty of assessing candidate qualities is the softness of information about these traits. Any action, statement, or appearance that candidates make may reveal something about their character or abilities. However, this information is usually open to many different interpretations. Obstinacy to one person may be steadfastness to another. Diplomacy to some is evasiveness to others. Evidence of compassion may also be read as evidence of weakness or gullibility. And differing interpretations of personal qualities are not as resolvable by reference to facts as beliefs about the candidates' policy positions might be.

Because candidates are known widely but not deeply, because voters have every reason to believe that they will never really know the candidate, and because information about candidate qualities is so malleable, first impressions of the candidates are often lasting impressions. This means that the campaign is unlikely to change many minds very much about this component of the vote decision. For those who see much stronger leadership qualities in one candidate relative to the opponent, the vote choice may be easy and early.

Perceptual Screens to the Campaign
Between easy voting based on partisan commitments and easy voting based on definite evaluations of the past record and candidate qualities, a substantial portion of the electorate is effectively removed from campaign influence before the campaign even begins. However, these are not the only limits on campaign effects. Campaign effects are further restrained among those who have not already firmly decided a vote choice because of the minimal effects conundrum and the effects of rationalization.

The general implication of the minimal effects conundrum, discussed at some length in chapter 1, is that those who are *most* likely to be influenced by the campaign are the *least* likely to pay attention to it because they have little interest in politics. Conversely, those who are *most* likely to pay attention to the campaign are the *least* likely to be influenced by it since they already have firm opinions.

Rationalization also diminishes the impact of the campaign among those who are not already firmly decided. Voters who lean toward one candidate or party over the other are likely to interpret events to be favorable toward their preference. In most cases the rationalization is not the extreme sort in which voters imagine scenarios that cast their favored candidate in a positive light and the opponent in a bad light. The more common form of voter rationalization is more subtle. There is almost always room for different reasonable interpretations or different degrees of importance given to new information about the candidates and, where there is room for alternative interpretations, voters are likely to choose the one that least challenges their preexisting opinions. All of this can take place quite subconsciously and without calculation. In effect, voters are their own "spin doctors." They try to reduce dissonance by not seeing it. This reduces the likelihood of a campaign changing the minds of even those somewhat open to change.

The resistance of voters to dissonant information is not lost on the candidates' campaigns and provides the basis for a campaign message version of the minimal effects conundrum. The logic is straightforward: the campaign messages that have the potential to make substantial changes in an election are the most extreme messages that, ironically, are also the least likely to be seen as credible by voters and are, therefore, the least likely to be offered by the candidates in their campaigns.[9]

While there are several forces impeding campaign effects and while many voters reach an easy and quick pre-campaign vote choice, the presidential vote decisions for many others are neither so easily nor so quickly made. While many see one presidential candidate as much more preferable to the other, some voters see strengths and weaknesses in both candidates. When partisanship, the record, and candidate qualities do not add up to an obvious choice, the voter faces a difficult decision. These tough vote decisions cannot be made so early and, if made tentatively early on, may be more open to change through the campaign. For these voters, the campaign may help to clarify matters, resolve uncertainties, and draw sharper distinctions between the candidates.

Systematic Factors Incorporated during the Campaign

There are two systematic factors that often help the voter who is undecided or indifferent at the outset of campaign season: the incumbency status of the candidates and the state of the election-year economy. These two factors establish the context of the campaign and, except for very late economic developments, are known prior to the beginning of the campaign, allowing the general course of the campaign to be predictable.

Presidential Incumbency

Incumbency is an advantage for presidential candidates in elections and is particularly advantageous during campaigns.[10] It is not, however, an automatic advantage. As studies of congressional incumbency make clear, incumbency provides opportunities and resources not normally afforded to other candidates, but they can be used effectively to garner votes or they can be squandered. Presidents who manage to avoid major policy failures or are fortunate enough to hold office while the nation generally enjoys peace and prosperity will be rewarded by voters. Some of these voters, judging national conditions to be generally favorable, will decide early on to renew the president's contract. Others, however, may see more of a mixed record or have other reasons that keep them from deciding to back the incumbent before the campaign gets under way.

While the advantages that most incumbent presidents enjoy are reflected in part in the vote intentions of voters who decided before the campaign, these advantages also affect the decisions of voters who reach their decisions during the campaign. As a result, one of the systematic effects of general election presidential campaigns is to incorporate the advantages of presidential incumbency into votes for the in-party presidential candidate. Put differently, all other things being equal, presidential campaigns tend to work to the benefit of in-party candidates.

There are several reasons why campaign effects favor incumbent presidents. Among the incumbent president's advantages are: (1) the trappings of the office and the role of the president as the national leader, (2) inertia among otherwise undecided voters, (3) the particular advantage that first-term presidential incumbents have in communicating a strong campaign message to voters, and (4) the easier road that incumbent presidents usually travel to receive their party's presidential nomination.

The primary advantage of incumbency is that, as the leader of the nation, the incumbent's stature in the eyes of many voters is higher than that of a mere politician. Even as cynical as many modern Americans have become, their patriotic feelings for the nation often become intertwined with their impressions of the president as candidate. It is difficult, if not impossible, to separate entirely feelings about the office from feelings about its current occupant.

From the candidate's perspective, all of the pomp and pageantry of the office can be used in the campaign while at the same time preserving the appearance of not campaigning, of rising above politics—the familiar Rose Garden strategy. More substantively, presidents can claim credit for specific accomplishments and government largess, whether it is delivering disaster relief or appearing with mayors who have been awarded additional federal funds to increase the size of their police force in a war against crime.

Voter inertia also works to the advantage of incumbent presidents. If voters are in doubt about which candidate to vote for, they may give the benefit of the doubt to the candidate who currently holds the office. The burden of proof, as it were, rests with the challenger, who has to make a convincing case for why voters should reverse the decision that they made at the previous election. Moreover, given the general psychological positivity bias of people (most people prefer to focus on the good rather than the bad), the challenger has a particularly difficult job of devising a convincing campaign message to displace an incumbent president.

A third major advantage of incumbent presidents is limited to incumbents whose party has been in the White House for only a single term. There are two perennially great themes in presidential elections: the stability theme ("stay the course" or "don't change horses in the middle of the stream") and the change theme ("it's time for a change" or "let's get the country moving again"). The stability theme's message is that the administration should have more time to enact and implement its program. The change theme suggests that one party has held power too long; we've tried it their way and there are still problems, so let's try something new. These are, respectively, the insider and outsider arguments for power.

Most candidates are limited to using one or the other of these themes but not both. A candidate from a party that has held the presidency for some time is well situated to use the stability theme but is poorly positioned to use the change theme. For instance, after Democrats had occupied the White House continuously since 1932, Harry Truman would have had a terrible time convincing voters that they should elect him in 1948 if they wanted change in the government. The situation is quite different for the out-party presidential candidate. It is in the interest of the out-party to make the case for change, but the stability theme is not normally in the challenger's interests.

Unlike in-party candidates after their party had held office for several terms and out-party presidential candidates, in-party candidates seeking a second term for their party can effectively make *both* the stability and change arguments for reelection. As the incumbent, the stability theme is naturally available to the candidate. The change theme can also be used by a candidate in this situation since his party has not been in office too long. After only four years in the White House, a party is new enough to the presidency to be still thought of as the outsiders. After two or more consecutive terms, the party's standard-bearer can no longer credibly lay claim to outsider status. Regardless of who it represents or what its policies are, after two terms in office a party becomes the establishment or status quo party.

A fourth advantage of incumbent presidents is that they generally have an easier time than other candidates in winning their party's presidential nomination.[11] Unified parties help and divided parties hurt their candidates. Not only do divisive party nomination contests absorb resources that might be more productively directed at winning the general election, but intraparty charges of candidates competing against each other can leave the eventual nominee's reputation bruised. There is little doubt, for instance, that George H. W. Bush's charge during the 1980 GOP presidential primaries that Ronald Reagan's tax-cut plan was "voodoo economics" hurt Reagan in the general election. Charges against a presidential candidate from within the party cannot be so easily dismissed as overcharged partisan rhetoric; they can come back to haunt the party when used by the opposition in the general election campaign. Candidates who get a "pass" for their party's nomination, as incumbents historically have, can avoid this problem. With their party's base united at the outset, their general election campaign can focus on attracting additional swing voters (J. Campbell 2007a).[12]

The Election-Year Economy
One of the most obvious factors affecting elections is the economy. Voters reward the in-party for robust economic growth and punish it for economic downturns. The economic record of an administration, of course, involves more than economic conditions in the election year itself, and it would be a mistake to think that most voters are so myopic that they do not take the pre-election-year economic record into account in their votes. Once an administration has been in office for long enough to have had an impact, voters hold it accountable for the health of the economy. However, like most other things, the past is weighted less than the recent in reaching decisions. Early economic woes may fade in memory if the economy recovers, but, by the same token, an early economic boom will not excuse a later economic bust.

The record of the pre-election-year economy has already entered into the vote deliberations of most voters well before the campaign. They have already had an ample chance to draw whatever political inferences they think appropriate from this economic information. More recent economic conditions, however, may not yet have been fully felt by voters and may not yet have affected views of the parties and candidates. These election-year economic developments become more completely felt by voters and are incorporated into their vote decision during the campaign.

Three particular aspects of election-year economic effects on the vote deserve clarification. First, economic developments themselves rather than economic reports are what drive economic influences on the vote. Voters live in the economy. What they do not experience personally, they nonetheless witness quite directly and in tangible terms. They see neighbors and friends get promotions or get laid off. They see prices rise or stabilize. Even if most voters paid close attention to the reported broad-based statistics of economic activity, and there is little reason to suspect that many do, these sterile facts would be no competition for experience. Because voters do not closely monitor the economy but rather acquire their information from informal economic impressions, there are lags between economic developments, voter evaluations of the economy, and political consequences for vote decisions.

Second, the effects of the economy on the vote extend beyond the narrowly economic. As the economy goes, so goes the voters' mood toward the in-party. That is, when the economy is doing well, the in-party benefits not only because voters have more money in their pockets but also because voters are generally more receptive to the in-party. Good economic times put voters in a good mood toward the in-party. In times of prosperity, voters may de-emphasize or forgive in-party shortcomings on noneconomic matters. By the same token, when the economy is doing poorly, the in-party may suffer for both noneconomic and economic reasons. If voters are upset with the administration over economic conditions, this disposition is likely to spill over to other matters as well. Thus, the state of the economy may have a significant systematic guiding effect on the course of presidential campaigns.

Third, responsibility for the economy is partly attributed to the party in the White House but also partly to the president personally. Presidents are held fully accountable in their reelection bids for what occurred in the economy during their term. However, voters do not hold a non-incumbent or successor candidate of the in-party accountable to the same degree. Though their party held power, they did not personally hold power and make the decisions that may have affected the economy. These successor candidates (e.g., George H. W. Bush in 1988, Gore in 2000) are only partially credited or blamed for economic conditions.

The Competitive Effect of Campaigns

The third component of the theory of predictable campaigns is that campaigns narrow the gap between frontrunners and trailing candidates. The presidential campaign, as Stephen Hess wrote, "serves as an equalizer" (1978, 47), and as Larry Bartels observes, "underdogs tend to gain ground" (1992, 264). The race routinely tightens up over the course of the presidential campaign, and the effect is to make the election more competitive (J. Campbell and Wink 1990; J. Campbell 1996; and Erikson and Wlezien 1996).[13]

There are five reasons that presidential campaigns reduce the leads of front-running candidates: (1) the campaign makes a bigger difference for candidates nominated by a divided political party and these candidates are usually the ones who are behind at the outset of the campaign, (2) presidential campaigns are intensely competitive contests that level the political playing field between the candidates, (3) frontrunners become the targets of increased scrutiny by both voters and the media, (4) strategically, frontrunners make a trade-off between securing their election and maintaining or extending their lead, and (5) late-deciding voters who had been undecided are likely to split about evenly between the two candidates.

Bringing the Disenchanted Back to the Fold

The first reason that campaigns reduce the lead of frontrunners is that candidates who are behind at the start of the campaign are often survivors of divided nomination contests. The general election campaign is of greater help to these candidates than to candidates who were nominated by an already unified party. Campaigns are especially helpful to candidates nominated by a divided party because they provide an opportunity to heal party wounds by shifting the focus from differences within the party to differences between the parties. Supporters of candidates who were defeated in the bid for their party's nomination are naturally often disgruntled and disenchanted with the party and its nominee. Voters who have focused on reasons not to support the party's eventual nominee and had a stake in defeating that candidate may find it difficult to support their recent foe in the general election. Many may flirt with defecting to vote for the opposition party's candidate. Others may suspend judgment. Time in the campaign allows the psychological barrier to supporting their party's nominee to weaken. Once they accept the disappointment of their first choice being denied the nomination, they may decide to come back, even if reluctantly, to support their party's candidate.

The focus of the general election campaign on the important policy and value differences between the political parties may also give the potentially disaffected second thoughts about voting for the opposition. These may set the relatively modest differences among candidates within the party, the differences of the nomination contest, into a larger context and provide voters with greater perspective. While some disaffected partisans will defect, others, after flirting with the possibility of defection, may simply decide to sit out the election. Still others may be gradually persuaded by the campaign to return to the fold if only to vote for "the lesser of two evils." The erosion of potential defectors by their return to their party's nominee or by their decision not to vote should be of greater help to trailing candidates than to frontrunners who normally enter the campaign season backed by an already unified party.

Competitive Campaigns

The second reason that presidential campaigns reduce frontrunner leads is that both campaigns draw on enormous resources and are roughly equally matched. With the grand prize of American politics at stake, both campaigns have highly visible and experienced national politicians as candidates, plenty of money, top-quality advisors, and receive a tremendous amount of coverage by the mass media.[14] Some campaigns are certainly run better than others, but the fact that presidential campaigns are such high-stimulus events means that any edge for one candidate's campaign over the other's usually does not mean so much.

To illustrate the point that campaign differences have a smaller impact as the intensity of the campaign increases, suppose that all resources in campaigns had definite dollar values attached to them. A half-million-dollar difference between candidates in a campaign in which the candidates spent two and a half million dollars is substantial. The difference is a fifth of everything spent on the campaign ($0.5/2.5 = 0.2$). Now suppose the half-million-dollar difference between candidate resources was in a campaign in which the candidates jointly spent twenty-five million dollars. In this case, the difference amounts to only 2 percent of all spending.

In presidential elections, because of the competitiveness of the national two-party system, the campaign finance laws, and the interests of the media and the public, the two presidential campaigns are quite competitive with one another and any difference between them is effectively diluted by the magnitude of the whole campaign. As a result, the battle between the two evenly matched and high-resource campaigns for the presidential candidates effectively narrows the vote gap between the candidates.

The impact of competitive or balanced campaigns on elections may be presented in formal terms. Following in the tradition of *The American Voter*'s distinction between long-term and short-term forces (A. Campbell et al. 1960), the vote can be understood as reflecting two sets of influences on voters: pre-campaign considerations (Pre-campaign) and considerations raised during the campaign (Campaign). The two-party national vote percentage for a candidate is some weighted average of these two sets of influences:

$$\text{Vote}_i = (\alpha \times \text{Campaign}_i) + ([1 - \alpha] \times \text{Pre-campaign}_i)$$

where α is the weight attached to campaign considerations ($1 \geq \alpha \geq 0$) and $[1 - \alpha]$ is the weight attached to pre-campaign considerations. The pre-campaign considerations and the considerations about the vote raised during the campaign are the percentage of the vote that would have been cast based purely on those deliberations. Since balanced or competitive campaigns should generally mean that campaign-affected preferences are closer to an even split than pre-campaign preferences (that $|$ Campaign $- 50 | < |$ Pre-campaign $- 50 |$), then the vote should approach an even division to the extent that the campaign plays a greater role in the voters' deliberations (as α increases).

One point about the balanced nature of presidential campaigns deserves clarification. A balanced campaign is *not* equivalent to not having a campaign. If there were no campaign, votes would be based only on the "pre-campaign" considerations of the above model ($\alpha = 0$, and therefore $[1 - \alpha] = 1$). However, in a balanced campaign, voters may weigh both what they knew about the candidates before the campaign as well as what they learned about them during the campaign ($\alpha > 0$). As long as the campaign enters the voting calculus at all, the greater balance in the campaign ought to drive the vote toward a more even division. *Balanced campaigns do not mean that campaigns are less important but that the elections are more competitive.*[15]

The Frontrunner as Target

The third reason for competitive campaign effects is that frontrunning candidates are subjected to increased scrutiny by the voters and the media. Once a candidate becomes the frontrunner, voters and the media ask tougher questions. Besides asking the superficial horse-race question of whether the candidate can win, the first questions of voters and the media are: Who is this candidate and what does he or she stand for? When a candidate becomes a clear frontrunner the question changes: Is this candidate worthy of being president? Most of the public at large have fairly high and often unrealistic standards of presidential worthiness. No candidate measures up or looks good enough. Flaws and weaknesses are brought into high relief. The initial glow from being the frontrunner dissipates as the would-be president is brought down a peg or two.

The media may have additional interests in reducing the lead of frontrunning candidates. It is clear that many journalists have adopted an adversarial role toward elected officials, and this approach may also be applied to what would appear to be nearly elected candidates. The media may also want to keep interest alive in the election story. Nothing dampens interest in a story as surely as knowing how the story will end. Members of the media scramble to be the first to announce the ending of the election story, but until that point they have an interest in maintaining the belief that the ending is in doubt.

The Frontrunner Plays It Safe

The fourth reason for the lead-reducing effect of presidential campaigns is that there is an obvious strategic tradeoff that candidates with large leads make late in the campaign. The tradeoff is between securing their election victory and preserving the size of their vote margin. Candidates with large leads become more cautious. They are less interested in the size of their victory and more interested in securing their victory. The situation is analogous to baseball or football teams with large leads late in the game. A baseball team with a three-run lead in the ninth inning does not care about giving up two runs, but does not want the tying or winning run to come to the plate. They will give up a run for an out. Football teams with big leads late in the game are conservative on offense, keeping the ball on the ground, and may use a "prevent defense," conceding modest gains by the opponent's offense. Playing it safe, presidential candidates with large leads may also be willing to lose some of their vote lead to avoid big mistakes and a chance of defeat.

Late Deciders Divide Evenly

The fifth reason that campaigns even up the race is that late-deciding voters who had held off making a decision are likely to divide fairly evenly. This is essentially a selection effect. Although there are a number of reasons why voters might postpone reaching a decision, many undecided voters are most probably torn between the two candidates. Many of these voters hold off declaring a vote intention because they see an appeal (or have a distaste) for voting for either candidate. The vote is a toss-up. As President George H. W. Bush put it, in a statement reminiscent of Yankee legend Yogi Berra, "it is no exaggeration to say that the undecideds could go one way or another."[16]

It seems reasonable to expect that some late deciders, when forced to make a choice if they intend to vote, will vote for the Democratic candidate and others will vote for the Republican candidate. If late-deciding voters remain truly torn between the two candidates (and are committed to voting), we should expect in general that their vote choice amounts to a flip of a coin and thus an even division of their aggregated vote. An even or near-even division should raise the vote share of the trailing candidate and reduce the lead of the frontrunner.

Narrowing Is Not Momentum

One point about the nature of the competitive, narrowing effect of the general election campaign warrants clarification: the narrowing effect of the campaign is not the same thing as political momentum. The distinction is important. The concept of momentum, a concept borrowed from physics, is that once public support begins to move in a particular direction it is likely to continue to move in that direction. A body set in motion tends to remain in motion. Holbrook (1996a, 130–32 and 142–43) claims that momentum plays a significant role in

Table 2.2. The Public Opinion Dynamics of Momentum and the Narrowing Effect

| | Candidate's Level of Support at: | | Expected Change from Time 2 to Time 3: | |
| | | | Expected from Momentum | Expected from Narrowing |
Case	Time 1	Time 2		
A	35	40	Gain	Gain
B	35	30	Loss	Gain
C	65	70	Gain	Loss
D	65	60	Loss	Loss

the effects of the typical presidential campaign, much like that found in presidential primaries (Bartels 1988). The theory of the predictable campaign, on the other hand, claims that the systematic narrowing effect of campaigns has been mistaken for momentum.

The distinction between the narrowing or competitive effect and momentum can be demonstrated by examining a set of four hypothetical campaign situations. These are presented in table 2.2. The first two situations concern trailing candidates, one who has gained ground in the polls from time 1 to time 2 (case A) and one who has lost further ground in the polls in this period (case B). The third and fourth situations involve frontrunners, a frontrunner who has increased his or her lead (case C) and one whose lead has recently diminished (case D). Momentum effects are more of the same. Those who have lost ground will lose more in their downslide (cases B and D). Those who have gained ground will have more voters jump on their bandwagon by time 3 (cases A and C). For the narrowing effect, the important point is not whether a candidate has recently become more or less popular but whether that candidate is ahead or behind the opponent. Candidates who are ahead can be expected to fall back a bit (cases C and D) while candidates who are running behind should be expected to gain ground (cases A and B).

In these hypothetical situations, the two processes of momentum and the narrowing effect anticipate the same change half of the time but anticipate a different change the other half of the time. In reality, however, once a narrowing effect occurs and continues, it should appear much like momentum. Trailing candidates will tend to see increase on top of increase, and frontrunners will tend to see their leads decline and then decline further. The telling point is that the changes are in the general direction anticipated by the narrowing effects of competitive campaigns. In contrast to a pure momentum process, support for even the most successful frontrunners does not skyrocket and support for the most clumsy trailing candidates does not completely evaporate. The effects of presidential campaigns are predictable, in part, because of their narrowing effect on the race rather than a momentum in the movement of the electorate. Since its direction cannot be anticipated before an initial movement by the public one way or the other, momentum alone would not make campaign effects predictable.[17] In contrast, the impact of the campaign's narrowing effect on the election can be anticipated at the outset of the campaign when it becomes clear which of the major-party presidential candidates is the frontrunner.

The Course of the Campaign

Presidential elections are predictable because presidential campaigns generally run a predictable course. Figure 2.2 depicts the three elements that structure most presidential campaigns: the stable context defining the starting point and limits of campaigns, the variable context affecting the systematic tilts to

Figure 2.2. The Development of the Typical Campaign According to the Theory of the Predictable Campaign

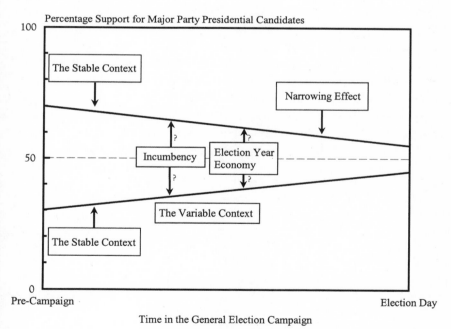

Percentage Support for Major Party Presidential Candidates

Pre-Campaign

Election Day

Time in the General Election Campaign

Note: The impact of the variable context of presidential incumbency and the election-year economy on the course of the campaign depends on whether an incumbent president is seeking election, the party of the incumbent, and the growth rate in the economy.

different campaigns, and the narrowing or competitiveness effect of presidential campaigns.

In part, campaigns are predictable because their net effects are limited. The course of a typical presidential campaign runs within relatively narrow bounds set by competitive national partisan politics with many voters reaching nearly irrevocable vote choices before the campaign begins. They know enough about the parties, the candidates, and the records to reach early vote decisions. They do not know everything, but they know what they like and do not like and both are clear enough to them before the campaign that they can settle on a choice.

Within the boundaries set by the early deciders, the campaign has three systematic effects on election results. First, it narrows the lead of frontrunning candidates. Large poll leads do not survive to the election. Second, the campaign tilts toward presidential incumbents reflecting the several advantages that presidential incumbents have over their challengers. Third, the campaign reflects the effects of the election-year economy on voter views toward the current presidential party. In addition to these systematic campaign effects, presidential campaigns may also have some unsystematic effects on election results. However, the theory of predictable campaigns argues that these unsystematic effects, idiosyncratic candidate gaffes or triumphs, are usually very limited in their impact on the vote.

The pre-campaign boundaries for presidential campaigns, each of the systematic effects of these campaigns, and the possibility of unsystematic campaign effects will be explored in some detail in subsequent chapters. However, before we undertake these explorations into the predictable campaign, we should clarify a few central concepts and examine the data that will be used throughout the analysis. Chapter 3 turns to these methodological matters.

★ *Chapter 3*

Studying the Effects of Campaigns

HOW A SUBJECT is defined, measured, and analyzed often plays a large role in the conclusions reached about it. So it is important at the outset to address four methodological matters about presidential campaign effects. First, several core concepts of the study are defined. Second, the data used to explore campaign effects are discussed. Third, the presidential elections examined in most of the analysis are reviewed. Finally, based on the vote, the polls, and data regarding the context of the elections, the extent of campaign effects in each of these elections is estimated.

Definitions and Measurements

Before addressing the question of whether presidential campaigns have particular systematic effects on the national vote, three concepts need to be pinned down. First, what exactly is the *presidential campaign?* What are included and excluded as parts of the campaign? Second, what are *campaign effects* and how are they best measured? Third, what are the *systematic* and *unsystematic* effects of the campaign on the election?

The Content and Timing of Campaigns

The presidential campaign refers to the general election campaign as distinguished from the campaigns for each party's presidential nomination. At first blush, the definition of the general election campaign would seem to be obvious. However, a few issues complicate matters.

Campaigns might be defined as strictly those activities of the candidates and their campaign operations. From the perspective of the candidate, the purpose of a campaign is to provide voters with convincing reasons to vote for the candidate. Any attempt to convey such reasons to potential voters is part of the campaign.[1] This view of campaigns from the perspective of the candidates, however, is quite limited.

Campaigns may alternatively be defined more broadly as extending beyond the candidates and their organizations. This more inclusive perspective is adopted here. Campaigns are more than a collection of discrete events and more than what the candidates and their surrogates do and say. Presidential campaigns, defined inclusively, consist of all those activities of the candidates, their running mates, their parties and personal campaign organizations, the press, and anybody else who seeks to influence in one way or another the decisions of potential voters. The intended influence of these campaign activities may range from attempts to reinforce, convert, or create a potential voter's presidential preference to activities designed to activate or demobilize potential voters to efforts merely to provide information (or even misinformation) to voters that may have one of the aforementioned effects. Included among these general election campaign activities are televised political advertisements; the distribution of leaflets, buttons, yard signs, and bumper stickers; websites and internet messages; campaign speeches and appearances by the candidates and their surrogates; candidate debates; and coverage of these activities by newspapers, magazines, radio, television, and the Internet. Campaigns include everything from these organized direct and indirect attempts to influence the choice of voters to the informal discussions of the candidates and issues by friends and acquaintances. Campaigns are electoral communications of all sorts, from slick advertisements on network television to neighbors exchanging views about the candidates over the back fence.

While the "what" of general election campaigns is so encompassing as not to exclude much (thus making decisions about what counts as campaign content less of an issue in the analysis), the "when" of presidential general election campaigns is both more difficult to determine and more important to defining the phenomena. The difficulty is that American presidential general election campaigns do not begin at a specific moment. Some say that they are perpetually in progress. As soon as one election is over, the next begins.

Even if you do not accept this inclusive definition of the general election campaign, it is clear that the line between the nomination season and the general election campaign season is not a sharp one.[2] Some candidates, like President Bill Clinton in 1996 or President George W. Bush in 2004, do not face opposition for their party's nomination and enjoy the luxury of effectively starting their general election campaign early. Moreover, presidential nominees of the political parties in the modern era are generally known in advance of their parties' nominating convention so both the public and the candidates can turn their attention to the general election before the parties officially make their nominations. The last presidential nomination requiring more than a single convention ballot was the Democratic convention of 1952 that nominated Adlai Stevenson, though several candidates since have had uncertain holds on their nomination going into the convention.[3] Most nominations are locked up weeks before the convention proceedings are gaveled to order.

All of these considerations leave the starting point of general election campaigns variable from election to election and even from candidate to candidate. While the start of the general election campaign is traditionally thought of as the first week of September or Labor Day (about two months before election day), this is several weeks after it has become clear who the respective parties would nominate and even after the two party conventions formally confirmed the candidates' nominations.

Since there is no definite starting date for the general election campaign and since the choice of candidates is usually clear sometime before the first convention, it is impossible to establish a precise starting point applicable to all general election campaigns. Most campaigns are gearing up prior to the first national party convention (held usually in mid-July to early August by the party not holding the White House); they all are getting off the ground after the second convention (held usually in mid- to late August by the president's party); and they are certainly under way by Labor Day. Because of these complications, we will opt to follow the tradition of claiming Labor Day as the start of the campaign but will also consider developments from before mid-July to early September as a campaign transition period during which the focus shifts from the nomination to general election contests.[4]

Campaign Effects and Vote Change

Whenever they begin, presidential campaigns may affect voters in many different ways (Lazarsfeld, Berelson, and Gaudet 1968; Holbrook 2006, 12–16). Most dramatically, campaigns may persuade voters to change their vote choice. Other voters who are undecided may reach a decision based on what they learn during the campaign. Less dramatically, campaigns may reinforce decisions of some voters to vote for a particular candidate. For others, the campaign may stimulate them to turn out to vote. Still others may be demobilized by campaigns. Campaigns may also broadly affect voters by informing or misinforming them, shifting their policy preferences, or even changing their minds about what issues they consider most important.

While the various possible effects of presidential campaigns on individual voters are important, the focus of this study is on the principal aggregate effect of the campaign: its impact on the division of the national popular presidential vote. Does the presidential campaign produce a net shift of votes from one candidate to another?

The question of whether campaigns affect election results is more complex than one might first imagine. Ideally, to determine whether campaigns made a difference one would want to know how the election would have turned out had there been no campaign. But, of course, all presidential elections have campaigns and so the problem is determining an appropriate baseline vote. A natural, if imperfect, baseline can be determined using trial-heat or preference poll results at the outset of the campaign.[5] The difference between the baseline and the actual vote can be attributed to campaign effects. Although the use of polls to assess campaign effects limits the analysis to those elections that have been held since scientific surveys were conducted early enough in the election year to achieve a pre-campaign benchmark, and even though poll results are not the same thing as actual election results, they are the best available evidence for making a comparison of pre-campaign and post-campaign voter decisions.

There are several alternative approaches to using preference polls to examine campaign effects. One is to use the polls in a time-series analysis within an election year or pooled across campaigns. That is, each poll result is treated as an individual observation and changes in the poll percentages for a candidate are interpreted as effects of the campaign. Following this approach, the dependent variable is the candidate's standing in the polls. This is the approach adopted by Holbrook (1996a) and Shaw (1999).[6]

The major problem with assessing campaign effects with a time-series of trial-heat polls is that it neglects the single most important piece of information about campaign effects: the actual vote division. To illustrate the point, Holbrook (1996a, 138) conducted a time-series analysis of average daily trial-heat polls in his examination of campaign effects in the 1988 and 1992 presidential elections.[7] For each election year he examined approximately 150 poll results. The actual election results are not included in the analysis, and even if they had been included, the actual results would represent only a single case out of the 150 examined.[8] Adopting this approach, it is quite possible for a model to do an excellent job of accounting for changes in the polls yet fail to explain changes that affect the actual vote.[9] The important campaign change is not from poll to poll but from poll to *vote*. This is the principal reason why the examination of a time-series of polls is an inappropriate approach to assessing the real effects of campaigns on the vote.

A second, and related, problem of assessing campaign effects by relying on poll data unanchored by the election results is that many changes in preference polls may not reflect changes in the final vote. Some changes in vote prefer-

Table 3.1. Campaign Effects and Four Types of Changes in Trial-Heat Polls

Relevance of Trial-heat Poll Change to Campaign Effects on the Election Results

Irrelevant poll change	*Relevant poll change*
Poll change without real public opinion change, resulting from measurement or sampling errors in the surveys	Change that lasts until election day caused by regular or systematic forces in the campaign
Temporary change in public opinion	Change that lasts until election day caused by unanticipated or unsystematic forces in the campaign

ences as expressed in opinion polls are real and lasting, but others are temporary blips in the polls or may reflect measurement and sampling errors in the surveys themselves. Table 3.1 itemizes the various types of changes in trial-heat polls by their relevance to the election results.

There are always some voters who are undecided or have lightly held preferences for a candidate.[10] For these voters, a slight breeze favoring one candidate may move them to say they favor that candidate, at least until the next campaign breeze. Poll movements based on these ephemeral shifts should not be taken seriously.[11] By the same token, all scientific surveys based on responses from samples of potential voters faced with the hypothetical question of who they would vote for if the election were held that day necessarily involve a degree of error (Crespi 1988; Asher 1998). As such, trial-heat polls may change from one day to the next without any real change in aggregate vote intentions.

Any examination of poll data over the course of an election year, especially early in an election year, reveals a good deal of volatility. A chart of poll numbers in some campaigns could easily be mistaken for an erratic electrocardiogram. Part of this volatility is real and reflects developments in the electorate's collective preferences for the candidates. However, a significant portion of it reflects fleeting changes in national preferences and differences caused by various measurement and sampling errors in the surveys. To no small degree, poll volatility, especially several months before the election, is noise (Wlezien and Erikson 2002, 978).[12] As such, great caution must be used in drawing inferences about campaign effects from changes in preference polls.

The analysis of presidential debate effects illustrates the danger of interpreting temporary or ephemeral shifts in the polls as meaningful campaign effects. According to Holbrook's (1996a, 108) analysis of presidential debates in 1984, there was a 17.3 percentage point pro-Reagan gap between Reagan and Mondale prior to the first presidential debate. After the debate the gap dropped to 13.8 percentage points, and this difference is read as a 3.5-percentage-point pro-Mondale debate effect. Before the second presidential debate that year, the pro-Reagan gap was 15.5 percentage points, and this expanded to 18.9 after the second debate, a 3.4-percentage-point change or "debate bump." With the focus on change between the pre- and post-debate polls, a second point is missed. In both instances, most of the bump in the polls following the debate dissipated shortly after the debate. By the time of the second presidential debate, the poll gap had drifted back (15.5 percent up from 13.8 percent) close to where it stood before the first debate (17.3 percent). Similarly, by the time of the vice presidential debate, much of the bump from the second debate had evaporated. Debate effects in the 1988 and 1992 elections also were mostly temporary in nature.[13]

Although there are dangers in using trial-heat polls to assess campaign effects, there is no alternative. To assess campaign effects we need readings of the electorate's intentions before and during the campaign, and polls are the best available information in this regard. There is an alternative, however, in *how* trial-heat polls are used to gauge campaign effects. Rather than using polls alone in a time-series analysis, trial-heat polls at various points in the election year can be compared to the actual election results for that year. Patterns in these comparisons can then be examined across a series of election years. Unlike time-series analysis, this approach anchors the analysis of campaign effects in the actual election results.[14] For instance, if candidates leading in the polls consistently receive smaller shares of the actual vote than their earlier poll standings, we would presume that something about presidential campaigns reduces the leads of frontrunning candidates. The conclusion about campaign effects in this case comes not from a comparison of one poll to another or even from a series of polls to later polls, but from polls at any given point during election years to the actual results of those elections.[15]

Sorting Out Influences on the Vote
Systematic campaign effects are only one of several types of influences on the presidential vote. Three types of influences on the vote can be distinguished: the pre-campaign context of the election, the regular or systematic developments of a campaign, and the idiosyncratic or unsystematic effects of a campaign. There are two sorts of systematic campaign effects: those that are regular developments of all presidential campaigns and those in which certain contexts of the campaigns "play out" or become incorporated into the voters' decisions over the course of the campaign. The competitiveness effect of presidential campaigns is an example of the former and the impact of the election-year economy is an example of the latter. Finally, any of these influences—pre-

Table 3.2. Classification of Influences on Presidential Elections

Category of Election Influence	Examples
I. Pre-Campaign Context	Partisanship
	Ideology
	Group attachments
	Pre-existing assessments of the candidates
	Pre-election-year economy
	"Favorite-son" phenomenon (localized)
II. Systematic Campaign Effect	
A. Regular Developments	Tightening up of the race
B. Incorporating the Context	Incumbency
	Election-year economy
III. Idiosyncratic Campaign Effect	Candidate gaffes or blunders
	Newly emerging issue
	Crisis or scandal

Note: Unless noted otherwise, all influences identified are presumed to be national in scope.

campaign contexts and systematic or idiosyncratic campaign effects—can be either national or local in scope. The impact of presidential incumbency on the election is a factor of national proportions while the home state or regional advantages of a "favorite son" candidate are by definition more localized in their impact. Table 3.2 summarizes these classifications of election influences.

As voting behavior studies since *The American Voter* have repeatedly made clear, voters enter campaigns with political preconceptions, the most important being their identifications with the major political parties. Presidential elections are partisan events that are significantly shaped by the standing partisan commitments of the electorate, commitments commonly bolstered by consistent ideological perspectives. The partisanship of the electorate has been and continues to be an important, widespread, and enduring characteristic of American politics. Most Americans are partisan, and most partisans vote for their party's presidential candidate in most elections. As such a force in the decisions of individual voters, partisanship in the aggregate is obviously an important influence on election results.

The national electoral history since the Civil War reflects the partisan character of presidential elections. Of the eighteen presidential elections from 1860 to 1928, during the period of the narrowly Republican third party system (1860–92) and the dominant Republican fourth party system (1896–1928), Republicans won fourteen elections and Democrats four. The rare Democratic presidential victories were close and under unusual circumstances. Grover

Cleveland won two very close elections, and Woodrow Wilson won two elections; the first was the consequence of Teddy Roosevelt's bolt from the Republicans, and the second was one of the closest elections on record.

Following the New Deal realignment in the 1930s, Democrats outnumbered Republicans, and this was reflected in presidential election results. Democratic presidential candidates won seven of the nine presidential elections between 1932 and 1964, a string of victories broken only by the two election victories of World War II's heroic general, Dwight Eisenhower (who had earlier been courted as a potential Democratic presidential candidate).

Since the late 1960s, with the gradual realignment toward the Republicans and creating a very competitive party system, Republican presidential candidates have won seven of the ten elections. Despite a Republican edge in victories, the era is better characterized as competitively balanced. Three of the Republicans' seven victories in this period were very closely decided contests (Nixon's victory in 1968 and George W. Bush's elections in 2000 and 2004). The record could easily have tipped in favor of the Democrats. The fact that Democrats usually are elected in Democratic eras, Republicans usually are elected in Republican eras, and neither party dominates in competitively balanced eras demonstrates the importance of the pre-campaign partisan context of an election.

The pre-campaign context of the campaign extends well beyond the longstanding partisan composition of the electorate. Before attention turns to the general election contest, the public's mood is inclined or disinclined toward a candidate by a host of factors, including the state of the economy, evaluations of the likely candidates developed from their previous service in office and prior campaigns, and their positions as incumbent or non-incumbent candidate seeking the presidency. Voters, like candidates, also enter the campaign season with political histories, and these histories set important parameters for the election. At the very least, the context of the campaign determines whether a candidate faces a friendly or hostile electorate, that is, one receptive or unreceptive to the candidate's case for election.

Although the pre-campaign context of an election is extremely important, elections seldom end up exactly where the campaign started. A candidate with a 20-percentage-point lead in the polls before the campaign usually does not win by that margin. There are two explanations for the difference. The first is that the fundamentals or the context of the election are not fully reflected in the public's thinking at the outset. A presidential candidate's incumbency or the state of the economy, for instance, may be established before the campaign begins, but these factors are worked into the voters' thinking over the course of the campaign. Put differently, the fundamentals or context of the campaign may set a predictable or systematic course to the campaign. That is, there may be certain regularities to presidential campaigns that should be anticipated at the outset of any particular campaign.

In accounting for campaign effects on the vote, it is also possible that the individual decisions of candidates, their campaign organizations, the media, and others attempting to influence voters may have unforeseen or idiosyncratic effects. Events beyond the candidates' control that would sway voters one way or the other may arise in any particular campaign. Alternatively, the particular decisions that candidates make in everything from off-hand remarks to the press to well-planned issue pronouncements may affect the voters' verdict. For instance, it would have been difficult to foresee, or to regard as any sort of regular feature of campaigns, the decision by the Dukakis campaign in 1988 to have the professorial-appearing candidate don an oversized army helmet and drive a military tank in front of press cameras (Jamieson 1992, 3–9). Unfortunately for the Dukakis campaign, the candidate became the object of ridicule. This is the stuff that keeps the blood pulsing through the veins of political journalists and keeps candidates and political consultants awake at night.

Usually, but not always, these unexpected or unsystematic campaign developments cancel each other out over the course of several months of campaigning. Each candidate scores unexpected points with the public and each makes political blunders that cost votes. Each candidate has good and bad days. However, it is unlikely that the good and bad days for both candidates balance out perfectly; one candidate may gain an edge from the give-and-take of any single campaign.

Although this study principally examines campaign effects in a national context, state and local conditions and campaign effects are also very important. They are made all the more so by the electoral college system and by the adoption in most states of a plurality winner-take-all provision in the awarding of electoral college votes.

From state to state and region to region, the voting public differs in partisanship and ideological leanings. State and regional economies differ in composition and growth rates. More particularly, one might expect that voters' familiarity with and pride in a home-grown candidate running for national office might be reflected in the vote. Moreover, there is the possibility that campaign events might have greater effects in some parts of the nation than in others. If a candidate made a statement during the campaign that suggested, for instance, support for policies anathema to the oil industry and favorable to oil consumers, he or she might expect a negative reaction in oil-producing states and more favorable evaluations in other states. Although some of these local campaign factors will be discussed in chapter 9, the attention of the study is directed primarily at the various national influences of the campaign.

One final point needs to be made about the distinction between systematic and unsystematic campaign effects. This concerns the apparent conflict between the early predictability of presidential election results and the impact of political campaigns on those results. It is commonly assumed that if elections are highly predictable well before the general election campaign gets under way, then the campaign must not make much of a difference. The prevailing view is that while the individual campaigns of the candidates may shift public opinion from time to time, overall and in the end, the campaigns together do not shift the vote very much from what it would have been without the campaigns. Some have suggested that the errors in forecasts reflect the magnitude of campaign effects and that accurate forecasts, in essence, mean that campaign effects are inconsequential (Holbrook 1996a, 31, 67).[16] The question is this: How can we predict an election before the campaign if the campaign matters? The answer is that campaign effects are predictable in the same way that elections are predictable. Most of the effects of campaigns are systematic and reflect the fundamentals included in the election forecasting models.[17] Viewing campaign effects as limited to their unanticipated effects as reflected in the forecast errors severely understates the impact of campaigns by restricting them to only their unsystematic component. The recognition of systematic campaign effects resolves the forecasting-campaign puzzle: *elections can be forecast in advance because the effects of campaigns can be largely forecast in advance.*

Data

This study uses three types of data: tabulations of the actual presidential popular vote, the aggregate results of trial-heat polls conducted before and during the campaigns, and individual-level survey data from the NES.

One issue that arises in the use of the aggregate poll and actual vote data is how to treat survey preferences for third-party or independent candidates and votes actually cast for these candidates. Since there is little stability in the emergence of significant third-party or independent candidates, examining the total poll or vote preference percentages rather than two-party percentages for major-party candidates might produce significant distortions in the analysis. A poor showing for a candidate in absolute terms (as a percentage of the total vote for all candidates) might simply reflect the personal decision of an independent candidate to run for president. This poor showing in the total vote percentage for a major party candidate may actually be a strong showing in the two-party vote percentage. Since the "real" contest in American politics is between the candidates of the two major political parties, the two-party percentage is the one that matters to the results and is the one that will be used in this analysis in measuring both poll preferences and the national vote.

The trial-heat poll data used are from the Gallup Poll. Since the late 1940s, national surveys conducted by Gallup have regularly included "trial-heat" questions asking respondents to reveal their vote preference prior to election day. These questions have been asked at irregular intervals before and during the campaign. To provide for comparability across elections, this analysis examines these poll results at seven periods during the election year: in early June, late July, after the national party conventions, early September, late September, mid-October, and just prior to the election in November.[18]

In examining some of the underpinnings of the theory of the predictable campaign we will use data from the American National Election Studies (NES). These data will be used to examine groups of voters: partisans versus independents, early versus late deciders, those with stable preferences versus those who changed their minds during the campaign. In keeping with the general approach of this analysis, the voting behaviors of these groups will be compared across elections. The use of the NES data across elections raises a problem: the survey data has a known and variable inaccuracy with respect to the presidential vote. The vote percentages for the candidates in the NES surveys do not match the actual vote percentages for these candidates.

Table 3.3 presents the reported (NES survey) and the actual vote percentages since 1952 for Democratic and Republican presidential candidates. Any survey entails some error and the amount of error in the NES surveys is not especially large. The mean absolute error in the NES reported two-party vote percentage is about 2.3 percentage points.[19] However, given that the average winning vote over this period was about 54.7 percent, a 4.7-percentage-point margin over an even vote split, the survey errors are proportionately substantial. Moreover, in several elections (1964, 1992, 1996), the survey errors were especially large.

The errors in the NES data, errors that are potentially quite problematic for comparisons across elections, can be corrected in the aggregate by weighting the data. The weights in each year for those who voted for different presidential candidates can be calculated by computing the ratio of the actual known vote for that candidate and the vote reported by the survey. If supporters of a candidate are underrepresented in the survey relative to their actual presence in the electorate, they are counted by a factor greater than one. Conversely, supporters of a candidate who are overrepresented in the survey relative to their share of the actual electorate are counted by a factor of less than one.

Table 3.3. *The Reported NES Presidential Vote Division and the Actual National Popular Presidential Vote Division, 1952–2004*

	Democratic Presidential Vote Percentage			Republican Presidential Vote Percentage		
Election Year	Reported	Actual	Difference	Reported	Actual	Difference
1952	41.85	44.38	−2.53	57.90	55.14	+2.76
1956	40.19	41.97	−1.78	59.49	57.37	+2.12
1960	48.72	49.72	−1.00	50.78	49.55	+1.23
1964	67.51	61.05	+6.46	32.31	38.47	−6.16
1968	40.86	42.72	−1.87	47.67	43.42	+4.25
1972	35.44	37.53	−2.09	63.49	60.69	+2.81
1976	50.11	50.07	+.04	48.14	48.00	+.14
1980	39.36	41.02	−1.66	50.83	50.75	+.08
1984	41.32	40.56	+.76	57.74	58.77	−1.03
1988	46.60	45.65	+.95	52.24	53.37	−1.13
1992	47.53	43.01	+4.52	33.92	37.45	−3.53
1996	52.87	49.24	+3.63	38.31	40.72	−2.41
2000	50.78	48.42	+2.36	45.59	47.91	−2.32
2004	48.59	48.27	−.33	49.94	50.73	−.79

Mean absolute error of reported presidential vote percentage = 2.17

Note: The vote percentage figures are of all presidential voters. The reported votes are from the American National Election Studies (NES). Actual and reported votes for third-party or independent candidates can be computed by subtracting Democratic and Republican votes from 100 percent. Actual vote percentages were calculated from Congressional Quarterly's *Guide to U.S. Elections*. The NES reported presidential vote percentages are of those voters who also responded to the party identification questions. The weightings used to adjust the data may be computed by dividing the actual vote percentage for a party's presidential candidate by the NES reported vote for that candidate. The mean absolute error is the mean annual errors for Democratic and Republican votes calculated separately.

The weighting procedure can be illustrated by the example of how the 1992 NES data were treated. The unadjusted 1992 NES data indicated that Bill Clinton received about 4.5 percentage points more of the vote than he actually received. It also erroneously undercounted votes for George H. W. Bush by about 3.5 percentage points. To correct for these inaccuracies, survey respondents indicating a Clinton vote were weighted by a factor of approximately .90 (43.01/47.53). In different terms, rather than counting each Clinton respondent as a whole vote, each was counted as nine-tenths of a vote. Respondents indicating that they voted for George Bush were weighted by 1.10 (37.45/33.92). Rather than counting each reported Bush voter as one vote, to compensate for the underrepresentation of Bush voters in the survey, they were counted as one and one-tenth of a voter. Through this weighting of the data, the survey data are brought into line with the known actual vote. The distribution of the adjusted party identification data for NES studies from 1952 to 2004 are presented in appendix A.

Fifteen Elections

In November of 2008, the United States will hold its fifty-sixth national election for the presidency, the forty-seventh since popular voting for the office became prevalent in 1824. The nation and the ways of electing presidents have changed enormously over this time. The election of the presidency first evolved from an elite-dominated to a popular-vote-based system (though retaining the electoral college). The evolution from elections with inactive candidates restrained by decorum from making personal appeals for votes to one with active and overt campaigning or "stumping" took even longer (Troy 1996). The technological developments of radio and then television further expanded the scope and intensity of modern campaigns.

Although a portion of the analysis in this study extends back to elections after the Civil War, most of the analysis deals with the fifteen presidential elections from 1948 to 2004. This series of elections is selected primarily because polling data necessary to examine campaign effects are not available for earlier elections, but also because the campaigns in these elections facilitate comparisons. Although the 1948 race between Truman and Dewey with its whistle-stop train stumping was quite different from the 2004 multimillion-dollar race between Bush and Kerry with its saturation of multiple media from cable television to the internet, all of the elections in this period were modern presidential campaigns. While campaign technologies continually evolved, the broad reach of the intensely fought, modern media-oriented campaign has remained the same.

Before drawing upon these fifteen elections to examine the theory of the predictable campaign, it is worth reviewing each of them to establish their historical contexts and the extent of relevant differences among them.

Truman's Surprise, 1948

The series begins with what might be regarded as the very antithesis of a predictable campaign: the miraculous come-from-behind victory of Democratic president Harry Truman over his Republican opponent, New York governor Thomas Dewey. Truman, who had served as Franklin Roosevelt's vice president, was elevated to the presidency upon Roosevelt's death. He oversaw the final victory of the Allies in World War II and led the country through the difficult transition to a peacetime economy. Dewey, who had been Roosevelt's Republican opponent in 1944, was renominated by his party to challenge Truman in 1948.

After four consecutive terms in the White House and having suppressed its divisions during Roosevelt's tenure and World War II, the Democratic Party was in disarray. The party splintered on both its left and right wings. Henry Wallace (who had served as vice president during Roosevelt's third term) and the progressives bolted from the left, and Strom Thurmond and the Dixiecrats, disgruntled over what they viewed as a party moving too far in the liberal direction on civil rights, bolted from the right. With the Democrats so divided, Dewey's election seemed a foregone conclusion. But with a very strong election-year economy and many Democratic bolters drifting back to the fold in the final days of the campaign, Truman narrowly defeated Dewey. To this day, one of the most memorable campaign images is that of a triumphant and beaming Harry Truman holding an early edition copy of the *Chicago Daily Tribune* with the premature headline, "Dewey Defeats Truman."

A War Hero President, 1952 and 1956

The 1952 and 1956 elections did not have quite the drama of 1948. Having lost five consecutive presidential elections, Republican leaders prevailed on General Dwight D. "Ike" Eisenhower, heroic commander of the Allied troops in World War II, to run for president as a Republican. The Republican nomination, however, was not his for the asking. He faced opposition from Senator Robert Taft of Ohio, known as "Mr. Republican" and generally acknowledged as the leader of the conservative wing of the party. Taft had unsuccessfully sought the GOP's nomination in 1940 and 1944. After a heated campaign for delegates extending right up to decisions about disputed delegate credentials at the Chicago convention, Ike narrowly defeated Taft for the Republican nomination.

Truman's decision not to seek a second full term of his own opened the

Democratic nomination to a wide field of candidates. Senator Estes Kefauver of Tennessee, raised to national prominence by his Senate Committee's hearings about organized crime, Senator Richard Russell of Georgia, former New York governor Averell Harriman, and Governor Adlai Stevenson of Illinois were the most prominent possibilities. After three ballots and Truman's endorsement, Stevenson was drafted as the party's nominee.

In the general election campaign, the erudite Stevenson fought an uphill battle against the plain-spoken Eisenhower. Although the economy was in fairly good shape and Democrats enjoyed a considerable advantage in partisanship, little else favored Stevenson's election. Eisenhower's personal popularity, embodied in his campaign's slogan "I Like Ike," as well as his down-home character, appealed to many voters. Moreover, with Democrats having held the presidency for two decades, many felt it was "time for a change." The issues of government corruption ("the mess in Washington"), rising prices, the Korean War, and the fight against communist subversion also generally favored Eisenhower's election (Morse 1953, 42–76). In the end, with a pledge that he would "go to Korea" and with party-reuniting overtures to the Taft forces, Eisenhower received a solid majority of the vote. The 1956 election rematched Eisenhower and Stevenson. Despite a weaker economy in 1956, Eisenhower was reelected by a slightly larger margin than in 1952.

The Kennedy-Nixon Contest, 1960

The 1960 election was one of the closest in history. There were several serious contenders for the Democratic nomination, among them Senators Hubert Humphrey of Minnesota and Lyndon Johnson of Texas. With a strong showing in the primaries, especially the West Virginia primary showdown victory over Humphrey, Senator John Kennedy of Massachusetts settled many doubts about the electability of a Catholic and captured the nomination, selecting Johnson as his running mate. On the Republican side, Vice President Richard Nixon, who had previously represented California in the U.S. Senate, received the Republican nomination without a serious challenge.

The race between Kennedy and Nixon was close throughout the election year. Kennedy held a slight lead in June, but Nixon pulled ahead slightly in July and maintained a slim lead through Labor Day. With a strong showing in the presidential debates, Kennedy regained a slight poll lead. On election day, with the campaign over and the ballots cast, the election still appeared to be a toss-up. The vote count went on well into the early hours of the next morning. Political chronicler Theodore H. White (1961) observed that the television networks did not declare a Kennedy electoral vote majority until 5:35 on Wednesday morning when they reported that Kennedy had apparently carried Michigan. Kennedy's popular vote plurality over Nixon was fewer than 115,000 votes, amounting to less than two-tenths of a percent of the nearly 69 million votes cast for president in that election.

The vote was so close that the Nixon camp for a time considered challenging the vote counts in several states, particularly in Illinois, where Chicago's Cook County Democratic machine was reported to have engaged in ballot tampering.

All the Way with LBJ, 1964

In sharp contrast to 1960, the winner of the 1964 election was never in doubt. Lyndon Johnson had ascended to the presidency upon the assassination of President Kennedy a little less than a year before the 1964 election, and he was unchallenged for his party's nomination. The Republican Party, on the other hand, renewed its internal battle between its northeastern moderates and midwestern and western conservatives. Party leaders tilting toward the party's conservative wing nominated fire-brand conservative Senator Barry Goldwater of Arizona, widely considered to be too conservative for the nation and regarded by some as "the minority candidate of a minority party" (Converse, Clausen, and Miller 1965, 322). Goldwater made inroads for Republicans in what had been the solid Democratic South, but ran far behind Johnson everywhere else. With the economy in strong shape, a very productive legislative record behind him, and the nation basically at peace (the urban riots and the major buildup of U.S. troops in Vietnam were still to come), the nation elected Johnson in a landslide. The peace, prosperity, and domestic tranquility, however, were not to last.

The Turmoil of 1968

The 1968 election was surrounded by more political turmoil than any modern presidential election. During Johnson's administration, the Vietnam War had escalated and the anti-war movement had grown beyond fringe student groups. The civil rights movement had also grown (both in its nonviolent and more militant wings) and, like the anti-war movement, had stimulated its own opposition. President Johnson faced opposition initially from Senator Eugene McCarthy of Minnesota, an opponent of the war in Vietnam, and later from Senator Robert Kennedy of New York, the younger brother, close advisor, and attorney general to martyred President Kennedy.

The 1968 election year was a series of shocking surprises. The first of these was President Johnson's declaration, delivered as an unexpected conclusion to a nationally televised speech on the evening of March 31, that he would not seek reelection. This opened the door for the candidacy of Vice President

Hubert Humphrey. Although both McCarthy and Kennedy ran strong in presidential primaries, the nomination system in 1968 was still largely determined by local and state party officials, and this favored Humphrey. Still, Humphrey's nomination was not a foregone conclusion, and Kennedy posed an especially serious challenge. Then, only minutes after addressing supporters who had gathered in Los Angeles to celebrate his victory in the winner-take-all California primary on June 4, Robert Kennedy's life was taken by an assassin's bullet. Still mourning the death of civil rights leader Reverend Martin Luther King Jr., who had been murdered in April as he stood on a balcony of a hotel in Memphis, and attempting to recover from the riots that followed, the nation was stunned. Senator George McGovern entered the race in Kennedy's place, but enough of Kennedy's support drifted over to Humphrey that the vice president secured the nomination. It was not an easy nomination. The Democratic convention in Chicago was perhaps the most divisive in history as police and anti-war protesters battled in the streets and tempers flared in the convention hall itself. Adding further to the divisions within the Democratic Party was the decision of Alabama's Governor George Wallace, a conservative Democrat, to make an independent run for the presidency in the Dixiecrat tradition.

The rancor within the Democratic Party made any conflict among Republicans seem inconsequential. The reemergence of Richard Nixon as the Republican nominee was another surprise of 1968. After narrowly losing the 1960 election to John Kennedy, Nixon ran and lost his 1962 race for the governorship of California. Upon this defeat, he had bitterly announced the end of his political career, telling the press, "You won't have Nixon to kick around any more, because, gentlemen, this is my last press conference" (White 1969, 51). Six years later, after turning back a challenge from Governor Nelson Rockefeller of New York on his left and from Governor Ronald Reagan of California on his right, a politically resurrected Nixon accepted the Republican Party's nomination at their convention in Miami.

Despite the bitter divisions among Democrats, allowing Nixon to gain a significant poll lead after the Democratic convention, the 1968 election turned out to be nearly as close as the election of 1960. Nixon's popular vote plurality over Humphrey was just over half a million votes out of more than 73 million cast (about seven-tenths of a percent of all votes cast). In one of the strongest third-party showings in this century, George Wallace drew 13.5 percent of the national vote.

Reelecting the President, 1972

The 1972 election was nearly the mirror image of 1964. President Nixon ran for reelection and, this time, the Democrats nominated a candidate generally regarded as being too far removed from the political mainstream. In a reformed nomination system that depended more on presidential primaries, Senator George McGovern from South Dakota wrested the Democratic presidential nomination from a crowded field of candidates that included, among others, the initial frontrunner, Senator Edmund Muskie of Maine, former vice president Hubert Humphrey, and Governor George Wallace.

McGovern, who had been an early opponent of the American involvement and conduct of the Vietnam War, was viewed by many as a candidate of the radical left. Although the Vietnam War continued to drag on into the 1972 election year, it had been somewhat defused as an issue since the Vietnamization of the war appeared to be extricating United States military forces from the conflict. In any event, McGovern's liberal image stemmed as much from domestic policies and his supporters as from his foreign policy. Nixon won in a popular vote landslide on par with Johnson's 1964 election and even more sweeping in terms of electoral votes. Nixon carried every state except Massachusetts (and the District of Columbia).

The Post-Watergate Election, 1976

The Watergate scandal, the resignation of the vice president under separate charges of illegal conduct, and the only resignation of a sitting president intervened between the 1972 and 1976 elections. The resignation of Vice President Spiro Agnew under charges of corruption, the subsequent appointment (pursuant to Section 2 of the 25th Amendment to the Constitution) of Representative Gerald Ford to replace Agnew as Nixon's new vice president, and President Nixon's resignation in early August, 1974, under threat of impeachment for Watergate-related offenses, led to Gerald Ford becoming the first unelected president in the nation's history. Although the public was appreciative of Ford's efforts to restore a sense of stability in a time of national crisis, his controversial pardon of Nixon weakened his standing. Although unelected and burdened by the pardon, Ford managed to fend off a very serious challenge by Ronald Reagan to win the 1976 Republican presidential nomination.

Perhaps buoyed by the prospects of a post-Watergate election, or enticed by the more primary-dominated nomination system, there was a crowded Democratic field of presidential hopefuls in 1976. A dark horse candidate, former Georgia governor Jimmy Carter, emerged from the field in the early caucuses and primaries. He gained enough momentum from these early victories to outlast his opposition and secure the Democratic nomination. Although he held large poll leads over Ford throughout most of the election year, Carter was elected with one of the smaller vote pluralities in recent history. Carter's vote plurality of 51 to 49 percent of the vote over Ford was greater than Kennedy's plurality in 1960 and Nixon's plurality in 1968, but not by much.

A Beleaguered President, 1980

The Carter administration was plagued with both domestic economic and foreign policy problems. Inflation and unemployment were high, and the economy was sluggish. The Iranians were holding American hostages, and the government appeared helpless. President Carter faced a very strong nomination challenge from Senator Edward Kennedy of Massachusetts, younger brother of John and Robert Kennedy, and just barely won renomination.

The 1980 Republican field of hopefuls was crowded. Ronald Reagan, the former governor of California and an outspoken conservative, broke away from the pack to win the party's nomination. He selected George H. W. Bush, his closest competitor for the nomination, as his running mate. Representative John Anderson of Illinois, a moderate who had also been a candidate for the Republican nomination, bolted to mount an independent candidacy.

Despite the many problems plaguing the administration and his very divisive nomination contest, Carter led Reagan in the polls from April through June. In the July polls, Reagan overtook Carter. By Labor Day, the gap had closed and the polls remained close right up to election day. The vote, however, was not so close. Reagan won by a respectable margin (about ten percentage points more than Carter's vote) and carried forty-four states. As Gerald Pomper described the proportions of Carter's defeat: "He received the lowest percentage of the popular vote of any incumbent Democratic President in American history and gained fewer electoral votes than any sitting chief executive except Taft, who lost most of his party to Theodore Roosevelt" (1981, 67). The election was generally interpreted as a rejection of President Carter rather than a mandate for Reagan's brand of conservatism, but the 1932 defeat of President Herbert Hoover by Franklin Roosevelt had been cast in similar terms, and that election was crucial to the New Deal realignment. Whatever motivated the Carter defeat and whatever latitude Reagan was granted by his victory, voters had answered the question that candidate Reagan had often posed to them throughout the campaign: "Are you better off now than you were four years ago?"[20]

Reagan's Reelection, 1984

The 1984 election ranks alongside the 1964 and 1972 elections as a modern-day landslide. Although President Reagan's approval ratings had dropped during the economic recession midway through his first term, the economy and his ratings had rebounded by the time of the election. He was renominated without opposition. On the Democratic side, Walter Mondale, Jimmy Carter's vice president, won the Democratic nomination over a field of opponents that included Senator Gary Hart of Colorado and the Reverend Jesse Jackson, a prominent civil rights activist.

The election was framed as a classic contest between a conservative and a liberal. In the face of mounting deficits, Reagan stood firmly behind the tax cuts of his first term and against "big government." Democrats attacked the unfairness of Reaganomics to those lower on the economic ladder, but as the party that had controlled Congress for decades and had built the modern American welfare state, they had difficulty fixing blame for big deficits on Reagan. Perhaps Mondale did more than anyone to define the campaign and determine the election results by his nationally televised acceptance speech at the Democratic convention. In addressing the budget deficit issue, Mondale told a national audience: "Let's tell the truth. Mr. Reagan will raise taxes, and so will I. He won't tell you. I just did" (Quirk 1985, 174). Many Americans heard this statement not as a challenge to Reagan's credibility but as a confirmation of the Republican charge that Mondale was a "tax-and-spend liberal." Reagan held healthy leads over Mondale in the polls throughout the election year. On election day, Reagan carried every state except Mondale's home state of Minnesota (which he nearly carried) and the District of Columbia.

The "Stay the Course" Election, 1988

Following President Reagan's second term, the presidential nomination in both political parties was hotly contested with crowded fields of candidates. George H. W. Bush, who had served as vice president to Reagan, successfully sought the Republican nomination as the natural heir to effectively extend the term of the Reagan administration. His most serious opponents for the nomination were Senator Bob Dole; Reverend Pat Robertson, the leader of the Christian right wing; and Representative Jack Kemp, the leading advocate of supply-side economics and tax cuts.

With several prominent party leaders opting not to run, including Governor Mario Cuomo of New York, Democrats turned to Governor Michael Dukakis of Massachusetts. Dukakis's closest rivals for the nomination were Senator Al Gore of Tennessee, Representative Richard Gephardt of Missouri, and the Reverend Jesse Jackson.

The success of the two Reagan campaigns had Republicans convinced that the 1988 campaign should once again be framed on the conservative-liberal axis, tagging their Democratic opponent with the dreaded "L-word." Linking himself firmly to the Reagan legacy, Bush pledged that under no circumstances would he raise taxes. Then, evoking the image of actor Clint Eastwood's hard-boiled Dirty Harry character, Bush declared that even when pressured to do so he would tell the opposition "Read my lips, no new taxes."

While the Republicans were intent on tagging Dukakis as a liberal, Dukakis was intent on directing attention away from ideology and toward performance. In his speech accepting the Democratic nomination, Dukakis declared that "this election isn't about ideology. It's about competence." Convention speaker Ann Richards of Texas carried the point further, mockingly excusing Bush gaffes because he was "born with a silver foot in his mouth." Republicans stuck to their game plan of portraying Democrats as soft on key American values, from respect for the flag to dealing just punishments to convicted criminals. To make the latter point they raised the case of Willie Horton. Horton was a black man who had been convicted in Massachusetts of murder, escaped from a furlough program run by the Dukakis administration, and committed several violent crimes. Although the Democratic campaign cried foul and claimed the ads were racist, the ads succeeded in raising doubts about Dukakis's toughness on the crime issue. Dukakis did not help matters when he answered in a coldly detached manner a hypothetical question in a debate about whether he would favor the death penalty if his wife had been raped and murdered. Although Bush never held a commanding lead, after Senator Dan Quayle's controversial nomination as vice president and after the conventions were over Bush led Dukakis for the remainder of the campaign. On election day, Bush won with a solid popular vote plurality, carrying forty states.

The Broken Promise Election, 1992

President Bush looked well positioned for reelection in 1992 following the Gulf War. His approval ratings were sky high, and, with these numbers in mind, several prominent potential Democratic opponents (most notably Governor Mario Cuomo, Senator Sam Nunn, Senator Bill Bradley, and Representative Richard Gephardt) decided not to run. The afterglow of the Gulf War approval ratings, however, proved short-lived. Besides the expected Democratic opposition, opposition to Bush arose among some Republicans and from the off-again, on-again independent candidacy of feisty Texas billionaire H. Ross Perot. President Bush survived the nomination challenge on the right from political commentator Pat Buchanan but did not get the free ride to renomination that most sitting presidents receive.

Despite the absence of several high-profile Democrats, there was still a strong field of Democratic candidates for the nomination. However, because of the increased "front-end loading" of the primaries, the "Super Tuesday" bunching of southern primaries, and the absence of strong southern competition for these "Super Tuesday" delegates, Governor Bill Clinton of Arkansas won these early March southern primaries convincingly, and his strong showing propelled him to the Democratic nomination.[21] In a move designed to help reverse Republican inroads in the South, Clinton chose Senator Al Gore of Tennessee as his running mate.

The 1992 election was dominated by economic issues. Clinton advisor James Carville reminded all to stay on message with his crude slogan, "It's the economy, stupid." But Bush's reelection chances were probably hurt more than anything by his having reneged on his memorable 1988 campaign promise not to raise taxes. As part of a 1990 budget deficit reduction compromise with congressional Democrats, the president went back on his "read my lips, no new taxes" pledge. For many this was unforgivable. Although President Bush led Clinton in the June polls, Clinton took the poll lead after the conventions and never relinquished it. He received better than 43 percent of the vote to less than 38 percent for Bush. The remaining 19 percent of the vote was cast for Ross Perot. It was the second-best showing for a non-major-party presidential candidate since the Republicans emerged as a major party in the 1850s.[22]

Clinton's Reelection, 1996
While the 1992 election appeared to be a personal rejection of President Bush, and despite considerable evidence of a realignment toward the Republicans (including the historic 1994 midterm congressional elections in which Republicans captured majorities in both the House and Senate), economic optimism buoyed President Clinton's reelection hopes. Although no Democratic president had been reelected since Franklin Roosevelt in 1944, Clinton had recovered from the 1994 setbacks and his approval ratings through the election year remained above 50 percent.

Senator Bob Dole of Kansas, the majority leader and former vice presidential candidate, was the Republican candidate.[23] Although he had faced primary opposition from the more aggressively conservative wing of his party, particularly from Pat Buchanan and Senator Phil Gramm of Texas as well as from wealthy businessman Steve Forbes and former Governor Lamar Alexander of Tennessee, the front-end-loaded primary system worked to Dole's favor as the early frontrunner. Though he finished second (by one percentage point) to Buchanan in the first-in-the-nation New Hampshire primary, he finished first in the other forty Republican state primaries. As his running mate, Dole selected former representative Jack Kemp.

President Clinton held a large lead in the polls over Dole throughout the election year. Although the polls right up to November suggested a near landslide victory, the actual vote was much closer. Clinton's popular vote plurality over Dole was just slightly larger than his victory over Bush four years earlier. Ross Perot, running again as a third-party candidate, received fewer than half as many votes as he had in 1992.

The Disputed Election of 2000

Not since the disputed election of 1876 between Rutherford B. Hayes and Samuel Tilden has an election generated as much controversy as the 2000 presidential election between George W. Bush and Al Gore. By several standards, the election was the most closely decided in American history. It was the first election since Grover Cleveland lost to Benjamin Harrison in 1888 in which the candidate winning the plurality of the national popular vote (Al Gore) failed to win a majority of electoral votes. It was only the fourth election in American electoral history that the candidate elected to the presidency with an electoral vote majority failed to receive a national popular vote majority. George Bush received 271 electoral votes (1 more than needed) with 49.7 percent of the national two-party vote.

Both parties sent their standard-bearers into the general election with highly unified bases of support. Having lost the 1992 and 1996 elections to Bill Clinton, Republicans were eager to set internal differences aside and unite behind a candidate. Party leaders and campaign contributors fell into line early behind George W. Bush, the governor of Texas and the son of former President George H. W. Bush. Although six Republicans joined the field of nomination hopefuls, the nomination race narrowed quickly to Bush and campaign finance reform proponent Senator John McCain of Arizona. Though McCain did well in contests allowing cross-over votes from independents and Democrats, especially in the Northeast, and extended the contest to early March, Bush clinched the nomination by winning seven of the eleven Super Tuesday primaries. He picked Richard Cheney, a long-time congressman from Wyoming and party elder statesman, as his running mate.

Democrats also had a serious contest for their party's nomination, despite the fact that Senator Bill Bradley of New Jersey failed to out-poll Vice President Al Gore in a single primary. Gore selected Senator Joe Lieberman of Connecticut as his vice presidential candidate, making Lieberman the first Jewish candidate on a national ticket. With both parties settling their nominations early, they pulled together well before their conventions to enter the fall campaigns solidly unified (J. Campbell 2007a).

The course of the 2000 election was unusual. Despite the fact that incumbent President Bill Clinton had been impeached and had barely survived removal by the Senate, his public approval ratings in July of 2000 stood at 59 percent (the median since 1948 is 49 percent), and the economy was experiencing robust growth. With the public generally happy with the performance of the administration, one would suppose the in-party candidate to run a conciliatory retrospective campaign, emphasizing the health of the economy and selectively using President Clinton where his popularity was greatest. Instead, Vice President Gore ran a more controversial class-politics, virtually Clinton-free, prospective campaign. For his part, Governor Bush ran as "Compassionate Conservative," simultaneously reassuring his base and reaching out to swing voters.

The campaign moved back and forth between the candidates, with Gore taking a small lead after the conventions, Bush retaking a small lead after the debates, and Gore pulling back to even in the closing weeks (J. Campbell 2001a, Johnston, Hagen, and Jamieson 2004, 17). In the end, with Gore failing to carry his home state of Tennessee and Clinton's home state of Arkansas, it all boiled down to the electoral votes of Florida. After disputed vote counts and multiple court cases, the contest ended with the Supreme Court's decision in the case of *Bush v. Gore*. The Court decided by a 7 to 2 vote that "there are constitutional problems with the recount ordered by the Florida Supreme Court that demand a remedy" and by a 5 to 4 vote that it was impossible to conduct another recount that would meet constitutional standards by the time required to cast the state's electoral votes. Effectively, this meant that Florida's 25 electoral votes would be cast according to the vote count certified by the state's secretary of state, awarding the state to Bush by a slim 537-vote plurality.

George W. Bush's Reelection, 2004

Several long-term changes in American politics took place over the years leading up to the 2004 election. The American electorate realigned from one in which Democrats dominated Republicans into one in which Republicans and Democrats were of nearly equal strength. The American electorate also became more ideologically polarized. More voters indicated either conservative or liberal inclinations, and these corresponded to their party identifications. As a result, in his 2000 election, George W. Bush became the only modern president to have received a majority of his vote from his ideological-partisan base (conservative Republicans) (J. Campbell 2007c). Reactions to President George W. Bush during his first term reflected this close level of polarized party competition. The partisan gap in presidential approval was at all time highs going into the 2004 election (Jacobson 2007).

While polarization in the electorate set the stage for another close election, the events of September 11, 2001, tilted the electorate in the president's direction. On that morning, Al Qaeda terrorists commandeered three commercial jetliners and crashed them into New York City's World Trade Center towers and the Pentagon outside of Washington, D.C. Passengers on a fourth high-jacked flight (United Airlines flight 93) prevented that plane from being crashed into either the U.S. Capitol or the White House. Like the Japanese attack on Pearl Harbor a generation earlier, the terrorist attacks of 9/11 awoke Americans to the fact that they were at war.

American and allied troops were sent to Afghanistan almost immediately to oust the Taliban government that had harbored Al Qaeda. Attention then turned to Saddam Hussein's brutal regime in neighboring Iraq that had failed to cooperate with U.N. inspectors as a cease-fire agreement from the Gulf War had required. Intelligence reports from the C.I.A. and other sources indicated that Hussein's government had developed an extensive biological and chemical weapons program (summarized as weapons of mass destruction) and raised anxieties that these could fall into the hands of terrorists. These reports, generally believed to be true by political leadership in both parties and around the globe, precipitated a chain of events that exhausted diplomatic efforts and led eventually to a preemptive invasion of Iraq by U.S. and allied troops. The "coalition of the willing" successfully deposed and later captured and tried Hussein but became bogged down battling insurgents in attempting to stabilize a newly elected Iraqi government. What had begun as a fairly bipartisan foreign policy increasingly became an element of the polarized politics of 2004. The long-term trend to heightened competition and polarization along with differences over the administration's foreign and domestic policies set the stage for another intensely fought presidential campaign.

After Al Gore decided not to run in 2004, Democrats were without an obvious frontrunner for the party's nomination. This void did not remain for long. Former Vermont Governor Howard Dean, a strident critic of the Bush administration and a candidate of what he termed as "the Democratic wing of the Democratic Party," emerged as the leader in a pack of ten hopefuls. Dean excited anti-war Democrats and was propelled by a highly successful, internet-based fundraising effort. As the Iowa Caucus approached, however, doubts about the candidate's ability to defeat President Bush in the general election caused many Democrats to desert Dean in favor of Massachusetts Senator John Kerry, who they thought was more electable.

With the parties highly polarized, both Bush and Kerry entered their fall campaigns with unified bases of support. Despite this internal party unity and competitive party balance, the electorate's slightly conservative tilt (J. Campbell 2005b, Jamieson 2006, 92–93) and its preference for the incumbent as being better able to handle the war against terrorism favored President Bush's re-election. Despite some ups and downs in the polls, the election wound up pretty much where it had started. President Bush was elected in 2004 with a popular vote majority, the first since his father's election in 1988 but with a smaller vote percentage than incumbents typically receive.

Very Different Elections

As the preceding synopses demonstrate, these elections are a very diverse lot in almost every way imaginable. They are diverse in their political and economic contexts, the competitiveness of the races, and the margins of victory. The richness in the variation of the elections upon which much of this study rests provides a good foundation for the analysis.[24]

The conditions under which these elections took place were often quite different. Most were conducted when the nation was at peace, but some were held while the nation was at war. The Korean War was under way when the 1952 election was held, the Vietnam War was in progress during both the 1968 and 1972 elections, and the war in Iraq and Afghanistan was underway during the 2004 election. Although the economy was healthy in most of these election years, it was booming in some (e.g., 1964, 1972, and 1984) and weak in others (most notably 1980).

There are also many differences with respect to the candidate situations in these elections. Aside from the many different personal strengths and weaknesses each candidate brings to the election, the elections differ by whether an incumbent is seeking reelection and whether there are significant third-party alternatives to the major-party candidates. As to presidential incumbency, ten of the fifteen elections included an incumbent president.[25] Seven of the ten incumbents won their elections and three lost (Ford in 1976, Carter in 1980, and Bush in 1992). Five elections did not involve an incumbent.[26] Although eligible, Truman decided not to run in 1952, and Johnson decided not to run in 1968.

Despite the predominance of the two-party system in American politics, several of the fifteen elections involved the presence of significant third-party or independent candidates. While nine were almost purely two-candidate contests, third-party candidates played a significant role in six elections. George Wallace received over 13 percent of the vote in 1968; John Anderson received almost 7 percent of the 1980 vote; and Ross Perot received 19 percent of the vote in 1992 and 8.5 percent in 1996. Although support for Strom Thurmond and Henry Wallace dwindled by the time of the election, their presence nevertheless may have significantly affected the 1948 campaign. Similarly, though Ralph Nader received less than 3 percent of the 2004 vote, the election was so closely decided that his candidacy may have made a difference as well.

The extent of competition in these fifteen elections is also quite varied. Four of the fifteen elections (1964, 1972, 1976, and 1996) had a strong frontrunner, a candidate commanding at least 60 percent support in the July and early September Gallup polls. In another four elections (1956, 1980, 1984, and 1992), a candidate held at least 60 percent of the prospective vote in one of these pre-campaign polls. In the remaining seven post–World War II elections (1948, 1952, 1960, 1968, 1988, 2000, and 2004), neither candidate had 60 percent of support in either the July or early September polls.

Competition as reflected in the actual election results is also varied. Four of the fifteen elections were landslides, with the winning candidate receiving 57 percent or more of the two-party vote. The four landslides were Eisenhower's 1956 reelection, Johnson's 1964 election, Nixon's 1972 reelection, and Reagan's 1984 reelection. At the other end the competitiveness spectrum were six elections that were especially close, with the winning candidate receiving less than 53 percent of the two-party popular vote. These close calls were Truman's come-from-behind election in 1948, Kennedy's razor-thin 1960 victory over Nixon, Nixon's 1968 election over Humphrey, Carter's narrow victory in 1976 over Ford, and George W. Bush's controversial election over Gore in 2000 and over Kerry in 2004. Victory margins in the remaining five elections in the series (1952, 1980, 1988, 1992, and 1996) were of moderate proportions, falling somewhere between very close and landslide elections.

The Extent of Campaign Effects

With the methodological groundwork in place, we can now turn to our two principal questions: do presidential campaigns affect election results and are these campaign effects on election results systematic or predictable? The next four chapters are devoted to examining the nature and extent of systematic campaign effects. Chapter 8 explores the impact of idiosyncratic campaign events. However, before we turn to those specific elements of the theory of predictable campaigns, we can first gain some perspective on the extent of the overall effect of presidential campaigns on their election results and the degree to which campaigns systematically or predictably affect the vote.

The overall net effect of the general election campaign and its systematic and unsystematic components can be estimated using the actual vote, the expected vote based on the factors identified as exerting a systematic influence on the campaign, and a survey measure of support for the candidates at the outset of the campaign. The net effect of the campaign is simply calculated as the difference between the level of support for a candidate before and after the campaign. The support before the campaign is measured by the pre-campaign trial-heat poll.[27] Using Labor Day as the start point for the campaign (and a case could also be made for using an earlier date), the early September poll standing of the candidates indicates how well the candidates would have done had the election been held before the campaign began. The actual November vote indicates candidate support after the campaign has been completed.

Table 3.4 presents both the before and after support levels for the in-party candidate in the fifteen elections from 1948 to 2004 and the difference that may be attributed to the intervening campaign. While the estimated total net effects of the campaign vary a good bit, ranging from less than one percentage point in 1960, 1988, and 2004 to nine percentage points in the Carter-Ford race of 1976, the average total effect of the campaign on the vote was slightly less than four percentage points. This is the average shift from the vote intention before the campaign to the vote actually cast at the campaign's end. In two election years (1948 and 1960) the net effects of the campaigns were apparently large enough to have reversed what otherwise would have been the outcome (J. Campbell 2001c). Using a more liberal view of when campaigns begin, either immediately before or immediately after the conventions, increases the average size of campaign effects to nearly five percentage points.

Even the more conservative estimate of campaign effects (from early September to election day) are considerably higher than estimated in previous analyses (Bartels 1992; Finkel 1993; Holbrook 1996a, 31).[28] One reason for this discrepancy is that previous studies considered campaign effects to be distinct from the effects of national conditions in place before the start of the campaign. As noted above, this study contends instead that much of the effect of national pre-campaign conditions on the vote is filtered through the campaign, affecting the course of the campaign and reactions to it.[29]

What portion of these campaign effects have resulted from the various systematic components of the campaign that we have discussed, and what portion are the result of the unexpected events and developments in these campaigns? Since the election forecasting model (table 1.5) includes the systematic elements of the campaign, it can be used as a benchmark to indicate how the election would have turned out had the campaign played out its systematic effects without any unsystematic effects.[30] Since we are not interested in the forecasting equation here for forecasting purposes, but instead for explaining campaign effects, we will adapt it to that purpose by using the most accurate recent measure of real GDP growth in the second quarter of the election year rather than the estimate of that growth released by the Bureau of Economic Analysis in August prior to the election. The difference between the initial level of candidate support and the (out-of-sample) expected vote is thus the extent of systematic campaign effects. The extent of unsystematic campaign effects can be calculated as the difference between the actual vote and the vote that would have been expected from purely systematic campaign effects. It is equal to the out-of-sample expected vote error.[31] It should be observed that since

Table 3.4. The Net Effect of Presidential Campaigns, 1948–2004

Year	In-Party	The In-Party Candidate's Support in Early September	The In-Party Candidate's Share of the Two-Party Vote	Net Effect of the Fall Campaign	The In-Party Candidate's Expected Share of the Vote	Net Effect of Systematic Aspects of the Fall Campaign	Net Effect of Unsystematic Aspects of the Fall Campaign
1948	Democratic	45.6	52.3	+6.7	51.7	+6.1	+0.6
1952	Democratic	42.1	44.6	+2.5	46.7	+4.6	-2.1
1956	Republican	55.9	57.8	+1.8	53.9	-2.0	+3.8
1960	Republican	50.5	49.9	-.6	49.4	-1.1	+.5
1964	Democratic	69.2	61.3	-7.8	60.9	-8.3	+.5
1968	Democratic	41.9	49.6	+7.7	47.8	+5.9	+1.8
1972	Republican	62.9	61.8	-1.1	60.6	-2.3	+1.2
1976	Republican	40.0	49.0	+9.0	46.5	+6.5	+2.5
1980	Democratic	48.7	44.7	-4.0	44.7	-4.0	-.0
1984	Republican	60.2	59.2	-1.1	58.1	-2.1	+1.0
1988	Republican	54.4	53.9	-.5	53.2	-1.3	+.7
1992	Republican	41.9	46.5	+4.6	48.8	+6.9	-2.2
1996	Democratic	60.8	54.7	-6.1	59.0	-1.8	-4.3
2000	Democratic	52.1	50.3	-1.9	52.7	+.6	-2.4
2004	Republican	50.5	51.2	+.7	52.4	+1.9	-1.1
Mean of Absolute Campaign Effects				3.7		3.7	1.7

Note: The net effect of the campaign is computed as the difference between the actual vote for the in-party candidate on election day and support for the in-party candidate at the beginning of the campaign (defined here as early September). The net effect of systematic aspects of the campaign (the effects of incumbency, the election-year economy, and the narrowing effect of the campaign) are calculated as the difference between the pre-campaign level of support and the vote expected as a result of systematic campaign effects (reflected in the out-of-sample expected vote using revised economic data instead of estimates available for forecasting prior to the election). The net effect of unsystematic aspects of the campaign are calculated as the difference between the actual vote and the vote expected to result from systematic campaign factors. The poll percentages used are of registered voters, not likely voters.

the systematic and unsystematic effects may be in opposite directions, their combined effects in absolute terms may be greater than the net total effects of the campaign.

The analysis indicates that systematic campaign effects, on average, produced nearly a four-percentage-point shift in the eventual vote. Systematic aspects in five of the fifteen campaigns shifted the vote by more than five percentage points. The unanticipatable events of campaigns also affected the vote, often to a significant degree, though generally to a much smaller degree than systematic effects. The net impact of unsystematic campaign developments, on average, affected the vote by less than two percentage points of the vote. The estimated impact of unsystematic factors exceeded three percentage points in two election years but was never as great as five percentage points in any of the fifteen elections.

While these broad parameters indicate that campaigns are important to the vote and that they have several systematic qualities that allow their effects and the election results to be predictable, from a different perspective campaign effects are quite limited. We now turn to the principal reason for this: the relatively stable context in which presidential campaigns take place.

Chapter 4

The Stable Context of the Campaign

EVERY ELECTION IS different but also part of a political past. No election can be understood purely by its own campaign or even by the general conditions of its particular election year. There is a continuity to electoral politics that is missed by examining elections as discrete or unique events. Although political observers tend to focus on what is new to each election, much remains the same. There is continuity in the political parties, the electorate and its beliefs, many of the issues, and often one or both of the presidential candidates.

The continuity of electoral politics allows many voters to decide quite early on who they will vote for, and this places limits on the potential effects of the campaign. With a substantial portion of the electorate set in their choice of candidate and essentially out of play for the campaign, possible campaign effects are restricted to affecting the choices of the subset of potential voters undecided or uncertain about their votes.

With portions of the electorate committed early on to the Democratic and Republican candidates, the campaign can be said to be played out within a stable context. The stability of the majority of the electorate is suggested in the aggregate by the historical parameters of the vote. In elections over the last half century, no matter how well a major-party presidential candidate has done in a campaign, he has not received more than 62 percent of the two-party national vote. Conversely, after even the worst campaign in this period by a major-party candidate, Democrat or Republican, the candidate still received at least 38 percent of the two-party national vote. Presidential election results are quite definitely bounded, between 38 and 62 percent of the national two-party vote.[1]

The pre-campaign poll numbers paint much the same picture. In the fifteen elections from 1948 to 2004, every major-party presidential candidate has had the support of at least 32 percent of respondents in the Gallup poll conducted in July of the election year. The leading candidate in the July poll, moreover, has held at least 46 percent of the two-party vote on election day. Thus, both the election and pre-campaign poll figures suggest that the stable context of the campaign probably constitutes *at least* 32 and 38 percent of the electorate on either side and apparently at least 46 percent of the electorate on the front-runner's side. This amounts to approximately three-quarters of the electorate voting for the major-party candidates.[2] By this accounting, the vote choice of about a quarter of the electorate would appear to be left open to possible influence by the campaign.

This estimate of the parameters of possible campaign effects is supported by self-reports of when voters decided their votes during the election year. As the figures presented in table 1.2 demonstrated, typically nearly two-thirds of the electorate indicate that they decided who they would vote for before or during the political parties' nominating conventions in the summer of the election year. Some additional voters may have effectively decided how they would vote but may have wanted to appear more open to additional information. Still others indicated that they decided immediately after the conventions but before the general election campaign got under way. In short, a large majority of voters regularly make up their minds how they will vote before the general election campaign starts. But why? Why do so many voters decide how they will vote before the campaign, before the candidates have a chance to make their cases for why voters should vote for them? What is the basis for this stable context in which the campaign takes place?

Easy Decisions Can Be Early Decisions

There are several reasons why many voters know how they will vote before the general campaign begins. What links these reasons together is that these early-deciding voters have enough information of different sorts on different dimensions of the choice to make them quite confident about their decisions. Before the campaign begins, they know all they need to know (or at least think that they do). For these voters, they can make an early decision because it is an easy decision.

Since *The American Voter* (A. Campbell et al. 1960), the landmark study of voting behavior, considerations that might affect the vote choice have been categorized as either long-term or short-term forces. Long-term forces are those that are carried from one election to the next, while short-term forces are those specific to a particular election year. Party identifications and ideological perspectives are the principal long-term considerations. Attitudes about various public policy issues and beliefs about the character and leadership abilities of the presidential candidates are usually classified as the principal short-term forces on the vote.

Early vote decisions based directly or (much more likely) indirectly on long-term considerations, such as partisanship and ideology, are certainly understandable. However, the analysis also suggests that many pre-campaign vote decisions are probably based on short-term considerations about issues and the qualities of the presidential candidates. Many considerations of the issues and candidates are not strictly short-term but are carried over from previous elections or are quite directly based on long-term dispositions, and many short-term evaluations are only short-term in the sense that they are made in the election year but not necessarily during the campaign. Some presumed short-term forces on the vote are not really so short-term.

Long-term Forces Affecting the Vote

Partisanship and the Vote

The American electorate has been and remains highly partisan.[3] As the figures reported in table 2.1 attest, partisanship is both wide and deep (and has become both wider and deeper). Most voters identify themselves more or less as Democrats or Republicans, and these voters loyally cast ballots for their party's presidential candidate. The extent of partisanship, even through a period of suspected partisan dealignment, is impressive. At least 90 percent of every electorate since 1952 has some level of identification with either the Democratic or Republican Party. On average, about half of the electorate in these elections were Democrats and about 40 percent were Republicans. The loyalty rates of these partisans are also noteworthy. In the typical election, about 78 percent of Democrats and 87 percent of Republicans voted for their party's presidential candidate.

Partisanship is also quite stable. Party identifications for the overwhelming majority of partisans do not appreciably change from one election to the next. Democrats remain Democrats and Republicans remain Republicans. Keith et al. (1992, 88–89), in analyses based on panel study surveys over periods of between four and nine years, found that better than 90 percent of strong partisans maintained their identification with their party over time, that between 80 and 90 percent of weak partisans remained identified with the same party over the years, and that roughly 75 percent of independents who lean toward a party years later indicate an identification with the same party. Of those few who changed their identifications, about as many adopted a neutral (or pure independent) position as indicated a new identification with the other party (Jennings and Markus 1984). Since individual partisanship changes often offset each other (as a few Republicans become Democrats and a few Democrats become Republicans), partisanship is even more stable in the aggregate.[4] The percentage of potential voters identifying themselves as Democrats or as Republicans has typically changed by only about two percentage points between presidential election years.[5]

The effects of partisanship on vote choice are both strong and mostly (perhaps almost entirely) indirect rather than direct.[6] Democrats do not vote for Democratic candidates because they are Democrats but because being Democrats means that they probably share some common perspectives about what government should and should not do. Partisanship has content. It is more than just a label. Democrats and Republicans see the world differently and, thus, react differently to the candidates and issues that arise in any election. Partisans share similar values and have similar political attitudes about issues and candidates. They also tend to interpret events in similar ways. These shared perspectives are the bonds that sustain partisan identifications and maintain the strong partisan loyalties in voting from one election to the next.

Partisanship thus establishes a stable context and boundaries for campaigns. As the authors of *The American Voter* put it, "Few factors are of greater importance for our national elections than the lasting attachment of tens of millions of Americans to one of the parties. These loyalties establish a basic division of strength within which the competition of particular campaigns take[s] place" (A. Campbell et al. 1960, 121).

Partisan Stability and Electoral Change
The pervasiveness of partisanship, its basic stability from one election to the next, and its importance in the decision-making of individual voters raises several interesting questions about the role of partisanship in affecting election results. If partisanship is so important and so stable, why doesn't the political party with the majority of partisans win election after election? As already noted, the majority party once did hold a virtual lock on the White House. Republicans won most presidential elections from 1860 to 1928 (fourteen of eighteen) and Democrats won most presidential elections from 1932 to 1964 (seven of nine). Since 1964, the American party system has undergone a staggered realignment, staggered because of the slow development of a Republican Party in the formerly solid Democratic South. This produced a system more evenly balanced between Republicans and Democrats (J. Campbell 2006). The shift was first evident in presidential voting beginning in the late 1960s, in party identification in the mid 1980s, and in congressional voting in the early 1990s. Over the period from 1968 to 2004, there were seven Republican presidential victories to only three for the Democrats, but this belies the fact that

three of the seven Republican victories (1968, 2000, and 2004) were near dead-heats and could have gone either way. Still, despite the importance of partisanship to shaping individual vote decisions and its stability in the aggregate, electoral change occurs. This raises the question of how party identification in the aggregate affects presidential election results.

The major effect of party identification on presidential election results is to constrain the results to a competitive range of the vote. The major political parties are quite competitive, despite the fact that Democrats outnumbered Republicans over much of this period, sometimes by a wide margin. In the 1964 NES survey, Democrats outnumbered Republicans by nearly two to one.[7] However, the effective Democratic Party lead in partisanship was greatly reduced by both the lower turnout rates and the higher presidential vote defection rates of Democrats. As table 2.1 indicated, since 1952 Democrats typically held about a ten-percentage-point edge over Republicans among reported voters (a 1.25 to 1 division). The greater likelihood of defection among Democrats further reduced their partisanship advantage. With the exceptions of the 1964 and 1992 elections (complicated by a strong Perot vote), Democrats have been more likely than Republicans to defect and vote for another presidential candidate.[8] In more recent elections, the Democratic lead in party identifiers has declined, but this has been accompanied by a commensurate decline in the Republican advantage in party loyalty. The net impact again is a more balanced partisan terrain. This effective parity between the parties in mass allegiances accounts, in part, for the lack of party dominance in presidential elections despite the importance and stability of partisanship.

A second reason that partisanship has not led to a single party dominating presidential elections in recent times is that, though partisanship is the single most important influence on the vote, it is by no means the only important influence. The votes of partisans (and even whether they will turn out to vote) cannot be taken for granted. Candidate qualities, policy issues, and group affiliations in any particular election can lead partisans to remain loyal, to defect, or even to stay away from the polls. If the circumstances of a particular election are favorable to a party, its partisans are more likely to vote and less likely to defect. Conversely, when circumstances are unfavorable to a party, those who identify with that party may feel cross-pressured and abstain from voting or even defect in greater numbers to vote for the opposition party's presidential candidate (J. Campbell 1997b, 90–97, 174–87). Some, though the numbers are normally quite small, may even change their party identifications between elections. In short, partisanship has not produced permanent presidential winners and losers because it is effectively balanced between the parties, and this competition allows other factors to play a greater role in affecting election results.

How Partisanship Enters the Fray

Although the sheer number of partisans does not necessarily lock one party into the White House, there remains the question of how partisanship affects election results. Both the loyalty in the vote choice of partisans and the turnout or partisan composition of the electorate affect the national vote for a party's presidential candidate. The presidential vote for a party can be thought of as a function of these considerations. The vote for the Democratic presidential candidate is expressed in these terms in the following equation:

$$DVOTE_T = (PID_D \times DVOTE_D) + (PID_I \times DVOTE_I) + (PID_R \times DVOTE_R)$$

where DVOTE is the percentage of the national two-party vote for the Democratic Party's presidential candidate, PID is the proportion of the electorate composed of a group of party identifiers, and the subscripts T, D, I, and R refer to the total, Democrats, independents, and Republicans, respectively.

The Democratic vote percentage nationally is a weighted average of the vote percentages of the three partisan groupings of voters. From a slightly different perspective, the equation essentially partitions the percentage of the total national Democratic vote into separate portions contributed by Democratic Party identifiers, independents, and Republican Party identifiers. The contribution of each party identification category to the national Democratic vote depends jointly on two considerations: the relative size of the party identification category and the proportion of its vote that is cast for the Democratic candidate.

While a party's presidential vote can be logically broken down into the votes it receives from each partisan grouping of voters, and while these partisan votes in turn depend jointly on the size (PID) and voting loyalties of the group (DVOTE), there remains the question of which of these factors plays a greater role in influencing the vote from one election to the next. We can explore the relative effects of these considerations of partisanship in a multiple regression analysis. The dependent variable in this analysis is the percentage of the two-party popular vote for the Democratic presidential candidate. The independent variables are the loyalty in presidential voting of Democratic Party identifiers, the percentage of the electorate who are Democratic Party identifiers, the percentage of Republican Party identifiers who defected to vote for the Democratic candidate, the percentage of the electorate who are Republican Party identifiers, and the percentage of independents who voted for the Democratic presidential candidate.[9] The analysis is conducted over the fourteen presidential elections from 1952 to 2004. A second regression using the net differences in party loyalty and partisan composition was also examined and produced similar findings.[10] The results of the more detailed regression are reported in table 4.1.

Table 4.1. The Partisan Composition of the Electorate, Partisan Defection Rates, Independent Voting, and the National Popular Vote, 1952–2004

Dependent Variable: The Two-party National Popular Vote for the Democratic Party's Presidential Candidate

Independent Variables	Unstandardized Coefficients	Standardized Coefficients
Percent of the electorate with Democratic Party Identification	.31 (3.64)	.19
Democratic Party Identifiers' *loyalty rate* on the presidential vote	.50 (21.18)	.71
Democratic vote percentage among Pure Independents	.09 (5.66)	.23
Percent of the electorate with Republican Party Identification	−.39 (4.31)	−.24
Republican Party Identifiers' *defection rate* on the presidential vote	.38 (8.31)	.28
Constant	.16	
N	14	
R^2	.998	
Adjusted R^2	.995	
Standard error	.450	
Durbin-Watson	1.369	

Note: The coefficients in parentheses are t-ratios. All coefficients are statistically significant at the p < .01 level, one-tailed. The data are from NES and have been adjusted (reweighted by the presidential vote) to correspond to the actual presidential vote division. Republican defection, the independent vote percentage for the Democratic candidate, and the Democratic loyalty rates only count votes for the presidential candidates of the two major parties. The percentage of pure independents is the baseline omitted category. It is omitted to prevent perfect multicollinearity among the independent variables.

The regression results reported in table 4.1 confirm the obvious: that Democratic presidential candidates fare better when more Democrats and fewer Republicans turn out to vote, when Democrats are more loyal and Republicans are more disloyal to their parties, and when independents provide a greater portion of their votes to the Democrat. Partisan loyalty, partisan turnout, and independent voting determines the presidential vote.[11] Beyond the obvious, however, the analysis indicates that one component in this period was more important than the others in determining the vote and that was *the loyalty of Democratic partisans* to their party's standard-bearer. The standardized coefficients indicate that the loyalty of Democratic Party identifiers was the strongest effect of any of the partisan components of the vote.

There are two reasons for the importance of Democratic partisan loyalty: Democratic identifiers were the largest group of voters in this period and their loyalty rates varied quite a bit.[12] In the 1972 McGovern debacle, only 61 percent of Democrats voted for the Democratic candidate. At the other extreme, in 1996, nearly 94 percent of Democrats voted for Clinton. Republicans' loyalty has been quite a bit more dependable, ranging from a low of 78 percent in Goldwater's 1964 crushing defeat to 95 percent in both of Eisenhower's elections and in Reagan's 1984 landslide over Mondale. The independent vote, though more variable than the vote of Democratic identifiers (as one would expect), is less important to the overall vote because independents constitute such a small portion of the electorate.[13]

The regression analysis answers the question of how partisanship can be both so important and stable while the results of presidential elections change from one election to the next. It indicates that though partisanship is extremely important and provides a great deal of stability, the parties are competitive enough, and their turnout and loyalty rates (especially those of Democrats) have varied enough that neither party has had a permanent lock on presidential elections.

Ideology, Values, and the Vote

Political ideologies, like partisan identifications, are long-term forces that shape the vote choice and allow many voters to make an easy and early vote decision. Voters who have very definite and very non-moderate ideological dispositions may have effectively decided how they will vote in an election long before the campaign, even long before both parties' presidential candidates are known. What is said, done, or revealed during the course of the general election campaign is largely of interest to these voters only as spectators. Barring some unexpected development, these votes have been locked up by one of the parties for some time.

The reason that many ideological voters are early deciders is that their ideologies are in place before the campaign and the parties remain consistent over time in their ideological leanings. This ideological character of the parties has strengthened in recent decades. A die-hard conservative voter knows there is no real option to a Republican vote. A committed liberal, likewise, has little real option to a Democratic vote.

For voters right of the more conservative candidate or left of the more liberal candidate the vote choice is not much of a choice at all. Unless there is something significant to persuade them to do otherwise, such as a scandal or an unacceptable administrative performance, there is little reason for the liberal to seriously consider a Republican or a conservative to consider a Democratic presidential candidate.

It is difficult to determine exactly how many early-deciding voters are ideologically locked in, but it is safe to say that there are a good many and that, in most of these cases, partisanship reinforces these early decisions. There are two points about the extent and nature of political ideologies in the electorate that suggest that they are decisive and early influences for many voters. First, though the evidence is clear that few voters have very sophisticated or articulated political ideologies and that many voters are not very conversant with or aware of the most common ideological labels (conservatism and liberalism), it is also clear that nearly all voters have some political values, some views of what is appropriate or inappropriate in government. These values guide their evaluations of politicians and issues. In this gut-level sense, all voters are to some degree ideological.[14]

The second observation suggesting that ideologies lead to many pre-campaign vote decisions is that most voters find themselves much closer ideologically to one of the candidates than to the other. Although the median voter is almost by definition a moderate, it does not follow that most voters are moderates. In fact, surveys generally indicate that most voters are not moderates. Self-described moderates are flanked by large numbers of conservatives and liberals (J. Campbell 2007b). In the 1970s, just fewer than half of voters in the NES said they were conservatives or liberals and some who were unaware of their ideological perspective may have nonetheless had one. Even many self-described moderates were probably not perfectly centrist. Since the 1990s, a clear majority of voters are self-described liberals and conservatives. Barring unusual circumstances, most of these non-moderates should have an easy time reaching a vote choice before the campaign gets under way.

Ideology's role in establishing a stable context for the election is suggested by evidence from the 1996 presidential election. The 1996 Voter News Service exit poll of voters found that while 47 percent described themselves as moderates, 20 percent said that they were liberals and 33 percent claimed to be conservatives.[15] Of self-described liberals who voted for a major-party presidential candidate, 88 percent voted for the Democrat, Bill Clinton. Of self-described conservatives who cast major-party presidential votes, 78 percent voted for the Republican, Bob Dole.[16] While some of these ideologically consistent voters may have wrestled with their choice, most probably never had any real doubt about how they would vote. Nearly two-thirds of ideologically consistent voters in the 1992 NES survey indicated that they had reached their vote decisions before the campaign began.

Not So Short-term Forces

Based on long-standing partisan commitments and definite ideological compatibilities with one of the parties, a number of voters reach their presidential vote decisions before the campaign begins. Other voters may reach early vote decisions because of considerations usually thought to be short-term. The issues, candidates, and circumstances of a particular election are commonly classified as being short-term in character, but voters may react to such factors in deciding their vote before the start of the campaign. Few short-term forces are strictly limited to the general election campaign season, and some may actually be carried over from previous elections. Most issues and candidates have histories, and this provides voters with information and the basis for impressions prior to the campaign. If these issue and candidate image impressions are compelling, some voters may draw upon them to arrive at an early vote decision.

The Perennial Issues

Most political issues that are important enough to make much of a difference to the vote choice are issues that, in one form or another, have been around for a while. These issues may be considered short-term in that they evolve over time, and some surface in different elections framed in different ways. The specifics of the policy debate on a general issue are often new to that election, but the basic conflicting priorities or perspectives embedded in the issues are often unchanged.[17] This fundamental continuity of issue differences between the political parties and their respective standard-bearers allows many voters to settle on an issue-based vote well before the campaign.

There is ample evidence of the fundamental continuity of issues.[18] A staple question of survey research for some time has been "the most important issue" question. Survey respondents are asked an open-ended question, that is, to name what they regard as the most important problem facing the nation. While the priorities shift from election to election, the list of problems is quite similar across election years. The economy in some form is always on the list, either as economic growth, inflation, or unemployment. A range of what are generally termed social issues also regularly appear on the list. Among these social issues are civil rights concerns, abortion policy, environmental concerns, and a number of other primarily noneconomic matters. Finally, foreign policy concerns and crises appear from time to time as conditions, and world tensions bring these issues to the forefront.

A good example of a perennial issue is tax policy. In recent years, Republicans have advocated lowering income tax rates or even abolishing the income tax altogether and funding government through a national consumption or sales tax.

They have also sought to reduce taxes on capital gains or investment-generated income in order to spur further private sector investment. Democrats, on the other hand, have either opposed tax cuts or have argued for more limited and targeted tax cuts aimed at those in the middle or lower end of the economic spectrum. In the 1984 election, Democratic candidate Walter Mondale went so far as to pledge, in his nomination acceptance speech, to increase taxes if elected. For the most part, however, the tax position of Democratic candidates has focused on the fairness of the tax cuts. This issue, in one form or another, seems to appear in every election. Voters have heard it all before, not necessarily the identical proposals, but proposals offering the same general thrusts. The positions of the parties' candidates are generally quite predictable. Most voters who have lived through the arguments about this issue in past campaigns do not need to pay close attention to the latest incarnation of the issue to know where they stand and which party stands with them.

There are many other perennial issues in modern American politics. The parties and their presidential candidates have staked out generally clear differences over the years on a wide variety of issues. Among these issues are spending on domestic programs, spending on national defense programs, the willingness to aggressively enforce environmental regulations, civil rights and affirmative action programs, abortion rights, approaches to reducing crime, gun control, the minimum wage, approaches to improving education, and the need for a balanced budget amendment. Table 4.2 identifies in a couple of words the general views that have come to be associated with candidates of the two political parties on these issues. Some appear in every election year and others (e.g., the minimum wage) emerge in some elections and not in others. Some become elevated to the focus of a campaign, and others become just one of a menu of issues that candidates speak to from time to time.

None of these issues should take even a marginally informed voter by surprise. If voters care enough about the issue for the candidates' positions to matter in deciding how to vote, then they most likely know where the parties' candidates have stood and will stand on the issue, and most of them will know with little doubt which party's candidate better represents their views on the issue.

In addition to the general stability of issues and party positions across election years, where candidates will stand on the issues is fairly well established before the campaign begins.[19] Despite the incentive of candidates to shift their positions between the nomination and general election campaigns in order to appeal to both a more ideological primary electorate and a more centrist general electorate, Page has demonstrated that large issue position changes are uncommon (1978, 149). Moreover, as Scammon and Wattenberg (1970, 318) suggest in their classic *The Real Majority,* a typical voter is likely to doubt

Table 4.2. The Parties' Positions on Issues in Recent Presidential Elections

Issue	Democratic Position	Republican Position
Income tax cuts	Oppose or favor if targeted to middle- and lower-income citizens	Support across the board and favor capital gains tax cuts
Domestic program spending	Favor more spending or smaller cuts	Favor holding the line or larger cuts
National defense spending	Favor holding the line or larger cuts	Favor more spending or smaller cuts
Environmental policy	Highly support, with no roll back	Favor reducing government regulation to help business and development
Civil rights and affirmative action	Support aggressive enforcement	Oppose quotas and reverse discrimination
Crime policy	Support rehabilitation, address societal reasons for criminal behavior	Emphasize swift, sure punishment that fits the crime
Gun control	Support	Oppose
Abortion rights	Support, "pro-choice"	Oppose, "pro-life"
Minimum wage	Favor keeping and increasing	Oppose increase because it would increase unemployment
Education	Favor more spending	Offer more parental choice, with vouchers for public or private schools
Health care	Favor greater government involvement and funding	Hold steady or reduce government role in, protect private health care system
Balanced budget amendment	Oppose, as obstacle to flexible fiscal policy	Favor as necessary discipline on federal budget makers
Assistance to state and local governments	Favor, targeting poorer communities, requiring compliance with national standards and policies	Offer less, giving funds and letting states and communities determine how to use them; more reticent about attaching strings to assistance

candidates' sincerity when they change their stand on issues midway through the campaign. Thus, even if candidates attempted to reposition themselves to better appeal to voters during the campaign, most voters paying attention to the issues know enough not to be so easily manipulated. Voters likely to be influenced by an issue are likely to know which candidate is closer to their position well before the general election campaign gets under way.

The Record and Valence Issues

When candidates' positions on issues are not well defined, the record of the party in office is usually clear and leads many voters to make an early decision. Many issues are valence or style issues, issues on which the parties agree about the policy goal but differ over the means or their ability to achieve the consensus goal.[20]

The economy is a classic example of a valence issue.[21] Everyone wants economic growth, low inflation, low unemployment, and low interest rates. However, the lack of differences between the parties on these policy goals does not mean that the issue cannot be used to arrive at a vote choice. Voters can evaluate the policies that parties advocate for achieving these goals, the level of commitment to the issue that the party and its candidates have, and, above all else, the past performance of the parties in reaching the goal. Americans are practical people and performance, more than promises or plans, counts.

Moreover, the information and experience that voters bring to bear in evaluating a party's performance on a valence issue does not require information generated in a campaign. Based on personal observation and the everyday information that they obtain from the media and in personal conversations, voters learn enough to make an early evaluation of the in-party's performance on major valence issues such as the economy. As Popkin (1991) has argued, voters use many information shortcuts and acquire significant information as a "*by-product* of activities they pursue as part of their daily lives" (23). Unless the record leaves them uncertain, with a mixed review, most voters can reach a pre-campaign decision about the in-party based on their reading of the record. After years of living with an administration and seeing the impact of its policies firsthand, most voters have definite views and few real doubts to be resolved by a campaign.[22]

Evaluating candidates on a valence issue is straightforward. If the current administration's performance on the valence issue is acceptable and there is no strong countervailing reason to vote for the other party's candidate, endorse this past performance with a vote for the in-party candidate. On the other hand (again barring a strong reason to vote otherwise or a suspicion that the other candidate would perform worse), if the in-party's performance on the important valence issue is unacceptable to the voter, the in-party's candidate should be rejected with a vote for the opposing party's candidate.

The economic issues in the 1980 and 1984 elections demonstrate the point. In 1980, under Democratic president Jimmy Carter, economic conditions were not very good and had not been very good for several years. Inflation was high. Interest rates were high. Unemployment was high. The "misery index," the combination of these rates, was higher than it had been in many years. Republican candidate Ronald Reagan asked voters the question that many had answered for themselves long before the campaign: "Are you better off today than you were four years ago?" It is the classic retrospective voting question. Forget promises; candidates will promise you anything. It is performance that counts and the performance of the Carter administration with respect to the economy was unacceptable to most voters. It cost Carter his reelection.

The other side of the retrospective valence issue is seen in the 1984 election. After a recession in the first years of the Reagan administration, the economy had rebounded. Taxes had been cut and the "misery index" dropped substantially. Satisfied with the economic developments under Reagan's watch, voters rewarded him with a landslide victory over his Democratic opponent Walter Mondale, who had been Carter's vice president. As both the 1980 and 1984 examples illustrate, voters had in the course of everyday life accumulated plenty of information regarding the performance of the administration on economic matters well before a campaign. While some may have remained uncertain or torn in their reactions to these observations, for many others nothing about the campaign would have made a difference. Their issue-based votes were settled before the campaign ever began.

Familiar Candidates

Although partisanship, ideologies, and issue preferences may point to a vote choice before the campaign, how can reasonable and thoughtful voters make up their minds before knowing who the candidates will be and before hearing their statements during the campaign? Are not voters who decide how they will vote before the nominating conventions or immediately after (and before the campaign) engaged in a reckless and irresponsible rush to judgment? Are early-deciding voters ignoring important personal qualifications of the candidates when they reach a pre-campaign decision?

The answer is that many voters have a fairly good idea about the personal qualifications of the candidates before the general election campaign and, in many cases, even well before the election year. Early-deciding voters may not know all there is to know about the strengths and weaknesses of the candidates, but they know them well enough and about as well as they will ever know them. Presidential candidates can only be known to voters at a considerable distance and usually under very controlled and artificial circumstances. Moreover, whatever voters see of the candidates and how they interpret what they see will be strongly conditioned by their partisan and ideological predispositions. Evaluations of character traits, because of the ambiguity of these traits, are especially susceptible to rationalization, to virtually effortless wishful thinking. Because of this, voters will never really know the candidates well, but even with a limited amount of information they can get enough of a reading about whether they *think* a candidate has what it takes.

Even voters who are not especially attentive to the campaign can learn about the candidates and form impressions of them before the general election. Ever since the early 1970s, when primaries became the predominant means of selecting convention delegates and nominating candidates, the national media has exposed voters to potential candidates from the beginning of the election year through the early months of summer. The Iowa caucuses and the New Hampshire presidential primary officially start the nomination campaign season in February of the election year, but the nomination campaign unofficially begins much earlier. In any case, whether voters learn about the candidates and gain impressions of their leadership skills before or during the nomination season, there are several months of media coverage of the most viable candidates prior to the start of the general election campaign.

Although voters can become quite familiar with the candidates through the media coverage of the nomination process, most voters should be familiar with many of the candidates long before this. The reason is that most presidential candidates are national figures of some prominence and with some sort of public record. Presidential candidates are usually not fresh faces to the public. Many candidates' records include either previous service as a president or vice president or a previous run for national office. Either way, they are known entities to most voters.

A review of Republican presidential and vice presidential candidates for the fourteen elections from 1952 to 2004 illustrates just how much continuity there has been in that party's ticket. With the single exception of 1964 (Goldwater and Miller), one of three last names—Nixon, Bush, or Dole—appeared on thirteen of these fourteen Republican tickets. Democrats had their own stable of repeat candidates, though they did not appear with quite the regularity of the Republicans. Four Democrats—Stevenson, Johnson, Mondale, and Clinton—were on nine of the party's fourteen tickets over this period.

Table 4.3 presents the list of the thirty major-party presidential candidacies from 1948 to 2004 and their previous national political experience in either serving as or running for president or vice president. In every presidential election

Table 4.3. Candidates Who Previously Ran for or Served as President or Vice President, 1948–2004

Election Year	Presidential Candidate	Served as President	Ran for President	Served as Vice President	Ran for Vice President	Served as or Ran for VP or President
1948	Truman (D)	✓	—	✓	✓	Yes
1948	Dewey (R)	—	✓	—	—	Yes
1952	Stevenson (D)	—	—	—	—	No
1952	Eisenhower (R)	—	—	—	—	No
1956	Stevenson (D)	—	✓	—	—	Yes
1956	Eisenhower (R)	✓	✓	—	—	Yes
1960	Kennedy (D)	—	—	—	—	No
1960	Nixon (R)	—	—	✓	✓	Yes
1964	Johnson (D)	✓	—	✓	✓	Yes
1964	Goldwater (R)	—	—	—	—	No
1968	Humphrey (D)	—	—	✓	✓	Yes
1968	Nixon (R)	—	—	✓	✓	Yes
1972	McGovern (D)	—	—	—	—	No
1972	Nixon (R)	✓	✓	✓	✓	Yes
1976	Carter (D)	—	—	—	—	No

Year	Candidate				
1976	Ford (R)	✓		✓	Yes
1980	Carter (D)	✓	✓		Yes
1980	Reagan (R)				No
1984	Mondale (D)	✓	✓	✓	Yes
1984	Reagan (R)				Yes
1988	Dukakis (D)				No
1988	G. H. W. Bush (R)	✓	✓	✓	Yes
1992	Clinton (D)				No
1992	G. H. W. Bush (R)	✓	✓	✓	Yes
1996	Clinton (D)			✓	Yes
1996	Dole (R)	✓	✓	✓	Yes
2000	Gore (D)			✓	Yes
2000	G. W. Bush (R)				No
2004	Kerry (D)				No
2004	G. W. Bush (R)	✓	✓	✓	Yes

Presidential candidates who had served as or ran for president or vice president 19 (63%)

Presidential candidates who had neither served as nor ran for president or vice president 11 (37%)

since 1948, with the single exception of 1952, at least one of the presidential candidates had some previous national political visibility of this sort and, in the one exceptional year of 1952, the Republican candidate Dwight Eisenhower was a household name as a war hero and the leader of the Allied armed forces in World War II. In five of the fifteen elections since 1948, both presidential candidates had previous national political experience. Nearly two-thirds of the thirty presidential candidates since 1948 had some high-visibility national political experience before their current candidacy. Ten of the thirty (a third of all candidates) were incumbent presidents. These candidates were certainly well known to most voters before the election year, and most voters could probably safely conclude that they were unlikely to learn anything from the general election campaign that would appreciably alter their impressions of these candidates.

Of the thirty major-party presidential candidacies from 1948 to 2004, ten had not previously run for or served as president or vice president (or been a major national war hero). While not having the advantages of these particular experiences to gain national name recognition and familiarity, all ten had held major public offices and had become well known to the public in the early stages of their nomination campaigns, if not before. Four of these candidates (Kennedy in 1960, Goldwater in 1964, McGovern in 1972, and Kerry in 2004) were U.S. senators. Kennedy had become nationally known and something of a political celebrity because of his family, his war record, and his contest for the 1956 Democratic vice presidential nomination. Goldwater had achieved national stature as the outspoken leader of the conservative wing of the Republican Party. Although McGovern was unknown to many before 1972, he had gained some visibility when he stepped into the 1968 Democratic nomination campaign in the breach left by Senator Robert Kennedy's assassination. Kerry had served in the U.S. Senate for twenty years and had achieved national visibility as a Vietnam War protester as early as 1971.

The remaining six candidates had served as governors (Stevenson in 1952, Carter in 1976, Reagan in 1980, Dukakis in 1988, Clinton in 1992, and George W. Bush in 2000). Of these six, Reagan and Bush were the best known before their nominations. Reagan had first become known as a movie actor and television host and later served as governor of California. He first appeared on the national political stage in 1964 with a nationally televised presentation in behalf of Barry Goldwater's candidacy. He went on to seriously challenge Richard Nixon for the party's 1968 nomination and nearly captured the 1976 nomination from incumbent President Gerald Ford. There is no doubt that he was a well-known political figure long before 1980. As the son and namesake of a former president, George W. Bush also had a good measure of recognition in the public before throwing his hat into the ring for the Republican Party's nomination in 2000.

Although eleven presidential candidates did not have the official national political experience of the other nineteen presidential candidates since 1948, a few had become nationally well known on other grounds and most had had enough political experience to have attracted a good deal of attention from the media and the electorate. During the campaign, additional voters would learn more about these candidates and be able to evaluate their leadership potential on the way to the party nominating convention. For most presidential candidates, however, voters could make these evaluations even sooner.

The Consistency of Voting Cues

Members of the electorate have a great deal to consider in deciding how to vote. Partisanship, a standing commitment to vote for a party's candidate, is a serious consideration, as is the compatibility of the candidates' ideological perspectives with those of the voter. The proximity of the candidates' issue positions to those of the voter on a variety of issues and the voter's evaluation of the candidates' personal qualifications and leadership abilities are also important matters. With all of these factors entering the voter's thinking, usually in quite unstructured and often subconscious ways, one might suspect that voters are often confused. Indeed a number are. Some voters may feel cross-pressured, pulled in one direction by some factors and in the other direction by other considerations.[23] Partisans may from time to time think that the opposition party's candidate is the better candidate and face the dilemma of loyally voting for their party's candidate even though they prefer the opponent or disloyally defecting to vote for the preferred candidate. The additional information and perspectives offered in the course of a presidential campaign may clarify matters for these cross-pressured voters and allow them to settle on a vote choice.

Most voters, however, do not confront major cross-pressures in deciding how they should vote. There is an abundance of evidence regarding the consistency of voting cues. For instance, analyses of partisanship, approval of the president's job performance, and retrospective issue evaluations indicate that most Democrats evaluate Democratic presidents and their performance on the issues more favorably than Republicans. Likewise, Republicans generally analyze their partisanship, candidate evaluations, and retrospective issue evaluations and line up to vote for their party's candidate (Abramson, Aldrich, and Rohde 2006).[24]

In the 1992 NES survey, for example, nearly half of the voters for Clinton and Bush could not mention a single reason why they would want to vote for the opposing candidate or against their preference. The vote choice, for these voters, was absolutely clear-cut, and most reached that decision early in the election year.[25]

One reason for the consistency among cues for voters is that many potential voters who confront major cross-pressures opt not to vote. If their partisanship pulls them in one direction and their evaluations of the candidates lead them in the opposite direction, they may avoid this inner conflict by not voting at all rather than feeling disloyal to their party or voting for a candidate whom they do not really like.[26] This self-selecting out of the process reduces the number of actual voters who find the vote decision to be difficult.

For a large number of voters, the vote is easy and can be decided early because they do not face cross-pressures. For most voters, the considerations of partisanship, ideology, issues preferences, and candidate evaluations are consistent in favoring one candidate over the other. Liberal Democrats are likely to find the Democratic candidate to hold more acceptable issue positions and have more of the leadership traits they want in a president. Similarly, conservative Republicans are likely to see the Republican candidate as being more admirable and in accord with their issue positions. This should not be surprising since the political parties are largely built around ideological and issue commonalities.

Moreover, the psychology of cognitive consistency causes voters to focus on agreeable information about their party's standard-bearer and to deemphasize information that makes the opposing candidate look good. Much of political information is open to varying interpretations, and partisans, acting as their own "spin doctors," will seek consistency and avoid dissonance in their evaluations whenever possible. They give the benefit of any doubt to their own party's candidate and are often ready to believe the worst of the opposition. Moreover, as the minimal effects conundrum suggests, those voters most likely to confront campaign information that might challenge their vote predisposition are usually the best equipped to defend their predisposition. Thus, there are both objective and subjective reasons for the consistency of the various considerations in the vote decision. Even so, some partisans may have a few qualms about their party's candidate and some may even be dissatisfied to the point of not voting or defecting. However, for most, the choice is quite clear; a vote for their party's presidential candidate is a foregone conclusion.

Evidence of the Stable Context in 2004

The stable context of the campaign is evaluated for the 2004 election in table 4.4. Using NES data for the 2004 election reweighted to actual presidential vote division, the table first separates early from late vote deciders. Early deciders are voters who indicated that they had decided how they would vote at or before the conventions and did not change their vote intention between the pre-election and post-election waves of the NES survey.[27] Late deciders

Table 4.4. Timing of the Vote Decision, Stability of the Vote Intention, Partisanship, and the Presidential Vote, 2004

Time of Decision, Stability of the Vote Intention, Partisanship, and the Vote Choice	Percent of the Electorate		
Early Deciders and No Change from Vote Intention	<u>70.7</u>		
Democratic Party Identifiers		33.1	
Voted for Democratic Candidate John Kerry			31.2
Voted for Republican Candidate George W. Bush			1.8
Voted for Others			.2
Pure Independents		2.3	
Voted for Democratic Candidate John Kerry			1.2
Voted for Republican Candidate George W. Bush			1.0
Voted for Others			.0
Republican Party Identifiers		35.2	
Voted for Democratic Candidate John Kerry			1.0
Voted for Republican Candidate George W. Bush			34.2
Voted for Others			.1
Late Deciders or Changed from Vote Intention	<u>29.3</u>		
Democratic Party Identifiers		14.5	
Voted for Democratic Candidate John Kerry			11.5
Voted for Republican Candidate George W. Bush			2.8
Voted for Others			.2
Pure Independents		3.2	
Voted for Democratic Candidate John Kerry			1.5
Voted for Republican Candidate George W. Bush			1.5
Voted for Others			.2
Republican Party Identifiers		11.7	
Voted for Democratic Candidate John Kerry			1.9
Voted for Republican Candidate George W. Bush			9.4
Voted for Others			.4
Total	100.0	100.0	100.1

Vote Division of Early Deciders: Kerry = 47.3, Bush = 52.3, Others = .4
Vote Division of Late Deciders: Kerry = 50.6, Bush = 46.8, Others = 2.6

Note: The percentages are of all voters grouped by time of decision, by time of decision and partisanship, and, in the far right column, time of decision and partisanship and vote choice. The data are from the 2004 NES and have been reweighted to the actual national presidential popular vote. The weights were the ratio of the actual presidential vote and the presidential vote in the unweighted NES data. The rounded weights were .99 for reported Kerry voters, 1.02 for reported Bush voters, and .66 for reported voters for other candidates. The intention change was computed from the reported vote intention in the pre-election wave of the NES survey and the reported vote in the post-election wave. Early deciders were those who said that they had decided during or before the last nominating convention in August (NES codes 1, 2, 3, 4, and 11). Late deciders were those who said that they decided in September or closer to election day (NES codes 5, 6, 7, 8, 9, or 10). Leaners are counted as party identifiers. N = 794.

are those who indicated that they had decided after the party nominating conventions or changed their preference between the pre-election wave of the NES survey and the vote that they reported in the post-election wave.[28] The early- and late-deciding groups are then broken down by the three basic party identification groups (counting "independent" leaners as partisans) and their presidential votes. Appendix B presents a similar, and generally confirming, breakdown of the vote for each election from 1952 to 2004 and the average breakdown of the vote for these elections.

As the table demonstrates, more than seventy percent of the electorate in 2004 had decided how they would vote for president before the general election campaign got under way. A third of the electorate were Democrats who had decided early how they would vote and stuck to that decision. About 95 percent (31.2 of 33.1) of these early-deciding Democrats decided to stand by their party's candidate. About 35 percent of the public were early and consistent Republican deciders and about 97 percent (34.2 of 35.2) of these early-deciding Republican voters were loyal to their party's candidate.[29] In contrast, the loyalty rates of late-deciding partisans, in both parties, were about 80 percent, as more of these voters struggled with their decision well into the campaign.

Taking the partisan loyalists into account and the few independents and partisans who had decided early on that they could not abide their party's candidate, President Bush had a 5-percentage-point lead over Senator Kerry among early deciders. George W. Bush entered the campaign season with commitments from 37 percent of the electorate. John Kerry, on the other hand, had commitments from about 33 percent of the electorate. Bush's lead among those who decided early was not insurmountable but forced Kerry into the position of having to make up considerable ground among the less than thirty percent of the late-deciding voters. In order to have offset his deficit among early deciders, Kerry would have needed to win the votes of about 56 percent of the late deciders, and 40 percent of these (11.7 of 29.3) were Republicans. The contours of the 2004 election had been set early.

Stability and Change in Political Experience

Presidential elections all differ in many ways. The political situation of the moment and the candidates and issues of the day are important influences on the results of the election. The Vietnam War and anti-war protests, the unrest in the streets, and the activism of the civil rights movement certainly made the 1968 presidential election different from those that came before and those that would come later. The terrorism of 9/11 and concerns about the course of the war in Iraq made the 2004 presidential election very different from others.

Every election has a different cast of characters and array of public concerns, and every election has its own particular context. However, focusing exclusively on the way elections differ from each other misses important continuities. Each election is to a great measure a product of past elections. The parties, issues, the voters, and even many of the candidates do not go away after an election or radically change from one election to the next. In a way, an election is better understood as a political battle in a continuing civil (and marginally civilized) war for control of the government, rather than a war unto itself. It is a distinct event, but also part of a continuous history that is in many respects quite stable.

There are of course important changes from one election to the next. Candidates emerge. The nature, framing, and salience of various issues change. The circumstances of the nation change. The opinions and moods of the electorate change. New voters enter the electorate and others leave, by choice or by mortality. Some of these changes are well known long before the general election campaign and can be evaluated early on. Such changes, along with the core partisan vote, establish a stable context of early decided votes, bounds within which the general election campaign is contained.

The other factors, those that make each campaign different, can be divided into two categories: those that are truly unique and those that are systematic. The effects of idiosyncratic or unique events and circumstances, such as a scandal or a foreign policy crisis emerging in the middle of a campaign, cannot be gauged in advance. The effects of systematic or routine differences in election settings, campaign advantages for incumbent presidents, or election-year changes in the nation's economic circumstances can be gauged in advance fairly well. The presence or absence of an incumbent and the growth or slump in the economy is known in advance of each campaign, and we can determine how these factors have systematically entered the decision-making of voters during past campaigns. The systematic playing-out of these pre-campaign conditions in the voters' decision-making, along with the stable pre-campaign context of early-deciding voters, allows both presidential campaigns and elections to be quite predictable. We now turn to an examination of the two most important systematic factors in campaigns: presidential incumbency and the economy.

Chapter 5

Presidential Incumbency

WHILE THE STABLE context of campaigns establishes the boundaries for possible campaign effects, several other pre-campaign circumstances affect not only vote decisions made before the campaign gets under way but also decisions reached during the campaign. The incumbency status of the candidates and the condition of the election-year economy are pre-campaign conditions that systematically shape the course of the campaign that follows. They are factors that help or hinder the campaigns of the candidates and that become incorporated into the decisions of voters during the fall campaign.

Presidential incumbency and the economy to some degree enter into the early vote decisions that establish the limits for the possible effects of the campaign. Retrospective evaluations of the administration and the economy certainly provide the rationale for many early vote decisions. A successful incumbent who has served during times of prosperity will have a sizable number of early-deciding voters already committed as the campaign begins. By the same token, a weakened president who has presided during troubled economic times will probably have few early adherents beyond rock-ribbed partisan loyalists. However, the effects of incumbency and the economy are not necessarily *fully* appreciated by voters before the campaign. Both incumbency and the economy, particularly economic developments during the election year, affect how campaigns are run and how receptive late-deciding voters are to these campaign appeals.

To the degree that considerations regarding presidential incumbency and the election-year economy are incorporated into vote choices during the campaign and establish the context in which other campaign events are evaluated, these factors systematically shape the course of campaigns. Like the stable systematic factors, presidential incumbency and the election-year economy, though variable from one election to the next, provide some further predictability as to what effects the campaign may have on the final vote. This chapter examines the impact of presidential incumbency on presidential campaigns and election results as well as the reasons why incumbent presidents have an electoral advantage. The effects of the election-year economy on the campaign are explored in chapter 6.

The Question of a Presidential Incumbency Advantage

Between the late 1960s and the early 1980s presidential incumbency seemed to be as much of a liability as it was an asset in presidential elections.[1] Of the four sitting presidents eligible to run for election between 1968 and 1980, two were defeated (Ford in 1976 and Carter in 1980), one decided not to run in the face of mounting opposition (Johnson in 1968), and one won reelection, only to resign in scandal shortly thereafter (Nixon in 1972). From the review of these cases, the election odds of an incumbent president do not look significantly better than those of a non-incumbent, and they may even look worse. In the early 1980s, after the successive defeats of Presidents Ford and Carter, some argued that incumbency had indeed become a hindrance to a presidential candidate, that the nation was ungovernable, that the problems of the nation were unsolvable, that any presidential record would be best remembered for its unkept promises and policy failures. Some speculated that the days of the two-term president were over and that the nation would see a succession of one-term presidents (Hargrove and Nelson 1985, 189; Burnham 1989, 15). Quite unlike the veritable mountain of evidence demonstrating the very considerable electoral advantage that accompanied congressional incumbency, these elections suggested that presidential incumbency was of dubious electoral value.

Experience since 1980 supports a less pessimistic but still unsettled view of the presidential incumbency advantage. Since the back-to-back defeats of Presidents Ford and Carter in 1976 and 1980, respectively, three presidents won reelection (Reagan in 1984, Clinton in 1996, and George W. Bush in 2004) and one was defeated (George H. W. Bush in 1992). Despite the fact that three incumbent presidents have been defeated and four have won reelection since the 1970s (not far from what would be expected in a competitive two-party system where incumbents had no appreciable advantage), the possible advantage of presidential incumbency may not be easily discounted. All three losing incumbents, after all, lost under unusual circumstances. President Ford has the distinction of being the nation's only unelected president, having been appointed to the vice presidency to fill the vacancy left by Vice President Spiro Agnew's resignation and then rising to the presidency upon President Nixon's resignation precipitated by the Watergate scandal. Moreover, President Ford's pardon of former President Nixon tainted him in the eyes of many voters and may have cost him the election. In large measure, President Carter was defeated in 1980 because of the unusually bad economic circumstances of the late 1970s. Finally, President George H. W. Bush lost in 1992 partly because he reneged on his "no new taxes" pledge of the 1988 campaign and partly because Texas billionaire H. Ross Perot mounted the strongest third-party candidacy since Teddy Roosevelt's Bull Moose Progressive campaign of 1912.

Does presidential incumbency make a difference to presidential elections and, more specifically, to the effects of the campaign on the election results? The answer to this question may not be so simple. The advantages of presidential incumbency may extend to all candidates or only a subset of candidates of the in-party. They may apply under all conditions or under particular conditions. Is incumbency an advantage for all candidates of the in-party or is it a personal advantage of an incumbent candidate? Does the advantage of presidential incumbency depend on how long a party has occupied the White House? Is it possible that the incumbency advantage is really not a systematic advantage at all, but a potential advantage that is highly dependent on the successes or failures of particular incumbents? In different terms, is incumbency merely an opportunity that is as likely to be squandered as exploited? Or is incumbency at times an outright liability for a candidate? Finally, to the extent that incumbency is a systematic advantage, why are candidates helped by it?

The Impact of Incumbency

The evidence suggests that presidential incumbency has been an advantage for presidents seeking a second term and for in-party candidates who are seeking a second consecutive presidential term for their party. Table 5.1 presents the record of incumbency and in-party candidates for the thirty-five presidential elections from 1868 to 2004. Table 5.2 further summarizes and examines the details of this record.

Presidents seeking reelection and any in-party presidential candidates seeking a second term for their party, as table 5.2 makes clear, seem to have an advantage over their opponents.[2] Two-thirds of the twenty-two incumbents seeking reelection were reelected. These incumbents typically received more than 53 percent of the two-party popular vote. Similarly, more than two-thirds of in-party candidates seeking a second term for their party were successful, and their mean vote was 55 percent of the vote. In-party candidates who were not incumbents or were attempting to extend their party's occupancy of the

Table 5.1. Presidential Incumbency and the National Vote, 1868–2004

Election	Presidential Candidate of the In-Party	Incumbent President Running	Incumbent Party Seeking a Second Consecutive Term	The Election Result and the Percentage of the Two-Party Vote	
1868	Grant (R)	✗	✗	Won	52.66
1872	Grant (R)	✔	✗	Won	55.93
1876	Hayes (R)	✗	✗	Won	48.47
1880	Garfield (R)	✗	✗	Won	50.01
1884	Blaine (R)	✗	✗	Lost	49.87
1888	Cleveland (D)	✔	✔	Lost	50.41
1892	Harrison (R)	✔	✔	Lost	48.26
1896	Bryan (D)	✗	✔	Lost	47.81
1900	McKinley (R)	✔	✔	Won	53.17
1904	T. Roosevelt (R)	✔	✗	Won	60.01
1908	Taft (R)	✗	✗	Won	54.51
1912	Taft (R)	✔	✗	Lost*	—
1916	Wilson (D)	✔	✔	Won	51.64
1920	Davis (D)	✗	✗	Lost	36.17
1924	Coolidge (R)	✔	✔	Won	65.21
1928	Hoover (R)	✗	✗	Won	58.80
1932	Hoover (R)	✔	✗	Lost	40.84
1936	F. Roosevelt (D)	✔	✔	Won	62.46
1940	F. Roosevelt (D)	✔	✗	Won	54.97
1944	F. Roosevelt (D)	✔	✗	Won	53.78
1948	Truman (D)	✔	✗	Won	52.32
1952	Stevenson (D)	✗	✗	Lost	44.60
1956	Eisenhower (R)	✔	✔	Won	57.75
1960	Nixon (R)	✗	✗	Lost	49.92
1964	Johnson (D)	✔	✔	Won	61.34
1968	Humphrey (D)	✗	✗	Lost	49.60
1972	Nixon (R)	✔	✔	Won	61.79
1976	Ford (R)	✔	✗	Lost	48.95
1980	Carter (D)	✔	✔	Lost	44.70
1984	Reagan (R)	✔	✔	Won	59.17
1988	G. H. W. Bush (R)	✗	✗	Won	53.90
1992	G. H. W. Bush (R)	✔	✗	Lost	46.54
1996	Clinton (D)	✔	✔	Won	54.74
2000	Gore (D)	✗	✗	Lost	50.26
2004	G. W. Bush (R)	✔	✔	Won	51.24
Summary		22 ✔	14 ✔	21 Won	
		13 ✗	21 ✗	14 Lost	

Note: ✔ indicates that the in-party candidate was the incumbent president or was seeking a second consecutive term for his party. ✗ indicates that the in-party candidate was *not* the incumbent president or was seeking *more than a second consecutive term* for his party. Because of the complication of the second-place finish of former Republican president Theodore Roosevelt's third-party candidacy in 1912, the 1912 Republican in-party vote is not computed here.

Table 5.2. The Record of Incumbency, Party Tenure, and the Personal Incumbency Advantage, 1868–2004

	Election Results		
Record of In-Party (vs. Out-Party)	*Won*	*Lost*	*Mean Two-Party National Vote*
All in-party candidates	21 (60%)	14 (40%)	51.9
Incumbent president			
Seeking reelection	15 (68%)	7 (32%)	53.2
Not running	6 (46%)	7 (54%)	49.7
In-party seeking			
Second consecutive term	10 (71%)	4 (29%)	55.0
Third or more consecutive term	11 (52%)	10 (48%)	50.6

Note: Because of the complication of the second-place finish of Theodore Roosevelt's third-party candidacy in 1912, the 1912 vote is not included in computing the mean votes, though it is counted as a loss for the in-party. Five incumbents seeking reelection had not previously been elected to the presidency (T. Roosevelt in 1904, Coolidge in 1924, Truman in 1948, Johnson in 1964, and Ford in 1976).

White House beyond a second term had no particular advantage (or disadvantage) over their opponents. These in-party candidates won about as often as they lost.

The impact of incumbency on the course of the campaign is also reflected in the election forecasting models. Table 5.3 presents the mean trial-heat standing in the polls for incumbent presidents running for election and the predicted vote for in-party candidates with a 50 percent standing in the polls at different points in the campaign. The forecasts are based on the trial-heat and economy model presented in table 1.5 (J. Campbell and Wink 1990; J. Campbell 1996). The table indicates that incumbents typically enjoy a healthy lead over their opponents throughout the campaign. Moreover, as the forecasts indicate, even without their poll leads, with a fifty-fifty split of preferences in the polls, in-party candidates were expected to narrowly win the election.[3]

Election forecasting models developed by Alan Abramowitz (1988, 1996) and by Helmut Norpoth (1996) also suggest a presidential incumbency advantage for candidates seeking a second presidential term for their party.[4] The Abramowitz forecasting model, introduced in chapter 1 (table 1.3), includes a

Table 5.3. The Presidential Incumbency Advantage and Campaign Effects, 1948–2004

Timing of the Preference Poll and Forecast Model	Mean Trial-Heat Standing of Incumbent Candidates	The Predicted Vote for the In-Party Candidate with 50 Percent of Support in the Polls
June	55.6	52.6
July	51.1	53.1
Post-conventions	54.3	51.9
Early September	53.6	52.2
Late September	54.4	52.0
October	54.2	51.7
November	55.0	51.0
The Actual Vote	53.9	52.5

Note: The mean trial-heat ratings of incumbents are based on the ten incumbent presidents who ran for election from 1948 to 2004. The five elections in this period without incumbents running for election were 1952, 1960, 1968, 1988, and 2000. The predicted vote is based on the trial-heat poll and economy model developed by J. Campbell and Wink 1990 and revised by J. Campbell 2004. The early September version of the model is presented in table 1.5. The forecast uses a median (annualized) second quarter economic change of 3.25.

predictor variable for whether the in-party presidential candidate is seeking a third term or more for the party. The analysis indicates that a candidate who is seeking *more* than a second term for the party can be expected to receive about 4.5 percentage points less of the vote than a candidate who is seeking a second consecutive term for the party.

This second-term effect, however, can be interpreted in two different ways. Either the candidate seeking a third party term is penalized by voters for this, or the candidate seeking a second party term has an advantage that is lost to the next in-party candidate attempting to extend the party's presidential tenure. These two interpretations can be distinguished by examining the predicted vote under average conditions for in-party candidates who are seeking a second party term as opposed to those seeking more than that. If there is a penalty for seeking more than a second consecutive term, we would expect that the predicted vote for "third-term or more" candidates under otherwise average conditions would be *below* 50 percent.

On the other hand, if the term variable is capturing a second-term advantage (lost to third party term candidates), the predicted vote for second-term candidates under otherwise average conditions would be *above* 50 percent. An analysis supports the interpretation that the Abramowitz model identifies a second-term advantage rather than a third-term (or more) disadvantage for in-party candidates. With an average approval rating and an average economy, the predicted vote is 55 percent for an in-party candidate seeking a second party term and 49 percent for an in-party candidate seeking more than a second party term. It is much more of a "don't change horses in the middle of the stream" model rather than a "time for a change" model.[5]

Helmut Norpoth's (1996) forecasting model also suggests a second party term advantage for in-party candidates. Norpoth's model predicts higher votes for candidates whose party did well in the last election but lower votes for candidates whose party did well in the election before that. The candidates expected to do best, according to the Norpoth model, are those whose party had won the last election but had lost the prior election: in-party candidates seeking a second consecutive term for their party.

Table 5.4 presents data regarding the fortunes of incumbents in presidential campaigns since 1948. Incumbent presidential candidates and in-party candidates seeking a second party term are compared to other candidates in the polls at the outset of the campaign (either after the conventions or around Labor Day) and on election day. The analysis indicates that incumbents and in-party candidates seeking a second term for their party are *more likely to have a larger lead going into the campaign and are somewhat more likely to hold on to a larger portion of their lead through the course of the campaign.*[6] The typical incumbent entered the campaign season with about a 60 to 40 poll lead over his opponent

Table 5.4. Presidential Incumbency, Pre-Campaign Poll Leaders, and Election Results, 1948–2004

| | Mean Support Level for Frontrunner When Campaign Starts | | | | | |
| | After Second Convention | | | Early September | | |
Pre-Campaign Poll Leader	Poll	Vote	Change	Poll	Vote	Change
Incumbent President	59.1	55.8	−3.3	61.8	59.0	−2.8
Challenger to President	56.8	50.7	−6.1	55.9	51.9	−4.1
No Incumbent	54.3	52.0	−2.3	54.6	52.0	−2.6
In-Party Candidate Seeking a Second Party Term	59.1	55.8	−3.3	59.8	57.7	−2.2
In-Party Candidate Seeking More than Second Term	53.2	51.4	−1.8	52.4	51.4	−1.0

Note: There were five elections with no incumbents (1952, 1960, 1968, 1988, and 2000). The poll-leading candidate after the second convention was the incumbent in seven elections and a challenger to an incumbent in three elections. The poll-leading candidate in early September was the incumbent in six elections and a challenger to an incumbent in four elections. The poll leaders by term sought were second-term seeking candidates in seven elections for the post-convention election start and six elections in the early September start.

and typically only lost about three points from this lead over the course of the campaign. Conversely, when incumbents are behind at the outset of the campaign (see row 2 of table 5.4), they are typically not as far behind the frontrunner and are more likely to close the gap on their opponent by election day. When challengers and multi-term in-party candidates have an opening poll lead, it tends to be smaller and more of it is whittled away by election day.

The advantage of incumbency before and during the campaign means that the vote for incumbents (and those running for a second party term) is shifted upwards. When incumbents win elections, they tend to win by larger margins (e.g., Eisenhower in 1956, Johnson in 1964, Nixon in 1972, and Reagan in 1984) and in the more uncommon elections when they lose, they tend to lose by narrower margins (e.g., Ford in 1976 and Carter in 1980). Of the sixteen elected incumbents who have sought reelection since 1868, only two were defeated in landslides and both were defeated under very unusual circumstances: President Taft in 1912 lost to Woodrow Wilson because of a badly fractured Republican Party and the third-party candidacy of former Republican president Theodore Roosevelt, and President Hoover in 1932 lost to Franklin Roosevelt in the midst of the Great Depression.

The more clear-cut decisions regarding incumbents are evident in the history of how closely elections have been decided with and without incumbents in the race. Table 5.5 presents the distribution of election closeness for these elections. The data indicate that very close elections have been quite unlikely when the incumbent president has been a candidate. Only three (14 percent) of the twenty-one elections with incumbents were near-dead-heat elections.

Table 5.5. Incumbency and Election Margins, 1868–2004

Size of the Popular Vote for the Winning Candidate	No Incumbent in the Race	Incumbent Was in the Race
Near Dead-Heats	6 (43%)	3 (14%)
Competitive	5 (36%)	10 (48%)
Landslides	3 (21%)	8 (38%)
Total	14 (100%)	21 (100%)

Note: Near-dead heats are elections in which the winning presidential candidate received 51.5 percent or less of the two-party vote. Competitive elections are those in which the winning candidate received between 51.6 percent and 57 percent of the two-party vote. Landslides are those in which the candidate received more than 57 percent of the two-party vote.

On the other hand, close elections have been quite common (6 of 14, 43 percent) in elections without an incumbent candidate. At the other end of the competitiveness spectrum, landslide elections have rarely occurred in openseat races and were nearly twice as likely when an incumbent was running.

Presidential Incumbency as an Opportunity

Although presidential incumbency is generally an asset for candidates, the reelection record of incumbents also suggests that presidential incumbency may best be regarded as an *opportunity* that can most often be used to electoral advantage, but can also be lost. Although voters are inclined for a number of reasons to look kindly on an incumbent president, presidents have a record, and if that record fails to meet the electorate's expectations then incumbency may not benefit the candidate in the campaign. Incumbents who find themselves in political trouble may even generate significant third-party opposition.[7]

Presidential approval ratings are one measure of how well an incumbent president has exploited the potential advantages of incumbency. For the ten incumbent presidents who ran for election between 1948 and 2004 the public's approval of the president's job performance in July of the election year, around the time of the national conventions, ranged from a low of a mere 21 percent for President Carter in 1980 to a high of 74 percent for President Johnson in 1964. The median approval rating for these candidate-presidents was 49.5 percent.

Both the variable nature of incumbency's effect and the general advantage of presidential incumbency are apparent in figure 5.1. The figure plots the July approval rating of the ten incumbent presidents running for election in this period against their share of the two-party November vote. As expected, the vote for the incumbent president has been proportional to the approval for the president's job performance ($r = .87$). Incumbency does not automatically bestow an advantage on the president as candidate, and any advantage that one president derives from incumbency is not necessarily equal to that of past or future presidents. That said, the relation between presidential approval and the later vote suggests that *incumbent presidents normally derive an advantage from incumbency.* The relationship between presidential approval ratings and the vote indicates that candidate-presidents have a good chance of winning election even with fairly low July approval ratings. Every president in recent times with an approval rating of more than 50 percent has gone on to win the election, but the historical record suggests that presidents do not need to reach the 50 percent approval threshold in order to win election (Brody and Sigelman 1983). Presidents with approval ratings higher than about 40 percent can ex-

Figure 5.1. Presidential Approval in July and the Incumbent's Two-Party Presidential Vote, 1948–2004

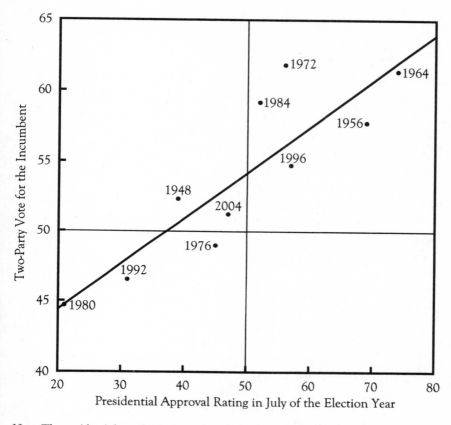

Note: The presidential vote for the incumbent is the percentage of the major two-party vote.

pect to win reelection, and, with the exception of Ford's narrow loss in 1976, all six candidate-presidents with this minimal level of popularity have gone on to electoral victory.[8]

As the plot of incumbent approval ratings and their vote percentages indicates, presidential incumbency is best thought of as an opportunity. It does not confer an automatic advantage on a candidate and is certainly no guarantee of reelection. Nevertheless, it is also an opportunity that can usually be converted into an advantage. Only failed incumbents, those who through their own doing or through circumstances beyond their control preside over national conditions below levels minimally acceptable to the public do not receive an advantage from incumbency. While highly successful incumbents obtain a sizable advantage from their status, even incumbents with a mixed record receive some benefit.

The Advantages of Presidential Incumbency

There are many reasons why presidents, particularly those seeking just a second term for their party, are likely to begin the campaign in a stronger position and may also fare well during the campaign. The list of systematic incumbent advantages, apart from any particular triumphs that an incumbent may have had in office, is quite extensive. From one perspective, everything that a president does in office is in preparation for reelection.[9] However, we can isolate some distinct advantages among the extensive array of resources at the incumbent's disposal. There are seven major advantages that are not available to non-incumbents.[10] Although most of these advantages help incumbents prior to their campaigns, they may also help incumbents hold leads through the course of the campaign.

Political Inertia
Simple inertia is one reason that candidates who are incumbents do well in re-election bids. If voters saw enough in a candidate to elect the candidate once, there is good reason to believe that they will do it again. The electorate usually does not change much from one election to the next, either in composition or in attitudes. Asked to make a judgment about a candidate that they previously elected, most voters will make the same decision. Some voters who had previously supported the incumbent will drift away and some who had previously opposed the incumbent may be won over, but a base of voters, who had provided the core of the winning coalition in the previous election, will remain committed to the incumbent.

Adding to the inertia or constancy that works to an incumbent's advantage is the natural reluctance of voters to admit that they had made a mistake in voting for the incumbent in the previous election. This tendency is reinforced by the general optimism of the public. Despite growing public cynicism toward institutions, most of the public wants to believe the best about individuals, including incumbents.[11] As a result, incumbents generally get the benefit of the doubt.[12] The logic is simple: "If it ain't broke, don't fix it." Challengers, on the other hand, have the burden of proof. They must convince voters that the job of president should be taken away from the incumbent, that it is "broke and needs fixing." With the status quo generally favoring the incumbent, challengers often have to run a more negative campaign. This has the potential of reversing opinions, but it is a high-risk strategy that can backfire with a public that seems to find political conflict and negativism distasteful.[13]

Learning from Experience

A second advantage of presidential incumbency is that the incumbent should have learned how to be a better presidential candidate from having run for and having served in the presidency. With the exception of incumbents who rose to the presidency from the vice presidency upon the death (or resignation) of a president, incumbent presidents have already successfully waged one national political campaign to win election. Not only does this mean that voters have accepted the candidate once and may be predisposed to reaffirm their decision four years later, it also means that most incumbents have done an acceptable job in assembling a campaign organization that mounted a campaign that allowed them to win the presidency. If they were able to do this once, they ought to be able to do it a second time. Moreover, having successfully run for the presidency once, these incumbents have had the opportunity to learn firsthand how they might improve their campaigning skills for the reelection effort. Although the evidence may fall short of compelling, the more memorable gaffes in late twentieth-century presidential campaigns—Ford's seeming denial of Soviet domination of Poland, Carter's interview statement about "lust in his heart," Dukakis's ridiculous appearance wearing an oversized helmet while driving a military tank—all happened to candidates who had not previously run for the presidency.

Incumbents not only have the advantage of learning from their previous successful campaign, but they may learn on the job what works and what does not work politically. They have the advantage of staking out a popular position before their opponent, but more importantly, they have the time and often the opportunity to correct their mistakes, an advantage that candidates in the heat of a campaign seldom have. Incumbents can send up "trial-balloon" proposals, see how the public reacts to them, and then either follow through with the proposals if the reaction is positive or drop the proposals and distance themselves from them if the reaction is negative.

Voters have also shown that they value experience in their candidates. When asked why they voted for one presidential candidate rather than another, one of the most frequent answers is the candidates' relative political experience. Voters appear to understand that presidents learn on the job and that anyone new to a job is more likely to make mistakes. If the risk of breaking in a new president can be avoided, why not? Thus, unless incumbents have demonstrably failed, experience is on their side, and this makes a difference for a significant number of voters. In his classic study *Choices and Echoes in Presidential Elections,*

Benjamin Page (1978) noted the advantage that experience provides to presidential incumbents: "The overriding importance of experience in the public mind gives a special advantage to incumbent presidents running for reelection. Other things being equal—that is, so long as times are reasonably good—people would rather stay with proven leadership than try someone new" (235).

The history of President Clinton's first term in office is a classic example of this advantage. By any account, the first two years of the Clinton administration were a mess. It began with the president's decision to allow homosexuals in the military, a decision met with widespread public disapproval. Subsequent developments were not much better. The hallmark of the first two years of the first Clinton administration was its failed attempt to radically overhaul the nation's health-care system, an initiative spearheaded by First Lady Hillary Rodham Clinton. Public dissatisfaction with the first two years of Clinton's first term was partly responsible for the devastating congressional losses Democrats sustained in the 1994 midterm election. The loss of fifty-two seats cost Democrats their forty-year control of the House of Representatives.

In the aftermath of the 1994 midterm election, President Clinton's prospects for reelection appeared dim. Commentators openly questioned the president's "relevance" for the remainder of his term. However, these critics underestimated the president and the opportunity afforded by the twenty-four months until the next election. President Clinton learned from his mistakes and took advantage of the available time to recover his political position. Republican congressional missteps helped in this recovery, but Clinton also helped himself. The 1994 midterm was a wake-up call. Elections are won in the political center and the administration had drifted markedly to the left. Political strategist Dick Morris was brought in to work "on repositioning Clinton" (Woodward 1996, 25). Gradually and without fanfare, the Clinton administration was able to move back toward the political center and, with the help of an overly aggressive Republican congressional majority and a healthy economy, President Clinton emerged from the political rubble of 1994 to win reelection in 1996.

A Unified Party Base

In addition to the incumbents' advantages of the public's political inertia and the opportunity to use what was learned in the first campaign and term of office, most incumbents also have had a united party behind them and clear sailing to their party's nomination. This is a considerable advantage going into the campaign. A candidate who receives his or her party's nomination without serious opposition can enter the general election unwounded by an intraparty battle and can focus full attention on winning in November. Rather than mending internal fences, the candidate enters the general campaign with a united and often enthusiastic base of support. The party's full resources, from its finances to the time and effort of its activists, can be devoted to the general election campaign. The difference between a candidate running with a unified as opposed to a divided party base is the difference between a candidate being well prepared for one election contest and a candidate scrambling for the party's nomination and then hurriedly regrouping, wounds and all, for another battle.

Divisive primaries and nomination contests generally weaken the party's eventual nominee and sap valuable resources that might have been spent in the general election campaign.[14] As we observed in chapter 4 (table 4.1), a presidential candidate needs to hold his or her partisan base, to secure their loyalty, and turn them out to vote.[15] With party loyalty rates as high as they are and with the independent vote as small as it is, a candidate cannot depend on partisans of the other party or on independents to assemble much of a winning coalition.

A divided nomination contest not only saps resources from the general election candidacy of the candidate but also supplies valuable ammunition to the opposition.[16] The nominee that emerges from a divided nomination contest is often haunted by the attacks made by fellow partisans in the heat of the intraparty battle. Perhaps the most memorable example of this was the characterization of Ronald Reagan's economic policy proposals in the 1980 campaign as "voodoo economics" by his nomination rival George Bush, who subsequently became Reagan's running mate. The Carter-Mondale campaign never tired of resurrecting the charge in that year's general election campaign. Attacks that come from within a party are accorded greater credibility and are used with relish by opponents in the general election campaign. Any candidate would like to avoid answering charges made from within the party, and incumbents are most likely to be in this position.[17]

The experience of recent incumbents demonstrates the impact of party unity and an easy nomination.[18] Since 1952 there have been ten incumbent presidents who could have run for election. Six received their party's nomination without serious challenge and went on to win the general election. Four of these incumbents won by landslide proportions (Eisenhower in 1956, Johnson in 1964, Nixon in 1972, and Reagan in 1984), the fifth won with a moderate plurality (Clinton in 1996), and the sixth narrowly won (George W. Bush in 2004). The four incumbents who faced a divided party either decided not to run (Johnson in 1968) or ran and lost in the general election. Two of these losing incumbents, President Ford in 1976 and President Carter in 1980, were seriously challenged for their parties' nominations. Ford managed to fend off a challenge from Ronald Reagan in 1976, and Carter survived a nomination challenge from Edward Kennedy in 1980.

The broader record of electoral history also demonstrates the importance of party unity to a presidential candidate and the greater likelihood that an incumbent president's party will be unified. Congressional Quarterly (1985, 324) examined the elections of the sixteen incumbent presidents who ran for reelection between 1900 and 1984 and found that all twelve who had "clear sailing" for their party's nomination won reelection while all four who had "tough sledding" for renomination were defeated.

Further evidence of the importance of party unity and its link to incumbency comes from an inspection of nomination conventions and the number of ballots necessary to nominate their standard-bearer. Although every presidential candidate since 1956 has won the party's nomination on the first convention ballot, multi-ballot conventions before 1956 were not uncommon. Eighteen of the forty-four presidential candidates nominated between 1868 and 1952 were nominated on a second or later balloting of their convention's delegates. Table 5.6 lists these multi-ballot nomination candidates, the number of ballots required for their nomination, their delegate strength on the convention's first balloting, and the outcome of the general election. Most of these

Table 5.6. *Multiple-Ballot Major-Party Presidential Nominating Conventions, 1868–1952*

Year	Political Party	Number of Ballots to Nomination	Nominee	Nominee's Delegate % on 1st Ballot	Election Outcome
1868	Democratic	22	Seymour	0% (—)	Lost
1876	Democratic	2	Tilden	54% (1st)	Lost
1876	Republican	7	Hayes	8% (5th)	Won
1880	Democratic	2	Hancock	23% (1st)	Lost
1880	Republican	36	Garfield	0% (—)	Won
1884	Democratic	2	Cleveland	58% (1st)	Won
1884	Republican	4	Blaine	41% (1st)	Lost
1888	Republican	8	Harrison	10% (4th)	Won
1896	Democratic	5	Bryan	15% (2nd)	Lost
1912	Democratic	46	Wilson	30% (2nd)	Won
1916	Republican	3	Hughes	26% (1st)	Lost
1920	Democratic	44	Cox	12% (3rd)	Lost
1920	Republican	10	Harding	7% (4th)	Won
1924	Democratic	103	Davis	3% (7th)	Lost
1932	Democratic	4	F. Roosevelt	58% (1st)	Won
1940	Republican	6	Willkie	11% (3rd)	Lost
1948	Republican	3	Dewey	40% (1st)	Lost
1952	Democratic	3	Stevenson	22% (2nd)	Lost

Note: There have been no multiple-ballot conventions since 1952.

Table 5.7. Effect of Multiple-Ballot Nominations on General Election Success of Nominee, 1868–1952

Number of Ballots to Select Nominee	Outcome of General Election for Party Nominee		
	Won	*Lost*	*Total*
Multiple-Ballot Nominations	7	11	18
	(39%)	(61%)	
First-Ballot Nominations	15	11	26
	(58%)	(42%)	

Note: If the three multi-ballot nominees who had first-ballot simple majorities are subtracted from the multi-ballot category, the win-loss record of multi-ballot nominees drops to five wins and ten losses. If post-1952 first-ballot nominations are dropped, the won-loss record of first-ballot nominees is fifteen wins and eleven losses. In four election years (1876, 1880, 1884, and 1920) both parties had multi-ballot nominations. The won-loss record of parties with multi-ballot nominations when the opposing party had a single-ballot nomination was three wins and seven losses, and one of these victories was Franklin Roosevelt's in 1932. Roosevelt had a first-ballot simple majority but lacked the extraordinary majority required for nomination under the Democratic party's two-thirds rule.

multi-ballot nominations involved four or more ballots. In short, these were parties that were significantly divided over the nomination.[19]

The evidence regarding multi-ballot presidential nominations indicates (1) that candidates who win their party's nomination after multiple ballots are much less likely to win the general election than those who were nominated on the first ballot, and (2) that incumbent presidential candidates have always won their nomination on the first ballot. Table 5.7 presents the election outcomes for candidates nominated after multiple ballots as opposed to those nominated on their party's first balloting of convention delegates. While a majority of first-ballot nominees went on to win their election, a sizable majority of multi-ballot candidates lost. As one would well expect, a party divided at the outset about its nominee is likely to remain divided enough that its candidate loses the election.[20]

Table 5.8 shows that none of the thirteen incumbents who ran for election from 1868 to 1952 were nominated in multi-ballot conventions. Every incumbent president who sought election did so with a party united enough to nominate him on the first ballot.[21] This undoubtedly helped many of these candidates (nine of the thirteen) win election.

An analysis of the breakdown of vote decision by the time of decision and partisanship (table 4.4 and appendix B) also provides evidence that incumbents usually enter their campaign seasons with a more unified party and that this early unity greatly enhances their prospects for a November victory (J. Campbell 2007a). The degree of early party unity is measured by the per-

Table 5.8. Incumbency and Multiple-Ballot Nominations, 1868–1952

Number of Ballots to Select Nominee	Was the Incumbent President Seeking the Party's Renomination?	
	Yes	No
Multiple-Ballot Nominations	0	18
	(0%)	(58%)
First-Ballot Nominations	13	13
	(100%)	(42%)
Total	13	31

Note: Since all nominations since 1952 have been on the first ballot, these cases are not included here. Adding the nominations for elections from 1956 to 2004 would add nine cases to the first-ballot incumbent seeking renomination category and seventeen cases to the first-ballot incumbent not seeking renomination category.

centage of early-deciding voters who voted loyally for their party's presidential candidate. With the exception of President Carter in 1980, each of the nine incumbent candidates since 1956 had a more unified party than their challengers. The median difference between the early unity for incumbents and their challengers (a party unity advantage) was about 9 percentage points. There was virtually no unity gap between incumbents and challengers among later-deciding voters. The early party unity advantage for most incumbents, however, proved important to their election. The median early party unity advantage of the six incumbents who won their elections was 14 percentage points. For the three losing incumbents since 1956, the median advantage was only 3 percentage points.[22] All of this evidence, from convention unity to survey data, sustains two related points: *an incumbent president is likely to have a more unified party at the outset of the election, and a unified party at the beginning of a campaign significantly helps a presidential candidate run a successful campaign.*

One final thought about incumbency and party unity: while having an incumbent in the race may discourage potential challengers for the nomination and encourage party unity, the in-party may not hold this advantage indefinitely. Not only does the 22nd Amendment to the Constitution prevent an incumbent from seeking a third term (thus opening the way for a battle over the successor nominee), but the in-party is likely to develop fissures over time. The longer a party is in office, the greater the likelihood that differences within the party will emerge. On the other side, a party that has lost a series of presidential elections may be more ready to set aside internal differences in order to improve its prospects. Nothing unites a party as much as being on the outside. This may explain, in part, the normally short series of consecutive presidential victories for either party (Norpoth 1995). After losing two or more presidential elections in a row (e.g., the Republicans going into 1952, the Democrats going into 1992), partisans may be ready to compromise among themselves in order to win an election.

Control of Events and the Agenda

Presidents have great powers that can be used to their political advantage. Indeed, the line between the president as president and the president as candidate is anything but clear, to the point that much of the president's campaign is now run directly out of the White House itself (Tenpas 2003). Governing and campaigning are inextricably linked in a democratic republic. From the time they take their oath of office, presidents make decisions that may affect their reelection prospects. For instance, discretion regarding government contracts or appointments or the details of policies and regulations can be used to target government benefits to electorally important constituencies. Presidential leverage over fiscal policy and indirectly over monetary policy can help stimulate the economy or settle a shaky economic situation before the election (Tufte 1978). The condition of the economy strongly affects voter reactions to the in-party candidate and incumbents usually do what they can to prime the economy for an upcoming election.[23]

While it is easy to exaggerate presidential powers and the ability of the president to control events, there is little doubt that the president has some control and can be quite public in his efforts to deal with national problems. Moreover, presidential decisions can be timed for maximum political impact, either to emphasize the positive or distract from the negative. In recent elections, at least since Secretary of State Henry Kissinger announced within weeks of the 1972 election that "peace was at hand" in the Vietnam War (White 1973, 330), political observers have been wary of presidential attempts to influence late-deciding voters with what has become known as an "October surprise."[24]

Although there is little evidence to suggest that these eleventh-hour presidential activities have had much impact, and while presidents do not have as much control over events as often believed, presidents as candidates do have a large amount of control over which issues receive attention on the national agenda. It is often said regarding the legislative process that the president proposes and the Congress disposes. The ability to propose legislation and to draw national attention to different issues is a great presidential power. No political figure in American politics has as much control over the national agenda as the president, and this power can be used to considerable electoral advantage. As Samuel Kernell (2006) well documents, presidents have realized that "going public" can advance their agenda and bargaining position with Congress.

There are always a variety of issues to which the public, the media, and Congress could devote their attention. Some of these issues may play to the president's political strengths and others may highlight a weakness. A president who can redirect national attention to favorable issues has the advantage of having the political battles of the next election fought on favorable grounds. Of course, some issues are always salient to the public—matters of the economy and matters of war and peace—and other issues are raised by circumstances and developments well beyond the president's control. However, if any presidential candidate has some control over what issues will become a major part of the debate, it would be an incumbent president.

The Rose Garden Strategy

Presidents in campaigns routinely employ the "Rose Garden strategy." In essence the Rose Garden strategy is when the incumbent president campaigns for election by simply appearing presidential (Tenpas 2003, 46–49). It amounts to campaigning without *overtly* campaigning. The media and the public are supposed to witness the president doing his job. The president is to be seen by voters as not merely another candidate crassly begging for votes but as a national and world leader.

The planned opening phase of Lyndon Johnson's 1964 campaign was a textbook case of the Rose Garden strategy. As Theodore White (1965) described it later, "the President would be 'Presidential' to start with—he would campaign from the White House, be on display, serenely coping with the business of the nation and the world, conferring honors or meeting great visitors in the rose garden; in this phase his field trips would be short, ceremonial, nonpolitical. . . . Lyndon Johnson was the Presidential Presence—and no challenger, at any time, can even approach the immense advantage that goes with being President" (372). Being seen simply doing the job, the president can campaign while appearing to be above politics and, at the same time, can deny the opponent the national stage as an equal contender for the office.

While the Rose Garden strategy, strictly speaking, suggests a non-campaign campaign from the steps of the White House, the essence of the strategy is much broader. The strategy is to connect the candidate with the office wherever possible. The presumption is that some of the esteem that voters patriotically have for the institution of the presidency will rub off on, or be transferred to, the incumbent personally. The image of the president as candidate becomes intertwined with that of the presidency and all the national symbolism that surrounds the office. Even prefacing the president's name with the title routinely reminds voters of the melding of the candidate and the presidency.

Nixon's reelection effort in 1972 pushed the point even more aggressively with his campaign cohort being named the "Committee to Re-elect the President." Signs along Nixon campaign motorcades reading "Right on Mr. President," "Hello Mr. President, Hang in there Sir," and "Nixon is Our President" (White 1973, 332) reflect the potency of the strategy.

In a nation that traditionally has been at best ambivalent about politics and has never been particularly embracing of politicians, the Rose Garden strategy is especially attractive and often effective. While the public is quite partisan, it does not appreciate partisanship. The Rose Garden strategy allows a candidate to advance the candidacy while still appearing to be above petty partisan politics. The presidency automatically elevates the status of a candidate above that of the challenger. Presidents as candidates realize that they can only benefit from reminding voters of this, and they seldom miss an opportunity to do so.[25]

It should also be noted that the prestige and trappings of the White House can also be exploited in a more politically tangible way. Even with public financing of presidential elections, one important advantage of presidential incumbency is the ease with which it allows candidates to raise additional campaign contributions to their party that indirectly (and sometimes not so indirectly) help their campaigns. The 1996 election, again, affords a good illustration of this advantage. As presidents in the past have done, but with much greater dedication, President Clinton's campaign effectively exploited the presidential office and its trappings to raise campaign money. Through a series of fundraising events such as coffees with the president in the White House, vice presidential calls to well-heeled potential contributors, and overnight stays in the White House's Lincoln Bedroom for particularly generous contributors, the Democrats raised a substantial bankroll for their 1996 campaign.[26]

The Disadvantage of the Challenger

While incumbents can surround themselves with all of the national symbols of the presidency and become associated in the minds of many voters with the nation itself, the images that voters have of non-incumbents are probably at their positive peak before they become active candidates. The initial information about a non-incumbent candidate is most likely to be strongly influenced by his or her campaign and, therefore, glowing. Once in the arena the candidate becomes just another politician and is subjected to greater media scrutiny and assaults by the opposition. The more that voters see of a candidate in different and uncontrolled situations, the more they are likely to glimpse various aspects of the candidate's character, not just what the candidate and his or her advisors want voters to see. As a result the more voters get to know a challenger during the campaign, the more likely they are to learn about or perceive the candidate's flaws. In short, presidential candidates look best before they are candidates and after they get elected.

Perhaps the 1992 third-party candidacy of Texas billionaire Ross Perot is most illustrative of this phenomenon. Early on in his 1992 venture into presidential politics, most voters regarded Perot as a no-nonsense, straight-shooting, tough-minded but reasonable alternative to "politics as usual." The longer Perot stayed on the national political stage, however, the more likely he was to reveal, and the more likely voters were to see, less attractive sides of his personality. His decision in 1992 to pull out of the presidential contest only to reenter weeks later, along with stories of his thin-skinned reactions to criticism, changed some views of his suitability for national political office (Germond and Witcover 1993, chapter 20).

Presidential candidates who challenge incumbent presidents are also generally in the unenviable position of running a more negative campaign than the incumbent. Incumbents must defend their records for reelection, claiming credit for various real or imagined accomplishments. Challengers, on the other hand, must attack the record to give voters a reason to displace the incumbent. Given that many voters prefer upbeat messages and have a distaste for conflict, the necessary negativity of the challenger's message may itself be a liability for the challenger's campaign. A candidate on the attack runs the risk of being seen by voters as having a "mean streak."[27]

Second Party Terms and Two Campaign Themes

Every presidential election is at least partially a referendum on the performance of the in-party over the previous four years. Voters routinely look to the past for guidance about who to entrust with power for the future, whether they want to renew their contract with the in-party. From a different perspective, voters ask themselves the question posed to them by Franklin Roosevelt (in 1934) and again by Ronald Reagan in 1980: "Are you better off than you were four years ago?" There are two basic campaign themes in presidential electoral politics that address the referendum question: *change* and *continuity*. When times are good and voters think that they are better off, candidates are at an advantage if they can persuade voters that they represent continuity, stability, more of the same. When times are not so good and voters think that they are worse off, candidates want to convince voters that they stand for change, for progress, for getting things moving again. The continuity theme is the appeal of the insider, the voice of experience. The change theme is the appeal of the outsider, the new voice. Both themes are simple appeals, easily communicated by candidates and readily grasped by voters.

At least one of the twin themes of change and stability has appeared in virtually every presidential campaign. Sometimes these themes are voiced quite explicitly, and at other times they form the subtext of a message. The change theme was explicit in Dewey's 1948 slogan "Had Enough?" (Kelly 1991, 218). It was also the clear centerpiece of the Kennedy campaign in 1960. As Theodore White (1961, 256) recounts in *The Making of the President, 1960*, the change theme was at the core of Kennedy's "grand theme that was to dominate and shape his campaign to the end: *America cannot stand still; her prestige fails in the world; this is a time of burdens and sacrifice; we must move*" (italics original).

Facing Vice President Hubert Humphrey and third-party candidate Governor George Wallace of Alabama in the 1968 election, Richard Nixon's campaign also focused on change. A high-level advisor to Nixon spelled out the mission in a campaign memo in July 1968: "we must convince the public that HH [Hubert Humphrey] is tied to the past, to policies that don't work, and that [he] stands for more of the same. More crises. More confusion. More wars. More inflation. More lawlessness. More loss of respect for the U.S. abroad. RN [Richard Nixon], on the other hand, stands for *change*. For new ideas, positive action, imaginative, workable programs that will help solve the problems now plaguing us. . . . Corollary to the above, we must play on the importance and frustration of today's voters. They *want* change" (McGinniss 1969, 233–34). The memo ends with the guiding theme for the messages of the campaign: "A change is urgently needed. There's only one candidate who stands for change: Richard M. Nixon" (236).

Ronald Reagan adopted the change theme campaign in his 1980 race against the incumbent, President Jimmy Carter. High interest, unemployment, and inflation rates and foreign affairs crises, including the administration's inability to secure the release of the American hostages held in Iran, filled a reservoir of public dissatisfaction with Carter that was there to be tapped. The change theme was a natural. As James Sundquist and Richard Scammon (1981) put it: "The central circumstance of the 1980 election was the unpopularity of Jimmy Carter" (20). It is little wonder that the tag line for the Reagan campaign advertising was "For a Change" (Pomper 1981, 77).

The theme of change was also prominent in Bill Clinton's 1992 campaign against President George Bush and independent candidate Ross Perot. While Clinton campaign advisor James Carville's colorful admonition regarding the economy is most frequently recalled, his first theme for the campaign was: "Change vs. more of the same."[28] The theme appeared clearly in one September televised spot ad in which Clinton, speaking directly to the camera, made the case for change: "Government just isn't working for the hardworking families of America. We need fundamental change, not just more of the same . . ."

(Arterton 1993, 99).[29] Clinton's claim to be the future-oriented candidate for change was spelled out even more clearly in the Fleetwood Mac song used extensively throughout the campaign: "Don't Stop Thinking About Tomorrow" (Germond and Witcover 1993, 346).

The stability theme also reappears throughout our electoral history. In the midst of the Civil War, Abraham Lincoln campaigned on the theme that the nation should not "change horses in mid-stream." The theme was repeated almost a century later in Franklin Roosevelt's 1944 campaign (Roberts and Hammond 2004, 168, 253). In 1900, Mark Hanna, speaking in behalf of President William McKinley, sounded the stability theme by asserting that voters should "let well enough alone" (Troy 1996, 109). Carrying forward the legacy of martyred President John Kennedy, President Lyndon Johnson in 1964 quite explicitly called upon the continuity theme. The key line of his nomination acceptance speech at the Democratic convention in Atlantic City, a line repeated throughout the campaign, was "Let us continue" (Faber 1965, 188).

President Reagan's 1984 reelection campaign, as Everett Ladd (1985b, 4) observed, also was organized around the stability or continuity theme. In his renomination acceptance speech before a nationally televised audience, President Reagan recalled the record of his first term and then highlighted the campaign message of continuity: "We bring to the American citizens in this election year a record of accomplishment and the promise of continuation" (Ladd 1985b, 4). Combining the stability and incumbency messages, the slogan for the campaign was "Leadership That's Working" (Abramson, Aldrich, and Rohde 1986, 51). George H. W. Bush, Reagan's vice president and successor, also unambiguously adopted and rode into office in 1988 on the stability theme, "Stay the Course" (Farah and Klein 1989, 109–10).

The twin campaign themes of continuity and change are common because they are simple and effective. They resonate with voters looking for a convincing and straightforward reason to choose one candidate over another. These themes may not pack a great deal of content (change to what?), but they may be enough to trigger a retrospective judgment. The applicability of the two themes is, however, determined by circumstances. Most candidates can only effectively use one of the themes in a campaign. In-party candidates running with a strong record behind them can make the case for continuity. Out-party candidates running when voters are particularly disgruntled with the administration's performance can make the case for change. Neither theme is likely to help in-party candidates in bad times or out-party candidates in good times. These candidates are best advised to direct voter attention away from retrospective considerations.

Although most candidates can, at most, use either the change or continuity theme, one type of candidate is in the enviable position of being able to use *both* themes: in-party candidates of a party seeking a second consecutive presidential term (recall the Abramowitz and Norpoth findings above). Assuming that the in-party record is an acceptable one, and the relationship of approval ratings and the vote suggests (figure 5.1) that voters are generous in judging acceptability, the in-party candidate can use the continuity appeal. This is not unusual. An in-party candidate in good times should be able to convert credit for that performance into future votes.

What is unusual is that an in-party that has been in office for less than four years can also claim that its candidate is an agent of change. Outsiders do not become insiders overnight, or even after four years. First-term incumbents can still convincingly claim that they are working to effect change in the system, that they need additional time to get the job of "change" done. The claim is credible because a first-term incumbent is not yet perceived by voters as the establishment candidate. Both Ronald Reagan in 1984 and Bill Clinton in 1996 shared this status. Each could appeal to voters who wanted stability and simultaneously appeal to voters who favored change. They were insiders to some but were still new enough on the job that they could portray themselves to others as outsiders, agents of change. After another four years in office, however, this claim would not have been credible.[30]

Is Incumbency Still an Advantage?

The record of incumbency, at least to a point, is clear. Presidential incumbency has been an electoral opportunity, an opportunity that has on occasion been squandered but has most often been used to considerable advantage both before and during campaigns. While the historical record suggests that incumbency has most often been an advantage, doubts persist about whether it remains so in modern presidential politics.

There are some good reasons for those doubts. Some have suggested, as G. Calvin Mackenzie has put it, that "in many ways the postwar presidency devours its incumbents" (1996, 125). The first reason to suspect that incumbency does not offer the advantage that it once did is the record of incumbency success itself. Of the seven president-candidates since 1968, four have won and three have lost. Second, presidents who were once virtually guaranteed renomination for a second term have been challenged within their own party. President Ford in 1976 and President Carter in 1980 were both very nearly denied their parties' nominations. Party reform and the proliferation of primaries have taken control of the nomination away from party professionals, who were dutifully respectful of presidents as the leaders of their parties, and given it over to primary voters, who do not have the same kind of stake in party unity or the electability of its nominee. Finally, the media may also have contributed to a decline in the incumbency advantage. Over the years, the relationship between the media and presidents has changed quite a bit. Whereas the old media (before the Vietnam War and Watergate) were respectful of (if not deferential to) the president, the new media are much more adversarial and combative. One could hardly imagine a Sam Donaldson shouting questions at President Franklin Roosevelt or the president willingly subjecting himself to these indignities. Of course, the difference in the media's coverage of the president goes well beyond matters of style and decorum. The media are more drawn to report negative news about the president and to suggest cynical political motives at every turn (Patterson 1994). Under this kind of media scrutiny, incumbent presidents might not look so noble to the public. It may not be merely a coincidence that public cynicism toward politicians and the political process has risen over this same period.

Although there are reasons to wonder whether sitting presidents continue to enjoy an electoral advantage, the reasons for suspecting a decline in the advantage should be tempered. First, though the recent record of incumbents has been less than impressive, this may be explainable. Presidential incumbency is an opportunity, and at least two of the three defeated incumbents may have squandered their opportunities. President Ford, the only president elected to neither the presidency nor vice presidency, was not the best of campaigners, ran with the baggage of the Nixon pardon, and barely survived an intra-party challenge for the GOP nomination. Even with these unusual circumstances, Ford only barely lost the 1976 election. Four years later, President Carter, having presided over a very weak national economy (the only shrinking election year economy between 1948 and 2004), with anemic approval ratings, and battered by a tough intra-party battle for renomination, lost to Ronald Reagan. The third defeated recent incumbent was President George H. W. Bush. The lesson of the Bush defeat is not that incumbents no longer have an advantage but that the advantage is not so great that they can renege on a clear promise to the public and get away with it. In 1988, George Bush told the American public, "Read my lips, no new taxes." He violated this very simple and very public promise, and this may well have cost him the 1992 election.

Because of party reform of the nomination process and the gauntlet of primary elections that prospective presidential nominees must run, recent incumbent presidents have been less likely to get the free pass to their party's nomination that their predecessors received. However, the nomination system did not stop changing after the Democratic Party's McGovern-Fraser reforms of the early 1970s. Subsequent changes may have actually (and quite unintentionally) worked to restore some of the advantages of incumbent presidents. Although party reforms of the nomination system in many respects set national standards for the delegate selection systems used in the states, the states were left with a great deal of latitude, including substantial control of the timing of their primaries and caucuses. Many states have used their discretion to have their delegate selections earlier in the election year. The result has been a bunching up or front-end loading of the nomination process. Whereas delegate selection in the post-reform system had been strung out over many months, allowing an outsider candidate to emerge and gain momentum, most delegates are now selected in a much shorter period. The result of this front-end loading is that frontrunners for the party nomination (and incumbents are usually in this position) have a significant advantage. The nomination process is more open to competition and intraparty battles than in the pre-reform days but not as much as it was in the post-reform wide-open system of the 1970s. In effect, incumbent presidents may not get the free ride to nomination that they once could count on, but neither are they likely to face the renomination struggles that plagued presidents in the 1970s.

Finally, though the political media are unarguably more aggressive in their treatment of presidents, and though voters are unquestionably more cynical about presidents than they once were, voters seem to still give presidents some benefit of the doubt. Voter skepticism applies to the media and the president's opponents as well as to the president.

★ *Chapter 6*

The Economic Context of the Campaign

THE HEALTH OF the national economy establishes a second important and systematic context for the presidential campaign. Long before President Clinton's campaign advisor James Carville concocted the slogan, "It's the economy, stupid," to remind Clinton campaign workers to stay "on message," political observers appreciated the political importance of the economy. As *The American Voter* (A. Campbell et al. 1960), the classic study of voting behavior, stated it: "Economic interest has long been seen as a primary motive impelling political action" (381).[1] The aggregate consequences of these individual economic judgments are clear. In his groundbreaking study *Political Control of the Economy*, Edward Tufte (1978) put it squarely: "as goes economic performance, so goes the election" (137).

There is no question that presidential elections and the direction that their campaigns take are significantly influenced by voter satisfaction or dissatisfaction with the in-party's management of the economy. The general condition of the national economy has a great deal to do with both the standing of the in-party candidate at the outset of the campaign and how that standing changes during the campaign. In-party presidential candidates fare much better when the electorate sees strong economic growth and experiences a higher standard of living and low unemployment, tax, inflation, and interest rates. A large body of research, using various measures of general economic conditions and examining different sets of elections, well documents the very substantial impact of the economy on presidential elections (Tufte 1978; Fiorina 1981; Hibbs 1987; Lewis-Beck 1988; Erikson 1989; Alesina and Rosenthal 1995, Lewis-Beck and Stegmaier 2000).

The basic point is simple: economic conditions strongly influence presidential elections. How and when the economy has its effects on the campaign is not so clear cut, however. Moreover, the impact of the economy on campaigns and elections is in some respects overstated and in other respects underappreciated. This chapter makes four observations about the role of the economy in making campaign effects on the election predictable.

First, economic performance both before and during the election year matters to election results, but only economic developments during the election year appear to affect what happens through the course of the campaign. The performance of the economy during the in-party's term prior to the election year affects the decisions of many early-deciding voters and thus helps to establish the stable context or parameters of the campaign. The performance of the economy during the election year affects whether the in-party or out-party is more successful at attracting votes *during* the campaign.

Second, though economic growth is undeniably important to campaigns and the election results, its importance is sometimes exaggerated. Presidential elections are more than matters of election-year economics. Voters are concerned about many things other than the economy. Exclusively economic perspectives on elections miss much of what concerns voters and affects election results.

Third, to the extent that the economy matters, the effects of economic conditions on the campaign are not strictly matters of dollars and cents or the economic well-being of voters. The condition of the economy affects the campaign indirectly through its impact on the public's general mood toward the in-party as well as directly through more strictly defined economic voting. Good economic times foster a positive general outlook, and hard times cast a shadow over everything the in-party does. In this regard, the political impact of the economy is sometimes underappreciated.

Finally, all in-party candidates are not held equally responsible by voters for the state of the economy. Incumbents are accorded full credit for a good economy and full blame for a bad one, but non-incumbents or successor candidates of the in-party are held only partially accountable for economic conditions. Voters draw a distinction between a president who personally controlled the levers of power that may have affected the economy and a successor candidate of the president's party who likely shares the outlook of the president but did not personally make presidential decisions.

The Importance of the Election-Year Economy

Although the economy throughout a president's term matters to voters and therefore has a bearing on the election, the economy during the year of the election is especially important to the impact of the campaign on the vote. The judgments of voters are likely to be most affected by the most recent information that they have about the administration's performance. Earlier information is relevant but less so than recent information. From one perspective, voters are asking the in-party candidate: what have you done for us lately? From another perspective, by more heavily weighing recent experience with the economy, they may be discounting to some degree the mistakes or the luck that an administration had early in its term, before it had a fair chance to get its economic program fully under way. Economic policies are not passed and implemented overnight, and their impact on the economy may take some time to be felt, but by the third year in office it is fair to hold the in-party responsible for economic conditions.[2]

The particular importance of the election-year economy to the election has long been recognized by presidential election forecasters. With one exception, every major forecasting model includes consideration in some form of economic conditions around the time of the election.[3] While there are differences among the models in the aggregate indicator of economic growth used and in the period of economic activity during the election year examined (first half of the year versus the second quarter), nearly every model quite explicitly takes the election-year economy into account in forecasting the election results, and the accuracy of each model would suffer significantly if the election-year economic conditions were not considered.

The impact of the election-year economy, as measured by the real growth rate in the GDP over the first six months of the election year, is demonstrated in figure 6.1. The figure plots the two-party vote percentage for the in-party presidential candidate against the economic growth rate for the first half of the election year for the fifteen presidential elections from 1948 to 2004.[4] Both bivariate and multiple regression lines (controlling for the in-party's September preference poll standing) have a statistically significant positive slope through the plot, indicating that, as expected, in-party presidential candidates fare better in stronger election-year economies. The fact that economic growth in the first half of the election year has a significant impact on the national vote over and above the impact of the pre-campaign public opinion as measured in the polls suggests that the economy affects how late-deciding voters change or make up their minds during the course of the campaign. Based on the multiple regression estimate of the relationship (the thicker line in the figure), in-party presidential candidates can expect to gain almost seven-tenths of a percentage point of the November vote for every additional percentage point of economic growth (annualized) in the first half of the election year.

The general history of election-year economies and the results of these pres-

Figure 6.1. The Election-Year Economy and the Incumbent Party's Two-Party Presidential Vote, 1948–2004

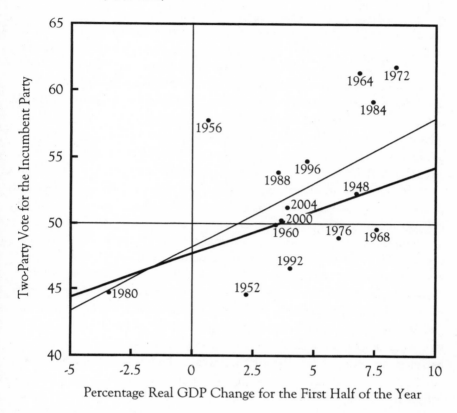

Percentage Real GDP Change for the First Half of the Year

Note: The presidential vote for the incumbent-party candidate is the percentage of the major two-party vote. The GDP change is the annualized percentage point change in the real GDP for the first two quarters of the election year as reported by the Bureau of Economic Analysis as of November 29, 2006. The thinner line is the bivariate regression line (b = .97). The thicker line is the multivariate regression line (b = .66) for a regression that also included the in-party candidate's standing in the early September preference poll and assumes an in-party candidate standing of 48 percent. This is the estimated neutral preference poll standing for an in-party candidate.

idential elections suggest that voters demand a certain amount of economic growth before they judge the in-party to be successful enough to return it to office. As a rule, voters seem to get at least a measure of the economic performance that they want from the in-party. The economy grew in the first half year in fourteen of the fifteen elections from 1946 to 2004 and exceeded three percentage points in twelve of these election years. The median GDP growth rate was about four percentage points annualized. One reading of the election-year relationship to the vote is from the estimated regression line. Its intersection of the 50 percent vote line suggests that the in-party candidate can generally expect to receive a majority of the two-party vote so long as first-half (annualized) economic growth is about 3.5 percentage points or greater. This estimate is calculated using a 48 percent preference poll standing, the estimated neutral point for in-party candidates. The lower cut-point indicated by the bivariate line (about 1.9 percentage points) does not take into account the presidential incumbency advantages documented in the previous chapter.

In-party candidates running with economic growth above 4.5 percentage points annualized have won more than two-thirds of the time (five of seven elections) and the two losses were very close elections (Humphrey in 1968 and Ford in 1976). In contrast, only one of the four in-party candidates running with weaker election-year economies (less than three percent growth) won election (Eisenhower in 1956).

The impact of the election-year economy would appear to be plainly evident in several elections. Of the fifteen presidential elections between 1948 and 2004, three were landslides and the election-year economies were booming in each case. The GDP was growing by 6.8 percentage points or better in the first half year leading up to Johnson's 1964 landslide, Nixon's 1972 landslide, and Reagan's 1984 landslide. At the other extreme, the 1980 election-year economy stands out among these elections as the only one in which economic activity declined during the first six months of the year. Such unusually poor economic conditions undoubtedly contributed to Carter's unusual defeat as a first-term elected incumbent.

The impact of the election-year economy on the campaign is also evident in the vote division of voters deciding during the campaign. The late-deciding voters tended to favor the in-party in proportion to how well the election-year economy was doing. The vote division and loyalty rates of late-deciding voters are calculated from the NES surveys (see Appendix B). The real GDP growth rate in the first half of the election year is positively correlated with the in-party vote percentage of late-deciding voters ($r = .20$) and the percentage of late-deciding partisans of the in-party voting for their party's standard-bearer ($r = .16$).

The real GDP growth rate in the second quarter of the election year is more strongly correlated to the late deciders' vote for the in-party candidate ($r = .60$) and the loyalty rate of late-deciding in-party partisans ($r = .31$). As both this and the more aggregated evidence indicate, many undecided voters are moved to a choice during the campaign by recent pre-campaign economic developments. This contributes to the predictability of the campaign's impact on the election.

There are three important caveats to the proposition that as the election-year economy goes, so goes the election. The focus on the election-year economy as being critical to the election may be too narrow in three ways. First, voters do not respond only to economics. To dust off an old maxim: "Man does not live by bread alone." Americans are very practical, and economics are thus very important to them. However, they do not care about economics to the exclusion of everything else. Second, to the extent that economic conditions are considered, American voters do not restrict their opinions to evaluations of the economy only in the election year. Economic conditions prior to the election year matter as well. Third, though voters consider many facets of the candidates beyond economics, the state of the economy may substantially affect how voters react to these noneconomic matters. Evaluations of the in-party on noneconomic matters take place within an economic context that primes voter reactions. In a sense, the impact of the economy is not *strictly* economic. There is a general spillover effect of economics, before and during the election year, which affects how voters evaluate the candidates on noneconomic issues and how they perceive the relative leadership qualities of the candidates.

Beyond the Economy

The impact of economics on the campaign and the results of the election is sometimes exaggerated. Some observers have almost an economic determinist view of elections, that the state of the economy determines whether the in-party wins or loses the election. This view both overstates the facts and oversimplifies the electoral process. Winning presidential elections does not depend exclusively on the economy. The economy affects elections, but the condition of the economy is not necessarily decisive in every presidential election.

Just as they indicate the extent of economic effects on election results, the election forecasting models also suggest the limits of economic effects. None of the various successful election forecasting models have relied exclusively on economic indicators to predict presidential elections.[5] Almost all of these forecasting models rely more heavily on general public opinion measures (either preference polls or presidential approval ratings) than on economic indicators to produce their election forecasts.[6]

In figure 6.1 the plot of economic growth during the first half of the election year and the in-party candidate's popular vote percentage also demonstrates the limited impact of the election-year economy. Although there is a definite positive relationship between the first-half growth rate in the real GDP and the November vote, the relationship is far from perfect. Many of the election years deviate a good bit from the regression line, and when other factors are taken into account, as they are in the multiple regression line (represented by the thicker line in the figure), the relationship between the election-year economy and the results of the election does not appear quite as strong.[7]

One reason that presidential election results are not simply reflections of election-year economies is that the condition of the economy is not the only thing important to voters. Other issues matter as well. Voters are not cash registers. Most voters care about issues and candidate qualities that are not directly related to economics. When asked what they consider to be the nation's most important problem or what they like or dislike about the presidential candidates, many voters offer answers related to the economy, but many do not and very few are focused on the economy to the exclusion of all other concerns.

Election results may also sometimes deviate from expectations based on the election-year economy because conditions may not provide grounds to render a clear-cut verdict on the in-party's performance. In six of the elections since 1948, economic growth during the first half of the election year was between approximately two and four percentage points (annualized). Voters apparently judge this economic performance to be middling, not necessarily weak enough to throw the in-party out of office, but not strong enough to guarantee it a vote of confidence. The in-party presidential candidate received a majority of the two-party vote in three of these elections (1988, 2000, and 2004) and lost the other three (1952, 1960, and 1992). In effect, even if the election-year economy were the only thing that mattered to voters, these conditions often are not so clear that they are decisive.

Economic Evaluations over Time

A second reason that the election-year economy is not all-important is that voters also care about, and hold the in-party accountable for, the condition of the economy before the election year. Some observers have the mistaken impression that presidents can win reelection simply by manipulating the economy just before the election. A simple interpretation of the presidential forecasting models, such as those examined in chapter 1, would appear to support this mistaken impression. Both of the models include only indicators of economic growth during the election year. The condition of the economy in earlier years is not directly included in either model. However, even though earlier economic conditions are not directly included in these models, their effects are felt indirectly. Voter reactions to the in-party's economic performance before the election year are embedded in their pre-campaign preferences. These pre-campaign preferences are reflected in the pre-campaign presidential approval ratings and preference polls that are included in the forecast models. In short, reactions to the in-party's economic performance before the election year are part of the stable context of the campaign.

Although voters seem to give greater weight in their thinking to economic developments during the election, the economic conditions during the earlier years of the presidential term also matter and are reflected in the standing of the candidates going into the campaign. Presidents cannot afford to preside over two and a half years of economic stagnation and then stimulate economic growth in the few months leading up to the election. Voters may not have the attention span for public affairs that some might desire and may not be able to recall specific information later on, but they are not amnesiacs either.

Figure 6.2 presents a causal model regarding how reactions to the economy are incorporated into the evaluations of presidential candidates by voters and eventually reflected in the votes they cast. The construction of the model is based on a good deal of research on economic voting, especially on Michael Lewis-Beck's impressive cross-national study *Economics and Elections* (1988). Lewis-Beck's research concluded that economic voting is both retrospective and prospective in outlook (examining past as well as likely future economic conditions), largely based on evaluations of the broad economy rather than the individual voter's personal finances and based on voters making an association between the government and economic conditions as opposed to voters automatically holding the in-party responsible for all economic developments.[8]

The starting point of the model is a change in either public policies or

Figure 6.2. A Model of Voters' Politicized Impressions of National Economic Conditions

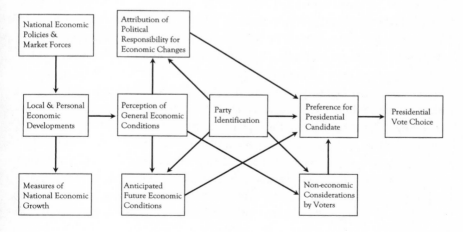

market forces that affect various economic decisions made around the nation. These decisions are of various sorts, covering the gamut from hiring or firing workers, increasing or cutting prices, lowering or raising interest rates, promotions or demotions, expansion or contractions of businesses, and many other individual economic matters. The measurement of national economic growth amounts to the cumulative impact of all of these individual economic decisions. Voters gain their impressions of the economy not so much from attention to the statistical measures reported by the government but from their personal day-to-day experiences and observations of how others they know are affected by the economy. If they see rising prices at the store, do not get their expected raise, hear about a neighbor getting laid off from work, and have relatives who are prevented from buying a house because of high mortgage rates, they have every reason to conclude that all is not so well with the economy. On the other hand, if they get a big raise, see businesses expanding in their city, and are able to buy the car they want because interest rates are low, they may well feel quite satisfied with the way the economy is going. Of course, no single event is likely to change voters' minds about how the economy is doing. However, a pattern of good or bad experiences, observations, and news over time may distill into a general impression. An important point to note is that it takes some time for voters, who are only passively and informally engaged in monitoring the economy, to form this perception. As important as the economy is to them, voters are not constantly monitoring it. Rather, they gradually develop impressions as different economic events come to their attention.

There are several further steps between the lagged perception of economic developments by potential voters and the impact of these perceptions on the presidential vote. Once voters form an impression about how the economy is doing, they then may at some time attribute some amount of credit or blame to the administration. They may also think ahead to what these recent economic developments portend for the future. Both the attribution of responsibility and the extrapolation from retrospective economic evaluations to anticipated future economic changes are undoubtedly colored by the partisan and ideological predispositions that voters hold. In tough economic times under a Democratic administration, for instance, Democrats may be less prone to think that economic difficulties are the fault of the policies of a Democratic president and may be less likely to believe that the future bodes more of the same.

The ramifications of this model for the theory of the predictable campaign are that the effects of economic conditions on the election are mediated by perceptions and predispositions. Their effects, therefore, take some time to be felt. Since voters are concerned about many things in daily life and are under no particular pressure to gather and make sense of the economic information they encounter while going about their daily routines, the impact of the economy on political preferences occurs haphazardly and over some period of time. Information about the economy is not automatically and instantaneously translated into election results.[9]

There is an imperfect lag in the impact of the economy on political preferences. It takes some time for economic conditions to be perceived as reflecting national conditions and to be evaluated for what they have to say politically to different voters. Information regarding economic conditions before the election year has already been digested by voters before the campaign begins. The economic conditions of the election year, however, are not yet fully digested. This lag in economic effects explains why the pre-election-year economy matters but is not directly included in most forecasting models (it has already been built into pre-campaign preferences) and why the election-year economy helps to shape the direction that the campaign takes in the months leading up to election day. Economic conditions before the election year have been perceived, evaluated for their political value, and incorporated into candidate preferences by the voters before the general election campaign begins. Economic conditions during the election year have not been so fully appreciated at the outset of the campaign.

Figure 6.3 presents the relationship between economic growth (as measured by the GDP in constant dollars) for the third year of the presidential term and the in-party candidate's poll standing in September of the election year for the fifteen elections from 1948 to 2004. The third-year growth rate is computed from the fourth quarter of the second year to the fourth quarter of the third year. Because of the lack of quarterly data for 1948, the third-year growth rate for that year is computed from annual data. The figure demonstrates that the condition of the economy during the third year of a presidential term appears to be somewhat related to the preferences of voters at the outset of the campaign (r = .51). Eight of the nine in-party candidates with third-year economies growing at 3 percent or more led their opponents going into September. Adlai Stevenson in 1952, running against war hero Dwight Eisenhower and after five consecutive Democratic presidential victories, is the only exception to the boost from a strong third-year economy. In contrast, only one of the six in-party candidates (Bill Clinton in 1996) with third-year economic growth rates below 3 percent entered the campaign ahead in the polls. Moreover, the effect of the third-year economy on the pre-campaign polls is also evident in the June and July election-year approval ratings (r = .63 and .58, respectively).[10]

Figure 6.3. The Third-Year Economy and the In-Party Candidate's Early September Trial-Heat Poll Standing, 1948–2004

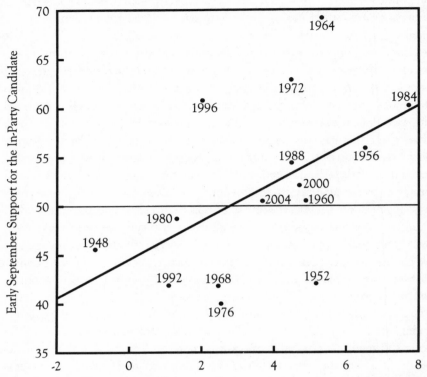

Percentage Real GDP Change for the Third Year in the Presidential Term

Note: The early September poll standing for the in-party candidate is the two-party division of registered voters. GDP change is the percentage point change in the real GDP from the eighth to twelfth quarter of the administration. The bivariate slope is 2.01 (p < .03) and r = .51. Because of the lack of quarterly real GDP data in 1946, the third-year growth rate for the 1948 election is based on annual data.

The Economic Climate

Economic conditions have an impact on the electorate beyond dollars and cents. To estimate the impact of the economy on the campaign by tracing only the extent of economic voting is to underestimate the more general effects of the economy. The economy goes a long way toward setting a general climate for an election. In a strong economy, the public may be more optimistic, less inclined to favor change, and more disposed to believe the best about the in-party candidates whose party has presided over and perhaps facilitated good economic times. In an economic downturn, the electorate's mood may turn grumpy. Voters may be more pessimistic, more responsive to calls for change, and more inclined to believe the worst about the in-party's candidate. The last thing that any in-party candidate wants to confront is an angry or surly electorate, and nothing puts the public in a worse frame of mind than the various personal problems linked to bad economic times. Voters who have had to endure economic hardships during an administration are unlikely to be very forgiving of in-party candidates or particularly receptive to their campaign messages.

This indirect effect of economic conditions, specified in figure 6.2 by the effect of voter perceptions of general economic conditions on their noneconomic considerations, need not even be directly associated with the economic policies of the in-party. If voters feel great insecurity because they know of people losing their jobs, or if they strain to make higher mortgage payments because of high interest rates, or if they cannot afford what they want to buy because of escalating inflation, they are more likely to look less kindly on whoever is in charge. Right or wrong, Americans hold the president responsible for the economy. Voters who are particularly worried about finances may take it out on the in-party candidate, and in a weak economy there are more voters in this predicament. Conversely, good personal experiences and observations of general economic well-being are likely to foster a more positive outlook and a more generous assessment of presidential leadership. In boom times, voters may be more forgiving of the in-party on other matters where they might have otherwise found fault.

The indirect impact of the economy should be especially evident in how voters are affected by what they learn from the general election campaign. The election-year economy may prepare an audience that is either friendly or hostile to the in-party's standard-bearer. During the general election campaign, voters hear from both major party candidates as well as many others interested in the election, from the media and interest groups to friends and neighbors. In this rich and diverse information environment, voters have tremendous latitude in deciding what to pay attention to, what to care about, and what to believe. With such discretion, the voter's predisposition, whether grounded in partisanship or an economically primed mood, can make a significant difference. This may be particularly true for voters who had not reached their vote decision prior to the general election campaign.

There seems to be little question that the economy affects the public's general mood and that this affects their evaluations of in-party candidates and their stands on many noneconomic issues. In the 1992 election, for instance, even after considering the voters' partisanship, views about both the state of the economy and the president's handling of it significantly affected judgments about President Bush's overall job performance.[11] The generalized impact of the economy is reflected in the well-established link between economic conditions and presidential job-approval ratings. An analysis of the 1984, 1988, and 1992 NES surveys indicates that between 80 and 90 percent of voters evaluated the president's overall job performance the same way they evaluated his handling of the economy.[12] More anecdotally, the resilience of President Clinton's job-approval ratings in the face of months of news regarding a wide range of scandal charges and his impeachment by the House of Representatives can be traced to the healthy economy over which he presided. Had the economy been less robust, the public might have been more disposed to take more seriously the various charges made against him. Similarly, the Iran-Contra scandal during President Reagan's second term might have been more damaging had the economy not been as strong as it was at that time.

Responsibility for the Economy

A critical link between voters experiencing real economic changes and their decision to support or oppose the in-party's presidential candidate is the attribution of responsibility for the economy. Although it is clear that presidents have limited abilities to control economic events, the public nonetheless holds them accountable for the economy's performance. While this may seem unfair to presidents, it provides presidents with a strong incentive to make the most of their powers to ensure that the economy is in good shape, particularly as elections approach. It should come as no surprise that in-party candidates who are not incumbents (successor candidates) are not accorded the same level of accountability as incumbents. While they share the party affiliation of the incumbent, successor candidates did not have the same personal control of presidential powers to steer the economy. As a result, voters accord successor candidates only partial credit or blame for the state of the economy.

There is now considerable evidence that voters do not attribute full accountability for the economy to successor candidates. Nadeau and Lewis-Beck (2001), in an examination of economic influences on the president vote in elections from 1956 to 1996 using NES data, found that "when no elected incumbent is running, economic effects [on the in-party vote] are much weakened" (171). In reexamining the trial-heat and economy forecasting model after the 2000 election, it was clear that successor candidates only received a portion of the credit or blame that would have gone to incumbents (J. Campbell 2001d, Campbell, Ali, and Jalazai 2006, 43). Finally, an inspection of figure 6.1 also demonstrates the stronger link between the economy and the vote for incumbents than for their would-be successors. Of the fifteen elections from 1948 to 2004, five involved successor candidates (Stevenson in 1952, Nixon in 1960, Humphrey in 1968, George H. W. Bush in 1988, and Gore in 2000). Incumbents ran in the remaining ten elections. The relationship of the GDP growth in the first half of the election year was stronger for incumbents (b = 1.01, r = .59) than for successor candidates (b = .38, r = .24). With the small number of elections involving successor candidates, it is unclear how much less credit or blame they receive than incumbents.[13] However, it is fairly clear that voters do not attribute full responsibility to a successor candidate for the economic record of the incumbent.

Electoral Economics

There are several factors that shape how general election campaigns affect the results of presidential elections. One very important factor is the election-year economy. The difference between where the candidates stand in the polls at the outset of the campaign and where they finish on election night is to a significant degree a result of voter responses to the state of the economy in the election year. Although economic conditions are only one component to making the course of campaigns predictable, campaign effects are systematic in part because campaigns tend to follow the money trail. In-party candidates tend to fare better than otherwise expected when the election-year economy is booming and to do less well when it is sluggish.

The impact of election-year economies is not as straightforward as one might think. It is not simply a matter of voters reacting immediately to changes in their personal financial situations. Voters react to broader economic developments, and their reactions are multifaceted and developed over time. They judge the president and the president's party by results. They give the in-party (the president or the successor in-party candidate) the credit or the blame for the state of the national economy as far as they can determine what that state is. Voters are not economists or economic reporters, but they do live in the economy. They experience and observe economic conditions firsthand. The economy affects the day-to-day lives of voters in so many ways that good economic times or bad economic times affect the general disposition of voters, which in turn affects the fortunes of the in-party presidential candidate.

While the election-year economy establishes an important part of the context for a campaign and affects the portion of late-deciding voters who cast their lot with the in-party candidate, the campaign is more than a matter of following the money trail of economics. Besides the important systematic influences of incumbency and election-year economics, campaigns have a general influence on the election results. Regardless of whether there is an incumbent president running for reelection and whether the election-year economy is booming or in recession, general election campaigns tend to narrow or compress the lead of the frontrunning candidate. In the next chapter this predictable competitiveness effect of campaigns and the reasons for it are examined.

★ *Chapter 7*

The Normal Course of the Campaign

THE CIRCUMSTANCES UNDER which presidential campaigns take place systematically affect how they develop and how they affect the November vote. Both presidential incumbency and the election-year economy establish important parts of the context for campaigns. Although these pre-campaign conditions are different in each election year, with incumbents running in some elections and not in others and with the economy booming in some years and faltering in others, they shape the course that campaigns take in ways that can be largely anticipated before campaigns begin.

In addition to incumbency and the economy, there is another factor that structures the campaign's effects on the vote: the fierce competition of presidential campaigns. Like the economy and incumbency, the intense competition of presidential campaigns makes campaign effects predictable. Because of the intense competition and the two-party system, campaigns usually narrow the lead of the frontrunning candidate. The normal course of the presidential campaign is for the race to tighten up by election day.

The Basis of Political Competition

Once the general election campaign begins in earnest, several aspects of competition whittle away at the frontrunner's lead and boosts support for the opponent. First, often unlike circumstances prior to the campaign, once the campaign begins, the candidates are on a fairly even playing field. Both receive a great deal of attention from the press and the public, have well-established campaign organizations behind them, and have top-rate professional advisors. Moreover, the campaigns for both candidates are run at such a high level of intensity, interest, and commitment, that any disparity that might exist is proportionately a small difference.

The competitiveness of presidential campaigns also provides a party with the opportunity to reinvigorate its partisans and bring back into the fold those who might have been disappointed with their party's nominee. While party nominations are sometimes decided with little contest, many are hotly contested, and some nomination battles leave deep internal party animosities. As the nomination hopefuls campaign for delegates, partisans take sides within the party. Since there can be only one nominee, when nominations are contested, there will be unsuccessful candidates with disappointed supporters. Some may be so deeply disappointed that they may consider not voting or may even flirt with voting for the other party's candidate.

Simply the passage of time would heal some internal party wounds, but competition between the parties in the general election campaign also provides candidates with an opportunity to solidify their partisan bases. Increasing party solidarity is the primary function of the first major events of the campaign, the party conventions. Through speeches, party platforms, and the selection of a vice presidential candidate, partisans are rallied to the candidate's side. Most speeches from the faction of the party winning the nomination are conciliatory in tone and stress the common values within the party and differences with the opposition. The rhetorical histories of both parties' national conventions are marked by rousing and reunifying speeches from party leaders.[1] Party platforms, often faulted for being general and full of platitudes, are precisely so because they are intended to smooth over any party divisions.[2]

Perhaps the most important part of a modern convention, particularly one nominating a non-incumbent, is the selection of the vice presidential candidate. Most presidential nominees are known to the public before the conventions and have been figured into vote decisions, but this is not the case for many vice presidential nominees. While the first rule in the selection of a running mate is to do no harm to the ticket, the vice presidential selection often helps to unify and energize the party faithful. By balancing the ticket, ideologically as well as regionally, a presidential candidate can make a meaningful overture to those who had supported other candidates for the nomination. Building party unity was clearly an element in Kennedy's selection of Johnson in 1960, Reagan's selection of Bush in 1980, Dukakis's selection of Bentsen in 1988, and Dole's selection of Kemp in 1996.[3] Like other convention decisions, the selection of the vice presidential candidate generally has a clear goal: to get the party's general election campaign off to a good start by presenting a united front.[4]

From the conventions to election day, the campaign reminds Democrats why they are Democrats and Republicans why they are Republicans. Partisanship is refreshed and restored. Internal party differences are set in perspective during the general election campaign when the larger differences between the parties are highlighted.[5] The campaign pulls partisans closer to their parties. As Ansolabehere and Iyengar observed: "campaign advertising does not manipulate people to vote against their political preferences. Partisans respond with renewed vigor to their parties' nominees. Over the course of the campaign, advertising will tend to strengthen the partisan bonds between candidates and the electorate" (1995, 81–82).

As a result of the partisan campaign, those who initially considered defecting in their vote may decide not to vote or even to return to vote for their party's standard-bearer. Those who were initially inclined not to vote because of dissatisfaction with their party's candidate may be persuaded to set those reservations aside.[6] This return of partisans to their party is consistent with Gelman and King's (1993) findings that presidential campaigns enlighten voter preferences, bringing them more into line with their underlying predispositions; with Erikson and Wlezien's (1998) notion that the campaign polarizes the distribution of voter preferences; with Gopoian and Hadjiharalambous's (1994) findings that late-deciding voters were both more likely to have supported a rival candidate for their party's nomination and were ultimately influenced by partisanship in their vote choice; and with my findings elsewhere (J. Campbell 2001b) that those who change their minds during the campaign are more likely to vote with their party than to defect to vote for the opposition's candidate. Even in the era of candidate-centered campaigns, presidential campaigns are party-reinforcing events.[7]

The return of straying partisans during the campaign has the effect of narrowing the race because the healing of internal party wounds usually helps the trailing candidate more than the frontrunner. The reason for this is that the candidate who is running behind quite often is running behind *because* of divisions within the party. In contrast, frontrunners are often not only strongly positioned against the opposing party but strongly positioned within their own party. As a result, with the party already firmly united, the frontrunner has relatively few straying fellow partisans to pull back into the fold. It is the trailing candidate who normally stands to gain the most from the parties becoming more unified during the campaign.

A third reason that the competitive context of the campaign may reduce the winning vote margin is that frontrunning candidates should strategically shift to a more cautious and defensive posture in the closing weeks of the campaign. The principal goal of a presidential candidate is to win the election. If a candidate is confident of a significant lead over an opponent, it only makes sense to protect that lead and not take any risks that might jeopardize the anticipated victory. A rational candidate would rather be certain of winning with 55 percent of the vote than risk losing for the chance of winning with 60 percent. The situation is akin to that of a football team with a large lead in the fourth quarter. When they have the ball, they protect it by running cautious plays. When the opposition has the ball, they go into a "prevent defense" that allows the other team to move the ball easily for short gains but prevents them from making long gains. In the same way, a presidential candidate with a significant lead willingly concedes some points to the opponent if it means avoiding a mistake that could conceivably lose the election. Candidates poised for victory become careful to a fault.

The fourth reason that campaigns typically narrow the vote margin of the winning candidate is that the media are likely to thoroughly scrutinize the frontrunning candidate, and this often reveals more controversial and less flattering aspects of the candidate (Hager 1996; Patterson 1994, 123). From the standpoint of attracting an audience, the media wants a close contest with an unknown ending. Although professionalism may restrain this motive, it is nonetheless an incentive to take an especially close look at the frontrunner. From a more professional standpoint, there is reason to want to know more about a candidate once it appears likely that the candidate will be president.

The final reason that campaigns normally cause an erosion of the frontrunner's lead is that late-deciding voters typically split more evenly than the rest of the electorate. Many late deciders are late in making up their minds because they are torn between the two candidates. They see the choice between the major-party candidates as a close call and are, figuratively, sitting on the fence. Therefore, it should not be surprising to see these late deciders typically splitting their votes roughly evenly. This more even division of late deciders narrows the frontrunner's lead.

The Evidence of a Narrowing Campaign

The historical accounts of several elections provide anecdotal evidence of the narrowing effect of presidential campaigns. For instance, though Goldwater lost in a landslide to Johnson in 1964, the November vote margin was much closer than the earlier, more lopsided polls had indicated. In 1968, Humphrey dramatically reduced Nixon's lead in the closing weeks of the campaign.[8] Similarly, Ford closed in on Carter in the last weeks of the 1976 campaign.[9] The 1992 and 1996 elections also reflect the narrowing effect. Clinton's winning margins over Bush in 1992 and Dole in 1996 were much smaller than his poll leads had been at the start of those campaigns.[10]

A more systematic examination of the evidence confirms the narrowing effect of campaigns. In comparing polls conducted from June through election day for the fifteen presidential elections between 1948 and 2004, the tendency of the frontrunner's lead to deteriorate is clear. The narrowing effects of campaigns are evident in the early September polls when the general election campaign has clearly begun, in the earlier effects of the parties' nominating conventions, and even in the often fluctuating summer polls when it is still unclear if the general election campaign is truly under way.

The Summer Polls

Polls conducted in the summer before an election should be read with great care. They are notoriously volatile (Crespi 1988, chapter 7; Asher 1998, 132; Wlezien and Erikson 2002). Even though many voters have already decided before the conventions, many others have not. Given the significant number who have not really focused seriously on the campaign, poll numbers can and often do change quite a bit.

Recall from table 1.4 that of the fifteen presidential elections since 1948, the June poll leader has gone on to win eight elections but has lost seven. This record is about what would have been produced by chance. Moreover, the mean differences between the vote and both the June and July polls (6.9 and 5.9 percentage points, respectively) are both larger than the errors from a purely naive guess of an even vote split (a mean error of 4.5 percentage points).

The summer polls do not just change from the summer to election day, they also change a good bit from one poll to the next throughout the summer. In their review of election-year polls from 1944 to 2000, Wlezien and Erikson (2002) observe that "the variance in the polls drops considerably as the election cycle evolves. This compression of variance is particularly pronounced after Labor Day, the unofficial beginning of the fall campaign" (974). This comports with my examination of polls in both the 1992 and 1996 elections. In both years, variance in the polls conducted up through the conventions was significantly greater than in polls taken after the conventions.[11] In effect, because of the number of potential voters still unsettled in their vote choice, the summer polls include a good bit of "noise," making them more unstable than later polls.

It would be a mistake, however, to write off the summer polls as entirely meaningless.[12] As figure 1.2 also shows, when the June and July polls are incorporated into forecasting models, their errors are considerably reduced. The summer polls alone in forecasting models have average errors of less than 3.1 percentage points, a significant improvement over the baseline errors of a naive guess of an even vote split.

With these reservations in mind, what do the summer polls say about the suspected narrowing effect of the campaign? Whether reflecting the systematic narrowing effects of the campaign or a simple regression to the mean, as expected, the leads of the June poll leaders rarely held up or expanded during the campaign.[13] Table 7.1 presents the record of the June poll leaders and their

Table 7.1. Change in Preference Poll Leads of June Frontrunning Candidates, 1948–2004

Year	Party of June's Frontrunning Candidate	June Gallup Poll for Frontrunning Candidate	June Frontrunner's Presidential Two-Party Vote %	Percentage Point Change for Poll Leader	Type of Change?
1948	Republican	56.3	47.7	−8.6	Reversal
1952	Republican	65.6	55.4	−10.2	Decline
1956	Republican	63.9	57.8	−6.2	Decline
1960	Democrat	52.1	50.1	−2.0	No Change
1964	Democrat	79.2	61.3	−17.8	Decline
1968	Democrat	53.2	49.6	−3.6	Reversal
1972	Republican	58.9	61.8	+2.9	Increase
1976	Democrat	59.8	51.1	−8.7	Decline
1980	Democrat	55.1	44.7	−10.4	Reversal
1984	Republican	54.6	59.2	+4.5	Increase
1988	Democrat	57.8	46.1	−11.7	Reversal
1992	Republican	53.5	46.5	−6.9	Reversal
1996	Democrat	59.8	54.7	−5.0	Decline
2000	Republican	51.1	49.7	−1.4	No Change
2004	Democrat	52.7	48.8	−3.9	Decline

Increased Leads	2
No Change	2
Declining Leads	5
Reversals	6

Frontrunning Party:	In-party 8, Out-party 7
Frontrunner's Election Outcome:	Won 8, Lost 7
Estimated Discount Rate of the June Poll Lead:	70%

Note: Both the poll and actual vote percentages are of major-party preferences. The "No Change" designation is assigned to elections in which the poll and the actual vote differed by two percentage points or less. The discount rate of the June poll $(1 - \beta)$ is based on a regression with the in-party's percentage of the two-party vote as the dependent variable and three independent variables: its June poll lead (poll − 50), the real GDP growth rate in the first half of the election year (with half credit for successor candidates), and a dummy variable for whether an incumbent president is running. The poll lead coefficient $(\beta = .30)$ was statistically significant ($p < .01$, one-tailed). The adjusted R^2 was .73.

eventual vote percentages. Support levels for June poll leaders eroded or vanished in eleven of the fifteen elections from 1948 to 2004. Four June frontrunners suffered double-digit losses and another two lost more than eight percentage points of their June lead. Only two June poll leaders (both incumbents) were able to build on their summer leads. Nixon added about three points to his lead in his 1972 landslide victory over McGovern, and Reagan added four and a half points to his lead in his 1984 landslide victory over Mondale. A regression analysis of the in-party vote as a function of in-party's June poll lead,

GDP growth in the first half of the year, and whether the incumbent was running indicates that the June poll lead should be heavily discounted (by about 70 percent). Although some portion of this discount may be attributable to the noise in the summer polls, it also reflects the narrowing effects of the campaign.

Initial signs of the narrowing effect of the campaign are also evident when using the July polls as a base. Table 7.2 presents the poll standings and eventual vote shares for the frontrunning candidate in the July polls. Frontrunners lost all or part of their July poll leads in twelve of the fifteen elections examined.

Table 7.2. Change in Preference Poll Leads of July Frontrunning Candidates, 1948–2004

Year	Party of July's Frontrunning Candidate	July Gallup Poll for Frontrunning Candidate	July Frontrunner's Presidential Two-Party Vote %	Percentage Point Change for Poll Leader	Type of Change?
1948	Republican	56.5	47.7	−8.8	Reversal
1952	Republican	53.4	55.4	+2.0	No Change
1956	Republican	62.2	57.8	−4.5	Decline
1960	Republican*	53.2	49.9	−3.3	Reversal
1964	Democrat	65.6	61.3	−4.2	Decline
1968	Republican*	51.3	50.4	−.9	No Change
1972	Republican	64.8	61.8	−3.0	Decline
1976	Democrat	68.1	51.1	−17.1	Decline
1980	Republican	60.8	55.3	−5.5	Decline
1984	Republican	56.4	59.2	+2.8	Increase
1988	Democrat	59.3	46.1	−13.2	Reversal
1992	Democrat*	62.9	53.5	−9.5	Decline
1996	Democrat	62.2	54.7	−7.5	Decline
2000	Republican	53.2	49.7	−3.5	Reversal
2004	Democrat	52.1	48.8	−3.4	Reversal

Increased Leads	1
No Change	2
Declining Leads	7
Reversals	5

Frontrunning Party: In-party 6, Out-party 9
Frontrunner's Election Outcome   Won 10, Lost 5
Estimated Discount Rate of the July Poll Lead: 67%

Note: Both the poll and actual vote percentages are of major-party preferences. The "No Change" designation is assigned to elections in which the poll and the actual vote differed by two percentage points or less. An asterisk indicates a switch in the frontrunning candidate since the June poll. The discount rate of the July poll $(1 - \beta)$ is based on a regression with the in-party's percentage of the two-party vote as the dependent variable and three independent variables: its July poll lead (poll − 50), the real GDP growth rate in the first half of the election year (with half credit for successor candidates), and a dummy variable for whether an incumbent president is running. The poll lead coefficient ($\beta = .33$) was statistically significant ($p < .01$, one-tailed). The adjusted R^2 was .71.

Five of the twelve frontrunners losing support ended up losing the election. The other seven losing support survived to win with a smaller margin. Although frontrunners in several elections suffered double-digit drops from their July levels, July frontrunners typically lost about four or five percentage points from their leads. There was effectively no change in two of the three elections in which July frontrunners did not sustain losses. In only one instance did the frontrunner expand his July poll lead (Reagan in 1984) and that was by less than three percentage points. The regression analysis of the July poll leads indicates that, like the June polls, they should be significantly discounted (by about two-thirds), but once partially discounted, they also provide important clues about the likely November vote margin.

The Convention Bumps

By the time the national party conventions take place, usually in late July and August, the choice to be offered to voters in the election has become clear and public opinion about the choice has begun to gel.[14] As we saw in table 1.2, typically about an additional fifth of the electorate moves from the undecided to the decided category during the conventions.[15] If the conventions have become the start of the general election campaign rather than the conclusion of the nomination contest, and if they are especially useful in helping to heal the wounds of the internal party nomination battles and spreading enthusiasm for the standard-bearer, then they ought to be particularly helpful to trailing candidates who are often survivors of more divisive nomination contests.

Aside from the opportunity to mend fences, conventions may also provide candidates with an important opportunity to present themselves and their case for election to the general public. Like the party-healing opportunity, the presentation opportunity may be especially important to trailing candidates, who often are non-incumbents. These trailing non-incumbents and their vice presidential running mates are usually less well known to voters. The conventions should be especially helpful to these candidates in providing them with an opportunity to become better known to the voters.

The relative impact of the conventions can be gauged by comparing the poll standings of trailing and frontrunning candidates before and after their parties' conventions. While we would expect conventions to generally help all candidates, we would expect that they would be of greater help to candidates trailing in the polls. Table 7.3 presents the poll standings of the presidential candidates of both major parties before and after their nominating conventions for the eleven elections from 1964 to 2004. Earlier election years are not included since polls between the conventions were not conducted and thus prevent the determination of each convention's separate impact.

Table 7.3. *Convention Bumps in Presidential Preference Polls, 1964–2004*

Year	In-Party	Democratic Party			Republican Party		
		Pre (%)	Post (%)	Change (%)	Pre (%)	Post (%)	Change (%)
1964	Democrats	**69.1**	**69.1**	0.0	20.8	33.7	+12.9
1968	Democrats	39.2	41.9	+2.7	46.8	60.8	+14.1
1972	Republicans	41.3	39.3	−2.0	**64.8**	**65.5**	**+0.7**
1976	Republicans	**59.6**	**68.1**	**+8.6**	35.2	42.5	+7.3
1980	Democrats	36.0	48.4	+12.4	**54.9**	**67.1**	**+12.2**
1984	Republicans	44.3	50.0	+5.7	**56.0**	**57.9**	**+1.8**
1988	Republicans	**53.4**	**59.3**	**+5.9**	46.5	52.7	+6.2
1992	Republicans	46.5	62.9	+16.4	40.4	42.4	+2.0
1996	Democrats	**56.8**	**61.8**	**+5.0**	36.6	46.1	+9.5
2000	Democrats	44.4	52.2	+7.8	**52.9**	**60.7**	**+7.8**
2004	Republicans	**52.1**	**50.0**	**−2.1**	49.5	50.5	+1.0

Positive Post-Convention Poll Changes (Convention Bumps): 86% (19 of 22)

Mean Percentage Change:
  All Conventions 6.2
  Democratic Conventions 5.5
  Republican Conventions 6.9
  First Conventions (Out-Party) 8.1
  Second Conventions (In-Party) 4.3
  Frontrunning Candidates' Conventions 4.4
  Trailing Candidates' Conventions 7.4
Estimated portion of net campaign bump surviving to election day: 29%

Note: The out-party traditionally holds its convention first in the campaign year. Frontrunners are in bold. The Net Campaign Bump is the difference between the candidates' poll standings before the first convention and after the second. The portion of the net bump surviving to the election is based on a regression of the in-party vote. The vote was explained in terms of the net convention bump, the preconvention poll percentage for the in-party candidate (before either party's convention), and the first-half growth rate in the GDP (with half credit for successor candidates). The adjusted R^2 was .84. The net bump coefficient was .29 ($p < .01$, one-tailed). The equation includes the fifteen elections from 1948 to 2004. Prior to 1964, polling data were not available between conventions that would permit the calculation of each convention's separate bump.

As the table demonstrates, the national party conventions regularly provide their nominees with a bump in the polls (J. Campbell, Cherry, and Wink 1992; Wayne 1997; Holbrook 1996a; Stimson 2004; and Johnston, Hagen, and Jamieson 2004). In nineteen of the twenty-two conventions examined, the nominee's standing in the polls improved following the convention. Candidates received an average convention bump of about six percentage points, though five conventions produced double-digit bumps. While Republicans tended to get slightly greater convention bumps than Democrats, the difference between convention bumps for the first convention (the out-party) and the second convention (the in-party) was more pronounced. The bump from an election year's first convention was typically almost twice as large as the bump from the second convention.

What is most interesting from the standpoint of the predictable campaign is that these convention bumps have typically been a bit larger for trailing candidates and smaller for frontrunners. Trailing candidates, on average, gained about 7.4 percentage points over their pre-convention poll standing while frontrunners, on average, gained only about 4.5 percentage points.[16] Four trailing candidates (Goldwater in 1964, Nixon in 1968, Carter in 1980, and Clinton in 1992) received double-digit boosts from their conventions. Among the frontrunners, only Ronald Reagan in 1980, having emerged as the nominee from a crowded field of Republican hopefuls, received a big boost from his convention. Convention bumps were understandably quite small for sitting presidents who were frontrunners and who had their parties solidly united behind them. Lyndon Johnson in 1964, Richard Nixon in 1972, Ronald Reagan in 1984 were already so politically strong within their parties and so well known (and popular) with the public that they had little to gain from the convention.

A review of the record of convention bumps also indicates that they are not automatic. Like presidential incumbency, conventions are an opportunity that can either be realized or wasted. Again like incumbency, conventions are an opportunity that normally is effectively exploited, but there have been at least three instances in which a party squandered its opportunity to use its convention to heal internal wounds and to present a convincing campaign message to a national audience. The three most notable cases of wasted convention opportunities were the strife-torn Democratic convention of 1968, the chaotic Democratic convention of 1972, and the Kerry-as-war-hero Democratic convention of 2004.

The 1968 Democratic convention in Chicago is one of the most memorable and disastrous conventions in American history. It is memorable for the bitter battles within the convention hall over the handling of the Vietnam War and for the bloody battles between police and war protesters in the streets of Chicago. The dominant image left by the convention was not of a jubilant nominee Hubert Humphrey and running mate Edmund Muskie but of Chicago's combative Mayor Richard Daley hurling epithets from the convention floor at Senator Abe Ribicoff of Connecticut, who had chastised Chicago authorities for their treatment of the protesters.

The 1972 Democratic convention lacked the vitriol of 1968, but as the first convention conducted under the more open rules of the McGovern-Fraser delegate selection reforms, it was very chaotic. Bain and Parris (1973, 332) noted, for instance, that there were a record number of challenges to delegate credentials that had to be settled with floor votes at the convention. Unlike the often carefully scripted conventions of recent years, the convention proceedings in 1972 were so out of control that the convention's nominee, Senator George McGovern, was unable to give his nationally televised acceptance speech until hours after most of the nation had gone to bed. When the 1968 and 1972 lost convention opportunities are set aside, convention bumps for trailing candidates have been almost twice what they have been for candidates who led in the polls going into their conventions.

In their 2004 nomination of Senator John Kerry of Massachusetts as their candidate, Democrats once again wasted their convention bump opportunity. As the first election following the terrorist attack of September 11, 2001, and with the nation at war in Afghanistan and Iraq, Democrats sought to neutralize President George W. Bush's advantage on the national security issue by organizing the convention around Senator Kerry's record as a decorated Vietnam War veteran. Emblematic of this theme was the opening line of the candidate's acceptance speech: "I'm John Kerry and I'm reporting for duty." Unfortunately for Senator Kerry, a thirty-year-old war record did not impress many voters as a convincing reason to support him. The Gallup Poll showed Kerry coming out of the convention with the support of two percent less of the electorate than he had when the convention began.

Aside from these three instances, conventions usually appear to help the nominated candidate. As with all campaign effects (recall table 3.1 and the discussion of illusory debate effects in chapter 3), however, there is the question of whether convention effects are real or ephemeral. Are convention bumps of any lasting consequence, or are they merely temporary reactions to conventions that are quickly forgotten?

Some portion of convention bumps is undoubtedly temporary. While most of the campaign involves a partisan debate in which both sides respond to points made by the opposition, the conventions are different. Apart from some media commentary and occasional partisan reactions from the opposition, during the conventions each party "holds the floor" for some time on its own. This one-sided campaign rally can create enthusiastic responses in voters that may barely survive the passing of the convention itself and further weaken when the other party is heard. As we have seen, with only a couple of exceptions, both parties receive a convention bump. Conventions are supposed to set the party's best foot forward, to reach out to the average American voter, and, with a few exceptions, they have done this. But after the convention, voters "sober up" and see the weaknesses as well as the strengths in a party and its standard-bearer.

While some portion of the bump from conventions is temporary, evidence indicates that part of it carries through to election day (J. Campbell, Cherry, and Wink 1992). The net in-party convention bump was calculated for the fifteen elections from 1948 to 2004. Although the lack of polls between the two conventions prevented the determination of the separate convention bumps in elections before 1964, the existence of polls before the first convention and after the second allow the determination of the net effect of the two conventions in pre-1964 elections. A model explaining the in-party candidate's share of the two-party vote as a function of the net convention bump, standings in the preference poll before the first convention, and the economic growth rate in the first half of the election year (halved for successor candidates) indicates that almost one third of the net convention bump (b = .29, p < .01, one-tailed) actually affects the election.[17] The impact of convention bumps, even discounted for the temporary nature of a portion of them, contributes to the general narrowing effect of campaigns since they generally favor trailing candidates.

The Fall Polls

Once both party conventions have nominated their presidential candidates, the general election campaign has clearly begun, and the American electorate has turned its attention to it. As we have already seen, by this point in the election year most voters have reached their decisions, thereby reducing volatility in the polls and making them more meaningful. The results of the polls conducted around Labor Day (the unofficial kickoff of the general election campaign) for elections since 1948 are presented in table 7.4. These poll results have been oriented in terms of the party of the candidate leading in the polls around Labor Day. The table also presents the eventual November vote for each of the poll leaders and the differences between the Labor Day polls and the November votes.

As we have already seen (table 1.5), the early September polls have themselves been useful predictors of the November vote and have been the basis for very accurate vote forecasts when combined with an indicator of the election-year economy. As the table indicates, the early September poll leader maintained enough of his lead to go on to win the election in all but two (1948 and 1960) of the elections examined, and the 1960 exception involved a poll change of less than a single percentage point, well within the margin of normal polling error.

The fact that opinion has begun to gel by Labor Day and that the early September poll standings of the candidates are highly predictive of the November vote does not mean, however, that the campaign from there on out has no effect. If campaigns made no difference, we would expect to see negligible differences between the September polls and the November votes. Instead, the

Table 7.4. Change in Preference Poll Leads of Early September Frontrunning Candidates, 1948–2004

Year	Party of Early September's Frontrunning Candidate	Early September Gallup Poll for Frontrunning Candidate	Early September Frontrunner's Presidential Two-Party Vote %	Percentage Point Change for Poll Leader	Type of Change?
1948	Republican	54.4	47.7	−6.7	Reversal
1952	Republican	57.9	55.4	−2.5	Decline
1956	Republican	55.9	57.8	+1.8	No Change
1960	Republican	50.5	49.9	−.6	No Change
1964	Democrat	69.2	61.3	−7.8	Decline
1968	Republican	58.1	50.4	−7.7	Decline
1972	Republican	62.9	61.8	−1.1	No Change
1976	Democrat	60.0	51.1	−9.0	Decline
1980	Republican	51.3	55.3	+4.0	Increase
1984	Republican	60.2	59.2	−1.1	No Change
1988	Republican*	54.4	53.9	−.5	No Change
1992	Democrat	58.1	53.5	−4.6	Decline
1996	Democrat	60.8	54.7	−6.1	Decline
2000	Democrat*	52.1	50.3	−1.9	No Change
2004	Republican*	50.5	51.2	+.7	No Change

Increased Leads   1
No Change   7
Declining Leads   6
Reversals   1

Frontrunning Party: In-party 9, Out-party 6
Frontrunner's Election Outcome: Won 13, Lost 2
Estimated Discount Rate of the September Poll Lead: 53%

Note: Both the poll and actual vote percentages are of major-party preferences. The "No Change" designation includes elections in which the poll and the actual vote differed by two percentage points or less. An asterisk indicates a switch in the Frontrunning candidate since the July poll. The discount rate of the September poll $(1 - \beta)$ is based on a regression with the in-party's percentage of the two-party vote as the dependent variable and two independent variables: its September poll lead (poll − 50) and the real GDP growth rate in the second quarter of the election year (with half credit for successor candidates). The poll lead coefficient $(\beta = .47)$ was statistically significant $(p < .01$, one-tailed). The adjusted R^2 was .89.

average difference, the typical change occurring over the course of the fall campaign, has been about 3.7 percentage points, and the difference has been nearly 6 percentage points or more in five of the fifteen elections.

Campaigns make a difference, and as in the analysis of the summer polls and the convention bumps, one of the most important differences made by presidential campaigns is the narrowing of the frontrunner's lead. From 1948 to

2004, the early September poll leads of the frontrunners were significantly reduced or essentially held constant in fourteen of the fifteen elections. While the degree of reduced leads has varied from one election to the next, the competitive effect of the fall campaign typically cuts the Labor Day frontrunner's lead just about in half. Based on a multiple regression accounting for variation in the in-party candidates' share of the two-party vote as a function of the frontrunner's early September poll lead, the second-quarter growth rate in the GDP (halved for successor candidates), and whether an incumbent was running, the early September poll lead should be discounted at a rate of .53.[18] That is, on average, approximately half of the September lead survives to the election.

The only frontrunner to expand his lead over the last months of the campaign was Ronald Reagan in 1980, and Reagan's slim 51-to-49 early September lead over Carter barely qualifies him as a frontrunner.[19] Experiencing by far the worst election-year economy in recent history (recall figure 6.1), voters in 1980 were looking for an acceptable alternative to President Carter. As the leader of the conservative wing of the conservative party, some voters had doubts that Reagan was acceptable as a vehicle to carry their votes expressing dissatisfaction with Carter. Some of these voters flirted with voting for former Republican congressman and independent presidential candidate John Anderson. In the closing weeks of the campaign, however, many of these reticent voters became convinced that Reagan was not too extreme ideologically to be an acceptable alternative to Carter. In particular, as Abramson, Aldrich, and Rohde (1982, 45–46) found, Reagan's debate performance may have shifted a couple of percentage points of the vote in his direction.

The widening of Reagan's small lead over Carter in 1980 is the exception that proves the rule of the narrowing campaign. First, Reagan did not have much of a lead to narrow. As it stood in September, the contest was already very tight. Second, despite the normal narrowing effect, Reagan's slim lead expanded because any narrowing effect was more than offset by late-deciding voters reacting to an unusually bad election-year economy. The politicization of these reactions was delayed because of concerns voters had about the out-party alternative. While typically only about 43 percent of voters reach their decisions after Labor Day (see appendix B), more than half of the electorate in 1980 were late deciders, and these divided more favorably to Reagan than did the early deciders. This occurred despite the fact that Democratic Party identifiers outnumbered Republican Party identifiers among this late-deciding group by almost two to one.

Other than the 1980 case and the very minor increase in Eisenhower's lead in the 1956 election and George W. Bush's lead in the 2004 election, general election campaigns have consistently tightened up the race between the frontrunning and trailing candidates. The drop in Clinton's 1996 lead over Dole (a decline probably illustrative of the effects of frontrunner caution), and the decline in Clinton's 1992 lead over George H. W. Bush are fairly typical. Not all campaigns have been so typical. The tightening has been only a modest percentage reduction in the frontrunner's lead in some elections. There were only modest percentage declines in Eisenhower's lead over Stevenson in 1952, Nixon's lead over McGovern in 1972, Reagan's lead over Mondale in 1984, Bush's lead over Dukakis in 1988, and in Gore's lead over George W. Bush in 2000. In other years, the competition of the campaign ate deeply into the fall frontrunner's lead. Besides the one case in which the lead disappeared altogether (Truman's famous comeback in 1948), there were proportionately large erosions in Nixon's lead over Humphrey in 1968 and in Carter's lead over Ford in 1976. Nonetheless, while the leads of frontrunners declined in some election years more than in others, the most important point is that, with but one exception (1980), to the extent that poll leads have moved at all during the fall campaign they have declined.

One aspect of the fall campaign deserves special note: the impact of presidential debates. To the extent that they have any lasting impact at all, and there are good reasons to be skeptical of their impact, presidential debates in general may contribute to the narrowing effect in the last weeks of the campaign.[20] Acknowledging the potential narrowing effect caused by candidates appearing as equals on the same platform, candidates with strong poll leads commonly seek to avoid debates altogether or keep them to a minimum. Moreover, expectations for the frontrunner generally run higher than for the trailing candidate, and trailing candidates "look good" if they merely hold their own. Thus, if both candidates perform about equally well in a debate and if the debate has any impact at all, it should benefit the trailing candidate and reduce the frontrunner's lead.[21]

Whether examining the change from the volatile summer polls to the November vote, the effects of convention bumps, or the change from the more stabilized fall polls to the November vote, a major systematic consequence of presidential campaigns appears to be their narrowing effect on the leads of candidates running ahead in the polls. The analysis has demonstrated that the campaign narrows the lead of frontrunners. We now turn to how campaigns reduce those leads.

Partisanship and the Narrowing Effect

One of the reasons suggested for the typical decline in the lead of frontrunners is that trailing candidates often come out of the more divided party and therefore benefit more from disgruntled partisans drifting back to support their party during the campaign. If this is the case, two patterns should be in evidence. First, a larger portion of partisans from the trailing candidate's party should put off deciding how they would vote until late in the campaign. Second, the trailing candidate should do better among late-deciding partisans than among partisans who have decided how they would vote before the campaign began. Thus, the trailing candidate should benefit disproportionately from the return of partisans to their roots.

Table 7.5 presents the mean distribution of partisans, their loyalty rates, and their votes for early- and late-deciding partisans of both the frontrunning and trailing candidates' parties in elections since 1952. Frontrunners in each of campaign were determined based on the candidates' poll standings in early September of the election year. Based on the findings of Keith et al. (1992), independents who say they lean toward a party are categorized as partisans. Only major party voters are included. The first column of the table presents the average percentage of the electorate made up by each of the four types of partisans (early deciders of the frontrunner's party, early deciders of the trailing candidate's party, late deciders of the frontrunner's party, and late deciders of the trailing candidate's party). The total of this column is 88.7 percent with the remaining 11.3 percent being independents and/or voters for third-party candi-

Table 7.5. Mean Partisan Vote for Frontrunning and Trailing Candidates by Time of Vote Decision, 1952–2004

Party Identifiers by Candidate Status and Time of Decision	Percentage of Voters Who Were Party Identifiers with	Party Loyalty Rates	Percentage of the Vote from Party Identifiers
Early Deciders of			
Frontrunning Candidate Party	28.3	96.0	30.8
Trailing Candidate's Party	26.5	86.3	24.0
Difference	+1.8	+9.7	+6.8
Late Deciders of			
Frontrunning Candidate's Party	14.4	80.9	17.2
Trailing Candidate's Party	19.5	72.1	16.8
Difference	−5.1	+8.8	+0.4

Note: N = 14. The mean total percent of all voters who were party identifiers (not pure independents) and who voted for a major party candidate was 88.7 percent. Frontrunners are determined by which candidate led in the early September preference poll. The election by election calculations on which these means are based are presented in table B.3 in appendix B. Typically, 44 percent of the trailing candidate's party are late deciders while only 35 percent of the frontrunner's party postpone their decisions. The percentage of the vote from partisans includes votes coming from the defectors from the opposition's party as well as the loyal partisans of the candidate's party.

dates. The second column presents the average loyalty rate for these groups. This is the percentage of party identifiers who reported that they voted for their own party's presidential candidate rather than the opposing party's candidate. The third column presents the mean percentage of voters who were loyal partisans of these groups. This is computed from the first two columns. The vote percentage from party identifiers is composed of two elements: loyal votes cast by partisans of the candidate's party and defecting votes cast by partisans of his opponent's party. For example, 96 percent of the 28.3 percent of early deciders in the frontrunner's party voted for the frontrunner and 13.7 percent (100 − 86.3) of the 26.5 percent of early deciders in the trailing candidate's party voted for the frontrunner. This means that typically about 31 percent of major party voters are early-deciding partisans who cast their ballots for the frontrunner. Table B.3 of appendix B presents the individual election breakdowns from which these averages were calculated.

As expected, in terms of the percentage of partisans in the electorate, frontrunners have an advantage among early deciders and less of an advantage or, more typically, a disadvantage among late deciders. About two percentage points more of the early-deciding electorate are partisans of the frontrunner's party.

Among late deciders, however, the advantage is with the trailing candidate. Typically, between 19 and 20 percent of late deciders are partisans of the trailing candidate, while only 14 or 15 percent of late deciders identify with the frontrunner's party. Put differently, while about 42 percent of partisan voters of the trailing candidate's party decided late in the process, only about 34 percent of the frontrunner's partisans hold off on their decision. With more of the trailing candidate's partisans still to decide during the campaign, the candidate is well positioned to gain ground on the frontrunner.

Compared to those who reached an early decision, late deciders are likely to be more disposed toward the trailing candidate. The question now is whether the strong appeal of the frontrunner with a friendly crowd of early deciders also sways the less friendly crowd of late deciders.

Several important aspects of partisanship in the campaign are reflected in the average party loyalty rates displayed in the table's second column. Most notably, all partisans, even late deciders torn about their decision and partisans of the less popular candidate's party, are more likely to support their own party's candidate than to defect. The mean loyalty rates ranged from about 72 percent for late-deciding partisans of the trailing candidate's party to 96 percent for early-deciding partisans of the frontrunner's party. The lowest level of support ever provided by partisans for their party's candidate was in 1972 among early-deciding Democrats whose candidate, Senator George McGovern, badly trailed

President Richard Nixon. Even in the face of that landslide defeat, about three out of five early-deciding Democrats cast ballots for McGovern.

While these high loyalty rates under various circumstances testify to the impact of partisanship, there are also quite definite differences in the degree of party loyalty for voters in different circumstances. As one would expect, party loyalty has been generally stronger for early deciders (about 91 percent) who see their vote choice as easy than for late deciders (about 76 percent) who do not see the choice as being so easy to make. Party loyalty also tends to be greater in the frontrunner's party (about 91 percent) than in the trailing candidate's party (about 80 percent). The greater loyalty within the frontrunner's party is evident among both early- and late-deciding partisans. Frontrunners hold a nearly ten point loyalty advantage among early-deciding partisans and nearly the same advantage among late deciders. The question is whether the composition advantage of trailing candidates among late deciders (in column 1) is sufficient to offset the loyalty advantage of frontrunners among late deciders (in column 2). Do trailing candidates fare better among late deciders, helping them narrow the lead built up by frontrunners among those reaching an early decision?

Generally speaking, trailing candidates do fare better among late-deciding voters than they had among early deciders. Considering both the electorate's composition and partisan loyalty rates, frontrunners typical have almost a seven-percentage-point lead among early-deciding partisan voters. Since early-deciding partisans normally constitute more than half of all voters, a lead of this magnitude is usually difficult to overcome with late-deciding partisans (usually about a third of voters) and independents (7 or 8 percent).

While the typical frontrunning candidate accumulates a healthy lead among early deciders, based on his own party's enthusiasm leading to early decisions at high loyalty rates, trailing candidates are able to offset this in part and narrow the frontrunner's lead by running about even among late-deciding partisans. Though frontrunners continue to engender greater loyalty than their opponents, even among the late deciders, more late deciders are from the trailing candidates' party and, even at reduced loyalty rates, a strong majority of these late deciders come home to their party on Election Day.

One way to look at the impact of partisanship in narrowing the frontrunner's lead is to think about how the typical election would turn out if only early-deciding partisans voted and how adding late-deciding partisans into the mix would change things. According to table 7.5, frontrunners would win 56.3 percent of the two-party vote if only early-deciding partisans voted (30.8/54.8). Adding the votes of the better than a third of late-deciding partisans reduces the frontrunners' average two-party vote among partisans to 54.1 percent

(48.0/88.7). From one standpoint, an average drop of 2.2 percentage points in the frontrunner's lead may not appear to be very much. They still remain comfortably above the 50 percent mark. On the other hand, a 2.2-percentage-point cut in a 6.3-percentage-point lead narrows that lead to only about two-thirds of what it was. Recall from the trial-heat forecasting model (table 1.5) and the analysis of the September polls (table 7.4), that the full narrowing effect of the campaign typically cuts the frontrunner's lead in half.

A More Even Division of Late Deciders

For the most part, late-deciding voters reach their decision late because the vote choice is not an easy one for them. As Gopoian and Hadjiharalambous observed, "late deciders, on average, see significantly lesser differences between the candidates than do other voters" (1994, 67). Individually, each of these voters could go one way or the other. The vote choice for some may in the end amount to a coin toss. Gopoian and Hadjiharalambous (1994) concluded as much in their study of influences on the vote choices of those who decided in the last couple of weeks of the campaign. According to their analysis, "late deciders behave in a near-random fashion in casting votes for president" (58).[22] We would expect that as a group, assuming that many go one way and many the other, the late deciders would divide fairly evenly, at least more evenly than voters who arrived at an early decision.

Table 7.6 presents the average vote margins between candidates for early- and late-deciding voters over the fourteen elections from 1952 to 2004. The votes of early- and late-deciding voters, independents as well as partisans, are from the corrected NES surveys. The table presents the average vote margin among early and late deciders for all elections and for those elections in which there was a clear frontrunner around Labor Day. Clear frontrunners are defined as those who have at least a 54 to 46 lead in the polls. This criterion excludes four election years, 1960, 1980, 2000, and 2004. Nixon's lead over Kennedy in 1960, Reagan's lead over Carter in 1980, Gore's lead over George W. Bush in 2000, and George W. Bush's lead over Kerry in 2004 were about 52 to 48 or less at the start of their campaigns. The vote divisions for each of the fourteen elections are presented in appendix B, table B.2.

The vote divisions of early-deciding and late-deciding voters are as expected. Voters who reach an early decision are much more likely to provide one candidate with a substantial lead over the opponent. The vote margin between candidates for early-deciding voters exceeded fifteen percentage points in six of the fourteen elections. Vote margins among late-deciding voters typically have been much smaller. The vote margin for voters deciding during the

Table 7.6. Mean Vote Margin between Major-Party Presidential Candidates,
1952–2004

	Mean Vote Percentage Difference between the Major-Party Presidential Candidates	
Time of Decision and the Stability of the Vote Intention	*All Elections*	*Elections with Clear Frontrunners*
Early Deciders and No Change from the Pre-Campaign Vote Intention	14.8 (12.3)	17.5 (13.5)
Late Deciders or Changed from the Pre-Campaign Vote Intention	8.0 (6.0)	6.9 (5.0)

Note: N = 14 for all elections and 10 for elections with clear frontrunners. The elections with clear frontrunners category includes all elections in which the leading candidate in early September had at least 54 percent of support among those supporting one of the two major-party candidates. This excludes four of the fourteen elections: 1960, 1980, 2000, and 2004. The standard deviations around each mean vote difference are in parentheses. The median differences were 9.8 percentage points for early deciders and 7.3 percentage points for late deciders. The median differences excluding 1960, 1980, 2000, and 2004 are 13.2 for early deciders and 7.3 for late deciders.

campaign exceeded fifteen percentage points only once, the late vote tide favoring Kennedy in 1960.

The average margin between candidates for early-deciding voters is almost twice as large as it is among late deciders (14.8 compared to 8.0). When the four elections without a clear frontrunner are set aside, the difference between the decisiveness of the early-deciding vote and the relative indecisiveness of the late-deciding vote is even clearer (17.5 compared to 6.9). Adding the more closely divided vote of those deciding during the campaign to the more one-sided vote of those deciding before the campaign narrows the overall vote margin for the winning candidate.

Competitive Campaigns Produce More Competitive Elections

One important reason that elections and campaigns are predictable is that competitive forces regularly reduce the leads of frontrunning candidates. The narrowing effect of campaigns is evident in changes from vote preferences of the summer polls to the actual vote on election day, in the convention bumps, in changes from vote preferences expressed in the fall polls to the actual vote, and in comparisons of the votes of early- and late-deciding voters. Not all campaigns have narrowed the frontrunner's lead, and some campaigns have narrowed the frontrunner's lead more than others, but there is a definite general tendency for the frontrunner's lead to narrow over the course of the campaign.

There are several reasons for the narrowing effect of campaigns. The more level playing field of the general election campaign, the healing of internal party divisions and the revitalization of partisan attachments, the cautiousness and scrutiny of frontrunners, and the indifference and even division of late-deciding voters may all play a part in ultimately reducing the leads of front-runners. While this analysis has not attempted to sort out the ultimate causes of the competitiveness effect among these plausible causes, it has established that presidential campaigns normally reduce the frontrunners' vote margins and then identified the proximate causes.

The proximate reason for the narrowing effect is that late-deciding voters offset the vote decision of early deciders in two ways. First, early-deciding voters are more likely to give lopsided majorities to one party while late-deciding voters either divide more evenly or split in favor of the trailing candidate's party. Frontrunners are often such clear choices within their own party that they pick up the lion's share of their support before the campaign begins. Conversely, potential supporters of the trailing candidate often struggle with their choice and only reach a decision during the campaign. The votes of late deciders countered or ran opposite to the votes of early deciders in six elections (1960, 1964, 1968, 1976, 2000, and 2004) (see table B.2 in appendix B). In the case of 1960, late deciders tilting to Kennedy actually countered the preferences of pre-campaign deciders who had tilted to Nixon to the point that they reversed what would have been the outcome and narrowly elected Kennedy. Those deciding during the campaign also provided Al Gore with a vote majority over George W. Bush in the disputed 2000 election. In the other four instances, differences between early and late deciders were not so great, and the result preserved a plurality for the candidate favored by the early deciders, though by a reduced margin.

The second proximate reason for the narrowing or competitiveness effect is that even when early and late deciders as groups favor the same candidate, the margin of support among late deciders is usually much smaller. The votes of late deciders essentially muted the votes of early deciders in six of the elections examined (1952, 1956, 1972, 1984, 1988, and 1996). In 1952, for instance, Eisenhower was the overwhelming favorite of early deciders, but his overall margin declined after dividing the late-deciding vote about evenly with Stevenson.

Either the countering or the muting effects of late-deciding voters in narrowing the leads of frontrunners were at work in twelve of the fourteen elections examined. There were only two elections in which late deciders favored by a wider margin the same candidate as the early deciders. In 1980, late deciders backed Reagan over Carter by a slightly bigger margin than early deciders had. Presumably, many late deciders required reassurance that Reagan was enough in the political mainstream to make him an acceptable alternative to Carter. It should also be noted that although Reagan led Carter in early September, his poll lead was quite slim and would not qualify him as being a clear frontrunner. In 1992, despite being a clear frontrunner, Clinton ran significantly stronger among late deciders. With many late-deciding voters electing to support independent candidate Ross Perot, late deciders who voted for major-party candidates sided more with Clinton against Bush than early deciders had.[23]

The analysis of the normal course of campaigns also has shed light on the dynamics of public opinion and the possible role of momentum in opinion change during the campaign. Momentum may play a role in the deterioration of the frontrunner's lead. Certainly an erosion of support is not good news for a presidential candidate and may convince undecideds to give the trailing candidate a second look. However, momentum is clearly not the driving dynamic in the campaign. Momentum would be as likely to push frontrunners to even greater heights as pull them to a more even division or even into defeat. The evidence indicates that the driving dynamic of campaigns is competition, which narrows the frontrunner's lead. As a result, a presidential candidate who has a large lead at the outset of the campaign normally comes out of the campaign season with only a fraction of that lead intact.

Chapter 8

Electoral Competition and Unsystematic Campaign Effects

WHILE FUNDAMENTAL POLITICAL forces systematically shape the course of presidential campaigns and election results, making both predictable, neither campaign effects nor election results are *perfectly* predictable. In addition to the systematic effects of campaigns, the particular decisions, strategies, and events that arise in campaigns may also influence their course. These idiosyncratic elements of campaigns may affect who votes and for whom they vote.

While unsystematic aspects of campaigns may make a difference, their impact is often marginal, especially in the aggregate. To some degree, the idiosyncrasies of a campaign are evaluated in light of the pre-campaign fundamentals of partisanship, incumbency, and the economy. Where there is room for varying interpretations about a campaign development (such as the Ford "Eastern Europe" gaffe or the Dukakis "tank trip") evaluations may tilt toward the candidate already favored on partisanship or other pre-campaign considerations, or toward the incumbent, or toward the candidate favored because of the economy. On most matters arising during the campaign, voters have the latitude to take the development seriously or to write it off as inconsequential. Moreover, in the aggregate, the idiosyncrasies of particular campaigns often neutralize each other (one event helping one candidate and another helping the opponent) and thus contribute to the narrowing effect of the campaign.

Even though the fundamentals that systematically shape decisions during the campaign generally have the greater impact on the vote and though the unsystematic aspects of a campaign may have only marginal effects, presidential elections are often competitive enough that even marginal effects of events unique to a particular campaign can be important and, in some cases, decisive. This chapter examines competition in presidential elections and estimates how often and in what particular elections the unsystematic events of campaigns may have affected the outcomes.

From Dead Heats to Landslides

In this analysis, we examine the thirty-five presidential elections between 1868 and 2004. The popular and electoral college votes in these elections are presented in table 8.1, ordered according to the national two-party popular vote for the candidate who was elected president.

The general point emerging from these returns is that American presidential elections are quite competitive. Of the thirty-five elections spanning almost 140 years of electoral history, Republican candidates won twenty-one times and Democrats won fourteen. The average two-party popular vote for the winning candidate has been just over 55 percent of the vote, a plurality of 5.2 percentage points (or a spread of between ten and eleven points between the votes for the winning and losing candidates). The typical election appears to be fairly competitive. The difference between winning and losing a typical election in this period is the difference between winning the votes of eleven out of twenty voters versus nine out of twenty voters.

The table also demonstrates that the typically modest popular vote margins are greatly magnified by the winner-take-all provisions employed by most states in awarding their electoral college votes. Thus, while the typical winning presidential candidate received about 55 percent of the popular two-party vote, he received almost three-quarters of the electoral votes. However, the close correspondence between the popular and electoral vote percentages is also evident. The correlation between a party's two-party share of popular and electoral college votes is strongly positive (r = .90).

The election results displayed in table 8.1 rather neatly divide into four groupings: near-landslide and landslide elections, moderately competitive elections, close contests, and near dead heats. Near-landslide and landslide elections are those in which the winning candidate's plurality of the two-party popular vote exceeded seven percentage points. Moderately competitive elections are those in which the winning plurality of the vote ranged from three to seven percentage points. Close contests were elections in which the two-party popular vote plurality exceeded one and a half percentage points but was less than three percentage points of the vote. Near-dead-heat elections were those in which the winning candidate received a two-party popular vote plurality of one and a half percentage points or less. These cut-points in part reflect general impressions

Table 8.1. Election Results Ranked by the Closeness of the Popular Two-Party Vote, 1868–2004

| | | | National Popular Two-Party Vote Percentage | | |
Election	Winning Candidate and Political Party	Losing Candidate	Vote	Plurality	Electoral College Vote % for the Winner
Near Dead Heats					
1876	Hayes (R)	Tilden	48.47	−1.53	50.1
1888	Harrison (R)	Cleveland*	49.59	−.41	58.1
2000	G. W. Bush (R)	Gore	49.73	−.27	50.5
1880	Garfield (R)	Hancock	50.01	.01	58.0
1960	Kennedy (D)	Nixon	50.08	.08	58.0
1884	Cleveland (D)	Blaine	50.13	.13	54.6
1968	Nixon (R)	Humphrey	50.40	.40	61.2
1976	Carter (D)	Ford	51.05	1.05	55.2
2004	G. W. Bush (R)*	Kerry	51.24	1.24	53.2
Close Contests					
1916	Wilson* (D)	Hughes	51.64	1.64	52.2
1892	Cleveland (D)	Harrison*	51.74	1.74	65.6
1896	McKinley (R)	Bryan	52.19	2.19	60.6
1948	Truman (D)	Dewey	52.32	2.32	61.6
1868	Grant (R)	Seymour	52.66	2.66	72.8
Moderately Competitive					
1900	McKinley* (R)	Bryan	53.17	3.17	65.3
1992	Clinton (D)	G. H. W. Bush*	53.46	3.46	68.7
1944	F. Roosevelt* (D)	Dewey	53.78	3.78	81.4
1988	G. H. W. Bush (R)	Dukakis	53.90	3.90	79.2
1908	Taft (R)	Bryan	54.51	4.51	66.5
1996	Clinton* (D)	Dole	54.74	4.74	70.4
1940	F. Roosevelt* (D)	Willkie	54.97	4.97	84.6
1980	Reagan (R)	Carter*	55.30	5.30	90.9
1952	Eisenhower (R)	Stevenson	55.41	5.41	83.2
1872	Grant* (R)	Greeley	55.93	5.93	78.1
Landslides					
1956	Eisenhower* (R)	Stevenson	57.75	7.75	86.2
1928	Hoover (R)	Smith	58.80	8.80	83.6
1932	F. Roosevelt (D)	Hoover*	59.16	9.16	88.9
1984	Reagan* (R)	Mondale	59.17	9.17	97.6
1904	T. Roosevelt (R)	Parker	60.01	10.01	70.6
1964	Johnson (D)	Goldwater	61.34	11.34	90.3

continued

Table 8.1. (continued)

| Election | Winning Candidate and Political Party | Losing Candidate | National Popular Two-Party Vote Percentage | | Electoral College Vote % for the Winner |
			Vote	Plurality	
1972	Nixon* (R)	McGovern	61.79	11.79	96.8
1936	F. Roosevelt* (D)	Landon	62.46	12.46	98.5
1920	Harding (R)	Cox	63.83	13.83	76.1
1912	Wilson (D)	Taft*	64.35	14.35	83.2
1924	Coolidge (R)	Davis	65.21	15.21	73.8
Mean	21 Republicans, 14 Democrats		55.17	5.17	72.2

Note: The popular two-party vote plurality is the two-party vote for the candidate winning the election less 50 percent. In 1876, 1888, and 2000, the pluralities are negative numbers, indicating that the candidates who received majorities of electoral college votes in these elections did not win pluralities of the popular vote. Asterisked (*) candidates are elected incumbents who sought reelection. Unelected incumbent presidents who sought election include Teddy Roosevelt in 1904, Coolidge in 1924, Truman in 1948, Johnson in 1964, and Ford in 1976.

of an election's closeness, but they also reflect natural divisions in the actual returns. Very few elections fall near a cut-point in this classification scheme.

The Landslides

At the bottom of table 8.1 are eleven elections, one-third of the series, that can be classified by the popular vote as landslides or near-landslides. Dwight Eisenhower's reelection in 1956 over Adlai Stevenson, in a rematch of their 1952 contest, was nearly of landslide proportions. Eisenhower added about 2.5 percentage points to his 1952 total and won nearly 58 percent of the two-party vote. With the possible exception of Woodrow Wilson's 1912 victory over President William Howard Taft (which was complicated by former Republican president Theodore Roosevelt's entry and strong showing in the race as the candidate of the Bull Moose Progressive Party), each of the remaining elections in this grouping measures up as a landslide. In each case there was at least a 17-percentage-point gap in the popular two-party vote between the winning and losing candidate.

Electoral landslides range from Herbert Hoover's pre-Depression 1928 victory over Governor Al Smith of New York, a Democrat and the first Catholic presidential candidate, to Calvin Coolidge's crushing defeat eight years earlier of John W. Davis. Davis was the dark-horse nominee of the Democratic Party who won his party's nomination on the 103rd convention ballot after a bitter struggle between Al Smith, who represented the ethnic, urban wing of the party, and William McAdoo, who represented the more rural, populist wing.

Both Franklin Roosevelt's first and second elections, in 1932 and 1936, respectively, during the depths of the Great Depression, rank as landslides. Although some evidence suggests that the New Deal realignment actually began with the 1928 election, the first two of Roosevelt's unprecedented four presidential victories were clearly part and parcel of a dramatic turn in American politics. The New Deal realignment raised Democrats from their minority or second major party status to that of the dominant majority party. Democrats would greatly outnumber Republicans for nearly the next fifty years. The juxtaposition of the 1928 and 1932 landslide elections demonstrates the political impact of the Depression on presidential politics. Herbert Hoover won in a landslide in 1928 and was turned out of office in an even slightly larger landslide four years and a stock market crash later.

Three elections in the second half of the twentieth century were clearly landslides. All three involved the election of a sitting president. President Lyndon Johnson, who was sworn in following Kennedy's assassination in 1963, overwhelmingly defeated his Republican opponent, Senator Barry Goldwater, in 1964. Johnson's popular vote plurality over Goldwater was more than eleven percentage points, and, aside from his home state of Arizona, Goldwater carried only five other states, all in the South. While some at the time questioned whether the Republican Party would survive the 1964 landslide, only eight years later Republicans would turn the tables. Richard Nixon's 1972 reelection over Senator George McGovern was devastating. Nixon had nearly a twelve-percentage-point vote plurality and carried every state except Massachusetts and the District of Columbia. Finally, President Ronald Reagan won reelection in 1984 by decisively defeating Democrat Walter Mondale, the former vice president to President Jimmy Carter. Reagan carried every state except Mondale's home state of Minnesota and the District of Columbia and had over a nine-percentage-point popular vote plurality (a spread of nearly nineteen percentage points).

Moderately Competitive Elections

The next ten elections, almost another third of the total, were moderately competitive. Five involved the reelection of an incumbent, including Franklin Roosevelt's bids for his third and fourth terms. Popular vote pluralities in this group range from more than 3 to nearly 6 percentage points. This amounts to vote spreads between winners and losers of between 6.5 and 12 percentage points. The closest of these moderately competitive elections was William McKinley's second victory over the populist Democrat William Jennings Bryan.

Bryan's third failed bid for the presidency, his 1908 defeat by William Howard Taft, was also moderately competitive. The most decisive victory in this group, from the standpoint of the popular vote, was Civil War general U.S. Grant's reelection over New York newspaper editor Horace Greeley, the nominee of the Liberal Republican and disarrayed Democratic Parties.

Several recent elections can be classified as moderately competitive. Both of Bill Clinton's presidential victories were solid victories. His defeat of George H. W. Bush in 1992 and Bob Dole in 1996 involved popular vote pluralities of 3.5 and 4.7 percentage points, respectively. In both cases Clinton's winning vote margins were about average. Similarly, George H. W. Bush's 1988 victory over Massachusetts's Democratic governor Michael Dukakis and Ronald Reagan's 1980 defeat of incumbent Jimmy Carter were victories at or just short of double digits in the spread between the candidates' vote percentages.

Close Contests

The third group of elections featured fairly close contests, with popular-vote pluralities of more than 1.5 but less than 3 percentage points. Five elections are in this category. Several of these are often recalled as close contests, such as Harry Truman's famous come-from-behind victory over New York governor Tom Dewey. Just a month before the election the *New York Sun* reported that "the main question is whether Governor Dewey will win by a fair margin or by a landslide" (Boller 1984, 278).

Truman's victory was surprising, in part, because the Democratic Party was so bitterly divided over civil rights, foreign policy, and further expansions of the welfare state that two minor parties had splintered from it. Strom Thurmond, the Democratic governor of South Carolina, ran as the candidate of the States' Rights Dixiecrat Party, and Henry Wallace, vice president during Franklin Roosevelt's third term, ran as the candidate of the left-wing Progressive Party. Both Wallace and Thurmond were expected to draw votes away from Truman, ensuring a Dewey victory. However, as the campaign progressed, many disgruntled Democrats initially attracted to Wallace or Thurmond drifted back to Truman.

While Truman's comeback in the 1948 campaign was remarkable, Grover Cleveland's comeback in 1892 after losing the presidency four years earlier is unprecedented. No presidential candidate before or since Cleveland has recaptured the presidency after having been defeated for reelection. Like both his 1884 victory and his 1888 defeat, Cleveland's 1892 victory was quite close, a margin of less than two percentage points. His comeback was all the more remarkable because it was accomplished despite a significant vote for third-party

Populist James Weaver, who most likely drew votes disproportionately away from Cleveland.[1]

The three other close-contest elections—the 1868, 1896, and 1916 elections—are often not remembered as such. With its strong base in the South, the Democratic Party was devastated by the Civil War. As of the 1868 election, three predominantly Democratic southern states (Virginia, Mississippi, and Texas) had not been readmitted to the Union and thus could not participate in the election. Moreover, since the 1864 election, President Andrew Johnson, a Democrat, had been impeached by the House and had narrowly escaped the two-thirds vote necessary to convict in the Senate. The Democrats in 1868 also did not immediately unite behind a strong candidate. The Democratic presidential candidate in 1868 was former New York governor and Reconstruction critic Horatio Seymour, who was reluctantly nominated by a very divided convention on the twenty-second ballot. *The New York Times*'s report of Seymour's nomination ran with the headline: "Unanticipated Result of the Five Days' Struggle." In contrast, the Republican Party became closely associated with the patriotic cause of the Civil War, received the public's sympathy for its martyred leader, Abraham Lincoln, and nominated as its presidential candidate victorious Civil War general Ulysses S. Grant. Nevertheless, even with the situation so unfavorable to Democrats and favorable to Republicans, Grant's popular vote plurality was less than three percentage points over Seymour.[2]

Most analysts of the history of American political parties regard the presidential election of 1896 as a realigning election in which a narrow Republican Party majority considerably expanded and left the Republicans in a dominant position over the Democrats. One would expect that an election that proved to have long-term consequences—making American politics less competitive for that era—would itself be less competitive. In fact, Republican William McKinley's 1896 defeat of thirty-six-year-old populist Democrat William Jennings Bryan was fairly close.[3] The race broke down on sharply regional lines reflecting the economic interests behind Bryan's soft-currency, pro-debtor and McKinley's hard-currency, pro-creditor policies. Bryan's populism swept the solidly Democratic South and the West, but McKinley swept the states in the more populous and urban northeast and midwest. In the end, McKinley won the election with less than a five-percentage-point spread over Bryan.

The closest of the five close-contest elections was Woodrow Wilson's 1916 reelection victory over Republican Charles Evans Hughes. Having run for and won the governorship of New York in 1906 at the urging of President Teddy Roosevelt, and having been appointed to the U.S. Supreme Court upon the nomination of President William Howard Taft in 1910, Hughes appeared well positioned to reunite the progressive and conservative wings of the Republican Party. The split of the Republican coalition had spawned Teddy Roosevelt's bolt from the party and had ensured Wilson's victory in the 1912 election. In 1916, the Republicans selected Hughes as their party's nominee on their convention's third ballot.

Despite continuing divisions in the Republican Party, Hughes very nearly defeated Wilson. The election was so close that both candidates went to bed election night believing that Hughes had been elected. Although Wilson's official popular vote plurality was only slightly more than 1.5 percentage points, the distribution of the vote made the election even closer than this national vote plurality suggests. In a front-page story the day after the election, the late city edition of the *New York Times* reported: "Although Charles Evans Hughes of New York had apparently been elected President and Charles W. Fairbanks of Indiana Vice President on returns received up to 3 A.M. today there were important shifts after that hour which leave the result undetermined, but indicating strongly the re-election of President Wilson. At this writing Mr. Wilson has 264 electoral votes and Mr. Hughes 251, with 16 still in doubt in two states. The still doubtful States are California with 13 votes and New Mexico with 3" (*New York Times,* November 10, 1916). The Hughes campaign waited until the Friday after election day, when the results of the California vote appeared more certain, before conceding the election to Wilson.

Table 8.2 presents a critical electoral vote analysis of the fourteen closest elections since 1868. The table indicates how many electoral votes the losing candidate needed to reverse the election outcome and how many properly located popular votes would have been needed to shift the critical number of electoral votes.[4] Hughes received 254 electoral votes, twelve short of an electoral college majority. If just fewer than two thousand voters in California had switched from Wilson to Hughes (less than one one-hundredth of a percent of the votes cast nationally in that election and less than one-fifth of one percent of the votes cast in California), Hughes would have carried California and its thirteen electoral votes and would have served as the twenty-ninth president of the United States.[5] From this perspective, the 1916 election was as close or closer than many elections with smaller winning popular vote pluralities.

It is not difficult to see the campaign as making the difference in the outcome of the 1916 election. Some historical accounts of the election trace Hughes's loss in California, and therefore his loss of the election, to what became known as the "forgotten handshake." Like the party generally, but only more so, California Republicans were sharply divided between the Roosevelt (progressive) and Taft (regular or conservative) wings. California's progressive Republican governor Hiram Johnson, who had been Teddy Roosevelt's 1912 running mate on the Bull Moose Progressive ticket, was running for a U.S. Senate seat in 1916. Hughes, anxious not to get entangled in internal California party politics, made the mistake of steering clear of Johnson to the extent that he did not even meet with him when they were at the same Long Beach hotel in late August during their respective campaigns (the "forgotten handshake"). Whether or not this was an intentional effort to avoid the appearance of taking sides in an intraparty contest for the Republican Senate nomination is unclear, but the failure to at least meet with Johnson was nevertheless interpreted by many as disrespectful.[6] Johnson won his Senate race with better than 60 percent of the vote. Californians cast nearly 575,000 votes for the Republican and Progressive Senate candidate Johnson in 1916 and only about 463,000 votes for Republican presidential candidate Hughes. The widespread impression that Hughes had snubbed Johnson quite probably cost Hughes several times the 1,711 vote margin by which he lost California.

Near Dead Heats

Nine elections have been decided by razor-thin margins. In the language of racing, these were near dead heats. The winner in three of these elections (Hayes in 1876, Harrison in 1888, and G. W. Bush in 2000) received electoral vote majorities without popular vote pluralities. In another four elections, the winning candidate received a popular vote plurality of less than one-half of a percentage point. As table 8.2 indicates, the losing candidate in each of these elections could have won an electoral college victory with a relatively small shift in electoral votes produced by very small popular vote swings in the appropriate states. The results in a majority of these elections hinged on fewer than thirty electoral votes narrowly decided in a couple of states or, in a few instances, a single state.

It is certainly not difficult to imagine that the outcomes of these elections may have been decided by the effectiveness or ineffectiveness of the presidential campaigns. Seven of the nine dead heats were decided by pluralities smaller than the median out-of-sample error of the trial-heat and economy forecasting model (.89, see table 1.5), and all nine elections were decided by margins of less than twice the model's median out-of-sample error.

While there are many differences among these contests, two characteristics are common among them. First, as noted in chapter 5 (table 5.5), six of these nine elections (67 percent) lacked an incumbent in the race (seven if only elected incumbents are counted). Of the remaining twenty-six elections decided by wider margins, only eight (31 percent) lacked an incumbent candidate. Presumably, the absence of an incumbent in the race increases voter uncertainty about his or her choice and this is collectively reflected in a more even division

Table 8.2. The Fourteen Closest Presidential Elections and Their Critical Votes, 1868–2004

Election	Presidential Candidates	Number of Electoral Vote Changes Required to Change the Election Winner	Minimum Vote Shift Necessary to Change the Critical Number of Electoral Votes	Total Popular Votes Cast Nationally	Minimum Vote Shift as a Percentage of the Total National Vote	Popular and Electoral Vote Shift States
2000	G. W. Bush-Gore	3	269	105,396,627	<0.001	Florida
1876	Hayes-Tilden	1	445	8,413,101	0.005	South Carolina
1884	Cleveland-Blaine	19	524	10,049,754	0.005	New York
1916	Wilson-Hughes	12	1,711	18,535,022	0.009	California
1976	Carter-Ford	29	9,246	81,555,889	0.011	Hawaii, Ohio
1960	Kennedy-Nixon	50	16,682	68,828,960	0.024	Hawaii, Illinois, New Jersey, New Mexico
2004	G. W. Bush-Kerry	16	57,787	122,295,778	0.047	New Mexico, Iowa, Colorado
1948	Truman-Dewey	77	29,294	48,793,826	0.060	California, Illinois, Ohio
1888	Harrison-Cleveland	33	7,187	11,383,320	0.063	New York
1880	Garfield-Hancock	30	9,409	9,210,420	0.102	Connecticut, Oregon, Indiana, Maine
1896	McKinley-Bryan	48	18,558	13,935,738	0.133	California, Indiana, Oregon, Delaware, Kentucky, West Virginia

1968	Nixon-Humphrey	79	145,559	73,211,875	0.199	Alaska, Delaware, Missouri, New Jersey, Ohio, Tennessee, Wisconsin
1892	Cleveland-Harrison	78	26,906	12,056,097	0.223	California, Delaware, Idaho, Illinois, Indiana, Kansas, West Virginia, Wisconsin
1868	Grant-Seymour	68	27,965	5,722,440	0.489	Alabama, Arkansas, California, Connecticut, Indiana, New Hampshire, Pennsylvania

Note: Elections are ordered by the minimum percentage of national vote that have to have shifted to change the election outcome. The first candidate in each pair won the election. The number of electoral votes required to change the election winner are the number of electoral college votes that, when added to the losing major-party candidate's electoral vote totals, would have produced an electoral vote majority. The minimum vote shift is the number of votes that would have changed state winners of electoral college votes. For example, a 445-vote shift from Hayes to Tilden in South Carolina in 1876 would have swung that state from Hayes to Tilden and provided Tilden with more than the one additional electoral vote that he needed to win the election. Similarly, a shift of 9,409 votes from Garfield to Hancock in 1880 in the four identified states would have shifted the electoral votes in those states to Hancock and provided him with at least the 30 votes that he needed for an electoral college majority. The minimum popular vote shift as a percentage of the total national vote is in percentage points. Except for 1868, each of these percentages is significantly less than one-half of one percentage point of the total national vote. In 2004, a shift of 59,300 vote in Ohio alone would also have changed the outcome.

Table 8.3. Incumbency Status, Partisan Parity, and Election Closeness, 1868–2004

Percentage of Elections that were Near Dead Heat Elections

		Incumbency Status of Election		
		Incumbent Running	No Incumbent in the Race	Total
Balance of Party Strength	One Party Dominant	0 (0 of 12)	17 (1 of 6)	6 (1 of 18)
	Parties Near Parity	30 (3 of 10)	71 (5 of 7)	47 (8 of 17)
	Total	27 (6 of 22)	46 (6 of 13)	

Note: The entries are the percentage of the joint category of elections that were classified as near dead heat elections. Near dead heat elections are those in which the winning candidate received less than 51.5 percent of the two-party national popular vote. The parties were considered near parity in elections from 1868 to 1892 and from 1968 to 2004.

of the vote. Second, near-dead-heat elections are concentrated in two eras of highly competitive party politics: from 1868 to 1892 and from 1968 to the present. These two eras account for nearly half of the post–Civil War presidential elections examined (17 of 35), but, with the single exception of the 1960 election, all of the near-dead-heat elections occurred in these periods when the major parties were of nearly equal strength.

Table 8.3 presents the percentage of near-dead-heat elections for four types of elections, with and without incumbents in the race and in party systems with and without a dominant party. As the table indicates, not one of the twelve elections in a dominant party period with an incumbent in the race have been extremely close. However, five of the seven open seat elections (71 percent) conducted when the parties were nearly evenly matched were near-dead-heat elections in which the campaigns could easily have made the difference between winning and losing.

The Disputed Election of 1876

The election of 1876 was one of the closest and most controversial in American history. The Republican contender was Rutherford B. Hayes, who was nominated as a compromise candidate in a divided convention. House Speaker James G. Blaine of Maine had generally been regarded as the likely nominee and led in the first six rounds of balloting. Blaine, however, had been under attack for his business dealings and had a few powerful enemies (most notably, New York political boss Roscoe Conkling) who prevented him from obtaining a majority of delegate votes (Cheney and Cheney 1996, 92). Hayes, the Republican governor of Ohio, was a distant fifth on the convention's first ballot but emerged in later ballots as the candidate able to rally the anyone-but-Blaine forces. He narrowly defeated Blaine on the convention's seventh ballot.

The Democrats nominated Governor Samuel Tilden of New York, a reform-minded opponent of New York City's Democratic Tammany Hall machine and its leader, Boss Tweed, on the second ballot. With a divided Republican convention, the aftermath of the economic panic of 1873, and the fallout from President Grant's scandal-plagued second term, the 1876 election-year climate seemed favorable for Democrats. However, Democrats continued to be at a long-term disadvantage due to their positions during the Civil War, positions that ranged from sympathy with the Confederate rebellion to criticism of Lincoln's handling of the war. Nevertheless, Tilden seemed in a relatively strong position to take advantage of the short-term conditions favoring the Democrats and to break his party's losing streak of four consecutive presidential elections.

On election night it appeared that Tilden had indeed defeated Hayes. With three states (Louisiana, South Carolina, and Florida) having a combined 19 electoral votes still too close to be determined, Tilden stood a single electoral vote away from victory.[7] He had 184 certain votes from seventeen states and Hayes had 166 from eighteen states. After learning that Tilden had carried New York and seeing the drift of the vote nationally, Hayes went to bed thinking that he had lost the election. Even the day after the election, with the votes in the three states still uncertain, Hayes said that he was "of the opinion that the Democrats have carried the country and elected Tilden" (Severn 1968, 173).

Both parties focused on the three remaining states that held the balance. Each of these states with disputed votes filed separate sets of vote returns, one set favorable to Tilden and another favorable to Hayes. Both parties found evidence of election fraud against the other side. With Congress divided by party, with Republicans controlling the Senate and Democrats the House, there was not even a politically expedient way to settle the impasse. Supporters of both candidates were frustrated and feared that the election was being stolen. Tempers ran so high that even the possibility of a second civil war seemed real.

Negotiations dragged on for weeks until each side agreed in the last week of January, 1877, to arbitration by an electoral commission. The commission was to be composed of five members from the House, five from the Senate, and five from the Supreme Court. Since this was a highly partisan matter, the partisan composition of the commission was evenly balanced with the two Democratic and two Republican Supreme Court justices selecting the crucial fifth judicial member of the commission who was likely to tip the balance on party-line votes.[8] The electoral vote count and commission proceedings lasted the entire month of February (Rehnquist 2004). In the end, the commission decided in favor of Hayes's vote count in each of the three disputed states, thus electing Hayes to the presidency by a single electoral vote and without a popular vote plurality.[9]

Although there will always be controversy surrounding the disputed vote counts in the three states, the 1876 election was certainly one of the closest presidential elections in American history.[10] Accepting the commission's vote count as accurate, Tilden could have won an electoral vote majority with a shift of fewer than five hundred votes in either South Carolina or Florida. Shifts of fewer than six hundred votes from Hayes to Tilden in the undisputed vote counts of either Nevada or Oregon also could have swung the election to Tilden. Questions of election fraud aside, there can be little doubt that the presidential campaign could easily have determined the outcome of a contest that was this close.

The Elections of the 1880s
The three presidential elections that followed the 1876 election were also extremely close. In 1880, the Republicans nominated Representative James Garfield of Ohio as their presidential nominee on the thirty-sixth ballot of their convention. The nomination had been deadlocked between former president Ulysses S. Grant (who would be seeking a third term), Senator James G. Blaine (who had narrowly lost the party's nomination in 1876), and Secretary of the Treasury John Sherman. Garfield emerged as the dark-horse alternative to Grant. Meanwhile, the Democrats nominated as their candidate former Civil War general Winfield Hancock on their convention's second ballot.

Although Garfield, unlike Hayes four years earlier, won a clear electoral majority, he actually carried two fewer states than Hayes and received a national popular vote plurality of fewer than two thousand votes out of more than nine million votes cast. The key to Garfield's clear electoral victory was that, unlike Hayes, he carried the big electoral vote states of New York (thirty-five) and Indiana (fifteen). A shift from Garfield to Hancock of fewer than ten thousand votes in four states or slightly more than ten thousand votes in New York state alone would have thrown the electoral vote majority to Hancock. As close as this election was, however, it was not nearly as close as the election that preceded it or the one that would follow it.

The presidential election of 1884 ranks as one of the closest in history. It also demonstrates more clearly than any election that campaigns can make a difference to an election's outcome. The 1884 election was bitterly fought. Governor Grover Cleveland of New York was the Democratic presidential candidate.

Cleveland received his party's nomination on the convention's second ballot. Although there was significant sentiment to renominate Samuel Tilden, whom many Democrats felt had been wrongly denied the presidency in 1876, he informed convention delegates in mid-June that he did not want to seek the office. Senator James G. Blaine of Maine, who had come close to winning his party's nomination in both 1876 and 1880, was the Republican candidate, nominated on his party's fourth convention ballot. His principal rival for the nomination was President Chester Arthur, who had served as Garfield's vice president and who had become president upon Garfield's assassination. Blaine's involvement in shady dealings with railroad companies during the Grant administration and Cleveland's personal life, including the fathering of an illegitimate child, supplied plenty of material for partisan invective during the campaign.

The critical events of the 1884 election would occur within a week of election day. As in the previous two closely decided elections, New York, the largest electoral vote prize in the nation, was again the pivotal state. During a rally for Blaine in New York City on the last Wednesday of October, a Presbyterian minister in addressing the crowd disparaged the Democratic Party as the party of "Rum, Romanism, and Rebellion."[11] Whether he did not hear the phrase or chose to ignore it, Blaine failed to denounce it at the time. Irish Catholics, a substantial voting bloc in New York, took offense. Blaine, himself of Irish ancestry, later distanced himself from the remark, but the damage had already been done.[12] Less than a week later, Cleveland carried New York and its 36 electoral votes. Largely as a result of this, he was elected president, the first Democrat elected president since the Civil War. A vote swing from Cleveland to Blaine of a mere 524 voters in New York, Cleveland's home state, would have reversed the election outcome. It would have swung New York to Blaine, providing him with 17 more electoral votes than he needed for election.[13] The minister's unfortunate remarks and the failure of Blaine to immediately condemn them probably cost Blaine at least 524 votes in New York and with them, the presidency.

The 1888 election also ranks as one of the closest ever. President Cleveland was nominated by acclamation as the Democratic Party's candidate. Matters were not nearly so clear for Republicans. The most likely nominee, 1884 Republican presidential candidate James G. Blaine, decided not to run. This left an open field. The leading candidate in the first round of balloting at the Republican convention was Senator John Sherman of Ohio, but the vote was widely split among six major and a number of minor candidates. By the sixth ballot, Benjamin Harrison, a former senator from Indiana and grandson of President William Henry Harrison, pulled nearly even with Sherman. On the eighth ballot Harrison won his party's nomination.

As noted above, Harrison went on to win the election without winning a plurality of the national popular vote. Cleveland received about one percentage point more of the popular vote than Harrison, but Harrison won 233 electoral votes to Cleveland's 168. Like the 1884 election, as table 8.2 shows, the outcome was again determined by New York. However, this time Republican Harrison carried the pivotal state.

The Closest of Modern Elections

Five elections in the modern era of American politics were near-dead-heat presidential races. Both of President George W. Bush's elections were quite close as were John Kennedy's victory over Richard Nixon in 1960, Nixon's victory over Hubert Humphrey in 1968, and Jimmy Carter's defeat of Gerald Ford in 1976. How close were these elections, what made them so close, and what may have decided their outcomes?

The closest of the five modern near-dead-heat elections was the 2000 disputed election between George W. Bush and Al Gore. By the standard of the fewest votes needed to change an election's outcome, the 2000 presidential election was the closest in American history, closer even than the 1876 Hayes-Tilden disputed election. The 2000 campaign saw each candidate rise and fall. Bush had an early poll lead that he lost to Gore after the Democratic Party's convention. Gore then lost his lead to Bush in the middle of the fall campaign and after several poor debate showings by Gore. In the closing weeks of the campaign, Bush's lead narrowed. By election day, it was a dead heat. It all came down to which candidate would carry Florida and its 25 electoral votes, and Florida itself was almost evenly divided in its votes. The election's outcome rested on the vote count in Florida and, even after recounts, there were enough disputed ballots to throw the matter into the courts. After a flurry of court battles, the U.S. Supreme Court decided on December 12, 2000, in the case of *Bush v. Gore* that the Florida Supreme Court could not set up its own "standardless manual recount" process. The vote previously certified by the Florida Elections Canvassing Commission stood—Bush was elected president by carrying Florida with a mere 537 more votes than Gore.

The context of the 2000 election suggested that it would be close but not nearly as close as it turned out to be. The generally even party balance between Democrats and Republicans as well as the growing ideological polarization of the electorate and the lack of an incumbent in the race were precursors of a close election. Although it appeared at the time that the economy was robust and would help the in-party Democrats (the August estimates for the first half of 2000 indicated a 5 percent growth rate for the real GDP), later measures of economic activity indicate that real economic growth in this period was just slightly below average for an election year. Revised GDP estimates from the Bureau of Economic Analysis indicated a 3.7 percent growth rate in the first half of 2000 (compared to a median rate of 4 percent in election years from 1948 to 2004).

One of the fundamentals, however, clearly favored the Democrats in 2000. Public opinion leading into the campaign favored the Democrats. Despite his impeachment by the House of Representatives, President Clinton's approval rating in July stood at 59 percent. Whether to distance himself from President Clinton because of Clinton's scandals or to establish his independence as a candidate after serving as vice president, Gore distanced himself from both Clinton and his record. This was a mistake that likely cost him support going into the fall campaign. This, along with poor performances in the debates and the siphoning of some votes to Ralph Nader's candidacy, may have cost Gore crucial votes in November and ultimately the presidency.

Prior to the 2000 election, the Kennedy-Nixon race of 1960 headed the list of narrowly decided modern presidential elections.[14] As table 8.2 shows, a swing of fewer than 17,000 voters to Nixon in four states could have reversed the election's outcome in 1960. Alternatively, as Theodore White observed, Nixon could have won an electoral vote majority with a vote swing to him of about 23,000 votes in Texas (out of nearly 2.3 million cast there) and fewer than 4,500 votes in Illinois. This assumes of course, and perhaps heroically, that the Democratic machines of Texas and Illinois would not have produced (by one way or the other) additional votes for Kennedy.

The pre-campaign conditions of the 1960 election prepared the way for a close election. Favoring the election of Vice President Nixon was the public's general approval of President Eisenhower, a mean approval rating from June though October of nearly 60 percent. On the other hand, economic conditions favored the election of Senator Kennedy. The economy during the election year was weak, actually shrinking by nearly two percentage points in the second quarter. These offsetting factors, and the lack of an incumbent in the race, set the stage for a closely fought battle.

While many decisions and events might have made a difference to the 1960 outcome, most observers trace the turning point in the election to the first of four nationally televised debates between the candidates.[15] Whether appearance or manner affected public evaluations, those who watched the September 26 debate tended to be pulled in Kennedy's direction.[16] White succinctly sums up the impact of the debates: "When they began, Nixon was generally viewed as being the probable winner of the election contest and Kennedy as fighting an uphill battle; when they were over, the positions of the two contestants were reversed" (White 1961, 318–19).[17]

Though the debate may well have been the proximate cause of Kennedy's slim victory, the candidate's delayed partisanship advantage was a deeper reason. Despite Democrats greatly outnumbering Republicans in 1960, there were about as many Republicans as Democrats among the early-deciding voters that year. Two-thirds of Republicans decided their votes early in 1960, and they overwhelmingly supported Nixon. As a result, Nixon held a 58 to 42 lead over Kennedy among early deciders. Many Democrats, on the other hand, were less certain about Kennedy and delayed their decision. Because of this, among late-deciding voters in 1960, Democrats outnumbered Republicans by more than two-to-one (see appendix B, table B.2). Whether his debate performance warranted it or not, it would be difficult to imagine the party composition of late deciders not tilting the campaign toward Kennedy. In sharp contrast to early deciders, late deciders divided nearly 61 to 39 for Kennedy.

The 1968 presidential election ranks as the third closest of modern elections in terms of the division of the national vote but is unsurpassed as the most turbulent in recent history. Republican Richard Nixon emerged from the political setbacks of his 1960 presidential loss to John Kennedy and his defeat two years later for the governorship of California to narrowly defeat Hubert Humphrey, Democratic candidate and vice president to President Lyndon Johnson, as well as George Wallace, third party candidate and governor of Alabama.

Going into the 1968 election, two conditions suggested a close election, another favored Humphrey, and two conditions favored Nixon. First, like 2000 and 1960, the lack of an incumbent in the race was a precursor of a close election in 1968. A second development that favored a close election was the long-term shift in partisanship that began in 1968 (J. Campbell 2006). The fragile New Deal coalition assembled by the Democrats in the 1930s and patched together in the 1940s and 1950s was unraveling and being replaced by a more competitively balanced party system. The deterioration of the New Deal coalition (dealignment) was evident by 1968, but the shape of the realigned party system would not be clear until the 1980s. In any event, the dissolution of the Democratic partisan majority increased the likelihood of 1968 being a close election.

Other conditions in 1968 tilted toward Humphrey or toward Nixon. Though overshadowed by the Vietnam War and civil rights issues, the economy in 1968 was strong enough that it should have helped Humphrey. The economic growth rate in the first half of 1968 was 7.6 percent, about what one would find in landslide election years. However, with growing sentiment against the administration's conduct of the war in Vietnam and increasing concern about unrest in the cities, strong economic numbers were not enough to salvage public support and party unity for the Democrats. These factors clearly favored Nixon. With an unpopular war and concern with civil unrest, President Johnson's mean approval rating from June though October of 1968 stood at only 40 percent. Having survived one of the most fractious conventions in American history, Humphrey's poll standing at Labor Day was only 42 percent. Governor Wallace had decided to run as a third-party candidate representing the conservative southern wing of the party, anti-war Democrats who had supported Senators Gene McCarthy or Robert Kennedy were contemplating sitting out the election, and only 37 percent of Democrats felt comfortable enough with Humphrey that they could reach an early decision to vote for him. The campaign allowed Humphrey to reunite a large part of the Democratic Party that was disaffected, but, in the end, unlike the Truman comeback of 1948, Humphrey's efforts fell short.

The 1976 election between Democrat Jimmy Carter and Republican Gerald Ford is the fourth-closest modern election in terms of the national vote but ranks even closer in terms of the number of votes that would have altered the outcome. A vote swing of fewer than 10,000 votes in Ohio and Hawaii from Carter to Ford, about one one-hundredth of a percent of all votes cast for president in 1976, would have provided Ford with an electoral vote majority.[18]

Though the issues and personalities in the 1976 election were very different than they were in 1968 and the Republicans were now the in-party, the conditions leading to a closely fought defeat for the in-party were in many respects similar. Although the in-party candidate in 1976 was the incumbent, Gerald Ford was an un-elected incumbent. He had been appointed to the vice presidency following the resignation of Vice President Spiro Agnew and became president upon the resignation of President Nixon at the height of the Watergate scandal. As in 1968, the economy favored the in-party in 1976, but public opinion favored the out-party candidate, Jimmy Carter in this case. The economy in the first half of 1976 was growing at an annualized rate of about 6 percent, though it had slowed to a more politically neutral 3 percent rate in the second quarter. Public opinion, on the other hand, tipped in favor of the Democrats. President Ford's approval ratings going into the election were in the mid-40s, near the break-even point. His standing in the pre-campaign preference polls, however, indicated far less support. At Labor Day, Democratic candidate Jimmy Carter held a 60 to 40 lead over the Republican incumbent. The scandal of Watergate and President Ford's pardon of former President Nixon was too heavy a burden to carry into the campaign. Additionally, Ford stumbled into a misstatement during his second presidential debate with Carter. At the conclusion of a response to a question about diplomatic relations with the Soviet Union, Ford said that "there is no Soviet domination of Eastern Europe, and there never will be under a Ford administration."[19] While he had apparently meant that the Soviets had not dominated the spirit of the people of Eastern Europe, people were not expecting this subtlety from President Ford and most interpreted his statement as a blunder. While Ford made up most of the lost ground to Carter during the campaign, this debate gaffe set back his campaign. As a result, he fell just short of replicating Truman's miraculous come-from-behind victory of 1948.

The final modern near dead heat is the 2004 election between President George W. Bush and Senator John Kerry. Like the 1976 election, the 2004 election ranks closer in the votes needed to change the electoral vote winner than in the national vote division. The pivotal state in the 2004 election was Ohio. A shift of fewer than 60,000 votes from Bush to Kerry in Ohio would have provided Kerry with the electoral vote majority.

Several factors contributed to the closeness of the 2004 election and tipped it toward the reelection of President Bush. In particular, three conditions shaped the course of the 2004 campaign: the terrorist attacks of September 11, 2001, and the war on terrorism that it precipitated, the increasing polarization of the electorate, and the partisan parity between the Democrats and the Republicans. The even division of partisanship and the divisions over the war in Iraq and the polarized views of the Bush presidency were evident in the presidential job approval polls well before the campaign. Job approval ratings for President Bush throughout the campaign hovered right around 50 percent (and the critical level of approval is closer to 40 percent). President Bush also entered the fall campaign just slightly ahead of Kerry in the preference polls. These lukewarm to mixed evaluations reflected long-term partisan differences, ideological polarization, and divided views about the administration's handling of the war in Iraq.

Ultimately President Bush's advantage on the war against terrorism (quite consistently at least a ten point margin over Kerry), his advantage on ideological perspectives in the highly polarized electorate with conservatives significantly outnumbering liberals (J. Campbell 2005b, 2007b, Jamieson 2006, 93), and the Republican voter mobilization efforts tipped the election to President Bush. Though Kerry came back effectively in the debates, recovering a good part of the ground he had lost in a weak convention send-off to his campaign, the campaign overall left voters pretty much where they started, perhaps adding no more than one percentage point of the vote to President Bush's column.

Campaign Effects and Close Elections

Dedicated campaign watchers examine each move made in a campaign as if it were a grand chess match. Campaign strategists, journalists, and political historians commonly see each campaign as something entirely different from its predecessors and believe that each maneuver could be crucial to the election's outcome. The point of this chapter is that this view, that the particular events and strategies of a presidential campaign determine who wins and loses, is probably *sometimes* right, and this is enough to take this aspect of campaigns seriously.

Unsystematic events of particular campaigns may be decisive in close elections. It is not difficult to imagine that if a certain New York Presbyterian minister in 1884 had characterized the Democratic Party as the party of "Rum and Rebellion," rather than "Rum, Romanism, and Rebellion," James G. Blaine would have defeated Grover Cleveland. If Charles Evans Hughes had been a bit friendlier to progressive Republicans in California in 1916, there is a very good chance that Woodrow Wilson would not have been reelected. If Richard Nixon and his advisors had better understood the mechanics of appearance on early television, Nixon might have prevailed over John Kennedy in 1960. If Gerald Ford had not stumbled so badly in describing the circumstances of Eastern Europe in his presidential debate, he may well have defeated Jimmy Carter. If Al Gore had focused more on Florida (or his home state of Tennessee), he might have defeated George W. Bush. It is not difficult to find elections in which a strong case can be made that particular events in the campaign made the difference to the election's outcome.

This is not to say, however, that any of these particular campaign events or the unsystematic component of any presidential campaign had large effects. To the contrary, the best evidence indicates that they do not. It is to say, however, that in close elections even small campaign effects may be very important. A significant number of presidential elections have been very close, close enough that some unsystematic factors of particular campaigns may have made the difference to the election's outcome.

How close does an election have to be for the unsystematic give and take of a campaign to make a difference? There is no easy or definitive answer to this question. It depends on the gravity of the unsystematic campaign development and the course that the campaign would have taken naturally as a result of the systematic factors of the election. Some campaign events, even those of considerable consequence, might simply serve to augment the expected outcome of the election. Others might reverse that direction. Moreover, as both the 2000 and 2004 elections certainly attest, the distribution of the vote across the states may affect how close an election really is.

One gauge of whether unsystematic campaign effects may have affected election outcomes can be obtained by a statistical analysis based on the election model (the forecasting model using the latest economic measures rather than those available at the time of the election). Assuming that the out-of-sample errors of the model reflect unsystematic campaign effects, the variation in these effects can be compared to what it would have taken to reverse each election's outcome. This allows us to estimate how likely it would be for any particular election's outcome to have been different from what the systematic factors would have produced. For instance, given that the typical unsystematic campaign effect (the median out-of-sample error) was about 1.2 percentage points of the vote with a standard deviation of the expected vote error of plus or minus 2.1 percentage points, it would appear that there was only about one chance in two hundred that Grant defeated Greeley in 1872 because of the particulars of that campaign. The estimate that Grant probably did not owe his reelection to unsystematic campaign effects is based on the fact that his popular vote plurality of nearly 56 percent of the national two-party popular vote is about three times the standard deviation of campaign effects.[20]

By this statistical gauge, we can gain a bit of a different perspective on campaign effects in the four categories of elections that we have examined. Table 8.4 presents a summary. It appears that unsystematic or particular campaign events probably made the difference in four of the nine near dead heats, perhaps one or two of the five close contests, but probably not in any of twenty-one moderately competitive or landslide elections.

First, among the nine near-dead-heat elections, there is almost a fifty-fifty chance that unsystematic campaign effects made the difference (in the popular vote winner) in any of these races. Since nine elections fall in this category, these odds suggest that campaign events probably decided four of these elections.

Table 8.4. The Likelihood that Unsystematic Campaign Effects Decided the Election Outcome, 1868–2004

Competitiveness of the Election Outcome	Number of Elections	Number of Elections Probably Decided by Unsystematic Campaign Effects
Near Dead Heats	9	4
Close Contests	5	1 or 2
Moderately Competitive	10	0
Landslides	11	0
All Elections	35	5 to 6 (14% to 17%)

Note: The estimated number of elections probably decided by unsystematic campaign effects is based on the combined analysis of the t-scores computed from the vote margin of an election and the standard deviation of the out-of-sample errors of the election equation (the trial-heat and economy forecasting equation with revised economic data) and historical studies of the particular elections.

Based on the expected votes from the forecasting model (table 1.6) and the vote difference between early- and late-deciding voters, the Kennedy-Nixon race in 1960 seems to be one likely case of a decisive campaign among these elections.

Second, the odds vary from between about one in four to one in nine that unsystematic campaign events swung any of the five close contest elections away from the candidate favored by the election's systematic fundamentals. The miraculous comeback of Truman in his 1948 race against Dewey may be a case of a decisive campaign among the close contest elections. Based on the historical analysis and the small number of votes involved in California, it would also appear that the campaign may well have also decided the close contest between Wilson and Hughes in 1916.

Beyond the dozen closest elections, however, the likelihood of unexpected campaign effects deciding an election's outcome is quite remote. The odds of unsystematic campaign events being decisive in moderately competitive elections range from one chance in thirteen (the 1900 election) to about one chance in two hundred (the 1872 election discussed above). There is no real chance that campaign events determined the outcome of any of the eleven near-landslide or landslide elections. The winning margin in each of these contests (or more accurately, non-contests) was about five to six times the typical net effect of unsystematic campaign events (11.3 versus 2.1 percentage points of the vote).[21]

Although this statistical analysis, like the historical analysis, suggests that the particular strategies, decisions, and events of a campaign can affect an election's outcome, this does not minimize in any way the importance of the fundamentals, or the pre-campaign context, in presidential elections. The particulars of a campaign may have been decisive in several cases *because* those elections were close and they were close *because* of the balance in the pre-campaign fundamentals. If the parties were not nearly at parity going into the 1884 election, for instance, James Blaine might well have survived the "Rum, Romanism, and Rebellion" indiscretion. If Republicans had not been so bitterly divided in 1912, Wilson might not have had incumbency in his favor in 1916 and Hughes's "forgotten handshake" in California might not have mattered. If the public was not already nearly evenly divided between Kennedy and Nixon going into the 1960 campaign (the July polls split about 53 to 47 in Nixon's favor), Richard Nixon's performance in the great debates probably would not have been as important to the election as it apparently was. In each of these instances, the pre-campaign context foreshadowed a very close election that would allow fairly small campaign effects to be decisive.

While unsystematic campaign effects may affect election outcomes in some instances, when the fundamental forces of an election are nearly balanced, and while these close elections are not altogether rare occurrences, it is important also to note that a large majority of presidential elections (about three-fifths of those since 1868) have been won by large enough popular vote margins that unsystematic campaign effects were not a factor in the outcome. Campaign strategies and events may have boosted or depressed the vote margin of the winning candidate, but the ultimate plurality vote winner depended entirely on political conditions in place before the general election campaign began.

★ *Chapter 9*

How Campaigns Matter

DO PRESIDENTIAL CAMPAIGNS affect election results? For campaign consultants and political pundits the answer is obvious: of course they do. Why else would anyone in his or her right mind devote the tremendous amounts of time and energy to devising intricate campaign strategies and to crisscrossing the country endlessly on speaking tours with a caravan of campaign workers and reporters? If they did not believe that campaigns affected the vote, why would candidates raise and spend the enormous amounts of money on consultants, national surveys, campaign appearances, and wildly expensive television advertising? For political scientists studying campaigns and voting behavior, the answer has not been so obvious. As discussed at the outset of this analysis, the research on presidential campaigns has concluded that their effects on the vote are "minimal." Being dedicated political observers as well as scientists, political scientists have never been comfortable with this finding. Nevertheless, the unsettling findings were there.

Also as observed at the outset, doubts about campaign effects have been renewed in recent years by the success of several election forecasting models. If elections can be accurately forecast before the campaign even begins, it might appear that the intervening campaign is of no real consequence. Individual campaign events may affect voters, but positive events for one candidate offset positive events for the opponent and the net effect is negligible, or so it is supposed. The canceling of these campaign effects may be imperfect in any particular election, but generally, even within an election year, the net impact of the campaigns is supposed to be minor. This supposition, however, understates the effects of campaigns.

The Impact of Presidential Campaigns

Presidential campaigns have significant effects, perhaps not as great or of the same sort as some campaign politicos might suppose, but significant nonetheless. The reason that elections are predictable is not that campaigns have no effect, but that campaign effects themselves are largely predictable. Campaign effects are predictable because their effects are limited and largely systematic. They are limited because of the large number of vote decisions reached before the campaign begins, decisions based on established partisanship, ideology, issue beliefs, and evaluations of candidate qualities. They are systematic because three fundamentals guide the course of the campaign and voter reactions to it, and these three fundamentals are in place before the campaign begins. Presidential incumbency and election-year economic conditions shape how receptive the voting public is to candidate messages. The political implications of the election-year economy are also gradually incorporated into the decisions of voters over the months leading up to the vote. The intense competition present in every presidential campaign also systematically puts pressure on frontrunners and typically costs them some portion of their lead.

These fundamental forces that have structured the effects of campaigns have done so over a long period of electoral history despite enormous changes in how campaigns have been conducted. The norms, styles, technologies, and intensity of presidential campaigning have changed tremendously over time. Yet throughout all of this history, partisanship has guided many voters to a choice before the campaign begins. The election-year economy, presidential incumbency, and the forces of political competition have systematically affected the evaluations of campaign events and the votes of those who decide during the campaign. Whether campaigns are conducted in a low-key manner from the front porches of the candidates' homes or through sophisticated focus-group-tested televised advertising, most voters rely on their partisan affinities and are affected by the circumstances of the election-year economy, incumbency, and the heated contest between the candidates regardless of how the campaign messages are delivered. There is little evidence to suggest that these fundamental factors have changed much over the years.

How Much Do Campaigns Matter?

The real question about presidential campaigns is not so much whether they matter but how much they matter. The extent of campaign effects on election results can be gauged in two ways. The first measure is the extent to which campaigns changed the vote margin for the candidates. The second measure is the frequency with which campaigns determined which candidate won a majority of the two-party popular vote.

The analysis found that presidential campaigns after Labor Day affect the national vote, on average, by about four percentage points (recall table 3.4).[1] In some elections the net effects of the campaigns have been nearly negligible; however, campaign effects have frequently exceeded six percentage points and in one election the campaign made a net difference of about nine percentage points.

How large or small should we consider these effects? From one perspective, an average effect of four percentage points might be judged to be rather small or minimal. The mathematically possible net effects of campaigns are much larger. At the extreme, with the average pre-campaign frontrunner standing at about 57 percent in the polls, an average change of 57 percent is arithmetically possible.[2] While this is an extreme, campaign effects in the double-digits are certainly thinkable. However, using more realistic benchmarks, the average campaign effect of four percentage points does not seem so small. The average two-party vote for winning candidates has been only about 4.5 percentage points over a fifty-fifty split, and the average change in the vote from one election to the next has been only about 6.4 percentage points.[3] Perhaps the best characterization of campaign effects is that they are neither large nor minimal in an absolute sense, but sometimes large enough to be politically important. This assessment comports fairly well with the individual election appraisals of campaign effects in the 1980s to 2004 by Abramson, Aldrich, and Rohde (1982, 1986, 1990, 1994, 1998, 2003, 2006).

Most of these campaign effects have been the result of the pre-campaign fundamentals that systematically structure the course of campaigns: incumbency, the election-year economy, and the competitiveness of the campaigns. The predictable "playing out" of these fundamentals over the course of the campaign often goes unnoticed in toting-up campaign effects, resulting in their underestimation. Although the effects of unsystematic or unanticipated developments of campaigns are much smaller, they also have made a difference to the vote. The unsystematic components of the campaign typically have made a net difference of about one to two percentage points of the vote.

Although presidential campaigns typically have a significant impact on the vote margins of the candidates, they usually are not decisive to who wins the election. Since most campaign influences are systematic and since one of the most important systematic effects is the narrowing (rather than the reversal) of the leads of frontrunners, the impact of campaigns as measured by their determination of the winning candidate is less than their impact on the vote margin. On the other hand, and this is what may be most important to those involved in the process, there is good evidence that campaigns have determined the popular vote winner in some elections. As indicated in table 3.4, campaigns appear to have been decisive in at least two of the last fifteen elections (13 percent). Truman's come-from-behind victory over Dewey in 1948 and Kennedy's razor-thin margin over Nixon in 1960 are probably both examples of campaigns that made the ultimate difference. Both of these were cases in which the winning candidate trailed at the outset of the campaign. While it is true that Kennedy was nearly even with Nixon as the 1960 campaign began, the analysis of late- and early-deciding voters reinforces the conclusion that Kennedy's bare majority was based on a strong showing among those who reached their vote decision during the campaign (appendix B, table B.2). Whether the first presidential debate tipped the scales to Kennedy or not, the scales were tipped in his favor during the campaign. Other recent elections—1980, 2000, and 2004 in particular—without clear frontrunners at their outset may also have been decided by the campaign (J. Campbell 2001c).

The analysis of unsystematic campaign effects (chapter 8) over a longer span of electoral history (1868 to 2004) arrives at a similar estimate of the frequency of decisive campaigns. That analysis, based on both the closeness of the elections and the distribution of systematic effects, indicates that unsystematic effects may have made the difference to election outcomes in something on the order of five or six (14 to 17 percent) of the thirty-five elections.[4] In addition to the disputed Hayes-Tilden and Bush-Gore elections of 1876 and 2000, this group might well include one or more of the very close elections of the 1880s, the Wilson-Hughes race of 1916, the Truman-Dewey race of 1948, the Kennedy-Nixon race of 1960, and the Bush-Kerry race of 2004.

Given that systematic factors related to the election-year economy and incumbency may have also been decisive in a few other elections, it would appear that campaigns have probably been decisive in roughly one out of every five elections (and likely more often in competitive partisan eras and when incumbents are not in the race). While from one standpoint this comports with a view that campaign effects are minimal, from another vantage point it indicates that campaigns can be decisive. This real possibility of decisive campaign effects is enough to fuel the hopes and fears of everyone involved in presidential campaign politics.

How Much Do Systematic Elements of the Campaign Matter?
The analysis in the preceding chapters indicates that campaigns affect the vote, that they do so largely in a systematic fashion, and that the systematic effects of campaigns reflect three factors: presidential incumbency advantages, evalu-

ations and the conditioning effects of the election-year economy, and the narrowing effect of campaign competition. What is unclear at this point is how these three systematic components of the campaign fit together. How much does each matter to the effects of the campaign and to what extent do they jointly account for campaign effects?

The three systematic components of presidential campaigns are brought together to explain variation in campaign effects in the regression results reported in table 9.1. The campaign effects regression is an adaptation of the vote forecasting equation (table 1.5, though using revised GDP data). The dependent variable is the amount of change in support for the in-party candidate that occurred during the fall campaign. It is computed as the difference between the level of two-party support for the in-party candidate in the Gallup trial-

Table 9.1. The Systematic Components of Campaign Effects on the National Vote, 1948–2004

Dependent Variable: Campaign Effects on the National Vote for the In-Party Presidential Candidate

Systematic Components	Unstandardized Coefficients	Standardized Coefficients
Early September margin in the preference polls	−.56 (8.09)	−1.01
Second-quarter growth rate for the real Gross Domestic Product (GDP) (annualized, half credit or blame for successor candidates)	.55 (3.76)	.47
Incumbent President Running	.50 (.42)	.05
Constant	−.46	
N	15	
R²	.86	
Adjusted R²	.82	
Standard error	2.04	
Durbin-Watson	1.30	

Note: The coefficients in parentheses are t-ratios. Campaign effects are computed as the difference between the pre-campaign support (two-party) for the in-party candidate as measured by the early September poll and the two-party vote for the in-party candidate. The early September margin in the preference poll is the two-party support for the in-party candidate in the Gallup poll around Labor Day minus 50 percent. The poll and vote figures are reported in table 3.4. The GDP growth are the latest available measures (December 2006) from the Bureau of Economic Analysis.

heat polls around Labor Day and the in-party's share of the actual two-party vote. These campaign effects were reported earlier in table 3.4. Each of the three systematic components of the election is included as an independent variable. The first systematic component is the narrowing effect of competition as measured by the in-party candidate's margin in the September poll. Bigger leads at the outset of the campaign should narrow, and this should be reflected in a negative coefficient for the September poll lead. The second systematic component is the election-year economy as measured by the real GDP growth rate in the second quarter of the election year. The third systematic component is presidential incumbency measured simply as an indicator of whether an incumbent president is seeking reelection (coded 1 if yes and 0 if no). The regression results reported in table 9.1 include the standardized as well as the unstandardized regression coefficients. The standardized coefficients may be interpreted as indicating the relative importance of the three systematic components affecting the campaign.

As the regression indicates, campaign effects largely reflect the three systematic components of the campaigns. They account jointly for about 82 percent of variation in campaign effects. Of the three fundamental influences on campaigns, the narrowing effect of competition typically has had the greatest impact. Frontrunners typically lose about half of their September leads by election day. Since the typical Labor Day frontrunner has had about a seven-point lead, the narrowing effect of the campaign typically has made about a 3.5 percentage point difference. The election-year economy, or more specifically, the economy in the three months leading up to the campaign, exerts the second-strongest influence on campaign effects. Based on the estimated impact of the economy and the typical growth rate of the election-year economy (median = 4.3 percent annualized when an incumbent is running), the election-year economy typically makes about a 2.4 percentage point difference in the campaign (and about 1.4 points when no incumbent is running). Presidential incumbency has the smallest impact of the three systematic components (though part of its impact is felt through the economy). All other things being equal, the advantages of an incumbent president have typically yielded about a half-percentage-point shift in the president's favor over the course of the campaign (more when the incumbent's greater credit for a good economy is considered).

Localized Campaign Effects

The analysis to this point has been concerned exclusively with the national electoral effects of the general election campaign on the two-party popular vote. However, the national impact of campaigns on the vote is not the only possible electoral effect of campaigns. Presidential campaigns may also have local-ized effects on the vote that, though important to the vote in one or several states, may affect the national vote in only a minor way. Such localized effects of campaigns may be especially important given that presidential elections are decided by electoral votes, which are generally awarded on a winner-take-all basis according to the popular vote plurality in each state. As a result, even a small localized effect of a presidential campaign may swing a substantial num-ber of electoral votes. Thus, neglecting to consider the distributional effects of the campaign on the vote would underestimate the impact of the campaign.

Like the national effects of campaigns, localized campaign effects systemat-ically reflect either the fundamentals in place before the campaign begins or the unsystematic developments that take place during the campaign. Among the systematic localized effects of the campaign are local variations of the national factors. Most noteworthy of these are the effects of the election-year economy, which may vary across the nation. Some states or regions may be better off, and voters in these areas may react differently to the candidates during the campaign season than voters in areas with depressed economic conditions. Elsewhere I have found that election-year economic growth in a state has a discernible, if slight, impact on state presidential votes, even after taking the election-year growth rate of the national economy into account (J. Campbell 1992, Camp-bell, Ali, and Jalazai 2006).[5] It is also quite likely that the narrowing effect of the campaign would be felt differently in different states. Since presidential candidates are likely to begin the campaign with greater strength in some parts of the nation than others, the withering of support under the pressure of campaign competition is likely to be greater where the candidate's initial sup-port was greater.[6]

There is a second set of conditions that may systematically affect the cam-paign without having a corresponding national impact. In addition to any pre-campaign advantage that candidates might enjoy by being the "favorite son" of their home state or region, they and their campaign messages may be more warmly received during the campaign by voters in their home states or re-gions. Voters take pride in candidates who emerge from their areas and may feel somewhat more familiar with, and empathetic toward, those candidates. Several studies (Rosenstone 1983, Lewis-Beck and Rice 1983, Holbrook 1991, and J. Campbell 1992) have found that presidential candidates gain an extra 4 to 7 percentage points of the vote in their home state and that vice presidential candidates typically add 1 to 2.5 percentage points.[7]

In addition to these systematic localized effects of the campaign, there are undoubtedly some that are unsystematic. A critical element in any presidential candidate's campaign strategy is where the candidate should put the greatest effort in attracting votes. Presidential campaigns target key swing states crucial to assembling an electoral college majority. Candidates spend more time, campaign workers devote more energy, and the campaign organization buys more media time for campaign messages in states regarded as vital to the candidate's victory. There would seem to be little doubt that these efforts, if only at the margin, make some difference either in persuading voters or in mobilizing supporters to vote.[8] Given that presidential campaigns direct their efforts at precisely those states where they might most likely affect voters and swing important electoral votes, these unsystematic localized campaign effects, as small as they might be in absolute terms, may be very important to the results of elections. Between the systematic and the unsystematic effects of campaigns on the distribution of votes, it seems likely that the analysis of the national effects of campaigns alone probably slightly understates how often campaigns have been decisive to elections.

Why Campaigns Matter

In the first chapter of this book I offered six reasons why there have been serious doubts about the impact of presidential campaigns on the vote: (1) the stability of individual vote choices, (2) the prevalence of early vote decisions, (3) the stability and pervasiveness of partisanship in the electorate, (4) the minimal effects conundrum in which those most open to influence by the campaign are least attentive to the campaign, (5) the fact that even issue voting is often largely retrospective and does not require attentiveness to promises made by candidates during the campaign, and (6) the fact that elections can be predicted fairly accurately prior to the campaign. The preceding analysis of the theory of predictable campaigns concedes each of these points yet also concludes that campaigns do make a difference to the vote. In fact, this analysis has found that presidential campaigns make a considerably larger difference than previous studies have claimed. How can the findings of significant campaign effects be reconciled with the reasons to suspect minimal campaign effects? Put slightly differently, why do campaigns matter?

First, the reasons noted above for doubting the effects of campaigns do serve to limit campaign effects. While we have found that campaigns on average have made a difference of about four percentage points in the vote and have been decisive in perhaps one in every five elections, given the tremendous efforts put into them and the possible extent of effects, the actual effects of campaigns might be regarded as marginal. There is little doubt that partisanship and other factors that can be considered before the start of the campaign make the vote choice easy for many voters and effectively restrict the campaign's potential movement of the electorate one way or the other.

Second, the theory of predictable campaigns quite explicitly reconciles the predictability of elections and the effects of campaigns. The pre-campaign factors that allow us to predict elections with some degree of accuracy do so because they help to systematically guide the course of campaigns. The developments of campaigns are to a significant degree products of fundamental pre-campaign conditions such as the economy and incumbency and the quite predictable intensity of competition between the candidates. Moreover, the election-year economy, presidential incumbency, and the high degree of competition between the candidates are important contexts in which voters evaluate the development of campaigns. In short, elections are largely predictable because campaigns are largely predictable.

The third way in which suspicions of minimal campaign effects can be reconciled with the findings of greater than minimal effects concerns the nature of campaign effects on individual voters. Since the classic study of voting behavior *The People's Choice* (Lazarsfeld, Berelson, and Gaudet, 1968, first published in 1944) presidential campaigns have been seen as frequently reinforcing the predispositions of voters, occasionally mobilizing them to turn out, and only rarely persuading them to change their vote choices. These findings would seem to support a view of minimal campaign effects in the aggregate. In particular, the most prevalent effect of presidential campaigns, reinforcement, might appear to be not much of an effect at all.

More may be going on under the rubric of reinforcement than is often thought. Classical reinforcement suggests that the initial preference for a candidate, often in line with longstanding predispositions (e.g., party identification), is simply buttressed by the information picked up during the campaign. Although this is an effect of sorts, no votes are changed as a result. Other forms of reinforcement, at least the reinforcement of the voters' predispositions if not initial preferences, do entail changing votes.

An example of another form of reinforcement is one in which voters at the outset of the campaign intend to defect from their predispositions (usually partisanship) but change their intention and remain loyal as a result of the campaign's reinforcement of their long-standing predisposition. In Gelman and King's (1993) terminology, the campaign enlightens voters as to their preferences.[9] In different terminology, the campaign reminds voters of the basis of their partisanship and restores the perspective that might have been temporarily skewed by the nomination battles. In other words, the campaign refreshes partisanship.

Partisans upset about their party's standard-bearer may initially indicate indecision or even a preference for the opposition. As we have seen, most of those influenced by the campaign (i.e., those reaching their vote decisions during the campaign) come home to their party. One important impact of the campaign is to reassert partisan differences after nomination contests that directed attention to differences within the parties. Party loyalty among late deciders is not what it is among early deciders, yet two-thirds of late-deciding Democrats and three-quarters of late-deciding Republicans decide to vote for their party's presidential candidate. Unlike classical reinforcement, this form of reinforcement of predispositions, perhaps better termed restoration, may result in changes in the vote.

Yet another variant of reinforcement involves voters who are initially unenthusiastic about their party's candidate and perhaps consider abstention. These potential voters may have their predispositions reinforced (reinvigorated) enough by the campaign to stimulate their turnout. Just as some voters may flirt early in the campaign with the idea of defecting to vote for the opposition's candidate, other potential voters unhappy with their party's nominee may seriously think about sitting out the election. By reminding voters of the reasons for their predispositions, the campaign may convince voters that voting for their party's standard-bearer is worth the effort. Through both the reassertion and reinvigoration of partisanship, the reinforcement of predispositions (and its sometimes related mobilizing effect) entails a change in the voter's intended behavior. In these instances, reinforcement can produce a real campaign effect on the national vote.

Some Implications of Predictable Campaigns

That campaigns have wide-ranging effects and that these effects are largely systematic in nature are important findings in that they enable us to better understand the overall impact of presidential general election campaigns. Presidential campaigns matter to a greater degree and evolve in a more systematic way than previously thought. However, these findings may also have implications for the candidates and how they run their campaigns, for the media and how it covers campaigns, and for voters and how they observe campaigns. Our better understanding of campaign effects might also affect overall evaluations of how well campaigns function for the political process.

Predictable Campaigns and the Candidates

What do the findings that campaigns are significant and largely predictable mean for the conduct of campaigns by the candidates? In one sense, they do not mean much. Presidential candidates always run as hard as they can. Although there have been a few unsuccessful candidates who have been able to secure their party's presidential nomination for a second run, most presidential candidates get only one shot at the presidency and they want to make the most of it.[10]

The systematic nature of campaign effects and their potential magnitude may make a difference in the strategies that candidates adopt and in the psychology of those working on their campaigns. The most important systematic aspect of campaigns is their general narrowing effect. Understanding this effect ought to help keep campaigns working at a high pitch and to help keep up the morale of those working on the campaigns of trailing candidates.

The perspective and motivation of everyone working on a campaign, from the candidate to the volunteer working the phone bank, are affected by their reading of how the campaign is going and the prospects for winning the election. It is difficult to motivate candidate supporters who think that their candidate is either a sure winner or sure loser. Certainty works against effort. Why bother to work hard for a candidate if you are quite sure that it will not make a difference? Supporters of candidates with seemingly insurmountable leads may be so confident that their candidates will coast to an easy victory that they slack off. On the other side, supporters of a badly trailing candidate may feel so disheartened that they cut back their campaign efforts.

There is good reason for the optimism of supporters of frontrunners and pessimism on the part of supporters of trailing candidates. Frontrunners usually go on to win their elections. However, since the leads of frontrunners usually shrink by election day, the supporters of frontrunners may be more confident and the supporters of trailing candidates more disheartened than they ought to be. Moreover, despite the odds strongly favoring the pre-campaign frontrunner and the narrowing effect of the campaign along with unsystematic campaign effects that can range as high as three or four percentage points, few trailing candidates can be counted out entirely. Presumably, if both sides realized that the race was likely to become much closer than the early polls suggested, then both would be more likely to work as hard as they possibly could right up to election day.

The predictable campaign also can inform the strategy that candidates might adopt, at least in so far as how aggressive they might want to be. Presidential candidates can gauge where they would end up as a result of a "normal" campaign and act accordingly. If a candidate is the likely winner of the election after a normal campaign, with a bit of a cushion for some unsystematic campaign effects that might go against him or her, the candidate might adopt a more cautious strategy in an attempt to solidify his or her base. On the other hand, if the fundamentals suggest that a candidate is likely to lose the election, his or her only real chance of winning may be to run a more aggressive campaign, hoping that voter reactions will break enough in his or her favor to overcome the systematic aspects of the campaign. In point of fact, candidates generally react in just this way. Candidates who are running behind or even with their opponents are the more likely to "go negative" than candidates who are safely ahead. It is worth noting that the implications of the predictable campaign for the morale of supporters and the strategies of the candidates are to reinforce the competitive effects of campaigns.

Watching Predictable Campaigns

What are the implications of the theory of the predictable campaign for those who watch campaigns—the media and the public? Both the public and the media, especially the media, have been widely criticized for focusing too much on who is ahead and who is behind in the polls at the expense of paying attention to the serious content of the campaign, the issue positions of the candidates that make a difference to how the country will be governed after the election. The candidates' positions, philosophy, and character are what the election is about. This is what voters need to know in order to make a well-informed vote choice. This is what the media ought to be reporting in order to help viewers do their jobs as citizens rather than providing inordinate amounts of "horserace" coverage of the ups and downs of the polls and the related "inside baseball" coverage of candidate strategies (Patterson and McClure 1976; Patterson 1994; Sigelman and Bullock 1991; Jamieson 1992). Our question is this: Should the predictability of campaign effects on the vote (which, after all, concerns the politics and not the policy content of campaigns) increase or diminish both the media's and the public's attention in matters such as poll standings and candidate strategies?

There is an argument that recognizing that the effects of presidential campaigns are largely predictable ought to diminish interest in following the ups and downs of the polls. Taking some of the surprise element out of the movement of the polls ought to lessen interest in them. If everyone understands in advance that the poll margins will shrink and that the movement of the polls will reflect incumbency and the growth in the election-year economy, then these expected poll movements become less newsworthy and attention can shift to the more important substantive differences between the candidates.

However, the theory of the predictable campaign suggests that increased coverage of campaign issues by the press and increased attention by the electorate will not affect the decisions of most voters. This is because most voters have already made up their minds or can be reminded of the basis of their partisanship. Most voters have an easy or relatively easy time reaching their vote choices. For the vast majority, additional information about the candidates, their records, and their issue positions would make little if any difference to their vote.

Nevertheless, increased attention to the content of the campaign may be helpful to a small but important minority of late-deciding voters. About 4 or 5 percent of voters for major-party candidates in typical presidential elections are late-deciding independents who might benefit from an increased focus on the issue positions and leadership qualities of the candidates. Additionally, about another 9 percent of voters in the typical election are late-deciding partisans who decide during the campaign to defect and vote for the opposing party's candidate. These voters struggle with their choice, and additional information may make a difference. Perhaps an equal number, or at least some number, of late-deciding party loyalists also struggle with their choice but eventually remain loyal to their party. In total, perhaps a fifth to as much as a fourth of the electorate might benefit from additional attention to the substance of the campaign. This is a distinct minority but an important one. Although the net effect on the national vote of changes among these voters is likely to be small in absolute terms, as the analysis of unsystematic campaign effects demonstrated, even a small shift can be important for elections commonly decided within the range of 55 to 45 percent of the vote. In any case, attention to the campaign horserace is at best entertaining and at worst useless while attention to substantive issues is at best useful to making a decision and at worst edifying.

Evaluations of Campaigns

American presidential campaigns have never been held in very high esteem by either the public or by many scholars and journalists. The circus-like atmosphere of campaigns—the anachronistic and non-deliberative national conventions, the rallies, slogans, bumper stickers, yard signs, television commercials, and stump speeches—seem hardly to be the proper form of serious public debate about the nation's future. Their seemingly interminable length and superficiality also open them up to ridicule. Critics in recent years have also derided campaigns for their expense and for their harshness and negativity. Yet, in a system that reaches out to those with only sporadic and marginal interest in politics, some show-business techniques and simplification have been necessary to get as much of the candidates' messages heard by as many voters as possible and to build as much enthusiasm in the electorate for the candidates as possible. Nevertheless, however necessary the techniques of presidential campaigns might be, as campaign historian Gil Troy observes, Americans have found presidential campaigns to be "too lengthy, too costly, too nasty, and too silly" (1996, 4).

How might campaigns be judged in light of the theory of the predictable campaign? First, the theory suggests that criticisms of the conventions may underestimate their role in the process. It is true that the national conventions have not played a deliberative role in determining their parties' nominees for many years. As we observed in chapter 5, not a single convention since 1952 has been forced to cast a second ballot to award its nomination. The elimination of the two-thirds rule in the Democratic Party, the increased reliance on primaries in the selection of convention delegates, and the compression, or front-end loading, of the primaries have all made it virtually inevitable that one candidate will have effectively locked up the nomination well before the convention begins. As such, the conventions no longer perform their original function of selecting the parties' nominees. Modern conventions simply ratify the choice already made. However, while the nomination function of conventions now appears perfunctory, they perform an important function for general election campaigns. Following sometimes very divisive nomination contests, conventions help to reunify each party. Since the candidate trailing in the polls is usually the survivor of the tougher nomination battle, the consequence of conventions, like the consequences of presidential campaigns in general, is to increase the competitiveness of elections.

Second, the theory provides perspective on concerns about the length, cost, combativeness, and entertainment value of campaigns. As they are and have been conducted, campaigns bring partisans back to their parties, make election outcomes closer, incorporate reactions to the election-year economy into vote decisions, and to a lesser extent, give the benefit of any doubt to incumbents. Any change in the electoral process that would reduce the length, cost, feistiness, or liveliness of campaigns might also reduce these effects. Certainly the length of general election campaigns allows disappointments about contested nominations to fade and reminds partisans that differences within the parties pale in comparison to differences between the parties. Similarly, if campaigns were somehow made more polite, the partisan contrast might not be as clear to voters. Finally, any reduction in the amount of money spent by the campaigns, or any change that might make them less accessible to a marginally interested electorate, would diminish campaign effects of any sort.

In the end, evaluations of presidential campaigns depend on what one looks for them to do. Changes in campaigns might make them both less partisan and less competitive. From a positive standpoint, weakened campaigns would make for more definitive election results. Winning candidates would probably win by large margins if the campaigns had less of a chance to narrow their leads. However, weakened campaigns would probably also mean that parties would pay an even greater price for tolerating contests over their presidential nominations. It would also mean that some significant number of voters, albeit a distinct minority, would decide how to vote without the critical information they needed or would base their vote on their disenchantment with their party's nominee. On the other hand, if voting with more complete and clear information and with intraparty and interparty differences put in their proper perspective is desirable, then campaigns are doing their job. If competition in elections is valued for the interest and efficacy generated among voters and the incentive for responsiveness that it provides candidates, then campaigns as currently conducted are working to make elections a more effective institution for democracy.

★ *Epilogue*

The 2008 Campaign

AS THIS IS being written, in the first week of January 2007, the dust is still settling from the 2006 midterm elections. Democrats gained thirty-one House seats, six Senate seats, and with them control of both House and Senate majorities for the first time since 1994. Though the members of the 110th Congress are only just about to begin their term, the 2008 presidential campaign is already on the horizon. About a year from now the Iowa caucuses, the New Hampshire presidential primaries, and a flurry of other state caucuses and primaries will select delegates for the Democratic and Republican conventions to be held in late August and into September 2008. (The conventions in 2008 have been scheduled later than ever to squeeze every advantage possible out of public financing of the general election campaigns by spending the set amount of money over a shortened period of time). At those conventions, delegates will nominate the major parties' presidential candidates. From then it will be two months of nonstop campaigning until voters head to the voting booths (if they had not already taken advantage of early voting opportunities) to elect the next president.

Between now and then, certainly a great deal will change that may affect how the campaigns are conducted, what their effects will be, and who emerges as the forty-fourth president of the United States. With these caveats in mind, what can this analysis and the theory of the predictable campaign tell us as we head into the presidential election of 2008? What might we anticipate?

It all begins with the nominations.

The Democrats

Buoyed by their midterm victories and President Bush's poor approval ratings (in the high 30 percent range as of December 2006), a bumper crop of Democrats have expressed an interest in or have been talked about as a possible Democratic presidential candidate in 2008. The frontrunner, and most likely nominee, is Senator Hillary Rodham Clinton of New York, wife of former President Bill Clinton. In the top tier of Democrats challenging Senator Clinton for the nomination are Senator Barack Obama of Illinois and former senator and 2004 vice presidential candidate John Edwards. Also in the pack of challengers are Governor Bill Richardson of New Mexico, Senator Joe Biden of Delaware, Senator Christopher Dodd of Connecticut, and several others. Former Vice President Al Gore and Senator John Kerry, the party's nominees in 2000 and 2004, decided not to join the race.

As the most likely nominee, Senator Clinton would bring a number of assets as well as several liabilities into the campaign. On the asset side of the ledger, she has a huge fundraising advantage over her Democratic opponents, being married to the political equivalent of an ATM. She is well known (unlike flash-in-the-pan Howard Dean in 2004) and highly admired in Democratic circles. While she has tried to steer a middle course in her Senate career, hoping to make herself more palatable to centrists, in the process of doing so, she may have tarnished her reputation among some in her party's very liberal base (especially her votes in support of the Iraq War). Though this may give pause to some of the more purist liberals, one would expect that most Democrats are likely to forgive her if they think she is their best hope of retaking the White House.

On the liability side of the ledger, Senator Clinton carries considerable baggage into the campaign. Other than President Bush, it is difficult to think of another political figure who polarizes Americans as sharply as Senator Clinton. While many Democrats are enthralled by Senator Clinton, many Republicans loathe her. She generates enthusiasm in the Democratic Party's base but may even do more to energize the Republican Party's base. Typically between 40 and 45 percent of Americans have a negative or unfavorable opinion of Senator Clinton, and this is outside the campaign context that can drive those numbers higher. Her political history includes plenty of fodder for her opposition: her mishandling of the health care plan in the early 1990s, questions about her cattle futures deal, the White House travel office controversy, and a number of controversial activities in her husband's administration from questionable fundraising methods to the highly criticized pardons he issued in the last weeks of his term.

The Republicans

The Republican nomination picture is even less clear. Four candidates have been in the party's top tier at one point or another. Rudy Giuliani, John McCain, Mitt Romney, and Fred Thompson. Former New York mayor Giuliani led most of the national polls leading up to 2008. His strengths were his impressive record as mayor, especially during the 9/11 attack on New York, and his strong stand on the war on terrorism. However, he also had some substantial liabilities. There was a real question of how his liberal positions on social issues, along with his three marriages, would sit with the party's conservatives.

Senator John McCain of Arizona was strong in early polling, though not with the party's conservative base. They viewed him as too eager to cut deals with Democrats. By the fall of 2007, McCain had slipped into fourth place in the polls.

Former Massachusetts governor Mitt Romney worked his way into the top tier by attempting to fill the conservative void left by the McCain and Giuliani candidacies. Though national polls placed him in the top tier and his ground game in Iowa and New Hampshire put him in good stead in these key states, many conservatives were unsettled by a record often inconsistent with his more conservative positioning for the nomination.

With no candidate exciting the party's base, former senator (and recent actor) Fred Thompson of Tennessee entered the race in September 2007 and immediately joined the top tier. With strong possibilities of resonating with the base and reaching out to moderates, Thompson seemed well positioned for the run, though it remained unclear if he had waited too long to start his campaign.

Several other Republicans, most notably former governor Mike Huckabee of Arkansas and Senator Sam Brownback of Kansas, also were in the field.

Ten Points

Though it is impossible to say with much certainty at this point who the Republican and Democratic Party presidential candidates will be in 2008, the theory of the predictable campaign offers some perspective on the general election campaign that will follow. As the theory suggests, many of the most important factors affecting a campaign and ultimately an election are in place well before the campaign takes place. Although this is being written before many of those early fundamentals are in place, ten points about the 2008 campaign can be made.

First, the way in which the parties settle their nominations is important to the election. A party's presidential candidate is better positioned for the election if the nomination is secured early and amicably with the party united behind the nominee. A candidate who can turn his or her attention to the general election earlier than the opposition has a significant advantage. Candidates who lack this initial united front generally gain ground on their opponent during the campaign, but the more important tendency is that they usually begin the campaign at a disadvantage that they rarely make up for during the campaign. Whichever presidential candidate gets the better start off of the starting block before and at the convention has a big advantage in winning the race.

Second, there are reasons to think that both parties will be firmly united behind their nominees in 2008. On the Democratic side, they have been out of the White House for eight years and, at the risk of understating the case, they have not held the Republican incumbent President Bush in very high esteem. Their approval rating for President Bush in 2006 in thirty-one Gallup Polls through the entire year of 2006 was only 9 percent. Democrats were hungry for a presidential victory in 2004, as evidenced by their quick abandonment of Howard Dean for John Kerry based largely on Kerry's perceived greater electability. Four years later, they should be hungrier still.

On the Republican side, though they have held the presidency for two terms and would perhaps take their hold on the office for granted, there are several reasons to think otherwise. First, the extent of polarization in American politics does not apply only to Democrats. Just as Democrats have been upset by the Bush presidency, most Republicans are upset at the very prospect of a Democrat in the White House, especially if that Democrat is Hillary Clinton. Second, both of the Bush presidential victories in 2000 and 2004 were near-dead-heat elections. Neither win provides much room to take victory for granted. And if Republicans had been lulled into complacency by their presidential victories, the Democrats' congressional victory in the 2006 midterm (and the issues that it has generated in the interim between elections) should get their partisan juices flowing again.

Third, the parties going into the 2008 election are probably near parity in party identification, and party identification is about as strong among voters as it was in the golden age of the 1950s. In the 2004 election, Democrats held a slight edge over Republicans among all voting party identifiers (from leaners to strong identifications) of 47.7 percent to 46.6 percent, but Republicans had an edge over Democrats among voting strong partisans of 20.9 percent to 18.6 percent. Party loyalty rates, as noted in appendix A, are about as high as they were in the 1950s. The consequence for 2008 is that partisanship should help to keep this election close.

Fourth, the lack of an incumbent president in the 2008 race is an important factor. The second-term advantage that President Bush enjoyed in 2004 is not available to his would-be successor. The 2008 election is all the more unusual in that it will most probably lack a candidate who has served as or run for either the presidency or vice presidency before. The last election in which incumbency was so lacking was the 1952 race between Dwight Eisenhower and Adlai Stevenson. The 2008 election, however, may include a unique twist on incumbency if Senator Clinton, the wife of a former incumbent, is the Democratic Party's standard-bearer.

Overall, the absence of an incumbent in the race, particularly in a competitive party era, should make the 2008 election quite competitive. As table 5.2 demonstrated, of the thirteen presidential elections without an incumbent in the race from 1868 to 2004, the in-party won six times and lost seven times. The record for the in-party seeking more than a second consecutive term in this period is eleven wins and ten losses. Together, these won-loss records suggest a toss-up in 2008.

The record of the vote in open-seat presidential contests, especially in periods of competitively balanced parties, is even more compelling. According to the evidence presented in table 8.3, five of the seven open-seat presidential elections in competitive party eras were near-dead-heat elections (decided with a winner's share of the two-party vote of less than 51.5 percent). The winning candidate's vote in the two exceptions (1868 and 1988, non-dead-heat elections) was less than 54 percent. In short, the odds are quite high that the 2008 election, like the 2000 and 2004 elections, will be very closely decided.

Fifth, as in every presidential campaign and election, the economy matters. At this point the economy is healthy, and this should help the Republican nominee. However, the impact of economic conditions before the election year is almost entirely factored into public opinion as it gels around the time of the national conventions. From the standpoint of tilting the campaign, the economic figures to watch are the GDP growth rates from the first half of the election year and particularly from the second quarter (from April to June). The effects of the election-year economy will become factored into voter thinking and affect voter receptivity to the in-party (Democratic) candidate's campaign message. A first-half-year GDP growth rate of 3.5 percent (annualized) or more should help the Republican candidate's campaign, and a GDP growth rate below that should help the Democrat's (see chapter 6).

Sixth, both the electorate's polarization and the strength and parity in its partisanship make the political conditions of 2008 especially inhospitable for third-party candidacies. With partisans on both sides wanting so desperately to win the presidency and with both being so close to doing so neither is likely to leave any stone unturned in appealing to voters with inclinations to stray to a third-party candidate. As a result, third-party candidates are unlikely to attract much of a vote, though even a small vote may matter in a close race.

Seventh, do not pay much attention to the summer polls until late July and just before the conventions, and even then understand that they are subject to substantial change. The summer preference polls are notoriously volatile. While they are not meaningless, they should be heavily discounted. In the summer months, the presidential approval ratings (even when the incumbent is not running) are probably more indicative of which way the electorate is heading. Bear in mind that the neutral point in the approval ratings is probably somewhere in the low 40 percent range, well below the 50 percent point.

Eighth, the post-convention and early September polls are crucial. Once it is clear who the major party candidates are, a large majority of voters have effectively decided their votes. Frontrunners around Labor Day rarely go on to lose. Most voters know which party's candidate more closely corresponds to their vision of what the national government ought to be doing and can reach a decision quite quickly once they know who the candidates are.

Ninth, if the 2008 campaign follows historical patterns, the margin between the frontrunning and trailing candidates in the post-convention polls will significantly shrink by election day. The daily polls will jump around, but these movements will for the most part be temporary blips. Because of the overriding competitive nature of presidential politics, we should anticipate that the election will likely be significantly closer than a literal reading of the polls would indicate.

Tenth, at their heart, campaigns are about candidates giving voters convincing reasons to vote one way or the other. This is the ball to keep your eye on. As noted in chapter 2, vote choices generally are determined by the evaluations of values and performance. Each party's candidate is likely to enter the 2008 campaign with an advantage on one of these dimensions and a campaign message to highlight the advantage for voters.

The Democratic Party's candidate is likely to have an advantage in evaluations of the in-party's performance. The key performance issue leading into the 2008 election is likely to be the conduct of the war in Iraq. At this point, support for the Bush administration's handling of the war is quite low. The average of four national polls conducted in December 2006 indicated only 28 percent of respondents approved of President Bush's handling of the war in Iraq. Though these numbers can change in a year, and a successor candidate may be able to put some distance between himself and his predecessor on the issue, the issue of the war in Iraq is likely to be a burden for the next Republican candidate.

The Republican candidate, however, is likely to have an advantage over the Democrat when it comes to the electorate's assessment of the values that the candidates would promote. In the median national election from 1996 to 2004, 41 percent of reported voters in the NES claimed to be moderates (or unaware of their ideology), 36 percent said they were conservatives, and only 22 percent indicated that they were liberals. This fourteen-point values gap between conservatives and liberals is especially valuable to Republicans at a time in which the parties are increasingly seen as ideologically distinct and when the presidential vote choice has become more closely associated with ideological perspectives (Abramowitz and Saunders 1998). The fact that more voters found George W. Bush's views ideologically acceptable, that he shared their values, contributed to his margin over John Kerry in 2004 (Campbell 2005). The values gap should be a concern for whoever the Democratic presidential candidate is in 2008.

Partisanship in the American Electorate

THE MOST IMPORTANT concept in understanding American voters, and consequently campaigns and elections, is partisanship. The purpose of this appendix is to assess both the extent and dynamics of partisanship in the American electorate since 1952, when the first American National Election Study survey was conducted. With the NES surveys from each election since, we now have a continuous series of national surveys that measure, among many other things, partisanship in the electorate over more than half a century.

Partisanship is grounded in a psychological identification with a political party. Voters are partisans not because they register as members, or pay dues, or simply like a particular party, or even vote for a party's candidates. Voters are partisans because they have formed some attachment to, or bond with, a political party. This bond of party identification has been measured since the first NES survey by a set of three branching questions. Survey respondents are first asked the following: "Generally speaking, do you usually think of yourself as a Republican, a Democrat, an independent, or what?" If the respondent indicates that he or she usually thinks of himself or herself as a Republican or Democrat, he or she is asked: "Would you call yourself a strong Republican [Democrat] or a not very strong Republican [Democrat]?" If the respondent in answering the first question indicates that he or she considers himself or herself an independent, has no preference, or is identified with another party, he or she is asked: "Do you think of yourself as closer to the Republican Party or to the Democratic Party?"

From the responses to these three questions, the NES devised a seven-point party identification measure. At each end of the scale are those who identify themselves as strong Democrats or strong Republicans. Working in from these endpoints, those who initially indicate an identification as either a Democrat or a Republican but who say that this identification is "not so strong" are classified as weak Democrats and weak Republicans, respectively. Those who initially indicate that they are independent or have no preference but then say that they regard themselves as usually closer to one of the parties, are coded as leaning Democrats and leaning Republicans. Those who say that they were independents or have no preference and then indicate that they are not closer to one party more than the other are coded at the center of the scale as pure independents.

Using this party identification measure, partisanship in the electorate can be measured by the percentage adopting an identification with one of the parties, the strength of that identification, and its use, particularly in deciding how to vote. A highly partisan electorate would be one in which most voters identified strongly with one of the political parties and voted loyally for their party's candidates.

Views of Partisanship

How partisan is the American electorate? Research regarding the extent and trends in partisanship has wrestled with this question for some time. The intellectual history of the matter can be roughly summarized as passing through three periods: *The American Voter* period, the revisionist or issue-voting period, and the restoration of partisanship period (Fiorina 2002).

The initial work on partisanship emphasized its importance in the vote choice. *The American Voter* (A. Campbell et al. 1960), the classic study of voting behavior, established the prevailing view of the American electorate as highly partisan. Most American voters identified in some way with one of the two major political parties, and most party identifiers loyally voted for their party's presidential candidate. Party identification did not necessarily directly dictate how a voter would vote, but it strongly shaped the various partisan attitudes that spanned vote choice considerations. Partisanship was at the core of what people thought and how they acted politically.

This view of the centrality of partisanship was seriously challenged by research conducted in the 1960s and 1970s. The revisionist view of the American voter suggested that *The American Voter* study was time-bound, a product of the unusual political calm of the 1950s. According to the revisionist view, partisanship was not so all-important to voters. Partisanship itself was often shaped by the issues and vote preferences of the particular campaign, rather than exerting a largely independent effect on these evaluations. It was not the "unmoved mover" supposed by *The American Voter* perspective. The independent impact of issues had been greatly underestimated and the impact of partisanship was not only overstated but in decline.[1]

According to this view, the 1970s and 1980s was as an era of partisan dealignment. Voters became increasingly independent of party, and partisans were increasingly free to vote for the other party's presidential candidate. Early observers of this trend include Walter Dean Burnham (1970), who wrote of the "onward march of party decomposition," and highly respected political columnist David Broder (1971), who titled his book on the subject *The Party's Over*. The assertion of a party dealignment became commonplace.[2] Ansolabehere and Iyengar (1995), for instance, report in their study of media effects on voters that "to be sure, the ranks of Independent voters have swollen since 1964" (2). Abramson, Aldrich, and Rohde (1998) concluded in their quadrennial report on voting behavior that "for the moment *dealignment* seems to be an accurate term to describe the American political scene" (259). Silbey (1998) stated the position most extremely. According to Silbey, since the 1890s, the political parties "have been in sharp decline throughout the nation's political system, plummeting to their present position of limited relevance to most people in an increasingly nonparty, candidate-centered age" (4). Moreover, by Silbey's reckoning, "partisan decay continued *in the electorate* throughout the 1990s as it had done for so long" (19).

Perhaps no single scholar has been more closely associated with the party dealignment thesis than Martin Wattenberg. In *The Decline of American Political Parties 1952–1994* Wattenberg accepted dealignment as a given and sought "to assess the extent of the decline of political partisanship in the electorate, the nature of the decline, and the reasons for it (1996, 5)." Wattenberg's thesis extended beyond the claim that more voters were independent of parties. He argued that this growing independence was based not on neutrality or even dislike of the two parties but on a perception that the parties were irrelevant to voters.

The latest wave of research has challenged the dealignment perspective, returning to a perspective more akin to that of *The American Voter* and restoring partisanship as the centerpiece of voting behavior theory (Miller 1991, Bartels 2000, Hetherington 2001). The key to this restoration is what would at first appear to be an arcane issue of how to measure party identification and, more specifically, how to interpret the responses of the so-called independent leaners. Are the independent leaners really independents who were pushed into indicating a fleeting preference for a party or are they partisans who are reluctant to reveal their partisanship (or perhaps attracted to the idea of thinking of themselves as "independent")? In *The Myth of the Independent Voter*, Keith et al. (1992) determined that the independent leaners are in nearly all important respects more like weak partisans and unlike pure independents. They are "closet partisans."[3]

Observing research on the partisanship of the American electorate is in some ways like watching a game of ping-pong. Partisanship is all important, then it is not, then it is. What are we to believe? How partisan are voters?

The analysis in this appendix focuses primarily on four basic questions about partisanship in the American electorate. First, what portion of the American electorate can be identified as partisan? Second, how loyal are partisans to their party's candidate in presidential voting? Third, how has the portion of the electorate identifiable as partisans changed over time? Finally, how has the loyalty of partisans in the electorate changed over time? Answers to these specific questions will help us answer the macro-electoral question of whether partisan dealignment, partisan realignment, or both realignment and dealignment have taken place. Is the electorate as a whole significantly less partisan than it was (dealignment) and has the partisan balance between Democrats and Republicans significantly shifted from what it was (realignment)?[4]

The Partisan Record

As discussed at length in chapter 3, there is a problem in using NES data, especially in over-time aggregate analysis. The problem is that the survey data are not as representative of actual voters as one would hope. Usually it is not possible or at least not very easy to check on the accuracy of survey data. However, it is possible and quite easy to see that the national presidential vote reported in NES surveys in some elections is quite different from that reported in the actual national presidential vote count. As table 3.3 indicates, there has been more than a two-percentage-point difference between the actual and NES vote for either the Democratic or Republican presidential candidates in eight of the fourteen elections from 1952 to 2004. In some years (1964, 1968, 1992, and 1996) the differences were much greater. While some vote irregularities in the vote count undoubtedly have happened over the years and may explain a slight portion of these differences, most of these discrepancies are probably the result of various errors inherent in survey research. For most individual and cross-sectional research, these errors may not be especially problematic, but they may cause more difficulties in aggregate time-series studies. Fortunately, since the error is known, adjustments for it can be made. The reweighting procedure discussed in chapter 3 is one method of correcting for the known inaccuracies. Throughout this analysis we will be examining the corrected or adjusted partisanship data.

Before proceeding, I should also note that the analysis examines only the partisanship of reported voters rather than the entire voting-eligible population. Since several studies have shown that independents are less likely to vote than partisans, partisanship among voters is likely to be a bit higher than for the general electorate.[5]

Table A.1 presents the distribution of partisans in the electorate from 1952 to 2004 for the seven party identification categories. Table A.2 presents the percentage of each of the seven party identification categories who reported voting for the Democratic presidential candidate. To facilitate comparisons over time, the vote in these categories is a two-party vote. To obtain Democratic vote defection rates, simply subtract their loyalty rates from 100. Conversely, to obtain the Republican loyalty rate, subtract the Democratic voting rate from 100.

There is much to learn about the partisanship of the American electorate by merely perusing these two tables. Most strikingly, they demonstrate just how partisan the American voter has been and continues to be. With the exception of 1976, fewer than nine percent of voters in any election since 1952 have been purely independent. Democratic presidential candidates have rarely received more than 20 percent of the vote of any Republican Party identification category and only once (1964) received more than a third of these votes. Democratic presidential candidates have never received as much as 5 percent of the vote of strong Republicans. Although Republican candidates have fared better among Democratic identifiers, they have never done well. Although Nixon came close to winning half the vote of weak Democrats in 1972, in most elections Republican candidates receive less than a third of the votes in any Democratic identification category. In short, most voters identify with a party and loyally vote for its presidential candidate.

Beyond the overall impression of partisanship, we can best extract more systematic information about the general partisan composition and loyalties of the electorates by examining these data statistically. Tables A.3 and A.4 present time-series regression analyses for the partisan composition of the electorate (table A.3) and for party loyalty in presidential voting (table A.4) for each of the seven party identification categories. The trend variable in each case is a simple counter variable, the last two digits of the election year (plus 100 in 2000 and after). A positive sign indicates a positive linear trend in the percentage of the electorate in that party identification category (table A.3) or in the loyalty rate in presidential voting (table A.4). Since pure independents by definition have no loyalties, they are excluded from table A.4. In the lower portion of these tables the expected percentage and loyalty rates of each of the partisan categories is calculated for the first (1952) and last (2004) elections in the time-series. In addition, the expected percentage and loyalty rates of partisans, regardless of the strength of their partisanship, are calculated for these elections.

Table A.1. *Partisan Composition of the American Electorate, 1952–2004*

Party Identification	Election														
	'52	'56	'60	'64	'68	'72	'76	'80	'84	'88	'92	'96	'00	'04	Mean
Strong Democrats	23.2	23.4	22.1	26.4	22.6	16.4	16.5	20.9	19.1	19.5	18.7	20.9	20.4	18.6	20.6
Weak Democrats	23.7	22.1	24.3	22.6	24.1	25.3	22.9	21.0	18.5	16.2	15.9	17.5	14.3	13.6	20.1
Leaning Democrats	10.5	6.4	5.9	7.6	9.6	10.4	11.8	11.0	9.2	10.9	13.4	11.4	13.3	15.5	10.5
Independents	5.2	8.9	8.1	5.3	8.5	8.8	10.4	8.7	8.1	6.9	8.8	5.7	7.4	5.7	7.6
Leaning Republicans	7.3	8.3	7.5	6.9	9.4	11.4	10.8	11.4	13.6	12.4	12.9	10.9	14.1	10.7	10.5
Weak Republicans	13.8	14.8	14.4	16.1	15.1	15.1	15.4	15.6	15.7	15.2	15.6	16.0	12.9	15.0	15.1
Strong Republicans	16.2	16.0	17.6	15.1	10.6	12.7	12.2	11.5	15.9	18.9	14.6	17.6	17.6	20.9	15.5

Note: The data are from NES for those respondents indicating that they had voted in the presidential election. The data have been adjusted by reweighting to conform to the actual national popular presidential vote.

Table A.2. *Presidential Voting of Party Identifiers, 1952–2004*

Party Identification	Two-Party Democratic Presidential Vote in the Election of														
	'52	'56	'60	'64	'68	'72	'76	'80	'84	'88	'92	'96	'00	'04	Mean
Strong Democrats	85.0	86.2	91.4	93.9	92.7	75.4	91.5	89.3	88.3	93.4	96.6	97.7	97.3	96.7	91.1
Weak Democrats	64.5	65.0	72.6	77.6	71.1	51.0	75.1	65.5	67.2	71.0	79.5	89.2	88.5	82.6	72.9
Leaning Democrats	63.5	69.2	90.3	87.2	66.8	63.0	76.0	61.5	78.3	87.5	89.9	91.6	76.8	86.8	77.8
Independents	21.4	17.7	47.1	71.8	33.4	32.2	43.4	26.9	26.8	34.5	59.4	45.6	47.6	52.8	40.0
Leaning Republicans	7.4	7.0	12.8	20.2	5.2	14.2	14.4	13.8	6.3	14.5	12.5	20.8	13.3	10.8	12.4
Weak Republicans	7.2	7.8	13.6	36.6	12.0	9.8	21.8	5.3	5.5	16.0	15.7	19.6	12.9	10.5	13.9
Strong Republicans	1.7	.5	1.7	7.6	2.9	3.7	3.2	4.8	3.1	1.7	2.9	4.2	1.9	1.7	3.0

Table A.3. Trends in the Partisan Composition of Presidential Electorates, 1952–2004

	Percent of Voters Who Are in a Party Identification Category:						
	Strong Democrats	Weak Democrats	Leaning Democrats	Independent	Leaning Republicans	Weak Republicans	Strong Republicans
Constant	27.49	36.72	.68	8.49	1.86	14.66	10.11
	(8.46)	(14.22)	(.30)	(3.90)	(.94)	(12.31)	(2.69)
Election Year	-.09	-.21	.13	-.01	.11	.01	.07
Trend Counter	(2.16)	(6.55)	(4.47)	(.41)	(4.47)	(.34)	(1.48)
Number of Cases	14	14	14	14	14	14	14
R^2	.28	.78	.63	.01	.62	.01	.15
Adjusted R^2	.22	.76	.59	.00	.59	.00	.08
Std. Error	2.46	1.96	1.70	1.65	1.50	.90	2.84
Durbin-Watson	1.43	.87	1.50	1.77	1.67	2.04	1.11
Expected in 1952	22.91	25.67	7.23	7.90	7.64	14.92	13.72
Expected in 2004	18.33	14.62	13.77	7.32	13.43	15.19	17.34
Change	-4.58	-11.05	+6.55	-.59	+5.79	+.27	+3.62
All Partisans (Not by Strength)							
Expected in 1952		55.81		7.90		36.29	
Expected in 2004		46.73		7.32		45.96	
Change		-9.08		-.59		+9.67	

Note: The data are NES data corrected in the aggregate to match the actual division of the national presidential popular vote. The trend variable is a counter for the last two digits of the election year (e.g., 52 for the 1952 election up to 104 for the 2004 election). The figures in parentheses are t-ratios.

Table A.4. Trends in the Party Loyalty of Partisans in Presidential Voting, 1952–2004

	Partisan Loyalty in the Presidential Vote of:					
	Strong Democrats	Weak Democrats	Leaning Democrats	Leaning Republicans	Weak Republicans	Strong Republicans
Constant	74.45 (11.06)	43.24 (3.89)	54.17 (3.93)	94.26 (15.17)	86.03 (7.61)	97.05 (40.08)
Election Year Trend Counter	.21 (2.53)	.38 (2.77)	.30 (1.75)	−.08 (1.09)	.00 (.01)	−.00 (.01)
Number of Cases	14	14	14	14	14	14
R^2	.35	.38	.20	.09	.00	.00
Adjusted R^2	.29	.33	.14	.01	.00	.00
Std. Error	5.10	8.41	10.44	4.71	8.56	1.83
Durbin-Watson	2.02	1.64	1.50	2.45	2.01	1.88
Expected in 1952	85.55	63.01	69.90	89.84	86.09	97.03
Expected in 2004	96.66	82.78	85.63	85.42	86.14	97.01
Change	+11.11	+19.77	+15.73	−4.42	−.05	−.02
All Partisans (Not by Strength)						
Expected in 1952		73.16			91.02	
Expected in 2004		89.07			90.03	
Change		+15.91			−.99	

Note: The data are NES data corrected in the aggregate to match the actual division of the national presidential popular vote. The trend variable is a counter for the last two digits of the election year (from 52 for the 1952 election to 104 for 2004). The loyalty of a partisan category is the percentage of those voting partisans who voted for their party's presidential candidate among those voting for a major-party candidate. The overall expected party loyalty rates are weighted averages using the expected proportions of partisans who are strong, weak, or leaning identifiers (from table A.3). The figures in parentheses are t-ratios.

Table A.3 indicates that there have been some significant changes in the partisan composition of the electorate since the 1950s. The electorate in the 2000s has many fewer strong and weak Democratic identifiers, a few more strong Republicans, and more leaning Democrats and Republicans. The numbers of pure independents and weak Republicans are essentially unchanged. There are two possible explanations for these changes. One interpretation would emphasize the rise in leaning partisans. Alternatively, as the summary figures at the bottom of the table indicate, one might point to the nine-percentage-point drop in Democrats and the nearly ten-percentage-point growth in Republican ranks. Democrats and Republicans are now almost at parity. Democratic numbers dropped from the mid-50 percent to the mid-40 percent range while Republican numbers rose from the mid-30 percent to the mid-40 percent range. Which interpretation one should accept depends on how leaning partisans are counted. As Keith et al. (1992) conclude and as the following analysis of party loyalties further demonstrates, leaners are partisans. Counting leaners as partisans suggests that the important difference emerging in table A.3 is the partisan shift from Democrats to Republicans—the realignment. The change is most clearly seen in the 2004 election. As table A.1 shows, for the first time since the NES was conducted, strong Republicans outnumbered strong Democrats among voters in 2004.

In revealing evidence of a realignment, table A.3 is good news for Republicans and bad news for Democrats. However, table A.4 offers some good news for Democrats (and more bad news for those who still claim party dealignment). Over the last half century, Democrats became more loyal and Republicans less loyal in their presidential voting. The loyalty of Democratic identifiers increased substantially from less than 75 percent to almost 90 percent. Republican loyalty declined very slightly from a bit over 90 to about 90 percent. Loyalty rates increased for Democrats and remained about steady for Republicans.[6] In the 1950s and 1960s, Republicans were generally much more loyal to their party's candidates than Democrats were to theirs. In the 1980s and 1990s, with the rise of loyalty among Democrats, Democrats and Republicans were about equally loyal to their parties. Overall, both were quite loyal.

As already noted, table A.3 offers some evidence regarding how partisan leaners might best be treated. The loyalty rates of partisan leaners, whether in the 1950s or 2000s, and whether Democratic or Republican, were about as high or higher than the loyalty rates of their weak partisan counterparts. This is much as one might expect from Keith et al.'s (1992) analysis of partisanship and again suggests that leaners should be considered as partisans on par with weak partisans.

Political observers have long debated whether the political system has undergone political dealignment or realignment. If partisan dealignment had taken place, we should have observed fewer partisans and more independents, and, among those partisans who remained, partisan loyalty of both Democrats and Republicans should have declined to low levels. On the other hand, if partisan realignment had taken place, we should have observed a decline in the number of partisans in one party and a rise in the other, with partisan loyalty remaining robust. The evidence could hardly be clearer: a realignment has taken place, and there is virtually no evidence of change in either identification or loyalty rates that supports the partisan dealignment conclusion.

Table A.5 offers a different summary of partisan change over the past six decades and allows a more refined examination of the realignment or dealignment question. The electorates from 1952 to 2004 are grouped into three periods, the first two of which consist of four presidential elections and the last includes six elections. The average percentage of the electorates who were pure independents, strong partisans of either party, Democrats, and Republicans are presented for each period as are the changes that occurred between each period and overall from the 1950s and early 1960s to the mid-1980s to 2004.

In examining partisan change in this way it is easier to see why many concluded (prematurely, we now see) that the system had undergone partisan dealignment. Not only had the number of leaning partisans increased in the 1970s (misinterpreted as an increase in independents), but the percentage of pure independents increased slightly and the percentage of strong partisans dropped by more than nine percentage points. Even counting leaners as partisans, both parties lost ground (though only slightly) to independents.

The partisan dealignment of the 1970s was, however, both slight and temporary. It was part of a larger and very gradual secular realignment that, to no small extent, counted on the conversion and generational replacement of some Democrats into Republicans.[7] Between the 1970s and 2004 the percentage of pure independents returned to the 1950s level and the decline in the percentage of strong partisans was mostly reversed. Returning to the table A.1, there is less than a one-percentage-point difference between the average percentage of strong partisans in 2000 and 2004 as opposed to 1952 and 1956. At the same time, Democratic numbers declined by about five percentage points and Republican numbers rose by about seven.

Over the whole period, comparing the party system of the 1950s and early 1960s to that of the late 1980s to 2004, Democrats lost almost 7 percent of the electorate and Republicans gained a like amount. The party system realigned,

Table A.5. Summary of Changes in Party Identification of the American Electorate, 1952–2004

Period of Elections	Mean Percentage of the Electorate Who Are:			
	Independents	Strong Partisans	Democrats	Republicans
1952–64	6.9	40.0	54.6	38.5
1968–80	9.1	30.8	53.1	37.8
1984–2004	7.1	37.1	47.8	45.1
Change				
1952–64 to 1968–80	+2.2	−9.2	−1.5	−.7
1968–80 to 1984–2004	−2.0	+6.3	−5.3	+7.3
Overall Change				
1952–64 to 1984–2004	+.2	−2.9	−6.8	+6.6

Note: Each of the first two periods includes four presidential elections. The most recent includes six. The data are adjusted from NES data to be reconciled with the actual vote. See note to table A.1. Independents are "pure independents." Democrats and Republicans include "leaning independents." Strong partisans include both strong Democrats and strong Republicans.

not as spectacularly as in the 1930s, but the balance of power between the parties changed appreciably away from the Democrats and toward the Republicans or, more accurately, toward party parity. Whereas the Democratic Party had clearly been the majority party from the 1930s to the 1960s, partisanship in the late 1980s to 2004 is more competitively balanced.

It is quite understandable that realignments are not recognized as such while they are underway. It is difficult to distinguish long-term change from short-term change without some historical perspective. The recent realignment, however, was especially difficult to detect because it did not resemble the archetypal New Deal realignment of the 1930s. It was certainly not as quick, not as large, and did not produce a clear majority party (J. Campbell 2006). The current realignment took several decades to complete (because of the lack of a Republican Party in the South), produced a shift in the normal vote of about half the size (5.7 percentage points as opposed to 10.5 percentage points), and left us with a competitive party system rather than one with a dominant Republican or Democratic Party.

There are two other reasons why the current realignment was not recognized more quickly. First, the staggered nature of the realignment meant that different components of it did not occur at the same time (J. Campbell 2006). Realigning change was evident first in presidential voting in the late 1960s (relatively unimpeded by the lack of a southern Republican Party), next in party identification in the early 1980s (recognized identifications lagging behind

Table A.6. Realignment in Macropartisanship, 1952–2004

Dependent Variable: Macropartisanship (Democrats as a Percentage of Partisans)

Independent Variables	Uncorrected NES Data	Corrected NES Data
1984 Realignment (pre '84 = 0, post '84 = 1)	−5.39* (6.33)	−7.23* (8.89)
Democratic percentage of the two-party vote	.33* (4.63)	.12 (1.69)
Constant	42.07	52.98
Adjusted R²	.81	.86
Standard Error of Estimate	1.57	1.50
Durbin-Watson	2.30	1.84

Note: N = 14. * indicates p < .05, one-tailed. The coefficients in parentheses are t-ratios. The macropartisanship measure counts leaning independents as partisans, but does not include pure independents.

behavior changes), and finally in congressional voting in the mid-1990s (upon the development of a Republican Party in the South). Second, the NES data problem, the inaccurate reflection of the vote, may have partially obscured the true extent of partisan change.

Table A.6 presents regression analyses of the macropartisanship of voters from 1952 to 2004. Macropartisanship is calculated as the percentage of major party identifiers who identified with the Democratic Party (MacKuen, Erikson, and Stimson 1989, 1128). The equations specify macropartisanship as a function of a dummy variable for elections before 1984 (zero in 1980 and before) and the presidential vote (Meffert, Norpoth, and Ruhil 2001). The presidential vote is included to determine the extent to which macropartisanship is sensitive to short-term forces. The first equation is conducted using uncorrected NES data and the second is conducted using the corrected NES data as explained in chapter 3.

Somewhat different pictures of partisan change emerge from the uncorrected and corrected data. The uncorrected data indicates that the realignment of party identification in 1984 shifted about 5.4 percent of partisanship toward the Republicans, with Democrats declining from being 58.6 percent to 53.2 percent of partisans. This is calculated using a 50 percent vote. According to this uncorrected data, short-term political forces were statistically significant, shifting partisanship by about a third of a point for every point of the vote. The analysis using corrected NES data indicates that macropartisanship shifted about 7.2 percentage points between 1980 and 1984, that this change accounts for 86 percent of the variation in macropartisanship over more than five decades, and that short-term forces did not significantly affect macropartisanship in this period. The corrected data indicates a shift from Democrats having a 59-percentage-point lead prior to 1984 to a 51.8-percentage-point lead thereafter. Partisan change in the uncorrected NES data is less clear than in the corrected data, especially if short-term forces are not taken into account.

★ *Appendix B*

Time of the Vote Decision and Partisan Loyalty

THIS APPENDIX PRESENTS in tables B.1 through B.3 year-by-year breakdowns of the reported presidential vote in NES surveys from 1952 to 2004. Table B.1 presents the vote in each election aggregated by the time of the vote decision (early-deciding voters in part A and late-deciding voters in part B), party identification, and the vote choice. The 2004 vote is similarly aggregated in table 4.4. In each election year, reported votes for each candidate were weighted to bring the NES aggregated vote percentages for each candidate into line with the actual division of the national vote. In accordance with the research of Keith et al. (1992) and the findings in appendix A, the so-called "independent leaners" are categorized as partisans.

The electorate for each election is broken down at three levels: (1) by time of decision (early- or late-deciding voters), (2) by party identification by time of decision, and then (3) by presidential vote choice by party identification by time of decision. For example, in 1952, 61.5 percent of all voters were early deciders. This 61.5 percent of voters who were early deciders breaks down to 31.3 percent who were early-deciding Democrats, 2.3 percent who were early-deciding independents, and 28 percent who were early-deciding Republicans. Each early-deciding party identification category is then broken down by their vote choice. The 31.3 percent of early-deciding Democrats were composed of 25 percent who voted for the Democratic candidate and 6.3 who defected to vote for the Republican candidate. Table B.2 reaggregates the vote to display the vote choice differences between all early- and late-deciding voters.

Although there is variation from one election to the next, table B.1 demonstrates several points about electoral behavior. First, it appears that in general a majority of voters, and in many cases a large majority of voters, decide their

Table B.1A. Timing of the Vote Decision, Partisanship, and the Presidential Vote, 1952–2004

Early Deciders

Party Identification and the Vote Choice	Percentage of Reported Voters														
	'52	'56	'60	'64	'68	'72	'76	'80	'84	'88	'92	'96	'00	'04	Mean
All Early Deciders	61.5	71.6	56.6	59.8	46.7	55.8	48.6	49.3	65.6	56.1	47.2	63.3	54.4	70.7	57.6
Democratic Party Identifiers	31.3	34.5	26.8	37.5	24.3	25.5	23.9	24.0	28.2	26.7	24.2	32.8	26.8	33.1	28.5
Voted for Democrat	25.0	28.7	22.0	35.8	21.0	15.1	20.2	20.4	23.8	24.3	22.5	31.2	24.9	31.2	24.7
Voted for Republican	6.3	5.8	4.7	1.7	2.7	10.4	3.6	3.5	4.4	2.3	1.7	.8	1.4	1.8	3.7
Voted for Other	.0	.0	.1	.0	.6	.0	.0	.0	.0	.0	.1	.9	.5	.2	.2
Pure Independents	2.3	4.3	3.5	2.5	2.0	3.9	2.4	3.1	3.7	2.0	1.7	.7	1.4	2.3	2.6
Voted for Democrat	.3	.6	1.1	1.7	.1	.8	.4	.6	.5	.7	.9	.5	.5	1.2	.7
Voted for Republican	2.0	3.7	2.4	.9	1.8	3.0	2.0	2.5	3.2	1.3	.7	.1	.8	1.0	1.8
Voted for Other	.0	.0	.0	.0	.1	.0	.0	.0	.0	.0	.1	.1	.1	.0	.0
Republican Party Identifiers	28.0	32.8	26.3	19.7	20.3	26.4	22.4	22.2	33.7	27.4	21.3	29.7	26.2	35.2	26.5
Voted for Democrat	.3	.7	.7	3.8	.4	.3	1.4	1.3	.6	.6	.7	2.2	.7	1.0	1.1
Voted for Republican	27.7	32.1	25.6	15.5	19.9	26.0	20.9	20.8	33.0	26.8	20.3	26.7	25.2	34.2	25.3
Voted for Other	.0	.0	.0	.5	.0	.0	.0	.1	.0	.0	.2	.9	.3	.1	.2

Table B.1B. Timing of the Vote Decision, Partisanship, and the Presidential Vote, 1952–2004

Late Deciders

Party Identification and the Vote Choice	Percentage of Reported Voters														
	'52	'56	'60	'64	'68	'72	'76	'80	'84	'88	'92	'96	'00	'04	Mean
All Late Deciders	38.5	28.4	43.4	40.2	53.3	44.2	51.4	50.7	34.4	44.0	52.8	36.7	45.6	29.3	42.4
Democratic Party Identifiers	26.1	17.8	26.1	18.8	31.9	26.3	27.1	28.9	18.5	19.8	23.8	16.9	21.3	14.5	22.7
Voted for Democrat	16.5	10.0	20.1	12.9	17.2	16.2	20.2	15.8	12.4	14.4	13.9	11.5	16.7	11.5	14.9
Voted for Republican	9.3	7.2	5.6	5.9	7.0	9.4	5.8	8.8	5.8	4.8	2.5	2.1	3.7	2.8	5.8
Voted for Other	.3	.7	.4	.0	7.7	.6	1.1	4.3	.3	.6	7.4	3.2	.9	.2	2.0
Pure Independents	3.0	4.6	5.1	2.9	6.6	5.0	7.8	5.6	4.3	4.9	7.1	4.4	5.8	3.2	5.1
Voted for Democrat	.8	.9	2.9	2.3	2.0	1.7	4.0	1.4	1.5	1.6	2.3	1.3	2.6	1.5	1.9
Voted for Republican	2.0	3.7	2.1	.6	2.6	2.5	3.7	3.1	2.6	3.0	1.5	1.9	2.3	1.5	2.4
Voted for Other	.2	.0	.1	.0	2.0	.7	.1	1.0	.1	.3	3.3	1.2	.9	.2	.8
Republican Party Identifiers	9.4	6.0	12.2	18.5	14.8	13.0	16.4	16.2	11.6	19.3	21.9	15.4	18.5	11.7	14.6
Voted for Democrat	1.5	1.1	2.9	4.6	2.0	3.3	3.8	1.4	1.6	4.0	2.8	3.4	3.0	1.9	2.7
Voted for Republican	7.9	4.9	9.1	13.9	9.3	9.3	11.9	12.0	9.7	15.1	10.7	9.8	14.5	9.4	10.5
Voted for Other	.0	.0	.1	.0	3.4	.4	.7	2.8	.3	.1	8.5	2.3	1.1	.4	1.4

Table B.2. Vote Division by the Time of the Vote Decision, 1952–2004

| | Vote Choice of | | | |
| | Early Deciders | | Late Deciders | |
Election Year	Democrat	Republican	Democrat	Republican
1952	41.6	58.5	49.5	50.5
1956	41.9	58.1	43.2	56.8
1960	42.0	58.0	60.8	39.2
1964	69.5	30.5	49.3	50.7
1968	46.8	53.2	52.8	47.2
1972	29.1	70.8	50.0	50.0
1976	45.3	54.7	56.7	43.3
1980	45.5	54.5	43.8	56.2
1984	38.1	61.9	46.2	53.8
1988	45.8	54.2	46.5	53.5
1992	51.5	48.5	56.1	43.9
1996	55.1	44.9	53.8	46.2
2000	48.8	51.2	52.1	47.9
2004	47.5	52.5	51.9	48.1

Note: The vote percentages of those deciding their votes either early or late and include only votes for major party candidates.

presidential vote by the time of the national party conventions and before the general election campaign. On average about 58 percent of voters indicated that they had decided by the time of the conventions and did not change their intention during the campaign. In five of the fourteen elections, more than 60 percent of the electorate decided their votes before the campaign.

Second, the table reveals an interesting pattern about partisan voting. Although party loyalty is evident in the vote choice of late deciders, it is generally even greater among early deciders. This finding is most clearly revealed in table 7.5. Early deciders evidently were satisfied with their party's standard-bearer and could reach an early and loyal vote decision. If voters had some doubts about their party's candidate, they held off deciding how they would vote. While some eventually decided to defect, most remained loyal.

Third, the table indicates that most third-party votes come from late deciders. Four of the elections since 1952 have had a significant third-party vote: 1968 for George Wallace, 1980 for John Anderson, and 1992 and 1996 for Ross Perot. Wallace in 1968, Anderson in 1980, and Perot in 1992 each received better than 90 percent of their votes from late deciders and Perot in 1996 received nearly 80 percent of his votes from late deciders. The conventional wisdom is that late-deciding voters might take the unelectability of the third-party

Table B.3. Party Loyalty for Frontrunning and Trailing Candidates by Time of Decision, 1952–2004

| | | Percentage of Voters Who Were Party Identifiers with | | | | Party Loyalty Rates | | | | Percentage of Vote from Party Identifiers (Including Defectors) | | | |
| | | Early Deciders | | Late Deciders | | Early Deciders | | Late Deciders | | Early Deciders | | Late Deciders | |
Year	Party of the Frontrunner	Front	Trail	Front	Trail	Front	Trail	Front	Trail	Front	Trail	Front	Trail
1952	Republican	28.0	31.3	9.4	25.7	99.0	79.9	84.3	64.0	34.0	25.3	17.2	18.0
1956	Republican	32.8	34.4	6.0	17.1	97.9	83.3	81.5	58.2	37.9	29.4	12.1	11.1
1960	Republican	26.3	26.7	12.0	25.7	97.3	82.3	75.5	78.1	30.3	22.7	14.7	23.0
1964	Democrat	37.5	19.2	18.8	18.4	95.4	80.4	68.7	75.0	39.6	17.2	17.5	19.7
1968	Republican	20.3	23.7	11.4	24.2	97.9	88.5	82.3	71.1	22.7	21.4	16.3	19.2
1972	Republican	26.4	25.5	12.6	25.7	98.7	59.2	73.8	63.1	36.5	15.4	18.7	19.5
1976	Democrat	23.9	22.4	26.0	15.6	84.7	93.6	77.7	75.7	21.6	24.6	24.0	17.7
1980	Republican	22.1	24.0	13.4	24.6	94.1	85.3	89.5	64.2	24.3	21.7	20.8	17.2
1984	Republican	33.6	28.2	11.3	18.3	98.0	84.2	85.9	68.2	37.4	24.4	15.5	14.1
1988	Republican	27.4	26.7	19.2	19.2	97.9	91.3	79.0	74.9	29.1	24.9	20.0	18.4
1992	Democrat	24.1	21.1	16.4	13.5	93.0	96.6	84.4	79.6	23.2	22.0	16.6	13.3
1996	Democrat	32.0	28.9	13.6	13.2	97.5	92.4	84.6	74.2	33.4	27.5	14.9	11.9
2000	Democrat	26.3	25.9	20.4	17.5	94.5	97.3	81.9	82.9	25.6	26.6	19.7	18.2
2004	Republican	35.2	33.0	11.2	14.3	97.2	94.5	83.4	80.2	36.0	32.2	12.2	13.3
Mean		28.3	26.5	14.4	19.5	96.0	86.3	80.9	72.1	30.8	24.0	17.2	16.8

Note: These percentages are calculated for major party voters. Front refers to those voters who identify with the party of the frontrunning candidate. Trail refers to those voters who identify with the party of the trailing presidential candidate. Frontrunners and trailing candidates are determined by which candidate led in the early September preference poll. The final set of columns is the percentage of the vote going to candidate from that candidate's partisans as well as defectors from the opposing candidate's party. For example, the 34 percent of the vote to the 1952 frontrunner from early deciding partisans includes the 27.7 (.99 × 28.0) percent-age points from his own party and 6.3 ([1 − .799] × 31.3) percentage points from early deciding partisans of the opposition who defected to vote for him.

candidate more into account and drift over to vote for a major-party candidate out of fear of wasting their votes. However, it appears that of those voters who do vote for a third-party candidate, many delay their vote choice perhaps because it is a more complicated three-way choice.

Fourth, the breakdown reaggregated in table B.2 indicates that the vote choice of late deciders is usually more evenly divided between the major-party candidates than it is among early deciders. As table B.2 demonstrates, late deciders were more evenly divided than early deciders in nine of the fourteen elections examined. Table 7.5 (composed from the year-by-year breakdown in table B.3) indicates that frontrunners and trailing candidates, on average, are about tied in the votes of late-deciding partisans while frontrunners typically have about a seven-point advantage among early-deciding partisans.

Finally, an examination of table B.2 indicates that the candidate leading among early vote deciders usually wins the election, a further indication of the importance of the stable context for the campaign. The leader among early deciders went on to win eleven of the fourteen elections. The only elections in which the candidate receiving a majority of the early-deciding vote then lost the popular vote were 1960, 1976, and 2000. The Nixon and Ford majorities among early deciders were more than offset by the Kennedy and Carter majorities among late deciders. In 2000, George W. Bush had a slight lead among early deciders, but this was more than offset by Al Gore's lead among late deciders.

Notes

Introduction

1. Holbrook's finding of strong momentum effects may be a result of two factors. First, the narrowing effect of the campaign may be mistaken for a general momentum effect. A rise in the polls for the trailing candidate may appear as simple momentum, though the positive movement for trailing candidates rather than for frontrunners suggests that competition is driving the process (see chapter 2). Second, because Holbrook examines a time series of polls, unmeasured campaign effects may spill across poll readings and may be "picked up" or measured by previous shifts in the polls.

Chapter 1

1. Attention to the 2008 presidential election began before the 2004 election was over. Speculation about Hillary Clinton's presidential ambitions date back to her husband's administration. Early speculation also centered on who would be the non-Hillary Democrat, with prospects including Barack Obama, John Kerry, Al Gore, John Edwards, and Russ Feingold. With President Bush completing his second term and Vice President Cheney having no presidential aspirations, early speculation about Republican potential candidates included John McCain, Rudy Giuliani, Mitt Romney, and others. Pollsters also wasted no time getting geared up for 2008. PollingReport.com reported six polls conducted between the November 2004 election and March 2005 about voter "preferences" among the possible field of potential candidates for the 2008 election fully forty-three months away.

2. In addition to the general studies of presidential voting behavior that touch upon campaigns secondarily and the specific studies of particular presidential campaigns, there are a number of excellent general studies of presidential campaigns. Among these are A. Campbell et al. 1966; Patterson and McClure 1976; Hess 1978; Patterson 1980, 1994; Popkin 1991; Kessel 1992; Finkel 1993; Gelman and King 1993; Holbrook 1996a; Just et al. 1996; Troy 1996; and Alvarez 1997. There are also several excellent treatments of presidential campaigns in texts on elections and voting behavior. Among these are Asher 1992; Polsby and Wildavsky 1996; and Wayne 1997. Also, though principally studies of individual elections, the election series by Paul R. Abramson, John H. Aldrich, and David W. Rohde (1982, 1986, 1990, 1994, 1998, 2003, 2006) since 1980 does an especially good job of setting an election and its campaign in context relative to previous

campaigns and elections. Finally, Boller (1984) presents an excellent and lively collection of anecdotes about presidential campaigns.

3. Ansolabehere and Iyengar nicely summarize the conventional academic wisdom about the effects of campaigns in observing that political scientists have "been hard-pressed to identify any effects and have concluded that campaigns in general and campaign advertising in particular are relatively unimportant determinants of electoral outcomes. In fact, political scientists routinely forecast presidential and statewide elections using models that ignore campaign-related factors altogether. Presidential elections, for instance, are thought to hinge on the state of the country's economy and the popularity of the incumbent president, with the competing campaigns having negligible effects on the outcome" (1995, 17).

4. Those voters who had an initial vote intention in the May survey wave and maintained it throughout the campaign were classified as constants by Lazarsfeld, Berelson, and Gaudet (1968, 67). After accounting for the three types of changers identified in the study, 49 percent of respondents are left as constants (65–66). In their examination of the consistency of vote intentions between May and October, 53 percent were identified as holding the same intention (102).

5. Forty-three percent of respondents were classified neither as truly stable nor as changers. Crystallizers (28 percent) were those who in May could not report a preference and later made a decision. The eventual votes of crystallizers split evenly between the Democrats and Republicans. Waverers (15 percent) indicated an initial preference, drifted away from it (usually indicating indecision, but sometimes indicating a preference for the other candidate), and then returned to their original preference.

6. I refer to the 8 percent of party changers as being *likely* cases of campaign-induced change rather than certain evidence of campaign effects because there are alternative explanations for all or some number of these changers. First, rather than the campaign causing these voters to change their minds, there is always the possibility of measurement error. That is, a few may have misunderstood the vote intention question or the surveyor may have made an error in recording the response at one point. Second, some of these voters may have changed their minds because they thought about their choice some more and not because of anything they heard or saw during the campaign. For example, a voter might have initially favored Roosevelt in the election and, working with the same information, might have changed his or her mind upon greater reflection and then favored Willkie. As Lazarsfeld, Berelson, and Gaudet concluded, "the figure for conversion is probably high. In any case conversion is, by far, the least frequent result . . . of the campaign" (1968, 104).

7. Six percent of voters shifted their vote intentions from Roosevelt to Willkie, and this was partially offset by a 2 percent shift from Willkie to Roosevelt.

8. The four out of five or 80 percent figure was calculated from chart 17 in *The People's Choice* (Lazarsfeld, Berelson, and Gaudet 1968, 54). *Voting* (Berelson, Lazarsfeld, and McPhee 1954, 18) presents a chart indicating that 64 percent of respondents in their 1948 survey indicated that they had made their final vote decision by June and that an additional 15 percent had decided by August of that election year. Corroboration from other studies was also noted in *Voting*'s inventory of findings appendix as finding number 176 (Berelson, Lazarsfeld, and McPhee 1954, 345).

9. *The American Voter* (Campbell, Converse, Miller, and Stokes 1960, 41) study

found that 65 percent of the 1952 electorate and 76 percent of the 1956 electorate indicated that they knew at or before the national party nominating conventions who they would vote for. If some voters regard reporting a late decision as being open-minded about the candidates, the reports of early decision-making by voters may be understated. Moreover, *The American Voter* study reported that 20 percent of survey respondents in 1952 and 11 percent in 1956 decided after the convention or during the campaign, though not in the last two weeks before election day. This category leaves a bit of ambiguity for our purposes since we might treat decision-making immediately after the conventions as distinct from decision-making fifteen days out from the election. The former might be considered as a pre-campaign decided vote and the later as a potentially campaign-influenced vote. In any case, this is another reason to regard reports of pre-campaign decision-making as low estimates. The conservative estimates of the time of vote decisions presented in appendix B indicate that typically about 58 percent of voters decided at or before the party conventions and reported voting for the candidate that they had previously said that they intended to vote for.

10. Does the fact that those voters who said that they decided early on in the election year mean that they "tuned out" the campaign and could not have changed their minds? No. Hypothetically, a development of great importance could have re-opened the decision for these voters and caused them to change their vote intention. However, as a practical matter, after the campaign ended these voters reported that their decisions were made very early in the year.

11. In *The American Voter* (1960), Campbell, Converse, Miller, and Stokes identified six kinds of partisan attitudes: those about the personal attributes of each of major-party presidential candidates, group interests, domestic policy issues, foreign policy issues, and "the comparative record of the two parties in managing the affairs of government" (33). Since these partisan attitudes are, collectively, highly determinative of the vote choice, we can safely infer that factors causing their stability would likewise cause stability in vote intentions. Also, there is a diverse literature regarding the minimal effects conundrum. See Lazarsfeld, Berelson, and Gaudet 1968; Klapper 1960; MacKuen 1984; and Zaller 1992.

12. At the extreme, some responses on surveys may not reflect opinions at all. Converse (1964) has characterized these responses without conviction as non-attitudes. Achen (1975), however, viewed instability in responses as indicative of internal variance in opinions and errors in our abilities to measure opinions. Of course, as in most things, with attitudes we are dealing with a continuum. In this case it ranges from random-like responses lacking any accompanying opinions to deeply rooted and firmly held convictions.

13. Patterson and McClure's (1976) finding that political advertisements have a greater impact than television news on voters nicely fits with this minimal effects scenario. Advertisements have a greater impact, among other reasons, because the audience that they reach contains many who are only marginally interested in politics whereas the news audience is self-selected of those who are already knowledgeable and relatively impervious to change.

14. Zaller (1992) elaborated upon and extended Converse's information flow model. Zaller's analysis suggests that those with medium levels of political interest and stored and new information are the most changeable. However, the more likely scenario is that those most likely to have an opinion change are those with relatively low levels of knowledge and relatively high levels of new information. This

combination of characteristics would seem to be common among many younger voters. Additionally, moderate voters would be closer to a tipping point between voting for one candidate or the other and so less of an opinion change would be necessary to change their vote. For a comparison of Zaller's and Converse's models see Campbell 1997b, 22–29 and 265–66.

15. Research on issue voting often draws a distinction between retrospective and prospective voting. Retrospective voting rewards or punishes candidates based on evaluations of their past performance on that issue (most commonly the economy, but the reasoning would apply to any issue). Prospective voting is based on what voters believe that the candidates would do if elected. Candidate platforms and promises come into play in prospective issue voting but not in retrospective voting. The distinction between retrospective and prospective, however, is really a false choice. Voters, like anyone making any decision, look to the past to learn about the future. Voters do not vote for a candidate simply to reward them for good past performance but because that past performance leads voters to believe that the candidate will continue to do a good job in the future. Similarly, voters are not so gullible that they take literally every promise that candidates feed them. Experience tells voters which promises might be sincere and which might lack credibility. Voters are neither purely retrospective nor purely prospective. They may have different time horizons and different rates for discounting old experiences, but they look to the past in order to learn about what candidates might do in the future so that they can make a reasonably intelligent choice in the present. In any case, the campaign supplies but a part of the needed information, and that information, in the context of the candidates' vote seeking, may also be substantially discounted by skeptical voters.

16. It should be noted that election forecasting is not without its detractors. For example, Philip Tetlock (2005) termed the 2000 election forecasts a "fiasco," writing that the modelers declared that Americans could ignore the campaign and that "Gore would defeat Bush by decisive, even landslide, margins" (25). It is true that two models in 2000 forecast a Gore landslide and that several others were well off the mark as well. However, no one has claimed that all forecasting models are strong and none claim perfection. That said, several models (including the ones examined here) were reasonably accurate in 2000 and predicted that Gore would win the popular vote, which he did (J. Campbell 2001d). The trial-heat and economy model, before it was revised to assign partial credit for the economy to successor candidates, was 2.6 percentage points off the actual vote in 2000. This was only two tenths of a point less accurate than the post-election NES vote distribution. Finally, a major point of this book, as well as Holbrook (1996a), is that campaigns matter and should not be ignored.

17. There is a clear ancestry of the Abramowitz (1988) popularity-economy-term forecasting model. The Abramowitz model essentially appends the third-term dummy variable to the popularity-economy model developed by Michael Lewis-Beck and Thomas Rice (1984). The Lewis-Beck and Rice model, in turn, is derived from Edward Tufte's (1978) popularity-economy model. Tufte's explanatory model was not explicitly constructed as a forecasting model and was not concerned with offering a forecast prior to election day. A second line of lineage for this model is Sigelman's (1979; also Brody and Sigelman 1983) analysis of presidential popularity and the presidential vote.

18. The presidential approval rating is the percentage of the public indicating in the

July Gallup poll that they approve of the way the president is performing his job. The growth rate in the economy is measured as the change in the Gross Domestic Product (GDP, in constant dollars) in the first half of the election year. The measure of the first-half GDP growth rate is reported by the U.S. Bureau of Economic Analysis in its August release.

19. The effects of the election-year economy and incumbency are also evident in most other presidential election forecasting models. See Lewis-Beck and Rice 1992 and the collection of forecasting articles in a special issue of *American Politics Quarterly* published before the 1996 presidential election. These presidential election forecasting articles include J. Campbell 1996; Abramowitz 1996; Norpoth 1996; Lewis-Beck and Tien 1996; Wlezien and Erikson 1996; and Holbrook 1996b. The impact of the economy, using various economic measures (opinions about the economy as well as actual economic activity), is explicitly a part of each of these models. The impact of incumbency is explicitly part of the Abramowitz and Norpoth models but is implicit in other models. It is implicitly included by the decision to orient the analysis in terms of the in-party (rather than Democrats versus Republicans). The in-party advantage (which is often the incumbent advantage) in these models can be determined by examining the predicted vote under neutral circumstances. In the case of the trial-heat preference poll and economy model, the in-party advantage can be determined by examining the predicted in-party vote with a fifty-fifty split of the preference poll and with a neutral amount of second-quarter economic growth.

20. In the thirty-four presidential elections from 1868 to 2004 (excluding the aberrant election of 1912 because of the split Republican vote for William Howard Taft and former Republican president Theodore Roosevelt), the winning candidate received more than 60 percent of the national two-party vote in only six elections (Theodore Roosevelt in 1904, Harding in 1920, Coolidge in 1924, Franklin Roosevelt in 1936, Johnson in 1964, and Nixon in 1972) and has never received more than 65.2 percent of the vote.

21. This refers to the presidential rose garden outside the Oval Office at the White House. The reference suggests that the president campaigns from the White House surrounding himself with all of the symbols of office, hoping that the electorate's respect and deference for the office of president influence their views about the person occupying the office.

Chapter 2

1. The indirect effect of these fundamentals on the election results is one of several important differences between the theory of predictable campaigns and other theories. Holbrook's (1996a) equilibrium theory, for instance, supposes that the fundamentals set some sort of "equilibrium" and "around this equilibrium level we expect to see campaign-induced shifts in public opinion" (46). Although Holbrook notes that "campaign events are hypothesized to function in such a way as to bring opinion into equilibrium" (65), the theoretical relation between the fundamentals and the campaign is unclear and the discussion and analysis generally suggest that the campaign is independent of the fundamentals. For example, in reviewing the success of forecasting models, Holbrook observed that "one possible interpretation of these results is that the difference between the actual outcomes and the forecast outcomes represents the effects of unspecified

variables, possibly the effects of the campaign" (31). Since the forecasts are constructed from the fundamentals or national conditions and the errors of the forecasts are statistically independent of the predictor variables (the fundamentals), Holbrook's association of campaign effects with the forecast errors suggests an assumption that campaign effects are unaffected by the fundamentals, though Holbrook also suggests that campaign effects draw public opinion toward the pre-campaign established equilibrium and this suggests an interactive relationship between the pre-campaign fundamentals and the campaign (56–57).

2. With half of the electorate susceptible to campaign effects, a two-thirds to one-third split of the vote would shift 33.5 percent to the candidate advantaged by the campaign and 16.5 percent to the opponent. The difference is a vote shift of 17 percentage points. In the more typical situation of one-third of the electorate open to the campaign, a two-to-one split would shift 22.1 percent to the candidate advantaged and 10.9 to the opponent, for a net shift in the vote of 11.2 percentage points. If one makes a more liberal assumption of a three-to-one campaign split, the net upper-bound effects would be 25 percentage points in the first instance and 16.5 percentage points in the latter.

3. The seventeen-percentage-point shift occurred in the 1976 election. About 45 percent of voters in that election indicated that they decided between the conventions and election day.

4. One piece of evidence that simultaneously illustrates the lack of political sophistication and knowledge in a large portion of the public are the responses to a 1986 NES question regarding President Ronald Reagan's ideology. Respondents were asked the very simple question of whether Reagan was a conservative, a moderate, or a liberal. After more than two decades on the national political stage as the most successful conservative politician in at least half a century, only about half (51 percent) identified Reagan as a conservative. The other half were unable to identify the most conservative president since the New Deal as a conservative. Twenty-two percent of respondents said that they could not answer the question, 11 percent said that Reagan was a moderate, and an astonishing 16 percent thought he was a liberal.

5. Bartels (1996) raises doubts about whether many voters know enough to cast a vote in line with how they would vote if they were fully informed. He contrasts how "fully informed" voters would have voted with how less than fully informed voters report having voted. He finds that the information shortfall has worked to the advantage of incumbent presidents by about five percentage points and to the advantage of Democratic candidates by about two percentage points. There are reasons to be skeptical of these findings. First, the simulation of the vote is based entirely on the relation of voter characteristics (age, race, gender, region, etc.) to the reported vote and excludes voter attitudes. Second, the probit simulated vote equation correctly classifies only between 68 and 75 percent of reported votes (Bartels 1996, tables 1 through 8). Third, though Bartels carefully addresses the matter of whether unmeasured characteristics (such as attitudes) may have produced different vote effects for the informed versus uninformed portion of a demographic category and claims that these unmeasured characteristics, in order to confound the analysis, must be "(1) strongly correlated with differences in political information, (2) *not* be *consequences* of differences in political information, and (3) operate distinctively in a particular demographic group" (215), it would seem possible that voters in certain groups with different attitudes might well be

judged to be less informed and, in fact, their different attitudes may cause them to see less need to become better informed. For instance, very liberal voters within a group may find little need to accumulate information in order to determine that they always favor the Democratic presidential candidate to the Republican. If their demographic group is predominantly Republican, the simulation might judge them to have voted for the Democratic candidate out of ignorance when, in fact, it was their preference. Luskin 2003 also raises a series of objections to Bartels' analysis. Though Lau and Redlawsk (1997, 2006) move away from Bartels' reliance on socio-demographics, they rely on the limited set of issue items in the NES studies (a small set of possible issues with a predetermined frame that may be inconsistent with the way that the voter sees the issue) as well as a limited set of social-group linkages. They find that only about 72 percent of voters typically cast "correct votes." Perhaps the severest challenge to these analyses is that nearly 90 percent of voters vote for candidates who are consistent with their statements regarding what they like or dislike about the candidates (see Kelley and Mirer 1974 and Kelley 1983). Some portion of these might have altered their vote with additional information, but to assert that these consistent voters are not voting correctly forces researchers to second-guess the voter about the voter's own beliefs and attitudes in response to open-ended questions.

6. The fundamental simplicity of the vote decision is well stated in Kelley and Mirer's "The Simple Act of Voting" (1974) and in Kelley 1983. Kelley and Mirer constructed and examined a preference index that they called the "voter's decision rule." The rule was based on a simple count of a respondent's number of responses to the NES questions about what the respondent likes or dislikes about each party's presidential candidate, with party identification serving as a tiebreaker. Their empirical analysis indicated that the vote expected by the voter's decision rule corresponded in most cases with the reported vote. It has also been argued that a rational vote choice is not only simple but can also be made with relatively low levels of information (Neuman 1986; Page and Shapiro 1992). The notion that a reasoned vote need not be a highly informed vote has been well made by Samuel Popkin (1991, 9) in his theory of "low-information rationality."

7. The weighting procedure used to bring NES data into line with the actual vote is explained in chapter 3.

8. The average absolute change of partisans from one election to the next was 2.2 percentage points for Democrats, 2.0 percentage points for Republicans, and 1.9 percentage points for independents. This may overstate the extent of change among all potential voters since these differences may be the result of turnout rate changes among partisans from one year to the next as well as changes in party identifications.

9. The campaign message version of the minimal effects conundrum deserves elaboration. The campaign information most likely to be believed by voters (to pass their perceptual screen) and therefore the most likely to be promoted by the candidates' campaigns is information that is most consistent with the voters preexisting beliefs about the candidates. Since this information is quite consistent with most views, it is unlikely to change those views. Information that would most likely challenge and possibly change preexisting beliefs is, ironically, unlikely to be believed and therefore unlikely to be offered by candidates. The fear of a backlash against outrageous claims reinforces this. The campaign strategies of presidential candidates tend to emphasize their positive stereotypes and

downplay their negative stereotypes. The campaigns are less likely to try to make major changes in the public's negative stereotypes of the candidates. Two examples illustrate the point. In the 1964 campaign, Johnson's campaign ran the infamous "daisy" ad only once. The ad, synchronizing the countdown to a nuclear explosion with a little girl picking the petals off of a daisy, outrageously suggested that Johnson's opponent Barry Goldwater was too trigger-happy to be trusted as commander-in-chief. The charge was too harsh and too outrageous to move voters and was aired only once. Similarly, James Farley recounted that, in the 1932 campaign, the Republicans overreached by trying to "sell the nation the idea that John Garner, Democratic candidate for Vice President, was a Red, or at least had Communist leanings" (1938, 162). According to Farley, the attempt failed miserably.

10. Aside from studies of presidential approval, there is relatively little literature on the presidential incumbency advantage. Among those who have addressed this advantage are Page (1978), Light and Lake (1985, 86), and Tenpas (2003).

11. The generally smoother road to renomination for incumbents may have a few potholes in the more open, post-reform nomination system. Although the nominating conventions for President Ronald Reagan in 1984, President Bill Clinton in 1992, and President George W. Bush in 2004 were more like coronations, Presidents Gerald Ford in 1976 and Jimmy Carter in 1980 faced very rigorous challenges from Ronald Reagan and Ted Kennedy, respectively. While the renomination of President George H. W. Bush in 1992 was never seriously in doubt, challenger Pat Buchanan did not make the road to renomination an easy one.

12. There is a fifth reason that presidential incumbents might run especially strongly in general election campaigns. Incumbents might fare better in general election campaigns because those that would not do well have early and definite signs of trouble and may decide not to run. That is, there may be some self-selection of more successful incumbents. Although most presidents who see political trouble in the next election choose to seek their party's nomination anyway, perhaps because of pride or hope from the advantages of incumbency, some decide to avoid a bitter fight and the real possibility of defeat. The most recent case of this sort was President Lyndon Johnson's decision not to seek renomination by the Democrats as their 1968 presidential candidate.

13. Evidence regarding the narrowing effect is reviewed at length in chapter 7, but the several studies cited have found evidence in the polls that the leads of frontrunners do generally shrink over the course of the typical campaign. Additionally, anecdotal evidence of this effect can be found in Irving Crespi's review of the accuracy of pre-election polls (1988). The highly regarded pollster Burns Roper is quoted by Crespi as observing that "almost without exception, the indicated front-runner in the polls fared worse than the polls said he would" (1988, 2).

14. Both campaigns are first-rate in the sense that there are no resource barriers to acquiring top-notch assistance, and both candidates have demonstrated an ability to secure their party's highly prized presidential nomination. To secure the nomination, a candidate must have either been a consensus choice of the party or have successfully competed against a field of prominent candidates for the nomination. In either case, the candidate has demonstrated considerable political strength and organizational acumen at least in the nomination process. There are cases in which campaigns are better run than others. However, the differences may appear greater than they really are. The campaigns of winning candidates

tend to be evaluated as better than they were and the campaigns of losing candidates are often seen as being more inept than they were. The reason for this distortion is that the fundamentals affecting each candidacy are usually not taken into account in evaluating campaign efforts. For instance, some have suggested that Dukakis's 1988 campaign was poorly run. Like most campaigns, it is safe to say that it could have been run better. Would this have made much of a difference in the vote? Probably not much. The context of the campaign, the raw materials of the election, substantially constrained the effect that the campaign could have on voters.

15. An analogy to batting averages in baseball may help clarify this point. Suppose two hitters both batted well above average over the first half of a baseball season. One went on to bat at the league's average for the remainder of the season and the second did not play the remainder of the season because of an injury. At the end of the season, the batting average of the first player would be lower than the average of the season-shortened second player. The first hitter's batting average for the season would be a weighted average of the above-average first half and the average second half (weighted by the number of at-bats in each half). The second hitter's batting average for the entire season would be equal to his average over the first half of the season since he did not have an at-bat in the second half of the season. The situation of the first hitter is analogous to an election with balanced campaign effects, while the situation of the second hitter is analogous to an election without a campaign. I thank Mike Mahar for suggesting this analogy.

16. I found this quotation on Compuwork's *Sounds* CD-ROM (1995). The recording of the quotation is referenced as NE0118.

17. It is also important to distinguish both the narrowing effect and momentum from the so-called bandwagon effect (Simon 1954). The bandwagon effect is reflected in Lord James Bryce's observation about American politics: "The maxim that nothing succeeds like success is nowhere so cordially and consistently accepted as in America" (1937, 211). When a candidate's election (or nomination before the general election campaign) appears inevitable, then undecideds and previous supporters of the opposition may be likely "to jump on the candidate's bandwagon." Both the level of support and the movement in that support would appear to be important to a bandwagon effect. A candidate high in the polls and moving upward is positioned for a positive bandwagon effect. Conversely, a candidate with low and declining poll numbers may have supporters jumping off the bandwagon. The narrowing effect of the campaigns suggests that bandwagon effects in general election campaigns are either nonexistent or are more than offset by the tendency of campaigns to tighten up competitively. Holbrook's analysis does not consider the possibility of a narrowing effect of the campaign and does not distinguish between momentum and the bandwagon effect (1996a, 130–31). While momentum could plausibly contribute to the narrowing effect of the campaign by raising the support level of the trailing candidate, the bandwagon effect would have produced an expansion rather than contraction in the winner's margin.

Chapter 3

1. Holbrook (1996a, 64) and Shaw (1998, Shaw and Roberts 2000) use an events-based definition of the campaign. This approach has several problems. Most

would agree that watching televised campaign messages or getting a phone call from a candidate's organization or agreeing to post a yard sign for a candidate are all part of the campaign, but none qualify as an "event." Holbrook also attempts to distinguish non-campaign events from campaign events. For instance, he cites Kiewiet and Rivers (1985) as finding "that changes in support for Reagan (as measured with trial-heat polls) during the 1984 campaign were clearly tied to changes in the unemployment rate, which is clearly not a campaign influence." This may not be so clear. If unemployment is an issue for some people, if the candidates or the media talk about it (even obliquely), it has been politicized and is part of the campaign. It is, moreover, futile to try to determine how the events themselves would have played out or affected the election somehow apart from their politicization through the campaign. It is hard to imagine how an event that has political repercussions during the course of the campaign would not be addressed in some way by the campaign. Given this, it appears futile to pursue an events-based definition and more productive to pursue a time-based definition.

2. The unending campaign is also not very helpful from an explanatory standpoint since all changes in the vote would be attributable by definition to the all-inclusive campaign effects. Some distinguishing limits on the time horizon of the campaign are necessary to make campaigns a meaningful concept. For campaign effects to be of interest there must be the logical possibility of non-campaign effects.

3. There were at least some doubts about both Gerald Ford's 1976 Republican Party nomination and Jimmy Carter's 1980 Democratic Party nomination when the respective conventions began, and certainly neither of these candidates could have afforded to shift their focus from the nomination to the general election prior to their conventions. Still, these are the exceptions.

4. Viewing a portion of the election year as a transition from the nomination contest to the general election campaign recognizes also that the nomination and general election campaigns of the candidates overlap. Each viable candidate for a party's nomination is also preparing the way for the general election. The focus may be mostly on securing the nomination, but at least a portion of the campaign's attention must look forward to positioning the candidate for a possible candidacy in the general election.

5. Because they contain a certain amount of error, trial-heat polls provide imperfect baselines. Beyond the normal amount of sampling error, some additional error is found in preference polls conducted earlier in the election year. This reflects the uncertainty in the preference of respondents and the fact that the polling situation may not entail for the voter the seriousness of the vote itself. This noise is likely to be greater in any single poll than in a group of polls, where errors in one direction may offset errors in an opposing direction.

6. Shaw and Roberts (2000) recognize the problems associated with the use of preference polls in measuring campaign effects (262). To avoid the poll problems, they use the Iowa Political Stock Market's price associated with a candidate's victory as a measure or prediction of the candidate's probability of winning the election. However, since these market prices share the short-term volatility of polls during the campaign, their use still does not anchor measures of campaign effects as reflected in the actual vote (Erikson and Wlezien 2006). In addition, the market measure may anticipate future campaign effects and thus muddy it as a measure of current effects.

7. Holbrook also examined campaign effects for the 1984 election with a "within

campaign" time-series but using different data (1996a, appendix A). For the 1988 and 1992 analyses, Holbrook interpolated data for days in which no polls were available. This inflated the sample size for his study and produces artificial positive autocorrelation problems. It also creates what might be termed a partial tautology problem when he uses the lagged poll data as an independent variable to "explain" data interpolated from that lagged poll.

8. Holbrook (1997, 22–23) defends his reliance on polls by observing that "some indication of the accuracy of these data can be gleaned by comparing the estimated outcome based on the last day of polling results to the actual election outcome. The last day (November 3) polling results were Clinton—50 percent, Dole—36.5 percent, Perot—9 percent, and the actual election results were Clinton—49 percent, Dole—41 percent, Perot—9 percent. The last day polling results were virtually right on target for Clinton and Perot but underestimated Dole's support." When recomputed to the two-party division, these last-day polls were more than three percentage points in error. To put the magnitude of this error in perspective, it is half the amount of the median real vote change from one presidential election to the next in elections since 1868 and about twice the out-of-sample error of several of the more accurate models that forecast election results several months before the election.

9. The weakness of the time-series of polls approach to studying campaign effects can be illustrated in several ways. First, from a regression analysis standpoint, even if the final observation of the 150 polls in an election year were the actual vote, the model might do an excellent job of accounting for variation in the 149 poll observations but a very poor job in accounting for variation in the final observation (the actual vote). The statistics of the model's performance would look exceptionally good, but it failed when it mattered. From a slightly different perspective, if the goal of an analysis is to explain how the campaign affected the vote, why would you want to construct a single model for that purpose that is also saddled with trying to explain 149 other poll movements, many of which might be temporary blips or the effects of sampling errors? Holbrook asserts that "by focusing on the ultimate outcome and ignoring the campaign period it is easy to misinterpret the process that led to the outcome" (1996a, 46). In response to Holbrook, one could say that by not focusing on the vote, he has constructed a model that may account for the ups and downs, the real and ephemeral poll movements during the campaign but not for the effects of the campaign on the actual vote. In short, the time-series analysis of polls does not necessarily answer the question of whether the campaign matters to the election results.

10. In the July and early September trial-heat polls typically 7 or 8 percent of the national Gallup poll sample (and never more than 12 percent) report being undecided. This probably understates the fluidity of the electorate. In the NES surveys typically more than 40 percent of respondents indicate that they reached their vote decision at some time during the campaign. As Shaw (1999, 351) notes, most polls ask undecideds which candidate they lean toward and then count those leaners as supporters. The difference between the proportion of undecideds in the polls and the proportion indicating a late decision in the NES surveys is important in assessing Gelman and King's (1993) dismissal of the thesis that campaigns involve the return of partisans to the fold. They noted that "the key evidence against this thesis is that the proportion of undecideds does not drop over the course of the campaign" (430). It would appear from both the fluidity of

preferences and reports regarding when the vote decision was made that the trial-heat questions may poorly measure the extent of indecision in the electorate.

11. My research with Lynna Cherry and Ken Wink (J. Campbell, Cherry, and Wink 1992) on convention bumps examined various decay functions that would assess the durability or lasting impact of convention effects. Shaw (1998) has also assessed the durability of campaign effects more generally in his poll-based time-series analysis of campaign events. His method was to examine poll changes at as many as ten days after a campaign event. This approach represents an improvement over previous analyses. However, it still falls short of gauging whether an event's impact survived to the election in whole or in part. An event's impact might well survive a week or so before it recedes or is even forgotten without so much as a residual effect on the vote.

12. By examining polls up to 150 days before the election, Holbrook's (1996a) analysis is particularly susceptible to treating campaign noise as real effects that affect the election results. A significant number of cases in Holbrook's analysis are in June and early July before either party's nominating conventions. Although real changes may take place at this point, a large part of any poll change this early in the election year is likely to be ephemeral.

13. In Holbrook's analysis of debate effects (1996a, table 5.3), he examines debates in 1984, 1988, and 1992 by determining the difference between pre-debate and post-debate polls. For both 1984 and 1988 he examines the apparent effects of two presidential debates and a vice presidential debate. In 1992 he examines the three presidential debates and a vice presidential debate. There are seven potential opportunities to examine whether the post-debate poll for a debate drifted back toward its previous level before the next debate. Since Holbrook's data indicate that there was effectively no change following the first debate in 1992 (less than half of a percentage point change), there are six real opportunities to determine if the debate bumps rather quickly evaporated. In all six cases the poll change from after a debate to before the next debate drifted back toward the pre-debate margin. In one case (after the second debate in 1992), the drift back was minor, but in the other five cases two-thirds or more of the "bump" receded before the next debate. In the 1980 campaign, CBS reporter Bruce Morton also noted the temporary nature of debate effects. In cautioning viewers about reading too much into post-debate poll changes, Morton observed that, "after the Reagan-Anderson debate we did a poll, and Governor Reagan bobbed up briefly and then settled about back to where he'd been" (Jamieson 1992, 194).

14. There are ways in which a time-series of polls can also be anchored to the actual election results. See J. Campbell, Cherry, and Wink 1992; and Erikson and Wlezien 1998.

15. As in other approaches, there is a potential bias in this approach that may favor the finding of campaign effects. The bias results from interpreting as campaign effects the difference between pre-campaign support for a candidate as measured by the polls and the post-campaign vote for that candidate. It is quite possible that there would be a change from the polls to the vote even without an active campaign. In the absence of a campaign, voters might change their minds. They might say one thing in responding to a survey question well before election day and another in the voting booth when their vote really matters.

16. By campaign effects, I mean the net effects of the campaign on the vote division.

After reviewing a model that accurately forecasts elections well before the start of campaigns, Holbrook, citing Bartels 1992, suggests that "one possible interpretation of these results is that the difference between the actual outcomes and the forecast outcomes represents the effects of unspecified variables, possibly the effects of the campaign. Because the forecasts are based on data from a period before the general election gets into full swing, the error in the estimates could be due to the intervening general election campaign" (1996a, 31). A caveat to this interpretation, as Holbrook points out, is that weaknesses in the model's specification, the measurement of its variables, and other non-campaign factors might also account for errors in the forecasts. Later, Holbrook notes that the discrepancy between the forecast outcome (he terms this an "equilibrium") and the actual outcome "may indicate the net effects of the campaigns above and beyond the effect of national conditions" (67).

17. This is one of several important differences between my theory of predictable campaigns and Holbrook's theory of campaign effects. Holbrook (1996a, 49) regards the fundamentals (the economy, etc.) as establishing a pre-campaign equilibrium and that the campaign is a competing influence on the vote that induces shifts in public opinion around the equilibrium. The theory of the predictable campaign, in contrast, argues that many of the effects of the fundamentals are funneled through the campaign, that they become politicized and relevant to vote decisions when they have been processed by the candidates, the media, and voters during the campaign.

18. The poll results examined are of registered voters. Because of the irregularity in the timing of surveys in the early years of this series, target dates were set in selecting polls in terms of days before the election (dbe). The target date for the June poll was 150 days before the election. The subsequent target polls in the election year are: 102 dbe for the late July poll; 60 dbe for the early September poll; 39 dbe for the late September poll; 20 dbe for the October poll; and 5 dbe for the November poll. The timing of the post-convention poll depended on the date of the second national convention, but it always fell between the late July and early September polls. Gallup poll data through 1996 were obtained from the Gallup Organization. The 2000 and 2004 polls were obtained from the Gallup Poll website (www.galluppoll.com).

19. The standard deviation of the absolute difference between the reported and actual votes is about 1.75 percentage points. This suggests a 95 percent confidence interval of about plus or minus 3.5 percentage points.

20. Reagan's question, asking voters to make a basic retrospective evaluation of national conditions as reflected in their personal circumstances and presumably reflective of the success of the administration's policies, powerfully framed the election's choice. Every voter could understand and answer the question, and the overwhelming majority would answer it to the candidate's advantage. There were no facts in dispute, no competing or abstract claims. The question in a slightly different form had been raised prior to the 1934 midterm congressional elections by President Franklin Roosevelt in a "fireside chat" on June 28, 1934. Roosevelt made the question the theme of his nationally broadcast radio address. After reviewing the accomplishments of the first year and a half of his administration, Roosevelt told his audience that "the simplest way for each of you to judge recovery lies in the plain facts of your own individual situation. Are you better off

than you were last year? Are your debts less burdensome? Is your bank account more secure? Are your working conditions better? Is your faith in your own individual future more firmly grounded?" (Buhite and Levy 1992, 48).

21. "Front-end loading" refers to the trend of states to move their primaries or caucuses to earlier in the election year (see Hess 1998, 68–69). After the Democratic Party's delegate-selection reforms formulated by its McGovern-Fraser commission after the 1968 election, states increasingly used presidential primaries to select delegates to the national nominating conventions. The fact that these primaries were spread out over several months allowed long-shot candidates (like Jimmy Carter in 1976) to build momentum (good press and money) for their candidacies. With the advent of the southern "Super Tuesday" in the 1980s and the shift of primaries to early in the nomination season (to avoid having a primary after the nominee has effectively been chosen), the system has evolved into a post-reform era. Although states still hold their individual contests and the compression of the delegate-selection process is not complete (as it would be in a national primary), the system is very advantageous for a frontrunning candidate. There is, in a sense, very little time to fall and little time for other candidates to gain much momentum.

22. The largest non-major-party presidential vote since the Civil War was for former president and Bull Moose Progressive candidate Theodore Roosevelt in the 1912 election. Roosevelt received 27.4 percent of the vote, finishing second to Democrat Woodrow Wilson and ahead of President William Howard Taft.

23. In order to devote full time to campaigning and to signal to the public that he was intent on winning the election, Dole resigned both his position as Senate Majority Leader and his seat in the Senate.

24. From an analytical standpoint one would like to have both a large number of cases or observations and a great deal of variance on all variables. Since the limitation imposed by the unavailability of early poll data restricts the number of observations (elections) that can be considered by this study, it is at least salutary to know that the very different elections in the series suggests substantial variation in variables among the cases that we have.

25. The ten elections involving incumbent presidents are: 1948, 1956, 1964, 1972, 1976, 1980, 1984, 1992, 1996, and 2004. In three of these elections, however, the incumbent president seeking election had not previously been elected president (Truman in 1948, Johnson in 1964, and Ford in 1976).

26. The sitting vice president ran as a presidential candidate in four of the five elections not involving an incumbent president. Nixon as Eisenhower's vice president ran in 1960, Humphrey as Johnson's in 1968, Bush as Reagan's in 1988, and Gore as Clinton's in 2000. Of elections since the 1930s, only the 1952 election (Eisenhower versus Stevenson) involved neither a sitting president nor vice president. The 2008 election will be the next.

27. Though there is no alternative to using survey data, there are unavoidable problems of sampling and measurement errors involved in using survey data as the indicator of pre-campaign levels of support. The uncertainty produced by random sampling and measurement error in these data, however, should not affect the averages of campaign effects. The effects in some campaigns may be overestimated, but the effects in others may be underestimated. These should balance out. Nonrandom error in the polls is more problematic. If the polls consistently overstate support for a candidate, for instance, the difference between the pre-

campaign poll and the vote will be inflated and campaign effects will be overestimated. One possible way to gauge whether this is a problem is to examine the difference between the polls and the vote at the time of the election. If the polls on election day overstate a candidate's support (as compared to the actual vote), there is reason to believe that the difference between the pre-campaign poll and the vote reflects a problem in the accuracy of the poll and not the effect of the campaign. Over the fifteen elections examined, the November Gallup trial-heat polls averaged .8 percentage points higher for the in-party candidate than the actual vote, though the November polls were lower than the actual vote in six election years. Although this difference is well within what might have been produced by random error or real changes in the last few days before the election, campaign effects were reestimated after adjusting the September poll by the November poll error. Unfortunately, this attempted fix did not improve the model's fit (see also J. Campbell 2001c).

28. In reviewing the differences between the actual vote and that predicted by his forecast equation, Holbrook (1996a) observes that the differences "could be due to the intervening general election campaign. If this is accepted as a real possibility, the net effects of presidential campaigns range from −.01 percentage points in 1984 to 2.59 percentage points in 1988—not very impressive" (31). At the end of his book, however, using his pooled model of candidate support (his table 6.4), Holbrook in table 6.5 estimates the net effects of campaigns to be .72 percentage points in 1984, 15.49 percentage points in 1988, and −4.39 percentage points in 1992. He does not explain the discrepancy between the two sets of estimates. Holbrook attributes the unusually high estimated campaign effects in 1988 to Bush's very "strong convention bump" and observes that the estimate "jibes well with the popular perception that the Bush camp ran a better campaign than the Dukakis camp" (147). My explanation is that the estimate greatly overstates campaign effects in 1988 because the analysis relies exclusively on polls rather than on an examination of the vote. The study overestimates the Republican convention bump (+11) and underestimates the Democratic convention bump (−4.6). While the estimates in my table 7.3 are in the same ballpark as Holbrook's estimates in his table 4.1, the estimates in his pooled analysis, especially the negative Democratic bump noted above, are out of line for both sets of estimates. Moreover, his estimates do not incorporate any deterioration in convention or debate effects from the event to election day.

29. Prior studies of campaigns (Bartels 1992; Finkel 1993; Holbrook 1996a) implicitly focused on the unsystematic effects of campaigns rather than their total effects. Holbrook explicitly separates the effects of pre-campaign national conditions from the effects of the campaign (144–46). His analysis does not acknowledge that pre-campaign fundamentals or national conditions affect the campaign, which in turn affects the vote (the possibility of systematic campaign effects). His estimate of campaign effects really measure only unsystematic campaign effects. The separate estimates of the average net effect of campaigns by Holbrook, Finkel, and Bartels are about what I estimate in table 3.4 to be the average *unsystematic* campaign effect. All range from about 1.5 to 2 percentage points.

30. The trial-heat and economy model (table 1.5 and J. Campbell 1996) includes all three systematic campaign effects indicated by the theory of predictable campaigns. The forecasting model explicitly includes the election-year economy. The trial-heat poll coefficient of approximately .5 reflects the narrowing effect of

the campaign. The incumbency advantage is reflected, in part, in the constant of the equation since the forecast is oriented in terms of the incumbent party. The forecast model can be respecified into a model to explain campaign effects with the dependent variable being the change in support for the in-party candidate from the early September trial-heat poll to the November vote. This model is examined in chapter 9, table 9.1.The campaign effects model also differs from the forecast model in the second-quarter GDP growth data used. The forecast model uses data available in August before the election, since a lead time is required for forecasting purposes. The campaign effects model uses post-election revised GDP data since its interest is in accurately explaining campaign effects rather than prediction.

31. The total net effects of the campaign can be mathematically apportioned into systematic and unsystematic effects as follows:

Total Campaign Effect = Unsystematic Effect + Systematic Effect
or Vote – Poll = (Vote – Expected) + (Expected – Poll)
where,

Total Campaign Effect = Vote – Poll
Systematic Effect = Expected – Poll
Unsystematic Effect = Vote – Expected.

Chapter 4

1. Election analyst and forecaster Louis Bean (1972) long ago noted the importance of the limited range of the presidential vote. As Bean observed, "the candidates of either party have usually won elections within the narrow range of 50 to 60 percent of the two-party vote. In only five cases in thirty since 1852 has a presidential swing gone as high as 61 to 65 percent" (7). The very limited range of the presidential vote would appear to be at odds with Holbrook's view that "there is a lot of variation in presidential election outcomes" (1996a, 23). The evaluation of variance in the presidential vote, of course, depends on what it is being compared to. There is variation, a great deal if compared to the fixed vote but very limited if compared to the potential spread across a zero-to-one hundred range.

2. It should be observed that the fact that the July frontrunning candidate received at least 46 percent of the November vote does not *necessarily* mean that this 46 percent of the electorate had firmly made up their minds in July. It is logically possible, though highly unlikely in reality, that the 46 percent voting for the July frontrunner in November had favored the opposing candidate in July and that the July frontrunner's supporters in July defected to the opposition *en masse* between July and November. Moreover, even without this implausible degree of individual vote intention instability, some voters with stable vote intentions may have not been entirely settled in their July preference. On the other hand, in most elections the July frontrunner held onto an even larger November vote share and many voters who say that they are unsettled in their preference may not really be so unsettled.

3. The contrast between the partisan attitudes and behavior of American voters and their beliefs about partisanship offers testimony to a troubling aspect of American political behavior: the purist streak of anti-partisanship and anti-politics. Americans are demonstrably partisan in their attitudes and behaviors, but many are reluctant to admit this because they dislike partisanship and the political conflict that

it entails. This has been observed by various scholars and journalists (see Ranney 1975; Dionne 1991; and Hibbing and Theiss-Morse 1995). The contrast also suggests the dangers of relying on voter self-reflection in examining their behavior. They may report what they would like to be the case rather than what is the case.

4. Change in the partisanship of individuals is only one of the two possible ways in which aggregate partisan change can take place. The second way is through changes in the composition of the potential electorate through new voters coming of age, immigration, and deaths of those previously in the electorate. Aggregate partisan change in the New Deal realignment, for instance, resulted largely from the mobilization of new voters (Andersen 1979; Campbell 1985, 1986; for an alternative view see Erikson and Tedin 1981, 1986).

5. The extent of aggregate partisan change includes both voters and nonvoters and was calculated from table 1.1 of Keith et al. 1992, 14. These data were obtained from the NES surveys. Data from the 1992 NES survey were also included. Leaning independents were counted as partisans. Change was calculated as the difference between the percentage of respondents claiming an identification with a party in one presidential election year and the percentage claiming an identification with that same party in the next presidential election year. Ten absolute differences were computed for the changes in the number of Democrats and in the number of Republicans. The median change between presidential elections for both parties was two percentage points. The mean (as opposed to median) change was 3.2 percentage points for Democrats and 2.4 percentage points for Republicans. Note that since nonvoters are counted in this mix there was no correction for the vote representativeness of the NES surveys. Also note that the mean change figures probably overstate true change during periods of nonrealignment, since the period under study includes the post–New Deal realignment away from the Democratic Party dominance toward greater party competition.

6. A number of studies examining the general election vote choice in well-specified causal models indicate that most of the effects of partisanship on the voter are exerted indirectly by the impact of partisanship on issue preferences and on evaluation of candidate characteristics, which in turn influence the vote decision (W. Miller and Shanks 1982, 346). That is, partisanship affects which candidate a voter regards as closer to him or her on the issues and which candidate is seen as having more admirable leadership traits (candidate image), and these issue and candidate image evaluations are major factors in the voter's decision-making. This interpretation is consistent with theory of *The American Voter* (A. Campbell et al. 1960) in which partisanship affected a set of "partisan attitudes" that included issues and candidate images, which in turn affected the vote choice. Most analyses of the vote have probably underestimated the indirect effects of partisanship. This is likely because of measurement error in issue preferences resulting from surveys that can only ask about a very limited set of issues framed in a very limited number of ways and because of the usual difficulties of asking marginally interested voters to express their political thinking on short notice for interviewers. In the 1996 NES survey respondents gave sixty-four different answers (different enough that they were coded differently) to the open-ended question of what was the nation's most important problem. Yet this very comprehensive survey could only include forced-choice issue questions (in one way or another) on fewer than twenty issues. For an elaboration of this argument that nearly all factors affecting the vote are "short-term" see J. Campbell 1997b, 29–34.

7.   Counting independents leaning toward a party as partisans, 61 percent of 1964 NES respondents indicated a Democratic identification and only 31 percent indicated a Republican identification. See Keith et al. 1992, table 1.1.

8.   As the figures in table 2.1 indicate, the Republican loyalty rate in 1992 dipped below that of Democrats, but these figures are complicated by votes for independent candidate Ross Perot. Among partisans who voted for either major-party candidate, Republicans in 1992 remained more loyal than Democrats. Among major-party voters in 1992 who were Democrats, 10.5 percent defected to vote for Republican candidate George Bush. Among major-party voters in 1992 who were Republicans, 10 percent voted for Democratic candidate Bill Clinton. Note that these NES defection figures have been adjusted (as described in chapter 3) to be consistent with the known national popular vote division.

9.   The final independent variable would be the portion of the electorate made up of independents; however, this variable must be excluded because it would have created perfect multicollinearity with the percentage of Democrats and Republicans in the electorate.

10. The second regression accounted for the national Democratic presidential vote using the net differences in the electorate's partisan composition and the net difference in the party loyalty in the voting of Democrats and Republicans along with the percentage of independents who voted for the Democratic candidate. The equation with three independent variables accounted for 99.6 percent of the variance in the Democratic presidential vote from 1952 to 2004 (adjusted R^2 = .989). The unstandardized (standardized) coefficients are as follows: net party loyalty .538 (1.016), net party identification composition .358 (.432), and Democratic vote among independents .016 (.039). The constant was 49.174 and the standard error of the equation was .646. Except for the vote of independents, all coefficients were statistically significant at p < .01 (one-tailed). The Durbin-Watson statistic for autocorrelation was 2.658.

11. This decomposition of the vote is suggested by Axelrod's (1972) analysis of group voting. Axelrod identified a group's contribution to a party's vote as the product of three terms: the group's size, its turnout rate, and its loyalty rate. By examining partisans as a proportion of voters this analysis essentially combines the first two terms, the number of partisans and their turnout rates. It is also interesting to observe that though the six partisan components of the vote (party composition and loyalty rates for the three party identification categories) are logically related to the national vote as a series of three interactions, as specified in the equation, the additive specification examined in the regression analysis (specified in that way to distinguish the relative impact on the vote of each of the components) nonetheless completely accounts for variation in the national vote. This is indicated by both the multiple correlation coefficient value of nearly 1.0 and the very low standard error of the equation. I have investigated the importance of partisan turnout, particularly as it relates to the party's success in congressional elections, elsewhere (J. Campbell 1997b).

12. Democrats outnumbered Republicans by more than ten percentage points in every election from 1948 to 1980. Since 1984, the gap has ranged from nearly zero in 1988 to over five points in 1996. Another reason that Democratic loyalty variation may have mattered so much is that variation in loyalty has a bigger impact on vote shares than variation in turnout. A one-percentage-point loss of loyalty costs a party two percentage points in its margin, since the party's candidate

not only loses the support but it is gained by the opposition's candidate. A one-percentage-point loss of turnout, on the other hand, hurts the party but does not help the opposition.

13.   The means and standard deviations of the six components of the vote are as follows: percent Democrats (mean = 51.3, sd = 3.69), Democratic loyalty (mean = 81.2, sd = 8.59), percent independents (mean = 7.6, sd = 1.60), independent vote for Democratic candidate (mean = 40.0, sd = 15.26), percent Republicans (mean = 41.1, sd = 3.81), and Republican vote for Democratic candidate (mean = 9.3, sd = 4.59). An alternative specification of the equation in table 4.1 that omitted the Republican portion of the electorate (as the baseline category) and included the independent portion of the electorate found that the percentage of electorate claiming to be purely independent was the *least* important of the six partisan components of the vote. Its standardized coefficient was only .07. The small impact is quite understandable given the small number and relative stability in the number of independents in the electorate over this period (see table 2.1).

14.   Studies of individual voting behavior have downplayed the impact of ideology on the vote choice. Many voters are not self-aware of their ideology, conversant with ideological terminology, or extreme in their ideological predispositions. Despite these findings, there is evidence that many voters are ideologically aware and consider these political values important enough to cast votes consistent with these predispositions. For example, of major-party presidential voters in 1992, almost 90 percent of liberals voted for the more liberal candidate Clinton, and, despite concerns about performance, nearly two-thirds of conservatives voted for the more conservative candidate Bush. About 85 percent of eventual major-party voters in that election could be directly identified (in the pre-election survey) to some degree as liberals or conservatives. Revealed values in questions about government spending and self-reliance helped to classify about another 10 percent of voters (ideologically voting with about the same consistency). As in the case of partisanship, most of the congruence of ideology and the vote is probably indirect. Ideological values affect perceptions and evaluations of the candidates, and their issue positions and these impressions affect the vote choice. The impact of ideology on the vote has probably been understated because of its abstract and complex nature and the reliance on self-awareness measures in surveys of often only marginally interested voters.

15.   The Voter News Service data used here were originally reported in the Roper Center's *America at the Polls, 1996* (Dougherty et al. 1997). This distribution of self-described ideological identifications in VNS polls has been quite consistent or stable across recent election years. When dealing with ideological labels, however, one needs to be quite cautious since many voters understand the labels to stand for different sets of principles or values, and these labels may mean very little at all to a significant number of voters. The ideological self-placements on NES surveys regularly generate about a quarter to a third of respondents admitting that they do not know how their views should be categorized. However, a lack of self-awareness of the appropriate label for their values does not mean that these respondents do not have political values. Moreover, among those who do respond, the percentage of moderates is probably exaggerated. Given the tendency under uncertainty to pick the middle position, the moderate category of voters is probably inflated. Recent NES efforts to probe further for voters' views indicate that the percentage of respondents with conservative or liberal inclina-

tions is much greater than previously thought (see note 14). Moreover, the impact of ideology probably has also been understated. To the extent that voter confusion about terms produces random error, the measured relationship of self-identified ideology and the vote is undoubtedly attenuated. Despite these obstacles, recent studies have documented a substantial increase in the link of ideology to partisanship and the vote (Abramowitz and Saunders 1998).

16.   When ideology and partisanship most strongly reinforce one another, as they do among conservative Republicans and liberal Democrats, voter loyalty is so strong that that itself suggests the ease with which the vote decision has been reached. The average two-party vote percentage for Republican presidential candidates among conservative Republicans from 1976 to 1996 was 94 percent. Among liberal Democrats the average two-party vote for the Democratic presidential candidate over this period was 90 percent. These figures were calculated from Voter News Service data reported in *The New York Times* (Nov. 10, 1996).

17.   A good example of an exception to the rule of issue continuity, an issue on which there has been discontinuity, is the civil rights issue in the 1950s and 1960s. Carmines and Stimson (1989) demonstrate that the Democrats had been the more conservative party and Republicans the more liberal party on civil rights until the mid-1960s. An influx of more liberal northern Democrats into its ranks shifted the Democrats to the left on this issue. This, in turn, increased African American identifications with the Democrats and shifted the party further left on a number of issues. Since the mid-1960s, however, there has been substantial continuity in the positioning of the parties despite the considerable evolution of the civil rights issue. In the 1950s and 1960s the issue involved the desegregation of schools, open housing laws, voting rights, non-discrimination in employment, and open public accommodations. The civil rights issue since the 1970s has involved affirmative action and policies in which employers and the government award preferences to minorities to create diversity and to compensate for a general historical record of discrimination.

18.   The NES surveys themselves offer evidence that issues have life spans longer than a single election. The NES has for some time asked specific issue questions. The existence of specific issue time-series data on a range of issues in a crowded survey instrument in which not all issue items could be accommodated suggests substantial issue continuity across time. Of course, if survey questions became anachronistic and meaningless to respondents, their continuity would suggest nothing more than repeated questioning, but there is little evidence from survey responses that these issues have disappeared as *real* issues or have become radically altered over this period. The general continuity of issues is also suggested by a number of studies examining changes in public opinion on these issues over time (see Smith 1990; Stimson 1991; and Mayer 1992).

19.   The stability of issues and candidates' positions on them would explain, in part, the neglect of issues by the news media. The news media is in the business of reporting news, what we know today that we did not know yesterday. Uninformed voters may need to learn where the candidates stand on the issues, but because of issue stability, these issue positions are not news to most modestly attentive voters and the news media. With this vacuum and because of the potential for exciting conflict, the news media report on the ever-changing "horserace" aspect of the election (Patterson and Davis 1985, 122).

20.   See Berelson, Lazarsfeld, and McPhee 1954; Stokes 1966; and Campbell and

Meier 1979. Issues on which the parties and candidates differ regarding the goals are termed position issues. The abortion issue is a good example of a position issue.

21. Another example of a valence issue would be the crime issue. Everyone wants to reduce crime but many have different ideas about the best way to achieve this goal. Some would favor solving social problems such as poverty and poor educational and employment opportunities in order to address what they regard as the root causes of crime. Others would do more to keep traditional two-parent families intact to keep troubled children from gravitating to criminal activity. Still others want government to encourage greater personal responsibility and protect public safety by keeping those convicted of criminal activities incarcerated for longer periods. In the case of the crime issue, parties and candidates are evaluated not only by their performance in reducing crime but also by whether their views of what constitutes justice comports with the voters' views.

22. Holbrook (1996a, 8) quotes V. O. Key on this point. In *The Responsible Electorate* Key (1966) wrote that "as voters mark their ballots they may have in their minds impressions of the last television spectacular of the campaign, but, more important, they have in their minds recollections of their experiences of the past four years" (9). Regarding voter uncertainty, Alvarez (1997) found that "uncertainty generally diminishes across the course of the campaign in response to issue and substantive information" (204). However, it appears that many voters may be sufficiently certain about the candidates' positions before the campaign to make firm pre-campaign vote decisions.

23. Elsewhere (J. Campbell 1997b, 90–97, 174–87) I have found that cross-pressures are an important factor in presidential turnout and vote choice. Partisans of losing presidential candidates are much more likely to feel cross-pressured about their vote decision, and many opt not to vote as a result. In related work, Marcus and MacKuen (1993) find that voter "anxiety" about the candidates and voter "enthusiasm" for a candidate affect vote decisions. They conclude that anxiety substantially weakens the voter's reliance on partisanship in deciding how to vote (677–78) and that enthusiasm for a candidate is important to deciding which candidate to support (677). These findings may also be interpreted from the standpoint of cross-pressure effects. If a voter is satisfied with his or her party's presidential candidate, he or she will feel enthusiastic about voting for that candidate. Enthusiasm is caused by the interaction of candidate evaluations and partisanship. On the other hand, a voter who is dissatisfied with his or her party's candidate will feel cross-pressured (the candidate evaluations pulling one way and partisanship the other) and this may produce anxiety. Anxiety is also caused by an interaction of candidate evaluations and partisanship. It is, however, not the anxiety itself that weakens the reliance on partisanship but the fact that the candidate evaluations of anxious voters contradict their partisanship and that vote choices are essentially determined by short-term forces (summarized in candidate evaluations) rather than *directly* by long-term partisanship (J. Campbell 1997b, 29–34).

24. Abramson, Aldrich, and Rohde (2006) examine partisanship, approval or disapproval of presidential performance (in general and with respect to the economy in particular), a summary measure of retrospective evaluations, and a balance of issue positions index and their relationship to the vote choice for elections from 1976 to 2004. The vote cues are clearly and positively related to one another in each year. Moreover, except in instances in which conditions were unfavorable to

a party (as they were for Democrats in 1980 and Republicans in 1992, for instance), substantial majorities of partisans find other cues to support a loyal party vote (see Abramson, Aldrich, and Rohde 2006, chapter 8).

25. NES pre-election respondents in 1992 were asked the following questions: "Is there anything in particular about Mr. (Bush/Clinton) that might make you want to vote (for/against) him?" Of eventual Clinton voters, about 48 percent said they could not think of any reason to vote for Bush or any reason not to vote for Clinton. Of eventual Bush voters, about 43 had no reservations whatsoever in their choice. Survey respondents who failed to mention any reason for or against either candidate were excluded from the analysis, so the above numbers represent those who were truly responsive to the survey questioning. Of 1992 voters without reservations, about 70 percent reached early decisions.

26. In a previous study (J. Campbell 1997b, 174–83), I examined a partisan disaffection index and its impact on the vote decision in NES surveys from 1952 to 1992. The index was based on the number of responses a survey respondent gave to NES questions about what they liked and disliked about their own party's presidential candidate and his opponent. The index ranged from –10 (a strong preference for the party's candidate, the maximum number of "likes" about the party's candidate and "dislikes" about the opponent) to +10 (a strong preference for the other party's candidate). Most partisans were quite satisfied with their party's candidate (relative to his opponent, anyway). The average disaffection index values for Democratic identifiers was –1.9 and ranged from –3.6 in 1992 and –3.5 in 1964 to –.2 in 1972. Among Republican identifiers the index average was –2.8 and ranged from –3.7 in 1956 to –.9 in 1964. The dependent variable was a trichotomous variable: a vote for the candidate of the respondent's party, abstention from voting, and a defecting vote for the candidate of the other party. Moderate levels of party disaffection, indicative of cross-pressures (since high levels would push the voter to the opposite camp), were significantly associated with nonvoting in each of the eleven presidential elections examined (see J. Campbell 1997b, table 8.3).

27. The pre-election wave of survey interviews began in early September and extended to the day before the election. In NES studies through 1996, the median time of the pre-election survey before the election was 30.5 days, or early October.

28. A vote change from the intended vote was used as a double check on those who claimed that they decided their vote early. Early deciders, as defined here, indicated that they had decided how they would vote at or before the last nominating convention, which was well before they would have been interviewed in the NES pre-election wave (which begins in early September and extends up to election day). Only nineteen respondents or 2.6 percent of those saying that they had decided their vote before the campaign changed their vote reported in the post-election survey wave from their intended vote reported in the pre-election survey wave. Since their reported time of the vote decision is contradicted by the mismatch of their intention and vote, these changers were grouped with the late deciders.

29. Early decisions regarding the vote are not limited to voters. Many nonvoters decided early on not to vote, though a majority of nonvoters indicated in the pre-election wave of the NES survey that they had intended to vote. Of those who reported not intending to vote or reporting that they did not vote, 52 percent said

that they intended not to vote and then reported having voted, 38 percent said that they would not and did not vote, and 11 percent said that they had voted despite earlier saying that they would not.

Chapter 5

1. Reasons to be skeptical about the advantage of presidential incumbency can also be found in earlier data. From 1868 to 2004, seventeen elected incumbent presidents have run for reelection. Nine improved their share of the two-party vote in their second run: Grant in 1872 from 1868, Cleveland in 1888 from 1884 (though he lost the electoral vote to Harrison in 1888), McKinley in 1900 from 1896, F. Roosevelt in 1936 from 1932, Eisenhower in 1956 from 1952, Nixon in 1972 from 1968, Reagan in 1984 from 1980, Clinton in 1996 from 1992, and G. W. Bush in 2004 from 2000. However, eight lost votes in their second run: Harrison in 1892 from 1888, Taft in 1912 from 1908, Wilson in 1916 from 1912, Hoover in 1932 from 1928, F. Roosevelt in 1940 from 1936 and 1944 from 1940, Carter in 1980 from 1976, and George H. W. Bush in 1992 from 1988.

2. Because of the two-term tradition and later the two-term constitutional limit, one might expect a strong relationship between candidates seeking a second party term and incumbent presidents seeking reelection. However, there is less overlap between incumbents seeking reelection and in-party candidates seeking a second party term than one might suspect. Although nearly all (eleven of twelve) non-incumbent in-party candidates were seeking more than a second term for their party (the exception being Bryan in 1896), nine of the twenty-one incumbents seeking reelection were attempting to extend their party's control of the presidency to more than a second term. The incumbency advantage appears strongest when the two conditions overlap, when incumbents are seeking a second term for their party. Nine of these twelve incumbents were reelected, and the average vote for these twelve was 55.9 percent of the two-party vote.

3. Examination of a personal presidential incumbency variable and a time for a change variable in the trial-heat and economy forecasting model produced weak results. In the early September model, a president seeking reelection was boosted by 1.05 percentage points though the estimate was not statistically significant at conventional levels ($p < .17$, one-tailed). In a separate analysis, a party seeking more than a second consecutive term was penalized .79 points, though the estimate was also not statistically significant at conventional levels ($p < .31$, one-tailed). A further analysis, specified with an interaction term between the September trial-heat and a dummy variable for an incumbent running had a coefficient in the expected direction ($+.021$), but it also fell short of conventional levels of statistical significance ($p < .19$, one-tailed). It appears that a substantial portion of the personal incumbency advantage is reflected in the early September trial-heat polls and the second-quarter economic growth rate. Of the fifteen elections, ten involved incumbent presidents seeking reelection (1948, 1956, 1964, 1972, 1976, 1980, 1984, 1992, 1996, and 2004) and five did not (1952, 1960, 1968, 1988, and 2000). The median trial-heat standing in early September for incumbents seeking reelection was 53.2 percentage points compared to 46.3 for non-incumbents of the in-party. The median second-quarter economic growth rate was 3.45 percentage points with an incumbent running and only 3.07 with a non-incumbent running.

4. Several other models also explicitly include incumbency effects. Holbrook's (1996b) forecasting model, as an adaptation of the Abramowitz (1988) model, also includes a second-term incumbency variable. Additionally, economist Ray Fair's forecasting model incorporates several aspects of incumbency (Fair 1978, 1982, 1988, and 1994; also see J. Campbell and Mann 1996, 30). Fair's model indicates that an incumbent president seeking a second term under average economic conditions should receive about 51.56 percent of the vote. However, an incumbent president seeking *more* than a second term appears to be penalized, receiving an expected 49.21 percent of the vote. Historian Allan Lichtman (1996, 3) also includes incumbency as one of his "Thirteen Keys to the White House." The keys are a set of thirteen pro- or anti-in-party questions whose answers, when combined into an index and a threshold applied, offer a prediction of which candidate should be expected to have won the election. While suggestive of many of the factors that may affect election outcomes, as a forecasting device the keys have several methodological shortcomings. First, all of the questions, including those regarding the economy, are simple forced and artificial dichotomies rather than interval measures. Second, each of the keys is arbitrarily weighted equally. Third, several of the keys are highly subjective in their coding. Several ask about "major" policy successes or failures, "significant" third-party activity, "serious" nomination contests, and "sustained" social unrest. These vague qualifiers allow for substantial ambiguity in the use of this method, as do the keys regarding whether either candidate is "charismatic."

5. The estimated model used to calculate these predicted votes was presented in table 1.3. The mean mid-July approval rating is 48.1 percent. The mean annualized real GDP in the first half of election years was 3.7 percent for a party seeking a second term and 4.1 percent for a party seeking more than a second term. Based on these averages and the estimated coefficients, the predicted vote for third or more party term seekers is 49.1 percent of the two-party vote. The predicted vote for second party term seekers is 54.7 percent of the two-party vote. Since we are examining the vote for the in-party, there are by definition no candidates seeking a first term for their party.

6. Much of the presidential incumbency advantage seems to be in place before the campaign. Voters are more likely to decide early and positively about incumbents who have successful terms. As the tables in appendix B reveal, almost 72 percent of voters were early deciders in 1956, and Eisenhower led Stevenson among this group by about 58 to 42 percent. Similarly, about 60 percent of voters in 1964 were early deciders, and Johnson led Goldwater among these voters by 70 to 30 percent. A smaller share of voters decided before the campaign in 1972 (56 percent), but Nixon led McGovern among those who did by a 71 to 29 percent division. Finally, Reagan led Mondale by a 62 to 38 split among the two-thirds of voters deciding early on in 1984. With their supporters easily backing successful incumbents very early in the election year, incumbents are in a sense doing well to divide the remaining vote evenly. Given the narrowing effect of the campaign and the substantial leads that these incumbents had going into their campaigns, we should have expected the poll-to-vote drop for these frontrunners to be larger than for those starting with smaller leads (given the proportionality of the narrowing effect). The fact that their percentage point drop was typically smaller rather than larger further suggests a presidential incumbency advantage.

7. Significant support for third-party presidential candidates has been rare, but it

appears to be a response to and largely at the expense of the incumbent party. The median vote for third-party candidates is about 2.8 percent of the total presidential vote, though it has exceeded 10 percent in six of the last thirty-five elections (1892, 1912, 1924, 1968, 1992, and 1996). The impact of third-party activity can be assessed through a regression with the in-party candidate's two-party vote percentage as the dependent variable and two independent variables: whether the incumbent was personally running and the share of the total vote for third-party candidates. The regression was estimated over the thirty-five elections from 1868 to 2004. The regression indicates approximately a 4.7-percentage-point boost for incumbents who are personally running and, most importantly, that the in-party candidate *loses* about .41 of a percentage point of the two-party vote for every percentage point of the total vote cast for the third-party candidate. Both effects were statistically significant (p < .02, one-tailed).

8.   The 40 percent threshold is based on the bivariate regression with the July approval rating as the independent variable and the incumbent's percentage of the two-party vote as the dependent variable. The regression's constant was 37.89, and the approval coefficient was .33 (p < .01, adjusted R^2 = .72, SEE = 3.31, N = 10). The critical approval rating (to produce an expected vote of 50 percent) was 37.2 percent. Including non-incumbent races in the estimation increases the critical approval rating to 40.5 percent. These estimates may slightly understate the approval rating needed for victory since the election-year economy is not taken into account, and that is normally strong enough to also help the in-party candidate.

9.   As an example, Bruno and Greenfield (1971, 15) recount how one of President Kennedy's ostensibly non-political trips in 1963 was also intended to touch base in states in which Kennedy as a candidate for reelection in 1964 would probably not be able to visit. As they observed, "there *is* no such thing as a non-political action by a President" (15).

10. There is also an eighth reason why incumbents might have stronger showings as candidates: electoral trouble should be more clearly evident to an incumbent and so weaker incumbents may drop out of the race before it begins. The decision not to seek reelection by some vulnerable incumbents amounts to a self-selecting out of incumbents and accounts in part for the stronger vote of the incumbents who do seek reelection. In other words, when we examine the vote for incumbents we are not examining the vote for all incumbents, but the vote for the subset of incumbents who have anticipated their chances of reelection to be great enough to make the run. This inflation of the apparent incumbency advantage is small since there have only been a few eligible incumbent presidents who have opted not to seek reelection. From 1868 to 2004 there have been only four incumbent presidents who had not been elected to two terms (excepting Franklin Roosevelt, the informal limit since Washington and the formal limit since the 22nd Amendment in 1951) and who decided not seek their party's nomination to a second elected term. These incumbents were Rutherford Hayes in 1880, Calvin Coolidge in 1928, Harry Truman in 1952, and Lyndon Johnson in 1968. Coolidge would have most probably won reelection. The case is less clear for the other three. One incumbent, Chester Arthur, sought his party's nomination but was denied it.

11. The positivity bias of many in the electorate is reflected in many ways, including the ratings of the presidential candidates on the "feeling thermometer" questions. Since 1968 the NES surveys have asked respondents to rate the candidates on a thermometer scale from 0 to 100 with a neutral point of 50. Twenty major-

party presidential candidates have been rated in the ten elections from 1968 to 2004. Despite the common lament that the vote is cast for the "lesser of two evils," most voters rate the individual candidates positively. It should be no surprise that mean thermometer scores for the ten winning candidates in these elections were greater than 50; however, it is notable that the mean thermometer rating for the losing candidate in each election (except 1972) also was greater than 50 degrees. The median rating exceeded 50 degrees for nineteen of the twenty candidates and equaled 50 degrees for the twentieth candidate (McGovern in 1972). See Knight 1984.

12. Bartels's (1996) research on the effects of information on the presidential vote in elections from 1972 to 1992 also suggests that incumbents may benefit from receiving the benefit of the doubt. Based on a simulated vote for a fully informed electorate, Bartels found that the vote for incumbent presidents was about 4.6 percentage points higher than it would have been had all voters been as fully informed as they could have been.

13. Many of the modern pathologies of American politics (the decline in voter turnout, decreased support for or approval of political institutions, and the greater reluctance of citizens to admit to their partisanship) may be traceable to a general turn away from politics and an aversion to political conflict. The lack of tolerance for or appreciation of the expression of political differences has long been a part of American political culture. Historian Richard Hofstadter (1969) observed this in his study of attitudes toward the first political party system. Much of the progressive tradition of political reform, from nonpartisan municipal elections to civil service reform, reflects a rejection of politics. Numerous studies have sought to explain this apolitical streak in American political culture (Hartz 1955; Boorstin 1953; Wilson 1960; Ranney 1975; Dionne 1991; and Hibbing and Theiss-Morse 1995).

14. There is an extensive literature on the impact of divisive primaries on general election results, in both presidential and subpresidential elections. See Hacker 1965; Pierson and Smith 1975; Bernstein 1977; Lengle 1980; Kenney and Rice 1987; Wattenberg 1991; Lengle, Owen, and Sonner 1995; and Atkeson 1998. Although the precise mechanism by which divisiveness affects the vote remains in dispute, it appears that divided nomination contests affect evaluations of the president which in turn affect the vote. The impact of party unity has also been included in election forecasting models. Lewis-Beck and Rice (1992) incorporated a divided party variable into their forecasting model, though the model did not fare well in predicting the 1992 election. They included a variable termed "candidate appeal," coded as a dichotomy, with presidential candidates receiving more than 60 percent of the total primary vote in their party considered strong candidates and those receiving less than 60 percent considered weak candidates. The estimated equation of the in-party candidate's share of electoral votes also included an economic variable (GNP change in the first half of the election year), the president's popularity as of July of the election year (as measured by the Gallup Poll's presidential job approval question), and a party strength variable (the in-party's seat losses in the prior midterm election). The estimated impact of candidate appeal was statistically significant and amounted to 19.7 percentage points of the electoral vote. In its popular vote equivalent, a strong candidate could expect to receive about 4.6 percentage points more of the popular vote than a weak candidate. Five of the eleven in-party candidates were counted as

weak candidates by the Lewis-Beck and Rice candidate appeal measure: Stevenson in 1952, Johnson in 1964, Humphrey in 1968, Ford in 1976, and Carter in 1980. The coding of Johnson as a weak candidate in 1964 makes the validity of this measure suspect. In 1964, Johnson received just under 18 percent of all primary votes, though he received more than any other candidate and the nomination system did not then depend heavily on the primaries. More than 43 percent of primary votes in 1964 were cast for unpledged delegates. The dichotomous nature of this variable may be in recognition that the primary vote is at best a crude measure of candidate appeal or party unity.

15. There is an interesting body of research regarding the mobilization and demobilization effects of contests over a party's nomination. The divisive nomination thesis is that partisans who had favored an unsuccessful candidate will be disgruntled and decide to sit out the general election (Southwell 1986). There would be reason to suppose that such voters would be more likely to feel crosspressured about their vote (since they had already found at least one candidate to be preferable to the nominee) and may opt not to vote (J. Campbell 1997b, chapter 8). Stone (1986) and Stone, Atkeson, and Rapoport (1992) offer a correction to the prevailing wisdom about divisive nomination contests. They found that there was a significant "positive carryover effect" from nomination contests, that "activity for a nomination contender—even when the activity is in support of a candidate who loses his or her nomination bid—increases the level of participation for the party's ticket in the fall campaign" (665). The authors conclude that "the literature overstates the effect of divisiveness and understates the positive effects of participation in nomination campaigns" (688). While it is worthwhile to note that nomination activity stimulates general election activity, it should be observed that the positive carryover effect was much stronger in every instance if the partisan supported the eventual nominee rather than a candidate denied the party's nomination (Stone, Atkeson, and Rapoport 1992, tables 2 and 3). Thus, the impact of divisive nomination contests exists. Each party would have less trouble mobilizing its partisans for the general election if most of them had sided with the nomination winner rather than a loser.

16. There remains an issue of whether divided parties reflect rather than cause weakness in the candidate. That is, a candidate perceived as beatable may attract competitors for the party's nomination. The link between party divisions and general election outcomes, according to this logic, may be spurious. The political vulnerability of the nominee portends weaker electoral results and generates party divisions. Party divisiveness, so the logic goes, is a side-effect of candidate weakness rather than a cause of poor electoral showings. It is quite likely, however, that both suppositions are correct—that party divisions occur when a nominee is seen to be vulnerable *and* that party divisions further contribute to the poorer general election outcomes for these candidates.

17. There is an extensive record of presidential candidates using charges made during the opposition party's nomination contest. President Reagan, campaigning in Ohio for reelection in 1984, repeated the following charges that were made by contending Democrats against the eventual Democratic nominee, former vice president Walter Mondale: "My opponent has done a very good job of slipping, sliding, and ducking away from his record. But here in Ohio during the primaries, Senator Gary Hart got his message through by reminding you, the Ohio voters, of the true record. And I quote—he said, 'Walter Mondale may pledge stable

prices, but Carter-Mondale could not cure 12 percent inflation.' 'Walter Mondale,' he added, 'has come to Ohio to talk about jobs, but Carter-Mondale watched helpless as 180,000 Ohio jobs disappeared in the period between 1976 and 1980.' Now I didn't say that. Those are Gary Hart's words" (Reagan 1987, 1511). This attack strategy has numerous advantages. The source adds some credibility to the charge, and the fact that the candidate is merely repeating a charge blunts the impression that the candidate is being mean or unfair to the opponent.

18. Evidence of the existence or absence of party unity can also be found in the general election. In many cases third-party presidential candidates emerge from a disgruntled faction of the incumbent's party. From 1900 to 1996, there were six presidential elections with significant third-party candidates: Teddy Roosevelt in 1912, Robert LaFollette in 1924, George Wallace in 1968, John Anderson in 1980, and Ross Perot in 1992 and 1996. The first three of these clearly came out of the in-party. Anderson's campaign came out of the Republican Party when the Democrats occupied the White House. Since Perot had not previously held office, it is more difficult to determine how his candidacy was related to party unity, though the timing suggests that it largely grew out of dissatisfaction with the presidency of Republican George H. W. Bush.

19. It is difficult to read a great deal into the number of ballots for nominations since the convention rules often extended the number of ballots necessary to secure the party's nomination. Until 1936, for instance, the Democratic Party required a two-thirds vote of delegates to win the party's presidential nomination. Thus, a multi-ballot nomination that was extended by this extraordinary majority requirement would thus not indicate as divided a party as one in which multiple ballots were required to gather simple majority. As table 5.6 indicates, three of the eighteen nominees produced by multi-ballot conventions had a simple majority of delegate votes on the first ballot. Two of these three won their elections.

20. While a contested nomination is for the most part a hindrance to a candidate in the general election, it may also help in some circumstances. As FDR's advisor James Farley reflected, the internal party contest that Roosevelt faced in 1932 helped to draw national attention to Roosevelt's candidacy (Farley 1938, 155).

21. One incumbent president, Chester A. Arthur, who wanted to run for election was denied his party's nomination in 1884. Arthur, a Republican, was elected in 1880 as James Garfield's vice president. He became president when Garfield was assassinated. President Arthur ran second to James G. Blaine in the Republican convention. Blaine won the party's nomination on the convention's fourth ballot.

22. Regression analyses also confirm the greater early unity for incumbents and the greater impact of the vote of early party unity. The dependent variable in the first regression was the difference in loyalty rates among early-deciding Democrats and Republicans. The independent variable was whether a Democratic president was running (scored 1), no incumbent was running (scored 0), or a Republican president was running (scored −1). The effect of incumbency was 8.3 percentage points ($p < .05$, one-tailed). A second regression with the Democrat's share of the two-party vote as the dependent variable and the party loyalty differences for early and late deciders indicated that about 34 percent of the early unity gap translated to the vote compared to 20 percent of the late unity gap. This may reflect, in part, the larger number of early-deciding voters.

23. Edward Tufte's analysis demonstrated that economic growth was greater in election years than nonelection years and that economic growth rates strongly

affect the election outcomes. According to Tufte, "solely because of the electoral-economic cycle, then, the incumbent president has typically started his bid for re-election with a lead of 52.4 percent to 47.6 percent over the candidate of the out-party. This is a very good start, and helps to explain why incumbent presidents rarely lose their bid for re-election" (1978, 135). The impact of the economy on the campaign and election is examined in chapter 6.

24.　White notes that in a Friday night televised speech just days before the election, McGovern hammered Nixon and Kissinger for suggesting that they were on the verge of a peace treaty with the North Vietnamese and the Viet Cong. McGovern called this a "cruel deception" (White 1973, 339). The Kissinger statement, however, comported well with views that Nixon was extricating America from that war. Stanley Kelley (1983, 108) quotes pollsters Frederick Steeper and Robert Teeter as reporting that in their polls they had "consistently found Nixon's biggest asset was that a clear plurality of voters perceived him as *de-escalating* the war." Kelley's analysis of responses to the NES open-ended "likes and dislikes" questions about the candidates also supports this view.

25.　Elizabeth Drew (1981) observes in her discussion of the presidential debate between Carter and Reagan in 1980 that "Carter, in his first answer, does his Presidential routine: 'I've had to make thousands of decisions since I've been President, serving in the Oval Office'" (322).

26.　The use of the White House for fundraising activities raises several ethical and legal issues that are not clear cut. Technically, conducting campaign fundraising activities on federal government facilities, such as the White House, is illegal. However, raising "soft money" for political party efforts such as voter mobilization and education was legal prior to 2004. After the 1996 campaign a number of Republicans called for a special prosecutor after it was revealed that Vice President Al Gore had solicited campaign contributions from his White House office that may have gone to the Clinton-Gore campaign rather than to the "soft-money" accounts of the National Democratic Party. Similarly, events staged at the White House for the purpose of raising campaign contributions or rewarding contributors (such as a night's stay in the Lincoln Bedroom) may skirt illegalities if the connection between the contribution and the White House perk is not explicit or if the explicit contribution solicitation is not made on the premises.

27.　The "mean streak" dilemma is not limited to challengers. It confronts any candidate whose strategic position compels him to go on the offensive. As Drew (1981, 306–308), Hunt (1981, 155–56), Abramson, Aldrich, and Rohde (1982, 41–42), and others observed, President Carter experienced the "meanness" dilemma in his 1980 race against Ronald Reagan. A number of observers at the time suggested that Carter's attacks on Reagan reflected meanness. As this case illustrates, the mean-streak problem confronts all candidates taking an offensive rather than defensive posture in a campaign. The Carter-Reagan case also suggests that the nature of the attack makes a difference. Unlike Carter, Reagan was able to attack his opponent without being labeled mean-spirited, since he was able to attack the Carter record without attacking the president personally.

28.　Carville's four rules for the 1992 Clinton campaign were: (1) "Change vs. more of the same," (2) "The economy, stupid," (3) "Don't forget healthcare," and (4) "The debate, stupid." These were listed on a white board in the Clinton campaign headquarters and can be seen at the end of the 1992 documentary film *The War Room*.

29. The Clinton campaign theme in 1992 might best be characterized as a blend of James Carville's "It's the economy, stupid!" and "change" (Troy 1996, 270). Presidential campaign historian Gil Troy writes that "Clinton interpreted his victory as a mandate for change" (1996, 271).

30. One candidate who defied the theme pattern was Warren Harding. His "Back to Normalcy" theme effectively combined both change and stability. Candidates of the majority party (as Republicans were in the 1920s) seeking to succeed a president from the minority party (in this case Woodrow Wilson) may be in the position to draw on both themes. On the other hand, the themes of continuity and change may also shed light on the difficulty that vice presidents have in seeking to win election in their own right. They face the dilemma of being poorly positioned to draw on either theme. As part of the past, usually a two-term administration, they cannot successfully portray themselves as the candidate of change. In adopting the continuity theme, on the other hand, they must adopt the agenda of the sitting president and thereby risk being perceived as lacking independent leadership abilities. Vice presidents as candidates are between the rock of disloyalty and the hard place of subservience.

Chapter 6

1. Among the entire range of conditions by which voters could retrospectively evaluate the performance of the in-party, only the issue of war and peace could conceivably rival the economy as a public concern. Voters reward candidates and their party for securing the twin goals of peace and prosperity. And, while the public generally rallies around presidents in time of war, they are not so forgiving of presidents during hard economic times. As a result, the failure to secure prosperity has a larger political price tag than the failure to produce peace. Thus, the difference between the potential political upside and downside of economic issues is greater than any other matter of regular public concern, including the great issue of war and peace.

2. Some might say that it is often unfair to hold the president accountable for the state of the economy, that there are too many factors that are well beyond any president's ability to control. In this sense, presidents are unfairly rewarded for strong economies and unfairly punished for weak ones. In a strict sense, this is true. However, from the voters' perspective it may be quite reasonable to act as if presidents controlled economic conditions. Knowing that they will be held accountable, presidents may make every effort within their powers to deliver a good economy to the voters. Without this pressure to deliver, presidents may be more inclined to make excuses than they otherwise would be.

3. For a compilation of seven prominent presidential election forecasting models see the October, 2004, issue of *PS: Political Science & Politics*. With the exception of Norpoth (2004), each uses either a broad-based objective index of economic activity like GDP growth or a measure of public opinion about the economy.

4. The real GDP growth rates are computed from the Bureau of Economic Analysis (BEA) of the U.S. Department of Commerce (2006). The annualized percentage change in real GDP is calculated from their quarterly GDP series in "chained" 2000 dollars. Since the purpose of the analysis is to determine the effect of the economy (rather than the effect of reports of the economy), the latest and presumably most accurate GDP estimates are used rather than the August

of the election year release used in the forecasting equations reported in chapter 1. The latest GDP change estimates correlate quite highly with the August BEA release ($r = .94$ for both first half year and second-quarter measures), but revised estimates generally indicate higher growth rates (a mean difference of a full percentage point between the second-quarter measures and about half of a percentage point between the first half measures). In addition, in particular years, there are notable differences between the contemporary and the revised estimates of growth. For instance, the reported first-half growth during the 1948 election was a bit over four percent, ranking seventh of the fifteen elections since that time. Revised estimates now set that GDP growth rate at nearly seven percent, ranking fifth of the fifteen elections. Conversely, the economy leading into the 2000 election appeared much stronger than revised estimates now indicate that it was. It had ranked sixth strongest of the fifteen elections, but ranked tenth in the revised GDP data.

5. J. Campbell and Garand 1999 presents a compilation of these models. We should also observe that the presidential election forecasting model that relied most heavily on economic indicators, the Fair model (1978, 1982, and 1988), was quite far off the mark in its 1992 forecast (Greene 1993) and was later significantly revised (Fair 1994). Also, Erikson's analysis (1989) of both Tufte's and Hibbs's measurements of per capita real income growth indicate that consideration of the economy alone only takes one so far in accounting for election results and that a more complete explanation is produced by combining economic indicators with a measure of general public opinion.

6. The standardized regression coefficients indicate the relative importance of each independent predictor variable in a forecasting equation. The election-year economy's position as a secondary predictor is evident in both models examined in chapter 1. In the Abramowitz model (table 1.3), the GDP growth rate in the first two quarters of the election year had a standardized coefficient of .36 compared to coefficients for July presidential approval of .52 and for the third-term variable of .33. In the trial-heat and economy model (table 1.5), the second-quarter GDP growth rate had a standardized coefficient of .42 compared to the September trial-heat poll standing's coefficient of .73.

7. It may be that the relationship between the election-year economy and the vote is nonlinear. While the election-year economy was quite strong in each landslide election in this period (1964, 1972, and 1984), the in-party vote in each instance was much greater than expected based on a linear relationship (bivariate or multivariate) between the economy and the vote. However, a nonlinear relationship would still leave several elections with large vote deviations from that expected based on their election-year economic conditions. A reviewer of the first edition suggested the possibility that the 1980 election was an outlier and that the three landslide elections were influence points. I reexamined the 1948 to 1996 data (a model with the first-half economic growth and the early September preference poll standing of the in-party's candidate) with a robust regression analysis (Rousseeuw and Leroy 1987). The regression diagnostic computed from a least median squares estimation detected one influence point: 1956. With 1956 out of the analysis, the estimated impact of the first-half growth rate in the election-year economy on the vote increases from a coefficient of 1.28 to 1.68. Thus, quite the contrary to the reviewer's concern, rather than overestimating economic effects the analysis may have underestimated them (though they re-

main in the robust regression clearly secondary in predicting the vote when compared to the preference poll).

8. The Lewis-Beck (1988) study was based on an analysis of voting behavior and economics in the 1980s in five European nations. He classified economic effects as personal versus collective, simple versus complex (involving an evaluation of the connection of the government to the economy as opposed to a simple evaluation of the economy), and retrospective versus prospective. He found that personal simple retrospective economic evaluations did not appear to affect the vote (57, 90, table 4.1), that the direct effect on the vote of collective simple retrospective evaluations was nearly negligible (tables 4.2, 4.3, and 4.4), and that personal complex retrospective evaluations of the economy had no direct effect on the vote (also tables 4.2, 4.3, and 4.4). On the positive side, he found that collective complex retrospective evaluations had a moderate direct impact on the vote (tables 4.5 and 6.1), that collective complex prospective evaluations of the economy had the strongest direct effect on the vote of any economic evaluation (tables 4.1 and 6.1, 83, 133), and that the total effects of retrospective and prospective evaluations (collective and complex) were about equal when the indirect effects of retrospective evaluations on prospective evaluations are taken into account. In somewhat different terms: (1) voters do not look only at their own pocketbooks when they vote but consider the broader economic conditions; (2) voters do not have a political reflex action about the economy but gauge whether the government was in some way responsible for the economic development; and (3) voters look to the past economic record (retrospective voting) to determine who might best serve their economic interests in the future (prospective voting).

9. The election forecasting models, especially the trial-heat and economy model (table 1.5, J. Campbell and Wink 1990; J. Campbell 1996, 2004b), are instructive on the gradual incorporation of economic considerations into vote preferences and ultimately on the vote. First, the trial-heat and economy model differs from the Abramowitz (2004 and table 1.3) popularity-economy-term model in a way consistent with the economic model of figure 6.2. The trial-heat model uses an early September trial-heat poll while the Abramowitz model uses July approval ratings. As a result of the different timing of their public opinion measures the models also have a different time frame for their measures of the economy (GDP change). Since the Abramowitz model is a bit earlier in the election year than the trial-heat model, it uses economic growth over the first two quarters of the election year. The later trial-heat model uses economic growth in only the second quarter of the election year. The difference would appear to be that the impact of first-quarter economic growth has not yet been fully felt in public opinion by the time July approval ratings are gathered but is incorporated into the early September trial-heat ratings. Thus the first-quarter economic conditions do not provide any guidance about the vote beyond that already provided by the September trial-heat poll. The forecasting models also provide corroborating evidence for figure 6.2 in another way. The trial-heat and economy model has been examined using trial-heat polls at different points during the election year, from June through November. There is a definite pattern for the contributions of the poll variable and the economy variable to the forecast. The closer the polls used are to election day, the more the polls matter to the forecast and the less the second-quarter economic growth rate matters to it. This does not mean that the second-quarter growth rate matters less to the election results. It means, rather, that the

second-quarter growth rate matters less *directly* to the forecast of the results. As the public gets further removed from the second quarter (ending in June) they have had a chance to process the economic information and incorporate it into the preferences they express in the polls.

10. It is unclear to what extent, if any, economic conditions in the first two years of an administration have on the vote. Hibbs (1982, 1987), Erikson (1989), and Erikson and Wlezien (1996) suggest that there is a cumulative effect of economic conditions over time but that there is a considerable discounting of economic growth rates earlier in the presidential term. My analysis, however, finds no significant relationship between economic growth, as measured over the first three years or the second and third year, with poll standings or approval rates before the general election campaign. Thus, it would appear that growth rates in the first half of a presidential term make at most a very minor impact on the next election.

11. A multiple regression using 1992 NES data with the president's job approval (a four-point scale from strongly approve to strongly disapprove) as the dependent variable and three independent variables—party identification, approval of the president's handling of the economy (also a four-point scale), and impressions of whether the economy was better or worse off over the past year (a five-point scale)—indicates a strong spillover effect of the economy. Each of the three independent variables was statistically significant ($p < .001$) and together they accounted for 50 percent of the variance in presidential approval ratings. The standard error of the estimate was 1.09. The standardized regression coefficients were .45 for approval of handling the economy, .11 for unmediated evaluations of the economy, and .30 for party identification. As one would expect, the independent variables were correlated with one another ($r =$ from .29 to .50), but they were not so highly intercorrelated as to produce multicollinearity problems.

12. Unfortunately, many of the questions asked over the years in the NES surveys regarding the economy are so relative as to be of very limited use in examining public evaluations of economic conditions. For instance, the question regarding retrospective economic evaluations is as follows: "How about the economy? Would you say that over the past year the nation's economy has gotten better, stayed the same, or gotten worse?" The possible answers are: "gotten better," "stayed same," or "gotten worse." This question and the answers are problematic because there are two embedded referents: what conditions were and what they are. A response that things had gotten better might be interpreted as positive for the in-party, but conditions may still be unacceptably bad to the voter if he or she thought conditions were horrible to begin with. Conversely, a response that things had gotten worse might be read as a verdict against the in-party, but not necessarily. If the economy had been booming, things may have gotten worse but still be quite acceptable. A slowdown from a growth rate of 6 percent to 4 percent is a slowdown, but an economy churning along at 4 percent growth is still quite strong. The NES questions regarding prospective economic conditions and both retrospective and prospective views of economic conditions are similarly relative measures rather than measures of satisfaction with economic circumstances.

13. A regression analysis on the in-party's vote share explained by GDP growth in the first half of the election year and an interaction term between the first-half GDP growth and whether the in-party candidate was an incumbent did not confirm the interaction effect ($p < .05$). However, the interaction was statistically significant for GDP growth in the second quarter of the election year in a state-level

forecasting model (Campbell, Ali, and Jalazai 2006, 50). Additionally, it appears that incumbents are especially attentive to the economy when they are seeking reelection. The median first half year growth was 5.4 percent when an incumbent was in the race and only 3.5 percent when a successor candidate was running.

Chapter 7

1. A good example is New York governor Mario Cuomo's stirring speech to the 1992 Democratic convention that nominated Arkansas governor Bill Clinton. The speech accomplished the two missions of any good convention speech: it emphasized the commonalities among all parts of the party and it energized the party to work to defeat the opposing party in the general election. See Germond and Witcover 1993, 344–45.

2. Wayne (1996) cites Dukakis's reaching out to Jackson in 1988 and Clinton's reaching out to Tsongas on rules and platform statements as efforts by the candidate to mend fences with fellow partisans following a nomination battle. Despite overtures of this sort, at times supporters of the losing candidates have been so disaffected that they hold back from enthusiastically endorsing the ticket. Most notably, divisions among Democrats were too wide to be bridged at their 1968 and 1972 conventions.

3. Though technically the decision of the convention's delegates, the last candidate to throw the vice presidential decision back to the convention was Adlai Stevenson in 1956. Presidential candidates have generally understood the potential divisiveness of an open contest for the vice presidential nomination and have recognized the value of using the decision either to appeal to another wing of the party or to energize the party. At the very least, finding an inoffensive nominee forestalls possible problems in the campaign. Among other post-1950 vice presidential nominees possibly selected to unify the party were Eisenhower's selection of Nixon in 1952, Nixon's selection of Henry Cabot Lodge in 1960, and Carter's selection of Mondale in 1976. The selection of some vice presidential candidates may have been intended more to energize than reunify the party. Mondale's selection of Geraldine Ferraro as the first female candidate on a major-party presidential ticket in 1984 may have been of this sort. Bush's selection of Quayle in 1988 may also have been an attempt to energize his campaign. Given that most vice presidential candidates running with non-incumbent nominees are not known to many in the public and that the first information available about a candidate is generally positive (before the opposition and the media have had a chance to dig up the negatives), the vice presidential nomination may be an important part of the convention bump and may also marginally affect the November vote. Wattenberg (1984), in examining the net impact of vice presidential candidates in elections from 1952 to 1980, found that they had an average effect of about three-quarters of a percentage point on the national presidential vote. Rosenstone (1983, 74), Lewis-Beck and Rice (1983), Garand (1988), and Campbell, Ali, and Jalalzai (2006) found that vice presidential candidates receive about a 2- to 2.5-percentage-point advantage in their home states.

4. Since 1968 the NES surveys have asked "thermometer questions," rating reactions from the most positive of 100 degrees to the most negative of 0, regarding the vice presidential candidates. With the exception of Dan Quayle in both 1988 and 1992, each vice presidential candidate has had a mean rating of 50 degrees or

higher. The mean thermometer scores in order of the strongest to weakest showings are: Muskie (D, 1968) 61, Gore (D, 1992) 57, Ferraro (D, 1984) 57, Cheny (R, 2000), 56; Lieberman (D, 2000), 56; Bush (R, 1980) 55, Bush (R, 1984) 55, Edwards, (D, 2004), 55; Agnew (R, 1972) 54, Mondale (D, 1980) 54, Bentsen (D, 1988) 53, Mondale (D, 1976) 53, Dole (R, 1976) 51, Agnew (R, 1968) 50, Cheney (R, 2004), 50; Shriver (D, 1972) 50, Quayle (R, 1988) 46, and Quayle (R, 1992) 42.

5. Reminding voters of the basis for partisanship is consistent with what W. Miller and Shanks (1982) found in their analysis of early opinion changes in the 1980 electorate. According to Miller and Shanks, "Between the time of the early primaries and the nominating conventions, liberals tended to alter their perceptions in a manner that increased the distance between them and Reagan and decreased the distance between them and Carter. In complementary fashion, more and more conservatives saw Reagan as the closer of the two candidates and uniformly, across all issues, increased their relative distance from Carter" (331). After the conventions, Miller and Shanks found that partisan perceptions continued to polarize, thus clarifying the voters' choice (332). The emphasis of the general election campaign on differences between the parties is also suggested by Jacoby's research on the priming effects of campaigns. In examining thermometer ratings of the candidates in 1980, Jacoby (1997) found that "over the course of the campaign, the salience of ideological distinctions among the candidates steadily increases, while their credibility becomes a less prominent component of the electorate's general perceptions" (28).

6. President Richard Nixon in remarks at a press conference on October 5, 1972 offered insights into the turnout component of the narrowing effect of the campaign:

> . . . the problem of a candidate that is ahead in the polls, and his organization, is a very significant one in this respect: It is the problem of getting his vote out. What we need above everything else is a big vote. In order to get a big vote, it means that people have to be stimulated to vote. That is one of the reasons that going to the country and participating will help get that big vote out, and when the time permits, I will go to the country in order to get the vote out, among other things.
>
> With the candidate who is behind substantially in the polls, he doesn't have that problem. With all the pollsters—and the pollsters always remember when they predicted right but never when they predicted wrong—this doesn't prove anything necessarily, because when the margins are up in the 60–40 range, on the fringes it is always quite soft either way.
>
> But in 1964 I was interested to find that Gallup never had Goldwater as more than 32 percent as against Johnson. In fact, Gallup's poll, taken one week before the election, showed Goldwater at 32 percent. He got 39 percent. Why? The Goldwater people voted, and many of the Johnson people thought they had it made (1972, 959).

President Nixon's observation about the softness of support when deviating too far from the normal vote is well taken. A significant portion of the support for the frontrunner with a large lead must come from potential defectors from the opposing party. I have found elsewhere (J. Campbell 1997b, chapter 8), however, that in the end, most disaffected partisans are cross-pressured and are more likely not to vote at all than to defect and vote for the opposing party's candidate.

7. Gopoian and Hadjiharalambous (1994, table 8, 64) found statistically significant "carryover effects" of the nomination (correlations between time of the vote decision and support for rival candidates for the party's nomination) in four of seven cases, and in each case the effect had the correct sign (indicating that supporters of rivals to the nominee were more likely to reach their general election vote decisions late). Although Gopoian and Hadjiharalambous (1994), like the present study (table 7.6), found defection rates to be higher among late deciders (1994, table 11), they were still consistently more likely to vote for their own party's candidate than the opposition's. Additionally, party identification had a statistically significant effect on the vote choice of late deciders in four of the five elections they examined (1972 through 1988). Moreover, Gopoian and Hadjiharalambous defined late deciders quite strictly as those indicating that they made their vote choice in the last two weeks of the campaign.

8. White (1969, 474) recounts that much of Nixon's lead over Humphrey, as measured in several polls, evaporated in the last week of October. Nixon's lead in the Gallup poll dropped from an eight-point lead as of October 21 to a statistically insignificant two-point lead on November 2. White notes that the polls also suggested a slight move back to Nixon in the last few days before the election. He attributes these changes to the Johnson administration's decision to halt bombing in Vietnam.

9. As Gerald Pomper (1977), among others, observed regarding the 1976 campaign: "The second phase of the campaign lasted through the month of September and at least through the first week of October. The polls registered a continuous decline in Carter's strength, with the contenders near a standoff by the end of the period" (67).

10. Regarding the 1992 election, though Pomper (1993, 144) noted a steadiness in preferences over the course of the campaign, Abramson, Aldrich, and Rohde (1994) noted that "the race tightened up considerably after Perot's reentry" (64) in late September.

11. The variance (as measured by the standard deviation in the two-party preference division of the trial-heat polls) was about 20 to 30 percent less in polls after the second convention. In 1992, examining all available national polls that included Perot as an option, the standard deviation of the two-party preference in pre-convention polls was 3.16 ($N = 34$) and the standard deviation in post-convention polls was 2.46 ($N = 104$). In 1996, the standard deviation of the two-party preference in pre-convention Gallup polls was 3.11 ($N = 36$) and the standard deviation in post-convention Gallup polls was 2.11 ($N = 47$).

12. The June and July trial-heat polls along with the second-quarter growth rate in the economy (real GDP, halved for successor candidates) account for more than 70 percent of the variance in the in-party's presidential vote for the fifteen presidential elections from 1948 to 2004. The standardized coefficients of the forecast regressions for both the June and July trial-heats indicate that the forecasts are more dependent on the trial-heat polls than the economic growth rates (J. Campbell 2004b).

13. The regression to the mean effect is one in which errors may have caused the initial deviation away from the mean. Assuming that the errors are random, the change computed from adjacent observations should tend to show a movement

toward the mean. Since we admit that errors in the summer polls are likely to be greater than in later polls and that this reflects the fact that many voters have yet to focus on the election, it is quite possible that part of the decline in the front-runners' numbers reflect the regression to the mean phenomenon. However, the fact that the separate June and July poll analyses both show a decline in front-runner support suggests that there may be more to the decline than simply a regression to the mean. This is also suggested by the evidence from several other areas that we will examine: the effects of the party conventions, changes from the fall polls to the election, and analyses of early- and late-deciding voters.

14. Most modern nominations are settled matters before the conventions. The trend toward the "front-end loading" of caucuses and primaries, selecting more of the delegates earlier in the election year, should only increase this tendency.

15. The number of voters who decide during the conventions is more impressive from the perspective of their proportion of all voters who had decided how they would vote. Before the conventions, typically a bit more than 40 percent indicate they have made their choice. Those who decide during the conventions typically bring the total of deciders up to about 63 percent of those who will eventually vote.

16. On two occasions (1968 and 1992), the frontrunner changed between the conventions. Nixon in 1968 received such a big boost from the GOP convention in 1968 that he was elevated from trailing candidate to frontrunner. Similarly, Clinton in 1992 pushed ahead of George H. W. Bush before the GOP convention, making Bush the trailing candidate going into his convention.

17. The regression specified the in-party candidate's share of the two-party vote as the dependent variable. The principal independent variable was the net convention bump, computed as the difference between the in-party candidate's standing in the Gallup preference poll (the two-party percentage) before the first convention and after the second convention. Two other independent variables were included in the equation: the in-party candidate's two-party share of support before the first convention and the second-quarter growth rate in the GDP (annualized, August release, and halved for successor candidates). The equation was estimated over the fifteen elections from 1948 to 2004. The adjusted R^2 of this model was .84, and the standard error of the estimate was 2.23. The coefficient of the net convention bump was .29 (p < .01, one-tailed; beta = .32). The coefficients were .43 for the pre-convention poll (beta = .75) and .67 for the economy (beta = .46). Both were statistically significant (p < .01, one-tailed). Using the June poll instead of the pre-convention poll in the equation boosts the net bump effect to .33 and the adjusted R^2 to .85. In a time-series analysis of second convention bumps, Stimson (2004, 121–26) surprisingly found the bump effects to be "permanent," showing no decay as the campaign moves forward.

18. The equation accounted for 89 percent of the variance in the in-party's vote (adjusted R^2). Alternative specifications indicate roughly the same discount rate for the September poll lead. The simple bivariate regression with the Labor Day polls as the independent variable and the November vote as the dependent variable yield a coefficient of .55 (a discount rate of .45).

19. While we define any candidate leading in the early September polls as the front-running candidate, some of these candidates were more definitely frontrunners than others. In particular, Nixon's lead over Kennedy in 1960 and Reagan's lead over Carter in 1980 were so slight that these elections could be classified as not

having frontrunners. In the remaining eleven elections, one candidate had a clear lead by early September. In all eleven of these cases, the poll leader in early September had led in the post-convention polls and, with one exception (1988), had led in the July polls as well.

20. Research on presidential debate effects generally indicates that most have had little impact on the vote, though a few (1960 first debate pro-Kennedy, 1984 second pro-Reagan, 1988 second pro-Bush, and 1992 third pro-Bush) may have had some effect (Abramowitz 1978; Geer 1988; Lanoue 1991; Shelley and Hwang 1991; Holbrook 1996a). In my review of Holbrook's debate analysis in chapter 3, I suggested that debate effects may be short-lived. The effects of one debate as measured by changes in the polls largely recede even before the next debate is conducted. In addition, of the seven presidential debates examined by Holbrook for the 1984, 1988, and 1992 elections, statistically significant effects were found in only three cases (and with changes in specifications, only two consistently significant cases: the second debates in 1984 and 1988). The estimated debate effects in these cases were also modest in magnitude (depending on the specification examined, less than 3.5 or less than 2 percentage points). Debate effects are likely to be small because of their lateness in the campaign season and because of their audience. Most debates are conducted in the closing weeks of the election year after most voters have settled on their candidate. The audience, moreover, is mostly attentive voters willing to set aside the time to watch it. These voters are even more likely than the average voter to have made up their minds. As a result, most debate watchers generally see their preferred candidate as having performed better in the debate and are less affected even when forced to admit that their candidate "lost" the debate. Even after Ford's infamous "Eastern Europe" gaffe in the second presidential debate of 1976, most Ford supporters thought that he had "won" the debate until overwhelming media commentary declared otherwise. In the face of this commentary, Ford supporters acknowledged as a matter of fact, rather than their own evaluation, that Carter had "won" the debate (Patterson 1980, 123). The first debate in 1984 between Reagan and Mondale is another strong example of how most debates have little, if any, effect on the election results. Despite Mondale's generally acknowledged stronger performance in the debate, it appeared to make little difference to the election results (Hunt 1985, 152–53; Kessel 1992, 222; Pika and Watson 1996, 97). It might have made a difference, however, if it had been followed by other debates or events that reinforced Reagan's poor showing.

21. Debates may also play a part in narrowing the leads of frontrunners by helping to bring disgruntled partisans back to their party. Debates tend to focus on position issues that separate the parties, thus reminding partisans of the issue basis for their partisanship. In general, however, based on previous findings of limited and undependable debate effects, debate effects might be best classified as a potential source of unsystematic campaign effects. Kennedy's strong showing against Nixon in the first debate of 1960, for example, could not have been anticipated and does not reflect any general effect that could be anticipated before other campaigns.

22. Gopoian and Hadjiharalambous (1994) examined identical comprehensive vote choice equations using NES data for voters reaching early, "middle," and late decisions in the five presidential elections from 1972 to 1988. While the models did an excellent job of accounting for variance in the vote choices of early deciders

and those who decided prior to the last two weeks of the campaign, they did not fare so well in explaining the vote choices of late deciders. In each of the five elections, the models correctly indicated the vote choices of 89 to 96 percent of the early and middle deciders. In contrast, the same models correctly classified only 61 to 71 percent of late deciders. They do not indicate how many voters the null model (the modal vote among late deciders) would have correctly classified, but it would probably be well in excess of 50 percent. The poor performance of the vote choice model among late deciders both in absolute terms and relative to voters reaching earlier decisions led Gopoian and Hadjiharalambous to conclude that there was a substantial random component to the individual decisions of voters who postponed their vote decision to the last two weeks of the campaign.

23. The unusually strong showing of independent candidate Ross Perot complicated matters in 1992. More than half of all voters in 1992 were late deciders, and about 35 percent of them voted for Perot. Only about 1 percent of early deciders supported Perot.

Chapter 8

1. The electoral vote difference between 1888, the election in which Harrison defeated Cleveland, and 1892, the election in which Cleveland defeated Harrison, is that Cleveland carried New York, Indiana, Illinois, and California in 1892 but had lost these states to Harrison in 1888. Harrison gained electoral votes in several states admitted to the Union between the elections, including Wyoming, Montana, and South Dakota. Other small differences resulted from some split electoral votes within states and electoral votes going to the Populist candidate James Weaver.

2. Although the 1868 election can be categorized as a close contest, it was the least close of this category. Lacking the restraint it would acquire in later years, the *New York Times*'s headline the day after the 1868 election declared: "Victory! Magnificent and Overwhelming Triumph." Grant received nearly three-quarters of the electoral votes, and, as the critical vote analysis in table 8.2 indicates, for Seymour to have won an electoral vote majority he would have had to have reversed the election outcome in seven of the thirty-four states voting that year. Still, Grant's 2.66-percentage-point plurality of the two-party popular vote is quite modest and more similar to the other close contest elections than to the moderately competitive elections.

3. The election was in fact close, though the *New York Times* at the time described the election outcome as one in which McKinley received "an enormous plurality of the popular vote" (Keylin and Nelson 1976, 92). After his 1896 defeat, Bryan would run and lose a second (1900) and a third (1908) time as the Democratic Party's presidential candidate.

4. The electoral vote count and the popular vote shift in states that would have changed the electoral college vote winner have been calculated from Congressional Quarterly's *Guide to U.S. Elections, Fifth Edition* (2005). Peirce (1968, 317–21) provides a similar sort of analysis of "Elections in Which Minor Vote Shifts Could Have Changed the Outcome" for elections from 1828 to 1960. The number of critical votes and some of the states involved differ a bit between Peirce's analysis and table 8.2. For instance, Peirce notes that "a shift of 1,983 votes from Wilson to Hughes in California would have cost Wilson the election" (1968, 321)

while I find that Hughes would have needed a shift of only 1,711 votes to tip California to him.

5. Alternatively, Hughes could have won an electoral vote majority with relatively minor vote shifts in several states other than California. Wilson would have been defeated in the electoral college with a shift of 14,069 votes from Wilson to Hughes in Kentucky, a shift of 14,347 votes in Missouri, or a combined shift of 10,535 votes in Maryland and New Hampshire.

6. The *New York Times*'s (Aug. 21, 1916, pp. 1, 7) story on the non-meeting of Hughes and Johnson on August 20, 1916, reported at the time that Governor Johnson was the Progressive candidate for Senate. In addition to opposition from both a Democratic and a Socialist candidate, Johnson was being opposed by Willis Booth, the Republican candidate. Booth apparently dropped out of the race before its conclusion. The election results in Congressional Quarterly's *Guide to U.S. Elections* reports Johnson as being both the Republican- and Progressive-endorsed candidate. There is some question among later analysts whether the supposed snub of Johnson cost Hughes the election. Gil Troy, for instance, concludes that "in blaming Hughes and the active stumping campaign for what was now considered a debacle, politicians were misled by both the dramatic quality of the Johnson snub and the high hopes that had imprisoned Hughes from the outset" (1996, 141). The closeness of the national vote and the vote numbers in California, however, as well as the general history of Republican presidential successes in the firmly Republican era (1896–1928, with the other exception of the Roosevelt and Taft split in 1912) suggest that the perceived snub may well have cost Hughes the 1916 election.

7. There were actually twenty disputed electoral votes. Nineteen were in the states of South Carolina (seven), Florida (four), and Louisiana (eight). The electoral votes in these states would be determined by the popular vote count in each respective state. A twentieth disputed vote came from Oregon, where the eligibility of a Hayes elector was in doubt because of his position as a U.S. postmaster. He resigned his elector and postmaster positions and was then reappointed to serve as an elector by the other Republican electors.

8. The congressional representation on the commission provided for three seats to the majority party and two to the minority in both the House and the Senate. There were peculiar developments in the Supreme Court representation. After two Democratic justices and two Republican justices were selected, the parties were anticipating the selection of Justice David Davis, a Republican appointee (by Lincoln) who was considered independent-minded, as the crucial fifth justice on the commission. However, before the selection was made, the Illinois state legislature elected Davis to the U.S. Senate, thus disqualifying him from the commission post. Justice Joseph Bradley, another Republican with an independent streak, was selected as the fifth justice. In the commission's deliberations, Justice Bradley was to vote with the Republicans on each of the three cases of disputed electoral votes.

9. There has been some speculation that southern Democrats put up less resistance to the commission's ruling for the Republicans than they might have because southerners made a deal with Hayes. In return for minimal resistance to Hayes's election, a Hayes administration agreed to ease up on post–Civil War Reconstruction policies, including the withdrawal of federal troops, and provide further assistance in rebuilding the southern economy (Severn 1968, 184–87). These

overtures, however, could also be seen as efforts to quell southern Democratic anger over Hayes's very narrow victory.

10. Democrats were convinced that the 1876 election had been stolen from Tilden. The House rejected the commission's rulings (though this had no effect since reversal of the rulings required a rejection by both the House and the Senate and the Republican Senate approved) and, also to no avail, passed a resolution declaring that Tilden had won the election. Sometime later, the Democratically controlled House appointed a committee to investigate fraud in the election. Known as the Potter Investigation (named after its chairman, Representative Clarkson Potter of New York), the committee concluded on purely partisan votes that Tilden had been wrongly denied election. However, the Republicans on the committee effectively argued that there had been substantial Democratic misconduct by those close to Tilden in the three disputed states. In defending the election of Hayes and in demonstrating Democratic election fraud, Representative Thomas Brackett Reed, a Republican member of the Potter Committee and years later Speaker of the House, offered the following observations to the House regarding Democratic misconduct:

> You can always tell something of the material of which the house is built by inspecting a portion of it. I had occasion to investigate one parish. I want gentlemen to draw their own inferences. I will not draw one, nor will I state a fact that either side can deny or dispute. In the parish of East Feliciana in the State of Louisiana, in the year between 1874 and 1876, there were fourteen persons murdered, and that fact no man doubts; no man can dispute it. The Democrats say that it was on account of cotton-seed stealing, and personal difficulties. The Republicans say that these murders were political. On these two points men differ, but here are the other facts equally undisputed. First, every man who was killed was a Republican; second, cotton-seed stealing and murder simultaneously ceased on election day; third, in 1874 that parish cast 1600 Republican votes against 800 Democratic—two to one. And in 1876, after these murders had taken place, there were 1700 registered Democratic votes, 400 unregistered, and one for Rutherford B. Hayes (quoted in McCall 1914, 73).

> Setting the voting patterns of the disputed states in historical context does not clarify matters much. It is historically true that none of these states would again cast an electoral vote for a Republican presidential candidate for the next *twelve* presidential elections. In 1928, more than half a century after the disputed 1876 election, Florida voted for Republican Herbert Hoover rather than for Democratic candidate Al Smith. However, prior to 1876, both Florida and South Carolina had voted for Grant in his 1868 and 1872 elections. Democrats won a plurality in Louisiana in 1868, but Republicans received a plurality in 1872.

11. The Presbyterian minister was the Reverend Samuel D. Burchard. Presumably the "rum" reference referred to those with the Democratic Party who opposed alcohol prohibition. The prohibition movement was well under way. The Prohibition Party had formed in 1869 and for the first time exceeded 1 percent of the national vote in the 1884 election. "Romanism" referred to the Roman Catholic Church. "Rebellion" referred to those who helped or sympathized with the Confederacy during or after the Civil War.

12. The evening of the same day as the "Rum, Romanism, and Rebellion" fiasco, Blaine attended a lavish dinner party with big business moguls. The dinner received a great deal of unfavorable publicity, portraying Blaine as cozying up to the wealthy and removed from the problems of the average voter. This exacerbated the Blaine campaign's problems.

13. A Blaine victory could also have been engineered by relatively small vote shifts in several other states. Blaine could have carried Connecticut and its 6 electoral votes with a vote swing of 645 votes, New Jersey and its 9 electoral votes with a vote swing of 2,156 votes, and West Virginia and its 6 electoral votes with a shift of 2,108 votes.

14. The election was so close that Nixon erroneously appeared to have won a narrow popular vote majority according to the NES survey. Although the vote divisions of these studies have on occasion differed quite significantly from the actual national vote (recall table 3.3), the 1960 election is the only election in which the NES indicated a plurality vote for a candidate who did not actually receive a plurality.

15. The visual presentation was very important to voter reactions to the debate. Those who watched it tended to think that Kennedy fared better, while those who listened to it on the radio tended to think that Nixon prevailed. For a number of reasons, including a recent illness, his famous five o'clock shadow, and a suit that faded into the black-and-white television background, Nixon appeared tired and sickly. In contrast, Kennedy appeared healthy and vigorous.

16. Going well beyond the long-suspected vote fraud of the Democratic Cook County machine, Seymour Hersch (1997) in *The Dark Side of Camelot* traces Kennedy's victory to more sinister influences. Hersch links Joe Kennedy, patriarch of the Kennedy family, with Mafia boss Sam Giancana about a year before the election and suggests that Mafia money and backing, including campaign contributions and work from the mob-controlled unions, helped John Kennedy carry Illinois and win the election (Hersh 1997, 131–54).

17. White (1961, 321–22) produces various survey evidence of the debates' effects, including a Roper poll conducted for the CBS television network. In Roper's national survey, 57 percent of voters indicated that the debates had influenced their vote decisions, and 6 percent indicated that their votes had been based on their evaluation of the candidates in the debates. Of this 6 percent who said that they were most strongly influenced by the debates, they favored Kennedy by three to one over Nixon. Extrapolating from the survey to the electorate, White estimates that about 2 million votes of Kennedy's margin over Nixon were attributable to the debates. Since Kennedy received only 114,673 more votes nationally than Nixon, the debate-based votes would seem to have made the difference in the national vote plurality. Subsequent research on the debates' effects (Katz and Feldman 1977) suggests that they changed far fewer votes, but even if the estimated effects are heavily discounted they were probably enough to have affected the results of such a close election.

18. Alan Ehrenhalt of *Congressional Quarterly* at the time wrote that "even though Carter's national popular vote margin was more than 10 times greater than Kennedy's in 1960 and more than twice as great as Richard M. Nixon's in 1968, the electoral college system came closer to misfiring than it did in either of those two years" (1976, 3115). Ehrenhalt went on to note that a small vote change in Ohio and Hawaii would have swung the electoral college vote to Ford.

19. For the full text of the questioning and responses see *The Presidential Campaign*

1976: Volume Three, The Debates (Washington: U.S. Government Printing Office, 1979, pp. 99–100). While Ford's gaffe in the debate may have proved costly, his campaign defended his participation in the debate, claiming that it was crucial in reducing Carter's large poll lead over Ford. Although incumbents often shy away from debates since they put the opponents on equal footing, the strategic decision of whether to participate in debates may have as much to do with the advantages of being the poll leader as it does with incumbency per se.

20. Ideally one would want to know the fundamental factors affecting each election as well as a direct measure of campaign effects for each election. Lacking this, it would be preferable to at least know the fundamental factors (public opinion, economic circumstances, and so forth) affecting the election and compare those to the actual vote to infer what otherwise unexpected effects the campaign may have had. Since pre-campaign public opinion measures, one of the key fundamentals, are not available for elections prior to the 1940s, we must resort to a less desirable strategy to determine whether idiosyncratic campaign events may have been decisive in a particular election. The strategy is to use information regarding the out-of-sample errors in the trial-heat and economy forecasting model (adapted to include revised economic data since the lead time is not an issue for explaining campaign effects). Assuming that the model captures all of the pre-campaign and systematic campaign effects on an election (such as narrowing leads and incumbency advantage), the difference between the expected and actual votes should be attributable to unsystematic or idiosyncratic campaign effects (such as Ford's misstatement about Eastern Europe in the debate). Based on the known distribution of these unsystematic campaign effects for elections from 1948 to 2004 and extending those to the pre-1948 elections, we can estimate the likelihood of campaign effects making the difference in the outcome by computing t-ratios (the winning margin divided by the out-of-sample standard error) and converting those t-ratios into probabilities. The standard error in this case was 2.12.

21. A t-ratio of more than 3.6 (and all landslides other than Eisenhower's 1956 near-landslide had t-ratio values of 4.0 or higher), suggests that there is less than one chance in two thousand that the campaign produced an actual vote that differed from the fundamental or expected vote by more than the margin of the plurality. For example, Hoover's 58.8 percent of the popular two-party vote in 1928 was 4.1 times the standard deviation of campaign effects (as gauged by the out-of-sample errors of the expected vote). The probability of a vote this large being due to campaign effects, assuming that the expected vote from the fundamentals and systematic campaign effects did not already favor the winning candidate, is less than .0001.

Chapter 9

1. It may be recalled from chapter 1 that one of the landmark studies of voting behavior, *The People's Choice* (Lazarsfeld, Berelson, and Gaudet, 1968, first published in 1944), found that the 1940 presidential election campaign shifted approximately 4 percent of the vote from incumbent Franklin Roosevelt to underdog Wendell Willkie. Although that study took a more generous view of the campaign period (using May as a start point), the net effects it found in the 1940 campaign are the average found in elections from 1948 to 2004. Moreover, and also

as the theory of the predictable campaign suggests, the shift in 1940 favored the candidate who was undoubtedly the trailing candidate in that race.

2. The 57 percent campaign change is the extreme case based on frontrunners losing all of their lead. A less extreme assumption of the frontrunner losing badly in a landslide, say with 38 percent of the vote, would yield a possible campaign effect of nineteen percentage points.

3. The average winning two-party vote in elections from 1948 to 2004 was 54.5 percentage points. The average interelection change over this period was 6.4 percentage points. The average interelection change in the fifteen elections from 1948 to 2004 is fairly typical throughout American electoral history. The average interelection change in the two-party percentage of the Democratic presidential vote in the thirty-four elections from 1872 to 2004 is 6.3 percentage points. In addition, the estimated effects are impressive when compared to previous estimates.

4. Allowing for some uncertainty in the statistical analysis, the numbers of elections decided by unsystematic campaign developments could be slightly higher or lower. An examination of the historical record suggests the possibility that the one or two additional elections may have been decided by idiosyncratic campaign developments.

5. I included in a forecasting model of the presidential votes in the states from 1948 to 1988 the first-quarter growth rate for each state's total personal income as reported in the Commerce Department's *Survey of Current Business* (J. Campbell 1992). The state economy effect was statistically significant, though its impact ranked among the weaker effects in the model. In a separate analysis of presidential voting in the states from 1960 to 1984, Holbrook (1991) included the growth in each state's real per capita income. Although Holbrook found the expected positive effect of state economic growth in his cross-sectional model, it did not reach conventional levels of statistical significance in his pooled model (103–104).

6. Of the three systematic effects of the campaign, the impact of presidential incumbency is likely to be felt most uniformly across the nation. The most plausible localized impact of incumbency may be produced by the incumbent directing more government largess to a state or the incumbent having a greater presence in a state either in person or in media appearances.

7. Elsewhere (Campbell, Ali, Jalazai 2006) I estimated the presidential candidate's typical home-state advantage at about 5.6 percentage points and about half of that percentage in the largest states. Holbrook (1991, 103) estimates it at about 6 percentage points, and Rosenstone (1983, 74) places it at just less than 4 percentage points. As to the vice presidential home-state advantage, Campbell, Ali, Jalazai (2006) found the vice presidential home-state advantage to be about 2.1 percentage points (again, about half that for the large states of California, Illinois, and New York). Holbrook (1991, 103) estimates the vice presidential home-state advantage at 1 percentage point in his pooled model. Additionally, both Rosenstone (1983) and I found that there has been a regional advantage of probably from 3 to 7 percentage points for presidential candidates from the South, though that does not appear to be the case after 1980 (Campbell, Ali, Jalazai 2006).

8. In one sense, the success in attracting votes through efforts that are part of the campaign strategies of the candidates may be considered a systematic effect of the campaign. However, in the sense used here, since the strategies and their effectiveness cannot be anticipated prior to the campaign itself, they are categorized as unsystematic effects.

9. Gelman and King (1993) argue that campaigns involve voters "coming home to their natural preferences" (431) but that this does not *necessarily* mean that they are "returning to the fold by party identification." This comports with the findings of this study. Many late-deciding partisans return to vote with their party, but others are torn by the issues and personalities of the campaign. The context of the campaign, significantly influenced by the economy and incumbency, shapes the preferences of many of these late deciders. Beyond this, however, there are some whose preferences are shaped in unanticipated ways or remain unclear after the campaign. These should generally divide evenly, but (as chapter 8 suggests) they occasionally prove important.

10. The first second-chance candidate, an unsuccessful presidential candidate who ran again, was Thomas Jefferson. Defeated by Adams in the election of 1796, Jefferson won the rematch in 1800. Other early presidential candidates who ran a second time after an unsuccessful bid were Federalist candidate Charles Pinckney, Andrew Jackson, Henry Clay (who ran in 1824, 1832, and 1844), and William Henry Harrison. In the second half of the nineteenth century, Grover Cleveland ran in 1892 after serving one presidential term and then narrowly losing his reelection bid to Benjamin Harrison. The record for failed presidential bids as a candidate of a major party is shared by Clay and William Jennings Bryan, who after losing to William McKinley in 1896 went on to lose to him again in 1900 and to William Howard Taft in 1908. Since Bryan, there have been three presidential candidates who lost and were given a second chance by their parties. Republican Thomas Dewey lost to Roosevelt in 1944 and four years later ran and lost to Harry Truman. Democrat Adlai Stevenson ran twice and lost twice to Dwight Eisenhower. Finally, eight years after Republican Richard Nixon was narrowly defeated in 1960 by John Kennedy, he was nominated by the Republicans and narrowly won election over his Democratic opponent Hubert Humphrey. Of the thirty-five presidential elections since 1868, only six (1892, 1900, 1908, 1948, 1956, and 1968) involved a non-incumbent candidate who had been defeated in a previous presidential election (L. Miller et al. 1972).

Appendix A

1. The debate over influences on macropartisanship, a concept akin to Converse's (1966b) concept of the "normal vote," further continues the debate about whether partisanship acts as "an unmoved mover" (Green, Palmquist, and Schickler 1998; Erikson, MacKuen, and Stimson 1998). The Erikson team finds evidence that short-term factors have a greater impact on partisanship, and the Green team finds a lesser impact of these factors. In either case, partisanship is quite stable, and from either perspective partisanship can be interpreted as "a running tally" of experiences, though a running tally of experiences seen and weighted from an already partisan vantage point and thus disposed toward reinforcing previous partisanship.

2. There is an extensive (and oftentimes frustrating) literature that finds, analyzes, or assumes a partisan dealignment. This literature includes Nie, Verba, and Petrocik 1979; Norpoth and Rusk 1982; Crotty 1984; Elshtain 1989, 123; Flanigan and Zingale 1998, 66; Holbrook 1996a, 13; Mackenzie 1996, 40–41; and Shea 1999. For a further discussion of research alleging a dealignment see J. Campbell et al. 1986.

3. It is important to note the strength of this finding. As conventionally measured

on the seven-point scale, leaners were thought to be between pure independents and weak partisans in their partisanship. The Keith et al. 1992 analysis suggests that it is not only inaccurate to collapse the leaners in with the pure independents but also inaccurate to draw a distinction between leaners and weak partisans (as the original NES coding did). The distinction between leaners and weak partisans is a distinction without a difference. The party identification scale should be a five-point scale, with leaners and weak identifiers with a party grouped together. W. Miller and Shanks (1996) present an analytic challenge to this finding. They claim that the independent leaners are acting as partisans but are not strictly speaking party identifiers since they deny that identification. Nevertheless, this situation may still be construed as a denial of their true identity rather than the absence of this identity.

4. The concept of partisan realignment has been a contested one. Some regard it as a shift in the critical issues that divide the political parties. Others interpret it as a change in the alignment of social groups toward the parties. Still others believe party realignment may be attributed to the balance of electoral power (or normal vote; Converse 1966b) between the parties. Among those taking this perspective there are further subdivisions between those who regard realignment as a change in which one of the major parties is the normal majority party and those who have a more relaxed standard, in which a realignment is regarded as any significant change in the balance of electoral power between the parties. This later definition is the one adopted here: a party realignment is significant change in the normal vote. A change in party identification is likely to accompany a party realignment but to lag behind as voters continue to hold on to old party labels for some time after their attitudes, beliefs, voting habits, and even underlying psychological identifications have changed. Partisan realignment should be regarded as a crude summary of an underlying continuous change in the normal vote variable. For an extensive discussion of the realignment concept see Shafer et al. 1991.

5. The nonparametric correlations (asymmetric Somer's d) between the intensity of partisanship (with weak partisans and leaners grouped together) has increased from between .05 to .09 in presidential elections from 1952 to 1972, to .14 to .19 in presidential elections from 1976 to 1992 (J. Campbell 1997b, 89). This suggests that turnout of pure independents has been dropping faster than that of partisans.

6. The inclusion of third-party votes as disloyal votes does not make much of a difference in early elections in the series, since between 1952 and 1964 there were no strong third-party candidacies to draw partisans into defection. Including third-party votes reduces the expected loyalty rates of partisans in both parties by about eight to ten percentage points for later elections in the series.

7. There is a growing literature that concludes that a Republican realignment has occurred or is in progress. The fact that the party system is no longer dominated by the Democratic Party as it was from the mid-1930s through the mid-1960s is well beyond dispute. Whether the newly aligned system is only a competitively balanced system between the Democrats and Republicans or will drift toward a Republican majority system is not yet clear. The realignment research includes Ladd 1985a, 1989, 1993, 1995b; Bullock 1988; Petrocik 1987; Stanley 1988; Carmines and Stimson 1989; W. Miller 1991; Abramowitz 1995; J. Campbell 1996, 1997a, 1997b, 2006; and Frymer 1996.

References

Abramowitz, Alan I. 1978. "The Impact of a Presidential Debate on Voter Rationality." *American Journal of Political Science* 22:680–90.

——. 1988. "An Improved Model for Predicting Presidential Outcomes." *PS: Political Science and Politics* 4:843–47.

——. 1995. "The End of the Democratic Era? 1994 and the Future of Congressional Election Research." *Political Research Quarterly* 48:873–89.

——. 1996. "Bill and Al's Excellent Adventure: Forecasting the 1996 Presidential Election." *American Politics Quarterly* 24:434–42.

——. 1999. "Bill and Al's Excellent Adventure: Forecasting the 1996 Presidential Election." Pp.47–56 in *Before the Vote,* ed. James E. Campbell and James C. Garand. Thousand Oaks, Calif.: Sage Publications.

——. 2005. "The Time-for-Change Model and the 2004 Presidential Election: A Post-Mortem and a Look Ahead." *PS: Political Science & Politics* 38:31.

——. 2007. "Disconnected, or Joined at the Hip?" Pp. 72–85 in *Red and Blue Nation? Characteristics and Causes of America's Polarized Politics,* ed. Pietro S. Nivola and David W. Brady. Washington, D.C.: Brookings.

Abramowitz, Alan I., and Kyle Saunders. 1998. "Ideological Realignment in the U.S. Electorate." *Journal of Politics* 60:634–52.

Abramson, Paul R., John H. Aldrich, and David W. Rohde. 1982. *Change and Continuity in the 1980 Elections.* Washington, D.C.: CQ Press.

——. 1986. *Change and Continuity in the 1984 Elections.* Washington, D.C.: CQ Press.

——. 1990. *Change and Continuity in the 1988 Elections.* Washington, D.C.: CQ Press.

——. 1994. *Change and Continuity in the 1992 Elections.* Washington, D.C.: CQ Press.

——. 1998. *Change and Continuity in the 1996 Elections.* Washington, D.C.: CQ Press.

——. 2003. *Change and Continuity in the 2000 and 2002 Elections.* Washington, D.C.: CQ Press.

——. 2006. *Change and Continuity in the 2004 Elections.* Washington, D.C.: CQ Press.

Achen, Christopher H. 1975. "Mass Political Attitudes and Survey Response." *American Political Science Review* 69:1218–31.

Alesina, Alberto, and Howard Rosenthal. 1995. *Partisan Politics, Divided Government, and the Economy.* New York: Cambridge University Press.

Alvarez, R. Michael. 1997. *Information and Elections.* Ann Arbor: University of Michigan Press.

American Institute of Public Opinion. 1972. *The Gallup Poll: Public Opinion 1935–1971.* 3 vols. New York: Random House.

——. 1978. *The Gallup Poll: Public Opinion 1972–1977.* 2 vols. Wilmington, Del.: Scholarly Resources.

American Survey. 1995–96. "And Here Is Your Next President." *The Economist* (December 23–January 5): 31–33.

Andersen, Kristi. 1979. *The Creation of a Democratic Majority, 1928–1936.* Chicago: University of Chicago Press.

Ansolabehere, Stephen, and Shanto Iyengar. 1995. *Going Negative.* New York: Simon and Schuster.

Arterton, F. Christopher. 1993. "Campaign '92: Strategies and Tactics of the Candidates." Pp. 74–109 in *The Election of 1992,* ed. Gerald M. Pomper, F. Christopher Arterton, Ross K. Baker, Walter Dean Burnham, Kathleen A. Frankovic, Marjorie Randon Hershey, and Wilson Carey McWilliams. Chatham, N.J.: Chatham House.

Asher, Herbert B. 1992. *Presidential Elections and American Politics.* 5th ed. Pacific Grove, Calif.: Brooks/Cole.

———. 1998. *Polling the Public.* 4th ed. Washington, D.C.: CQ Press.

Asher, Herbert B., and Andrew R. Tomlinson. 1999. "The Media and the 1996 Presidential Campaign." Pp. 125–42 in *Reelection 1996,* ed. Herbert F. Weisberg and Janet M. Box-Steffensmeier. Chatham, N.J.: Chatham House.

Atkeson, Lonna Rae. 1998. "Divisive Primaries and General Election Outcomes: Another Look at Presidential Campaigns." *American Journal of Political Science* 42: 256–71.

Axelrod, Robert. 1972. "Where the Votes Come From: An Analysis of Electoral Coalitions, 1952–1968." *American Political Science Review* 66:11–20.

Bain, Richard C., and Judith H. Parris. 1973. *Convention Decisions and Voting Records.* 2nd ed. Washington, D.C.: Brookings Institution.

Bartels, Larry M. 1988. *Presidential Primaries and the Dynamics of Public Choice.* Princeton, N.J.: Princeton University Press.

———. 1992. "The Impact of Electioneering in the United States." Pp. 244–77 in *Electioneering,* ed. David Butler and Austin Ranney. Oxford: Clarendon Press.

———. 1996. "Uninformed Votes: Information Effects in Presidential Elections." *American Journal of Political Science* 40:194–230.

———. 2000. "Partisanship and Voting Behavior, 1952–1996." *American Journal of Political Science* 44:35–50.

Bean, Louis H. 1948. *How to Predict Elections.* New York: Knopf.

———. 1972. *How to Predict the 1972 Election.* New York: Quadrangle Books.

Beck, Nathaniel. 1992. "Forecasting the 1992 Presidential Election: The Message Is in the Confidence Interval." *The Public Perspective* 3, no. 6 (September/October): 32–34

———. 1999. "Evaluating Forecasts and Forecasting Models of the 1996 Presidential Election." In *Before the Vote,* ed. James E. Campbell and James C. Garand. Thousand Oaks, Calif.: Sage Publications.

Benedetto, Richard. 1992a. "Polling Likely Voters Narrows the Margin." *USA Today,* October 28, 8A.

———. 1992b. "Gap Jumps to 8 Points, Poll Says." *USA Today,* November 2, 7A.

Bennett, Stephen Earl, and Linda L. M. Bennett. 1993. "Out of Sight, Out of Mind: Americans' Knowledge of Party Control of the House of Representatives, 1960–1984." *Political Research Quarterly* 46:67–80.

Berelson, Bernard B., Paul F. Lazarsfeld, and William N. McPhee. 1954. *Voting.* Chicago: University of Chicago Press.

Bernstein, Robert A. 1977. "Divisive Primaries Do Hurt: U.S. Senate Races, 1956–1972." *American Political Science Review* 71:540–45.

Boller, Paul F., Jr. 1984. *Presidential Campaigns.* New York: Oxford University Press.

Boorstin, Daniel. 1953. *The Genius of American Politics*. Chicago: University of Chicago Press.

Broder, David S. 1971. *The Party's Over*. New York: Harper.

———. 1992. "Pundits' Brew: How It Looks." *The Washington Post*, November 1, C1.

Brody, Richard, and Lee Sigelman. 1983. "Presidential Popularity and Presidential Elections: An Update and Extension." *Public Opinion Quarterly* 47:325–28.

Bruno, Jerry, and Jeff Greenfield. 1971. *The Advance Man*. New York: William Morrow.

Bryce, James. 1937. *The American Commonwealth*. Vol. 2. New York: Macmillan.

Buhite, Russell D., and David W. Levy, eds. 1992. *FDR's Fireside Chats*. Norman: University of Oklahoma Press.

Bullock, Charles S., III. 1988. "Regional Realignment from an Officeholding Perspective." *Journal of Politics* 50:553–74.

Burnham, Walter Dean. 1970. *Critical Elections and the Mainsprings of American Politics*. New York: Norton.

———. 1989. "The Reagan Heritage." Pp. 1–32 in *The Election of 1988*, ed. Gerald M. Pomper, Ross K. Baker, Walter Dean Burnham, Barbara G. Farah, Marjorie Randon Hershey, Ethel Klein, and Wilson Carey McWilliams. Chatham, N.J.: Chatham House.

Campbell, Angus, Philip E. Converse, Warren E. Miller, and Donald E. Stokes. 1960. *The American Voter*. New York: Wiley.

———, eds. 1966. *Elections and the Political Order*. New York: Wiley.

Campbell, James E. 1985. "Sources of the New Deal Realignment: The Contributions of Conversion and Mobilization to Partisan Change." *Western Political Quarterly* 38:357–76.

———. 1986. "Voter Mobilization and the New Deal Realignment: A Rejoinder to Erikson and Tedin." *Western Political Quarterly* 39:733–35.

———. 1992. "Forecasting the Presidential Vote in the States." *American Journal of Political Science* 36:386–407.

———. 1996. "Polls and Votes: The Trial-Heat Presidential Election Forecasting Model, Certainty, and Political Campaigns." *American Politics Quarterly* 24:408–33.

———. 1997a. "The Presidential Pulse and the 1994 Midterm Congressional Election." *Journal of Politics* 59:830–57.

———. 1997b. *The Presidential Pulse of Congressional Elections*. 2nd ed. Lexington: University Press of Kentucky.

———. 1999a. "The Science of Forecasting Presidential Elections." In *Before the Vote*, ed. James E. Campbell and James C. Garand. Thousand Oaks, Calif.: Sage Publications.

———. 2001a. "The Curious and Close Presidential Campaign of 2000." Pp. 115–37 in *America's Choice 2000*, ed. William Crotty. Boulder, Colo.: Westview.

———. 2001b. "Presidential Election Campaigns and Partisanship." Pp. 11–29 in *American Political Parties: Decline or Resurgence?* ed. Jeffrey E. Cohen, Richard Fleisher, and Paul Kantor. Washington, D.C.: CQ Press.

———. 2001c. "When Have Presidential Campaigns Decided Election Outcomes?" *American Politics Research* 29:437–60.

———. 2001d. "The Referendum that Didn't Happen: The Forecasts of the 2000 Presidential Election." *PS: Political Science & Politics* 34:33–38.

———. 2004a. "Introduction: The 2004 Presidential Election Forecasts." *PS: Political Science & Politics* 37:733–35.

———. 2004b. "Forecasting the Presidential Vote in 2004: Placing Preference Polls in Context." *PS: Political Science & Politics* 37:763–67.

———. 2005a. "The Fundamentals in U.S. Presidential Elections: Public Opinion, the

Economy, and Incumbency in the 2004 Presidential Election." *Journal of Elections, Public Opinion and Parties* 15:73–83.

———. 2005b. "Why Bush Won the Presidential Election of 2004: Incumbency, Ideology, Terrorism, and Turnout." *Political Science Quarterly* 120:219–41.

———. 2005c. "Evaluating the Trial-Heat and Economy Forecast of the 2004 Presidential Vote: All's Well that Ends Well." *PS: Political Science & Politics* 38, no.1 (January 2005): 33–34.

———. 2006. "Party Systems and Realignments in the United States, 1868–2004." *Social Science History* 30:359–86.

———. 2007a. "Nomination Politics, Party Unity, and Presidential Elections." Pp. 74–90 in *Understanding the Presidency, Fourth Edition,* ed. James P. Pfiffner and Roger H. Davidson. New York: Pearson Education.

———. 2007b. "Polarization Runs Deep, Even by Yesterday's Standards." Pp. 106–16 in *Red and Blue Nation? Characteristics and Causes of America's Polarized Politics,* ed. Pietro S. Nivola and David W. Brady. Washington, D.C.: Brookings.

———. 2007c. "Presidential Politics in a Polarized Nation: The Re-election of George W. Bush." *The George W. Bush Legacy,* ed. Colin B. Campbell, Bert A. Rockman, and Andrew Rudalevige. Washington, D.C.: CQ Press.

Campbell, James E., Syed Ali, and Farida Jalazai. 2006. "Forecasting the Presidential Vote in the States, 1948–2004: An Update, Revision, and Extension of a State-Level Presidential Forecasting Model." Pp. 33–57 in *Campaigns and Political Marketing,* ed. Wayne P. Steger, Sean Q Kelly, and J. Mark Wrighton. New York: The Haworth Press.

Campbell, James E., Lynna L. Cherry, and Kenneth A. Wink. 1992. "The Convention Bump." *American Politics Quarterly* 20:287–307.

Campbell, James E., and James C. Garand, eds. 1999. *Before the Vote.* Thousand Oaks, Calif.: Sage Publications.

Campbell, James E., and Thomas E. Mann. 1992. "Forecasting the 1992 Presidential Election: A User's Guide to the Models." *Brookings Review* 10 (Fall): 22–27.

———. 1996. "Forecasting the Presidential Election: What Can We Learn from the Models?" *Brookings Review* 14 (Fall): 26–31.

Campbell, James E., and Kenneth John Meier. 1979. "Style Issues and Vote Choice." *Political Behavior* 1:203–15.

Campbell, James E., Mary Munro, John R. Alford, and Bruce A. Campbell. 1986. "Partisanship and Voting." Pp. 99–126 in *Research in Micropolitics.* Vol. 1, ed. Samuel Long. Greenwich, Conn.: JAI Press.

Campbell, James E., and Kenneth A. Wink. 1990. "Trial-Heat Forecasts of the Presidential Vote." *American Politics Quarterly* 18:251–69.

Carmines, Edward G., and James A. Stimson. 1989. *Issue Evolution.* Princeton, N.J.: Princeton University Press.

Cavanagh, Thomas E., and James L. Sundquist. 1985. "The New Two-Party System." Pp. 33–67 in *The New Direction in American Politics,* ed. John E. Chubb and Paul E. Peterson. Washington, D.C.: Brookings Institution.

Cheney, Richard B., and Lynne V. Cheney. 1996. *Kings of the Hill.* Rev. ed. New York: Simon and Schuster.

Congressional Quarterly. 1985. *Guide to U.S. Elections.* 2nd ed. Washington, D.C.: Congressional Quarterly.

———. 1989. "Official 1988 Presidential Election Results." *Congressional Quarterly Weekly Report* (January 21): 139.

——. 1993. "Official 1992 Presidential Election Results." *Congressional Quarterly Weekly Report* (January 30): 233.

Converse, Philip E. 1964. "The Nature of Belief Systems in Mass Publics." Pp. 206–61 in *Ideology and Discontent,* ed. David E. Apter. New York: Free Press.

——. 1966a. "Information Flow and the Stability of Partisan Attitudes." Pp. 136–57 in *Elections and the Political Order,* ed. Angus Campbell, Philip E. Converse, Warren E. Miller, and Donald E. Stokes. New York: Wiley.

——. 1966b. "The Concept of the 'Normal Vote.'" Pp. 9–39 in *Elections and the Political Order,* ed. Angus Campbell, Philip E. Converse, Warren E. Miller, and Donald E. Stokes. New York: Wiley.

Converse, Philip E., Aage R. Clausen, and Warren E. Miller. 1965. "Electoral Myth and Realty: The 1964 Election." *American Political Science Review* 59:321–36.

Converse, Philip E., and Gregory B. Markus. 1979. "Plus ça change . . . The New CPS Election Study." *American Political Science Review* 73:32–49.

Converse, Philip E., Warren E. Miller, Jerrold G. Rusk, and Alan C. Wolfe. 1969. "Continuity and Change in American Politics: Parties and Issues in the 1968 Election." *American Political Science Review* 63:1083–1105.

Crespi, Irving. 1988. *Pre-Election Polling.* New York: Russell Sage Foundation.

Crotty, William J. 1984. *American Parties in Decline.* 2nd ed. Boston: Little, Brown.

Delli Carpini, Michael X., and Scott Keeter. 1996. *What Americans Know about Politics and Why It Matters.* New Haven, Conn.: Yale University Press.

Dionne, E. J., Jr. 1991. *Why Americans Hate Politics.* New York: Simon and Schuster.

Dougherty, Regina, Everett C. Ladd, David Wilber, and Lynn Zayachkiwsky, eds. 1997. *America at the Polls, 1996.* Storrs, Conn.: Roper Center for Public Opinion Research.

Downs, Anthony. 1957. *An Economic Theory of Democracy.* New York: Harper and Row.

Drew, Elizabeth. 1981. *Portrait of an Election.* New York: Simon and Schuster.

Ehrenhalt, Alan. 1976. "Carter and Democrats Move into Control." *Congressional Quarterly Weekly Report* (November 6): 3115.

Elshtain, Jean Bethke. 1989. "Issues and Themes in the 1988 Campaign." Pp. 111–26 in *The Elections of 1988,* ed. Michael Nelson. Washington, D.C.: CQ Press.

Erikson, Robert S. 1989. "Economic Conditions and the Presidential Vote." *American Political Science Review* 83:567–73.

——. 1990. "Economic Conditions and the Congressional Vote: A Review of Macro-level Evidence." *American Journal of Political Science* 34:373–99.

Erikson, Robert S., Michael B. MacKuen, and James Stimson. 1998. "What Moves Macropartisanship? A Response to Green, Palmquist, and Schickler." *American Political Science Review* 92:901–12.

Erikson, Robert S., and Kent L. Tedin. 1981. "The 1928–1936 Partisan Realignment: The Case for the Conversion Hypothesis." *American Political Science Review* 75:951–62.

——. 1986. "Voter Conversion and the New Deal Realignment: A Response to Campbell." *Western Political Quarterly* 39:729–32.

Erikson, Robert S., and Christopher Wlezien. 1996. "Of Time and Presidential Election Forecasts." *PS: Political Science and Politics* 29:37–39.

——. 2006. "Are Political Stock Markets Really Superior to Polls as Election Predictors?" manuscript.

Faber, Harold. 1965. *The Road to the White House.* New York: The New York Times.

Fair, Ray C. 1978. "The Effect of Economic Events on Votes for President." *Review of Economics and Statistics* 60:159–73.

——. 1982. "The Effect of Economic Events on Votes for President: 1980 Results." *Review of Economics and Statistics* 64:322–25.

——. 1988. "The Effect of Economic Events on Votes for President: 1984 Update." *Political Behavior* 10:168–79.

——. 1994. "The Effect of Economic Events on Votes for President: 1992 Update." Cowles Foundation Discussion Paper, No. 1084, Yale University.

Farah, Barbara G., and Ethel Klein. 1989. "Public Opinion Trends." Pp. 103–28 in *The Election of 1988*, ed. Gerald M. Pomper, Ross K. Baker, Walter Dean Burnham, Barbara G. Farah, Marjorie Randon Hershey, Ethel Klein, and Wilson Carey McWilliams. Chatham, N.J.: Chatham House.

Farley, James A. 1938. *Behind the Ballots*. New York: Harcourt, Brace.

Finkel, Steven E. 1993. "Reexamining the 'Minimal Effects' Model in Recent Presidential Campaigns." *Journal of Politics* 55:1–21.

Finkel, Steven E., and John G. Geer. 1998. "A Spot Check: Casting Doubt on the Demobilizing Effect of Attack Advertising." *American Journal of Political Science* 42: 573–95.

Fiorina, Morris P. 1981. *Retrospective Voting in American National Elections*. New Haven, Conn.: Yale University Press.

——. 2002. "Parties and Partisanship: A 40-Year Retrospective." *Political Behavior* 24: 93–115.

Flanigan, William H., and Nancy H. Zingale. 1998. *Political Behavior of the American Electorate*. 9th ed. Washington, D.C.: CQ Press.

Frymer, Paul. 1996. "The 1994 Electoral Aftershock: Dealignment or Realignment in the South." Pp. 99–113 in *Midterm*, ed. Philip A. Klinkner. Boulder, Colo.: Westview Press.

Gallup Poll. 1999. Data file with preference polls for presidential elections from 1936 to 1996 (excel file).

——. 2005. Preference polls from Gallup Poll archives, www.galluppoll.com.

Garand, James C. 1988. "Localism and Regionalism in Presidential Elections: Is There a Home State or Regional Advantage?" *Western Political Quarterly* 41:85–104.

Geer, John G. 1988. "The Effects of Presidential Debates on the Electorate's Preferences for Candidates." *American Politics Quarterly* 16:486–501.

Gelman, Andrew, and Gary King. 1993. "Why Are American Presidential Election Campaign Polls So Variable When Votes Are So Predictable?" *British Journal of Political Science* 23:409–51.

Germond, Jack W., and Jules Witcover. 1993. *Mad as Hell*. New York: Warner Books.

Gopoian, J. David, and Sissie Hadjiharalambous. 1994. "Late-deciding Voters in Presidential Elections." *Political Behavior* 16:55–78.

Green, Donald, Bradley Palmquist, and Eric Schickler. 1998. "Macropartisanship: A Replication and Critique." *American Political Science Review* 92:883–99.

Greene, Jay P. 1993. "Forewarned before Forecast: Presidential Election Forecasting Models and the 1992 Election." *PS: Political Science and Politics* 26:17–21.

Hacker, Andrew. 1965. "Does a Divisive Primary Harm a Candidate's Election Chances?" *American Political Science Review* 59:105–10.

Hagen, Michael G. 1996. "Press Treatment of Front-Runners." Pp. 190–219 in *In Pursuit of the White House*, ed. William G. Mayer. Chatham, N.J.: Chatham House.

Hargrove, Erwin C., and Michael Nelson. 1981. "Presidents, Ideas, and the Search for a Stable Majority." Pp. 45–63 in *A Tide of Discontent*, ed. Ellis Sandoz and Cecil V. Crabb, Jr. Washington, D.C.: CQ Press.

———. 1985. "The Presidency: Reagan and the Cycle of Politics and Policy." Pp. 188–214 in *The Elections of 1984*, ed. Michael Nelson. Washington, D.C.: CQ Press.

Hartz, Louis. 1955. *The Liberal Tradition in America*. New York: Harcourt, Brace.

Hersh, Seymour M. 1997. *The Dark Side of Camelot*. Boston, Mass.: Little, Brown.

Hess, Stephen. 1978. *The Presidential Campaign*. Rev. ed. Washington, D.C.: Brookings Institution.

———. 1998. *The Little Book of Campaign Etiquette*. Washington, D.C.: Brookings Institution.

Hetherington, Marc J. 2001. "Resurgent Mass Partisanship: The Role of Elite Polarization," *American Political Science Review* 95:619–31.

Hibbing, John R., and Elizabeth Theiss-Morse. 1995. *Congress as Public Enemy*. Cambridge: Cambridge University Press.

Hibbs, Douglas A., Jr. 1982. "President Reagan's Mandate from the 1980 Elections: A Shift to the Right?" *American Politics Quarterly* 10:387–420.

———. 1987. *The American Political Economy*. Cambridge, Mass.: Harvard University Press.

Hofstadter, Richard. 1969. *The Idea of the First Party System*. Berkeley: University of California Press.

Holbrook, Thomas M. 1991. "Presidential Elections in Space and Time." *American Journal of Political Science* 35:91–109.

———. 1996a. *Do Campaigns Matter?* Thousand Oaks, Calif.: Sage Publications.

———. 1996b. "Reading the Political Tea Leaves: A Forecasting Model of Contemporary Presidential Elections." *American Politics Quarterly* 24:506–19.

———. 1997. "Did the Campaign Matter?" Paper delivered at the Annual Meeting of the Midwest Political Science Association.

———. 2006. "Do Campaigns Really Matter?" Pp. 1–21 in *The Electoral Challenge: Theory Meets Practice*, ed. Stephen C. Craig. Washington, D.C.: CQ Press.

Hunt, Albert R. 1981. "The Campaign and the Issues." Pp. 142–76 in *The American Elections of 1980*, ed. Austin Ranney. Washington, D.C.: AEI Press.

———. 1985. "The Campaign and the Issues." Pp. 129–65 in *The American Elections of 1984*, ed. Austin Ranney. Durham, N.C.: Duke University Press.

Jacobson, Gary C. 2007. *A Divider, Not a Uniter: George W. Bush and the American People*. New York: Pearson Longman.

Jacoby, William G. 1997. "Public Preferences during a Presidential Campaign: Sources of Stability and Change." Paper presented at the Annual Meeting of the Midwest Political Science Association.

Jamieson, Kathleen Hall. 1992. *Dirty Politics*. New York: Oxford University Press.

———. 1996. *Packaging the Presidency: A History and Criticism of Presidential Campaign Advertising*. New York: Oxford University Press.

———, ed. 2006. *Electing the President 2004*. Philadelphia: University of Pennsylvania Press.

Jennings, M. Kent, and Gregory B. Markus. 1984. "Partisan Orientations over the Long Haul: Results from the Three-Wave Political Socialization Panel Study." *American Political Science Review* 78:1000–18.

Johnston, Richard, Michael G. Hagen, and Kathleen Hall Jamieson. 2004. *The 2000 Presidential Election and the Foundations of Party Politics*. New York: Cambridge University Press.

Just, Marion R., Ann N. Crigler, Dean E. Alger, Timothy E. Cook, Montague Kern, and Darrell M. West. 1996. *Crosstalk*. Chicago: University of Chicago Press.

Karmin, Monroe W. 1987. "Economic Outlook: Who Will Win in 1988?" *U.S. News & World Report* (October 26): 45.

Katz, Elihu, and Jacob J. Feldman. 1977. "The Debates in the Light of Research: A Survey of Surveys." Pp. 173–223 in *The Great Debates,* ed. Sidney Kraus. 1962. Reprint, Bloomington: Indiana University Press.

Keith, Bruce E., David B. Magleby, Candice J. Nelson, Elizabeth Orr, Mark C. Westlye, and Raymond E. Wolfinger. 1992. *The Myth of the Independent Voter.* Berkeley and Los Angeles: University of California Press.

Kelley, Stanley, Jr. 1983. *Interpreting Elections.* Princeton, N.J.: Princeton University Press.

Kelley, Stanley, Jr., and Thad W. Mirer. 1974. "The Simple Act of Voting." *American Political Science Review* 68:572–91.

Kelly, Kate. 1991. *Election Day.* New York: Facts on File.

Kenney, Patrick J., and Tom W. Rice. 1987. "The Relationship between Divisive Primaries and General Outcomes." *American Journal of Political Science* 31:31–44.

Kernell, Samuel. 2006. *Going Public.* 4th ed. Washington, D.C.: CQ Press.

Kessel, John H. 1992. *Presidential Campaign Politics.* 4th ed. Pacific Grove, Calif.: Brooks/Cole.

Key, V. O. 1966. *The Responsible Electorate.* New York: Vintage Books.

Keylin, Arleen, and Eve Nelson. 1976. *If Elected. . . .* New York: Arno Press, Random House.

Kiewiet, D. Roderick. 1983. *Macroeconomics and Microeconomics.* Chicago: University of Chicago Press.

Kiewiet, D. Roderick, and Douglas Rivers. 1985. "The Economic Basis of Reagan's Appeal." Pp. 69–90 in *The New Direction in American Politics,* ed. John E. Chubb and Paul E. Peterson. Washington, D.C.: Brookings Institution.

Klapper, Joseph. 1960. *The Effects of Mass Communication.* New York: Free Press.

Knight, Kathleen. 1984. "The Dimensionality of Partisan and Ideological Affect: The Influence of Positivity." *American Politics Quarterly* 12:305–34.

Ladd, Everett Carll. 1985a. "As the Realignment Turns: A Drama in Many Acts." *Public Opinion* 7 (no. 6): 2–7.

———. 1985b. "The Ladd Report #1: The Election of 1984." New York: Norton.

———. 1989. "The 1988 Elections: Continuation of the Post–New Deal System." *Political Science Quarterly* 104:1–18.

———. 1993. "The 1992 Vote for President Clinton: Another Brittle Mandate?" *Political Science Quarterly* 108:1–28.

———, ed. 1995a. *America at the Polls, 1994.* Storrs, Conn.: Roper Center for Public Opinion Research.

———. 1995b. "The 1994 Congressional Elections: The Postindustrial Realignment Continues." *Political Science Quarterly* 110:1–23.

Lanoue, David J. 1991. "The 'Turning Point': Viewers' Reactions to the Second 1988 Presidential Debate." *American Politics Quarterly* 19:80–95.

Lau, Richard R. 1994. "An Analysis of the Accuracy of the 'Trial Heat' Polls during the 1992 Presidential Election." *Public Opinion Quarterly* 58:2–20.

Lau, Richard R., and David P. Redlawsk. 1997. "Voting Correctly." *American Political Science Review* 91:585–99.

———. 2006. *How Voters Decide: Information Processing during Election Campaigns.* New York: Cambridge University Press.

Lazarsfeld, Paul F. 1944. "The Election Is Over." *Public Opinion Quarterly* 8:317–30.

Lazarsfeld, Paul F., Bernard Berelson, and Hazel Gaudet. 1968. *The People's Choice.* 3rd ed. New York: Columbia University Press.

Lengle, James I. 1980. "Divisive Presidential Primaries and Party Electoral Prospects: 1932–1976." *American Politics Quarterly* 8:261–77.

Lengle, James I., D. Owen, and M. W. Sonner. 1995. "Divisive Nominating Campaigns and Democratic Party Electoral Prospects." *Journal of Politics* 57:370–83.

Lewis-Beck, Michael S. 1985. "Election Forecasts in 1984: How Accurate Were They?" *PS: Political Science and Politics* 18:53–62.

———. 1988. *Economics and Elections.* Ann Arbor: University of Michigan Press.

Lewis-Beck, Michael S., and Tom W. Rice. 1982. "Presidential Popularity and Presidential Vote." *Public Opinion Quarterly* 46:534–37.

———. 1983. "Localism in Presidential Elections: The Home State Advantage." *American Journal of Political Science* 27:548–56.

———. 1984. "Forecasting Presidential Elections: A Comparison of Naive Models." *Political Behavior* 6:9–21.

———. 1992. *Forecasting Elections.* Washington, D.C.: CQ Press.

Lewis-Beck, Michael S., and Mary Stegmaier. 2000. "Economic Determinants of Electoral Outcomes." *Annual Review of Political Science* 3:183–219.

Lewis-Beck, Michael S., and Charles Tien. 1996. "The Future of Forecasting: Prospective Presidential Models." *American Politics Quarterly* 24:468–91.

Lichtman, Allan J. 1996. *The Keys to the White House, 1996.* Lanham, Md.: Madison Books.

Light, Paul C., and Celinda Lake. 1985. "The Election: Candidates, Strategies, and Decisions." Pp. 83–110 in *The Elections of 1984,* ed. Michael Nelson. Washington, D.C.: CQ Press.

Luskin, Robert C. 2003. "The Heavenly Public: What Would a Fully Informed Citizenry Be Like?" Pp. 238–61 in *Electoral Democracy,* ed. Michael B. MacKuen and George Rabinowitz. Ann Arbor: University of Michigan Press.

Luttbeg, Norman R., and Michael M. Gant. 1995. *American Electoral Behavior.* Itasca, Ill.: F. E. Peacock.

Mackenzie, G. Calvin. 1996. *The Irony of Reform.* Boulder, Colo.: Westview Press.

MacKuen, Michael. 1984. "Exposure to Information, Belief Integration, and Individual Responsiveness to Agenda Change." *American Political Science Review* 78:372–91.

MacKuen, Michael B., Robert S. Erikson, and James A. Stimson, 1989. "Macropartisanship." *American Political Science Review* 83: 1125–42.

Marcus, George E., and Michael B. MacKuen. 1993. "Anxiety, Enthusiasm, and the Vote: The Emotional Underpinnings of Learning and Involvement during Presidential Campaigns." *American Political Science Review* 87:672–85.

Markus, Gregory B. 1982. "Political Attitudes during an Election Year: A Report on the 1980 NES Panel Study." *American Political Science Review* 76:538–60.

Mayer, William C. 1992. *The Changing American Mind.* Ann Arbor: University of Michigan Press.

McCall, Samuel W. 1914. *The Life of Thomas B. Reed.* Boston: Houghton Mifflin.

McGinniss, Joe. 1969. *The Selling of the President 1968.* New York: Trident Press.

Meffert, Michael F., Helmut Norpoth, and Anirudh V. S. Ruhil. 2001. "Realignment and Macropartisanship." *American Political Science Review* 95: 4, 953–62.

Meyer, Phil. 1992. "Numbers Turn on Undecided Voters." *USA Today,* November 2, 7A.

Miller, Lillian B., Beverly J. Cox, Frederick S. Voss, Jeannette M. Hussey, and Judith S. King. 1972. *"If Elected. . . ."* Washington, D.C.: Smithsonian Institution Press.

Miller, Warren E. 1987. "The Election of 1984 and the Future of American Politics."

Pp. 293–320 in *Elections in America,* ed. Kay Lehman Schlozman. Boston: Allen and Unwin.

———. 1991. "Party Identification, Realignment, and Party Voting: Back to the Basics." *American Political Science Review* 85:557–68.

Miller, Warren E., and Teresa E. Levitan. 1977. *Leadership and Change.* 2nd ed. Cambridge, Mass.: Winthrop.

Miller, Warren E., and J. Merrill Shanks. 1982. "Policy Directions and Presidential Leadership: Alternative Interpretations of the 1980 Presidential Elections." *British Journal of Political Science* 12:299–356.

———. 1996. *The New American Voter.* Cambridge, Mass.: Harvard University Press.

Miller, Warren, and Santa Traugott. 1989. *American National Election Studies Data Sourcebook.* Cambridge, Mass.: Harvard University Press.

———. 1991. "American National Election Studies Data Sourcebook, 1952–1990." Mimeographed.

Moos, Malcolm, and Stephen Hess. 1960. *Hats in the Ring.* New York: Random House.

Morin, Richard. 1992. "Pollsters' 'Nutty' Calculations Added up on Day that Counted: In Academia, However, One Well-Known Political Crystal Ball Lies Shattered." *The Washington Post,* November 5, A37.

Morse, Joseph Laffan, ed. 1953. *The Unicorn Book of 1952.* New York: Unicorn Books.

Nadeau, Richard, and Michael S. Lewis-Beck. 2001. "National Economic Voting in U.S. Presidential Elections." *Journal of Politics* 63:159–81.

Neuman, W. Russell. 1986. *The Paradox of Mass Politics.* Cambridge, Mass.: Harvard University Press.

Nie, Norman H., Sidney Verba, and John R. Petrocik. 1979. *The Changing American Voter.* Enlarged ed. Cambridge, Mass.: Harvard University Press.

Nixon, Richard M. 1972. "The President's News Conference of October 5, 1972." Pp. 952–60 in *Public Papers of the President.* Washington, D.C.: U.S. Government Printing Office.

Norpoth, Helmut. 1995. "Is Clinton Doomed? An Early Forecast for 1996." *PS: Political Science and Politics* 28:201–207.

———. 1996. "Of Time and Candidates: A Forecast for 1996." *American Politics Quarterly* 24:443–67.

———. 2004. "From Primary to General Election: A Forecast of the Presidential Vote." *P.S. Political Science and Politics* 37:737–40.

Norpoth, Helmut, and Jerrold G. Rusk. 1982. "Partisan Dealignment in the American Electorate: Itemizing the Deductions since 1964." *American Political Science Review* 76:522–37.

Page, Benjamin I. 1978. *Choices and Echoes in Presidential Elections.* Chicago: University of Chicago Press.

Page, Benjamin I., and Robert Y. Shapiro. 1992. *The Rational Public.* Chicago: University of Chicago Press.

Patterson, Thomas E. 1980. *The Mass Media Election.* New York: Praeger.

———. 1994. *Out of Order.* New York: Vintage Books.

Patterson, Thomas E., and Richard Davis. 1985. "The Media Campaign: Struggle for the Agenda." Pp. 111–27 in *The Elections of 1984,* ed. Michael Nelson. Washington, D.C.: CQ Press.

Patterson, Thomas E., and Robert D. McClure. 1976. *The Unseeing.* New York: Putnam.

Peirce, Neal R. 1968. *The People's President.* New York: Clarion.

Petrocik, John R. 1987. "Realignment: New Party Coalitions and the Nationalization of the South." *Journal of Politics* 49:347–75.

Pierson, James E., and Terry B. Smith. 1975. "Primary Divisiveness and General Election Success: A Reexamination." *Journal of Politics* 37:555–62.

Pika, Joseph A., and Richard A. Watson. 1996. *The Presidential Contest*. 5th ed. Washington, D.C.: CQ Press.

Polsby, Nelson W., and Aaron Wildavsky. 1996. *Presidential Elections*. 9th ed. Chatham, N.J.: Chatham House.

Pomper, Gerald M. 1977. "The Presidential Election." Pp. 54–82 in *The Election of 1976*, ed. Gerald M. Pomper, Ross K. Baker, Charles E. Jacob, and Wilson Carey McWilliams. New York: David McKay Company.

———. 1981. "The Presidential Election." Pp. 65–96 in *The Election of 1980*, ed. Gerald M. Pomper, Ross K. Baker, Kathleen A. Frankovic, Charles E. Jacob, Wilson Carey McWilliams, and Henry A. Plotkin. Chatham, N.J.: Chatham House.

———. 1993. "The Presidential Election." Pp. 132–56 in *The Election of 1992*, ed. Gerald M. Pomper, F. Christopher Arterton, Ross K. Baker, Walter Dean Burnham, Kathleen A. Frankovic, Marjorie Randon Hershey, and Wilson Carey McWilliams. Chatham, N.J.: Chatham House.

Popkin, Samuel L. 1991. *The Reasoning Voter*. Chicago: University of Chicago Press.

Quirk, Paul J. 1985. "The Economy: Economists, Electoral Politics, and Reagan Economics." Pp. 155–87 in *The Elections of 1984*, ed. Michael Nelson. Washington, D.C.: CQ Press.

Ranney, Austin. 1975. *Curing the Mischiefs of Faction*. Berkeley: University of California.

Reagan, Ronald. 1987. *Public Papers of the Presidents of the United States*. Washington, D.C.: U.S. Government Printing Office.

Rehnquist, William H. 2004. *Centennial Crisis: The Disputed Election of 1876*. New York: Knopf.

Roberts, Robert North, and Scott John Hammond. 2004. *Encyclopedia of Presidential Campaigns, Slogans, Issues, and Platforms*. Westport, Conn.: Greenwood Press.

Rosenstone, Steven J. 1983. *Forecasting Presidential Elections*. New Haven, Conn.: Yale University Press.

Rousseeuw, Peter J. 1984. "Least Median Squares Regression." *Journal of American Statistical Association* 79:871–80.

Rousseeuw, Peter J., and Annick M. Leroy. 1987. *Robust Regression and Outlier Detection*. New York: Wiley.

Scammon, Richard M., and Ben J. Wattenberg. 1970. *The Real Majority*. New York: Coward, McCann & Geoghegan.

Scher, Richard K. 1997. *The Modern Political Campaign*. Armonk, N.Y.: M. E. Sharpe.

Severn, Bill. 1968. *Samuel J. Tilden and the Stolen Election*. New York: Ives Washburn.

Shafer, Byron, et al. 1991. *The End of Realignment?* Madison: University of Wisconsin Press.

Shanks, J. Merrill, and Warren E. Miller. 1991. "Partisanship, Policy and Performance: The Reagan Legacy in the 1988 Election." *British Journal of Political Science* 21:129–97.

Shaw, Daron R. 1998. "A Study of Presidential Campaign Event Effects from 1952 to 1992." Manuscript.

———. 1999. "The Effect of TV Ads and Candidate Appearances on Statewide Presidential Votes, 1988–96." *American Political Science Review* 93:345–61.

Shaw, Daron R., and Brian E. Roberts. 2000. "Campaign Events, the Media and

Prospects of Victory: The 1992 and 1996 U.S. Presidential Elections." *British Journal of Political Science* 30:259–89.

Shea, Daniel M. 1999. "The Passing of Realignment and the Advent of the 'Base-less' Party System." *American Politics Quarterly* 27:33–57.

Shelley, Mack C., II, and Hwarng-Du Hwang. 1991. "The Mass Media and Public Opinion Polls in the 1988 Presidential Election: Trends, Accuracy, Consistency, and Events." *American Politics Quarterly* 19:80–95.

Sigelman, Lee. 1979. "Presidential Popularity and Presidential Elections." *Public Opinion Quarterly* 43:532–34.

Sigelman, Lee, and David Bullock. 1991. "Candidates, Issues, Horse Races, and Hoopla." *American Politics Quarterly* 19:5–32.

Silbey, John H. 1998. "'From Essential to the Existence of Our Institutions' to 'Rapacious Enemies of Honest and Responsible Government': The Rise and Fall of American Political Parties, 1790–2000." Pp. 3–19 in *The Parties Respond*. 3rd ed., ed. L. Sandy Maisel. Boulder, Colo.: Westview Press.

Simon, Herbert A. 1954. "Bandwagon and Underdog Effects and the Possibility of Election Predictions." *Public Opinion Quarterly* 18:245–53.

Smith, Eric R. A. N. 1989. *The Unchanging American Voter.* Berkeley: University of California Press.

Smith, Paul A. 1986. "Electoral Campaigns." Pp. 65–98 in *Research in Micropolitics.* Vol. 1, ed. Samuel Long. Greenwich, Conn.: JAI Press.

Smith, Tom W. 1990. "Liberal and Conservative Trends in the United States since World War II." *Public Opinion Quarterly* 54:479–507.

Southwell, Priscilla L. 1986. "The Politics of Disgruntlement: Nonvoting and Defection among Supporters of Nomination Losers, 1968–1984." *Political Behavior* 8:81–95.

Stanley, Harold W. 1988. "Southern Partisan Changes: Dealignment, Realignment, or Both?" *Journal of Politics* 50:64–88.

Stimson, James A. 1991. *Public Opinion in America.* Boulder, Colo.: Westview Press.

———. 2004. *Tides of Consent.* New York: Cambridge University Press.

Stokes, Donald E. 1966. "Some Dynamic Elements of Contests for the Presidency." *American Political Science Review* 60:19–28.

Stone, Walter J. 1986. "The Carryover Effect in Presidential Elections." *American Political Science Review* 80:271–80.

Stone, Walter J., Lonna Rae Atkeson, and Ronald Rapoport. 1992. "Turning On and Turning Off? Mobilization and Demobilization Effects of Presidential Nomination Campaigns." *American Journal of Political Science* 36:665–91.

Sundquist, James L., and Richard M. Scammon. 1981. "The 1980 Election: Profile and Historical Perspective." Pp. 19–44 in *A Tide of Discontent,* ed. Ellis Sandoz and Cecil V. Crabb, Jr. Washington, D.C.: CQ Press.

Tenpas, Kathryn Dunn. 2003. *Presidents as Candidates: Inside the White House for the President's Campaign.* New York: Routledge.

Tetlock, Philip E. 2005. *Expert Political Judgment.* Princeton, N.J.: Princeton University Press.

Troy, Gil. 1996. *See How They Ran.* Rev. and exp. ed. Cambridge, Mass.: Harvard University Press.

Tufte, Edward R. 1978. *Political Control of the Economy.* Princeton, N.J.: Princeton University Press.

U.S. Department of Commerce, Bureau of Business Economics. 1960, 1964, 1968. *Survey of Current Business* (July).

U.S. Department of Commerce, Bureau of Economic Analysis. 1989. *The National Income and Product Accounts of the United States.* Vols. 1 and 2. Washington, D.C.: U.S. Government Printing Office.

———. 1972, 1976, 1980, 1988, 1992. *Survey of Current Business* (July and August).

Wattenberg, Martin P. 1984. "And Tyler, Too." *Public Opinion* (April/May): 52–54.

———. 1990. "From a Partisan to a Candidate-centered Electorate." Pp. 139–74 in *The New American Political System.* 2nd ed., ed. Anthony King. Washington, D.C.: AEI Press.

———. 1991. *The Rise of Candidate-Centered Politics.* Cambridge, Mass.: Harvard University Press.

———. 1996. *The Decline of American Political Parties.* Cambridge, Mass.: Harvard University Press.

Wayne, Stephen J. 1997. *Road to the White House, 1996: The Politics of Presidential Elections.* Postelection ed. New York: St. Martin's Press.

White, Theodore H. 1961. *The Making of the President 1960.* New York: Atheneum.

———. 1965. *The Making of the President 1964.* New York: Atheneum.

———. 1969. *The Making of the President 1968.* New York: Atheneum.

———. 1973. *The Making of the President 1972.* New York: Bantam Books.

———. 1982. *America in Search of Itself.* New York: Harper and Row.

Wilson, James Q. 1960. *The Amateur Democrat.* Chicago: University of Chicago Press.

Wlezien, Christopher, and Robert S. Erikson. 1996. "Temporal Horizons and Presidential Election Forecasts." *American Politics Quarterly* 24:492–505.

———. 2002. "The Timeline of Presidential Election Campaigns." *Journal of Politics* 64:969–93.

Woodward, Bob. 1996. *The Choice.* New York: Simon and Schuster.

Zaller, John R. 1992. *The Nature and Origins of Mass Opinion.* Cambridge: Cambridge University Press.

Index

Atkeson, Lonna Rae, 259n15
Atlantic City, N.J., as site of the 1964 Democratic Party convention, 124
attitude change, 10. *See* stability of individual vote intention or vote choice
Axelrod, Robert, 250n11

"Back to Normalcy," 1920 Harding campaign slogan, 262n30
Bain, Richard C., 152
balanced budget amendment, as a campaign issue, 89
bandwagon effect, 46, 241n17
Bartels, Larry M., 41, 238n5, 245n16, 247n29, 258n12
Bean, Louis H., 248n1
Before the Vote, xvi
Bentsen, Lloyd M. Jr., 144, 267n4
Berelson, Bernard B., 234n4, 234n6
Berra, Yogi, 45
Biden, Joseph (Joe), 206
big government, as a campaign issue, 68
Blaine, James G., 176, 177, 178, 179, 185, 187, 260n21, 274n12, 274n13
Boller, Paul F. Jr., xxi, 233–34n2
Booth, Willis, 272n6
bounded the national vote, 79
Bradley, Bill, 69, 71
Bradley, Joseph P., 272n8
Broder, David S., 215
Brookings Review, xvi
Brownback, Sam, 207
Bruno, Jerry, 257n9
Bryan, William Jennings, 169, 170, 171, 255n2, 271n3, 277n10
Bryce, James, 241n17
Buchanan, Patrick J., 69, 70, 240n11
budget deficits, as a campaign issue, 68, 70
Bull Moose Progressive Party. *See* Progressive Party; Roosevelt, Theodore
Burchard, Samuel D., 179, 185, 273n11
Burnham, Walter Dean, 215
Bush, George, H. W. 15, 34, 40, 41, 45, 61, 67, 68–70, 74, 93, 97, 103, 104, 115, 123, 126, 140, 141, 144, 146, 157, 164, 170, 240n11, 246n26, 247n28, 250n8, 254n25, 255n1, 260n18, 266n3, 266–67n4, 269n16, 270n20

Bush, George W., 15, 50, 56, 61, 71–73, 75, 93, 96, 100, 103, 115, 153, 156, 157, 161, 163, 173, 180, 184, 185, 192, 206, 208, 209, 210, 211, 232, 233n1, 236n15, 240n11, 255n1

California: 96; in the election of 1892, 271n1; in the election of 1916, 172, 173, 187, 271–72n4, 272n5, 272n6; gubernatorial election in 1962, 65, 182; home-state advantage in, 276n7; primary in 1968, 65
campaign, presidential: as a chess match, 184; as communication process, 50; as a debate, 12; definition of, xix, xxi, xxii, 49, 50, 51, 241–42n1, 242n2, 244n15, 246n15; denigration of, xx, 4, 201, 202; doubts about the impact of, xx, 5–21, 58, 189; and governing, 119; length of (perpetual campaign), 3, 4, 50, 201, 242n2; resources in, 42, 43
campaign effects: xvi, xix, 23, 43, 49, 52, 54, 57, 58, 238n2; constraints on (limits to), xix, 21, 24, 26, 28, 29, 36, 37, 47, 48, 49, 75, 76, 79, 80, 102, 196, 197, 240–41n14; healing of internal party divisions, 42, 144, 145, 150, 158, 163, 170, 198, 202, 277n12 (*see also* reinforcement effect of campaign, of partisanship; restoration of partisanship by the campaign); journalistic perception of, xx, 184, 185, 189, 190; localized, 25, 55, 56, 57, 58, 127, 194–96, 265n13, 276n6; measurement of, 75–78, 192–94, 242n6, 244n15, 246n27, 248n31; mobilization of voters, 4, 50, 51, 144, 184, 196, 197, 198, 261n26; polarizing effect of, 145, 267n5; political science perception of, xx, xxi, 189, 234n3; size of, xix, xx, xxi, 4, 5, 6, 7, 9, 12, 13, 23, 49, 52, 154, 155, 173, 186, 189, 190, 191, 192, 193, 194, 196, 199, 234n3, 244–45n16, 247n28, 248–49n30, 248n31, 276n2, 275n21; systematic nature of (predictability of), xix, xx, 21, 23, 26, 27, 28, 37, 38, 47, 48, 49, 54, 55, 57, 58, 75, 76, 78, 101, 102, 128, 142, 143, 157, 165, 187, 190, 191, 194, 195, 196, 199,

Clinton, William (Bill) Jefferson, 15, 27, 50, 61, 70, 71, 72, 86, 87, 93, 96, 97, 103, 114, 115, 121, 123, 124, 125, 128, 137, 140, 146, 152, 157, 164, 170, 181, 206, 240n11, 243n8, 250n8, 251n14, 254n25, 255n1, 261n26, 261n28, 261n29, 266n1, 266n2, 269n16, 271n16, 273n24

close contest elections, 166, 170–73, 186, 187, 271n2

closeness of presidential elections, 24, 25, 63, 71, 74, 75, 79, 83, 106, 109, 110, 165, 166–88, 191, 201, 202, 203, 208, 210, 248n1, 271n2, 272n6, 274n17, 276n3

CNN (Cable News Network), xviii

cognitive consistency, 98. *See also* rationalization of voters

Committee to Re-elect the President, 121

communist subversion, as a campaign issue, 63, 240n9

compassionate conservatism, as Bush 2000 campaign theme, 72

competence (capabilities) of presidential candidates, 26, 36, 44, 69, 74. *See also* candidates, presidential, assessment by voters of; leadership abilities of candidate

competitiveness effect of presidential campaigns. *See* narrowing effect of presidential campaigns

Compuwork, 241n16

Confederacy, 177, 273n11

conflict, political, public distaste for, 113, 122, 248–49n3, 258n13. *See also* apolitical streak in American political culture; purist orientation toward politics

confusion of voters, 97, 251–52n15

Congressional Quarterly, 116, 271n4, 272n6, 274n18

Conkling, Roscoe, 176

Connecticut, in the election of 1884, 274n13

consequences of elections and campaigns for governing, 4, 25, 34, 203

conservatives, 30, 33, 62, 64, 65, 67, 68, 70, 72, 73, 86, 87, 98, 156, 172, 183, 184, 207, 211, 238n4, 251n14, 251n15, 252n16, 252n17

consistency of voting cues, 97, 98, 239n9, 252n17, 254n25, 254n26

continuity: of candidates over time, 79, 89, 93; of electoral politics over time, 79, 86, 101, 112; of ideology and party association over time, 86; of issues over time, 79, 89

convention, the national nominating, of the political parties, 6, 7, 16, 29, 51, 65, 72, 80, 92, 110, 116, 117, 150, 151, 153, 154, 171, 205; Democratic Party convention of 1920, 168; Democratic Party convention of 1968, 65, 152, 183, 266n2; Democratic Party convention of 1972, 152, 266n2; Democratic Party convention of 1992, 266n1; Democratic Party convention of 2004, 152; lack of deliberation in, 51, 201, 202; multiple ballots for nomination cast in, 51, 116–17, 168, 171, 172, 176, 177, 178, 179, 202, 260n19, 260n21; order of, 51; presentation of the nominee as a function of, 150; as rallies for the general election campaign, 150, 266n1; and the selection of the party's vice presidential candidate, 150, 266n3

convention bumps (effects), xv, xvi, xxii, 150–54, 155, 162, 244n11, 269n13, 269n17; in the election of 1968, 152; in the election of 1972, 152, 153; in the election of 1988, 247n28; in the election of 2004, 153; for frontrunning and trailing candidates, 153, 154; for incumbents, 152; and the narrowing effect of campaigns, 147, 150, 157; net effect on the election, 154, 244n11; temporary or lasting effect, 150, 153, 154, 244n11, 244n12, 269n17; and vice presidential selection, 266n3

Converse, Philip E., 9, 10, 235n11, 235n12, 235–36n14, 277n1

Conversion effect of campaign, 50, 51, 59, 197, 234n6, 234n7

Cook County (Ill.) Democratic Party machine, in the election of 1960, 64, 181, 274n16

Coolidge, Calvin, 168, 237n20, 257n10

"correct votes," 238–39n5

correcting survey data: National Election Study data to reflect the actual vote, 31, 59–61, 98, 161, 216, 224, 225, 227–32, 239n7, 250n8, 274n14; Gallup data, 246–47n27

corruption in government, as a campaign issue, 63, 66

creation effect of campaign, 50

Crespi, Irving, 240n13

crime: as a campaign issue, 39, 69, 89, 123; as a valence issue, 253n21

cross-currents in presidential campaigns, 29, 57, 165, 189

cross-pressures, effects of on potential voters, 83, 97, 98, 253n23, 254n26, 259n15, 268–69n6

crystallizers, 234n5

Cuomo, Mario M., 68, 69, 266n1

cynicism of public toward politics, 38, 112, 126, 127, 236n15

"daisy" ad, 1964 Johnson campaign ad, 240n9

Daley, Richard J., 152

Davis, David, 272n8

Davis, John, W., 168

dealignment (decline), of political parties, xxii, 24, 31, 33, 81, 182, 215, 216, 222, 277n2

Dean, Howard, 73, 206, 208

death penalty, as a campaign issue, 69

debate, effect of presidential, xxi, xxii, 53, 54, 72, 157, 244n13, 270n20, 270n21; in 1960 campaign, 63, 181, 182, 192, 270n21, 274n17; in 1976 campaign, 183, 184, 185, 269–70n19, 270n20; in 1980 campaign, 156, 244n13, 261n25; in 1984 campaign, 54, 244n13; in 1988 campaign, 69, 244n13; in 1992 campaign, 244n13, 261n28; in 2000 campaign, 181; and narrowing effect of campaigns, 157, 270n21; temporary or lasting effect, 54, 244n13; vice presidential 54, 244n13

decisiveness of campaign effects, 185–88, 189, 191, 192, 196

Decline of American Political Parties, 215

Demobilization effect: of campaign, xx, 4, 50, 51, 54; of nomination contest, 259n15

Democratic Party, 5, 9, 31, 33, 39, 45, 51, 56, 63, 72, 73, 84, 89, 121, 177, 179, 181, 185, 205, 208, 234n5, 246n21, 250n7, 250n8, 250n9, 250n10, 250n12, 252n17, 260n18, 261n26, 272n8, 278n7; candidates of, 5, 9, 27, 29, 30, 55, 59, 62, 79, 82, 85, 87, 92, 93, 97, 98, 136, 137, 144, 166–69, 206, 207, 209, 210, 211, 227–32, 233n1, 237n19, 238–39n5, 239–40n9, 252n16, 271n3, 273n10, 277n10; coalition, 33, 182; conventions of, 65, 151, 152, 153, 168, 180, 183, 205, 247n28, 266n1, 266n2; delegate selection reforms of, 126, 246n21; and electoral commission of 1876, 177, 272n8, 272n9; identifiers with, 24, 71, 72, 81, 82, 83, 84, 97, 98, 100, 119, 136, 144, 156, 159, 169, 182, 183, 198, 213–25, 227–32, 239n8, 251n13, 252n16, 254n26; internal divisions of, 33, 62, 83, 170, 171, 182, 208; loyalty of identifiers with, 83, 84, 85, 86, 100, 144, 198, 217–21, 227–32, 250n8, 250n10, 250n12, 251n13; nomination campaigns of, 63, 67, 68, 69, 125, 242n3; and party system, 56, 171, 216, 221–25, 249n5, 250n12, 278n7; policy positions of, 89–91, 252n17; political machine of, 177, 274n16; two-thirds rule for nomination by, 202, 260n19. *See also* southern Democrats

democratic theory, 30, 119, 203

Depression, the Great, 109, 168, 169

desegregation, as a campaign issue, 252n17

deviating election, 9, 10

Dewey, Thomas E., 61, 62, 123, 170, 187, 192, 277n10

Dirty Harry (movie character), 69

disaffected (disgruntled) partisans, 144, 158, 203, 254n26, 259n15, 267–68n6, 270n21

disaster relief, 39

distribution of the vote, 185, 195

District of Columbia: in the election of 1972, 66, 169; in the election of 1984, 68, 169

INDEX • 297

dissonance reduction, 37, 98

divided (divisive) nomination contests, 27, 38, 40, 42, 50, 64, 65, 67, 114–19, 126, 150, 170, 171, 176, 177, 183, 197, 198, 202, 203, 240n11, 256n4, 258n14, 259n15, 259n15, 259n16, 260n22, 266n2. *See also* internal party divisions

divisive primaries, 115, 258n14

Dixiecrats, 62, 65, 170

Do Campaigns Matter?, xvi, xxi

Dodd, Christopher, 206

Dole, Bob, 27, 68, 70, 71, 87, 93, 144, 146, 157, 170, 243n8, 246n23, 266–67n4

Donaldson, Sam, 126

"don't change horses in the middle of the stream," campaign theme, 39, 108

"Don't Stop Thinking About Tomorrow," 124

Drew, Elizabeth, 261n25, 261n27

Dukakis, Michael S., 57, 68, 69, 96, 113, 144, 157, 165, 170, 241n14, 247n28, 266n2

early deciders of vote choice, xv, xix, 7–9, 23, 26, 27–31, 33, 34–38, 48, 59, 79–81, 86–88, 91, 92, 97–102, 117, 118, 129, 147, 156, 158–64, 182, 183, 187, 190, 192, 196, 198, 227–32, 234n8, 234–35n9, 235n10, 248n2, 253n22, 254n25, 254n28, 254n29, 256n6, 269n13, 269n15, 270n20, 270–71n22, 271n23

ease of vote choice, 30–33, 35, 36, 80, 86, 87, 197, 200, 252n16

Eastern Europe debate gaffe by Ford, 113, 165, 183–85, 270n20, 274–75n19, 275n20

East Feliciana, Parish in Louisiana, 273n10

Eastwood, Clint, (actor) 69

economic conditions, 22, 25, 27, 31, 40, 41, 56, 57, 63, 64, 67, 70–72, 74, 88, 91, 101, 102, 120, 126, 128–42, 180, 261n28, 262n29, 262n1, 262n2, 262n3, 265n12, 275n20; assigning responsibility for, 41, 130, 135, 136, 139, 140, 262n2, 264n8, 265n11; before the election year, 27, 56, 129, 134–37, 265n10; in election year, xix, xx, xxi,

13, 14, 15, 19–24, 27, 37, 38, 40, 41, 48, 54, 56, 62, 74, 102, 103, 108, 114, 129, 130, 134, 143, 154, 156, 165, 180, 181, 182, 183, 190–95, 197, 202, 209, 234n3, 236n17, 237n18, 237n19, 247n30, 255n3, 256n4, 257n8, 258n14, 263n6, 263n7, 268n12, 269n17, 276n5, 277n9; and the Great Depression, 109, 168, 169; indirect effects of news about, 136, 139; lag in voters reaction to, 41, 135, 137, 156, 264n9; limited effects of, 133; measures of used in election forecasting, 130, 185, 263n5; and panic of 1873, 177; perceptions of, 136, 264n8, 265n11, 265n12; public expectations of, 131, 265n12; recession in the early 1980s, 67, 92; relative impact in election forecasting models, 263n5, 263n6; spillover effect of, 133, 265n11; state and regional, 57, 195. *See also* prospective evaluations of the economy; retrospective evaluations

economic policies: as a campaign issue, 22, 70, 92, 115, 119; effects of, 130, 134, 139

Economics and Elections, 135

economic voting, 135; causal model of, 135; cross-national analysis of, 135, 264n8; theory of, 135–37, 264n8

education as a campaign issue, 89, 253n21

education of voters by campaign, 4

Edwards, John, 206, 233n1, 267n4

Ehrenhalt, Alan, 274n18

Eisenhower, Dwight D., xv, 15, 22, 56, 62, 63, 75, 86, 96, 109, 115, 132, 137, 156, 157, 163, 168, 181, 209, 246n26, 255n1, 256n6, 266n3, 275n21, 277n10

efficacy, of potential voters, 203

election, presidential: of 1796, 277n10; of 1800, 277n10; of 1824, 61, 277n10; of 1832, 277n10; of 1844, 277n10; of 1864, 171; of 1868, xxii, 171, 209, 255n1, 271n2, 273n10; of 1872, 186, 187, 255n1, 273n10; of 1876, 71, 173, 176–80, 192, 273n10; of 1880, 178, 179, 257n10; of 1884, 170, 178–80, 185, 187, 255n1, 257n10, 260n21, 273n11; of 1888, 71, 170, 173, 179, 180, 255n1, 271n1; of

Elections and the Political Order, 9, 10
electoral college, 198; critical vote analysis, 172, 271n2; disputed votes in, 177, 178, 272n8; vote's association to popular votes, 166; votes of, 57, 61, 166, 172, 173, 177–79, 181, 183, 184, 194, 196, 258n14, 271n1, 271n2, 271n4, 272n5, 272n7, 272n8
electability of nominee, 126, 208
electoral commission for election of 1876, 177, 178, 272n7, 272n8, 272n9, 273n10
enlightening of voters by the campaign, 145, 197
enthusiasm, about the candidate choice, 115, 201, 253n23. *See also* cross-pressures, effects of on potential voters
environment as a campaign issue, 13, 89
equilibrium theory of campaigns, xvi, xxii, 237n1, 244–45n16, 245n17
Erikson, Robert S., 145, 147, 237n19, 263n5, 265n10, 277n1
Erie County, Ohio, 5
experience: of incumbent as candidate, 113–14; of incumbents valued by voters, 122; voters gaining information through everyday, 30, 35, 41, 96, 130, 136, 137, 140, 141, 236n15, 277n1. *See also* information, political, short-cuts

Fair, Ray C., 256n4, 263n5
Fairbanks, Charles W., 172
Farley, James A., xxi, 5, 240n9, 260n20
Farley's Law, 5
"favorite son" candidacies. *See* home-state (or region) advantage
"feeling thermometer" survey questions, 257n11, 266–67n4
Feingold, Russ, 233n1
Ferraro, Geraldine A., 266n3, 267n4
financing presidential campaigns, 21, 27, 43, 112, 121, 201, 202, 205, 206, 261n26. *See also* soft money
Finkel, Steven E., 12, 233n2, 247n29
fireside chats of F. Roosevelt, 245n20
fiscal policy, as a campaign issue, 119
flag, respect for: as an issue, 69

Fleetwood Mac, 124
Florida: Election Canvassing Commission, 180; in the election of 1876, 177, 178, 272n7, 273n10; in the election of 2000, 72, 180, 185; State Supreme Court, 72, 180
focus group tested campaigning, 190
"For a Change," 1980 Reagan campaign slogan, 123
Forbes, Steve, 70
Ford, Gerald R. Jr., 15, 66, 67, 75, 96, 103, 109, 111, 113, 115, 126, 146, 157, 165, 180, 183, 184, 185, 232, 240n11, 242n3, 246n25, 270n20, 274n18, 274–75n19, 275n20
forecasting elections (forecasting election models), xv, xvi, xxi, 5, 13, 21, 23, 58, 76, 101, 103, 106, 108, 130, 133, 134, 137, 147, 154, 161, 173, 185, 187, 189, 196, 197, 234n3, 236n16, 236n17, 237n19, 237n1, 244–45n16, 247n28, 248n1, 256n4, 258n14, 262n3, 262–63n4, 263n5, 263n6, 264n9, 265–66n13, 268n12, 275n20, 276n5; critics of, xvi, 236n16; errors in, 237–38n1
foreign policy as a campaign issue, 67, 88, 101, 123, 170, 235n11. *See also* peace or war, the nation at
"forgotten handshake" in election of 1916, 172, 173, 187, 272n6
framing effects, 24
front-end loading of nomination system, 69, 70, 127, 202, 246n21
front porch campaigning, 190
frontrunner candidate (in preference polls): clear (unambiguous), 74, 161, 162, 192, 232, 269–70n19; in general election campaign, xx, xxii, 15, 21, 25, 27, 29, 41, 42, 44, 46, 75, 80, 109, 142, 143, 145, 146, 149, 150, 152, 156, 157–63, 191, 192, 194, 199, 210, 233n1, 240n13, 248n2, 256n6, 267n6, 269n13, 269n16, 270n21, 276n2; for nomination, 70, 73, 127, 206, 246n21; softness of support for, 266n6; strategy of, 145, 163
fundamentals of campaign context, xix, xxi, xxii, 10, 21, 23, 27, 56, 57, 58, 76, 79, 165, 181, 187, 188, 190, 191, 194,

liberals, 33, 62, 66, 68, 72, 86, 87, 98, 184, 206, 207, 211, 238n4, 238–39n5, 251n14, 251n15, 252n16, 252n17

Lichtman, Allan J., 256n4

Lieberman, Joseph, 71, 267n4

Light, Paul C., 240n10

"likes and dislikes" survey questions, 239n6, 261n24

Lincoln, Abraham, 124, 171, 177, 272n8

Lincoln Bedroom of the White House, use of for campaign fundraising, 121, 261n26

lock on presidential election by a political party, 24, 82, 83, 84, 86

Lodge, Henry Cabot, 266n3

Long Beach hotel, in the 1916 election, 173

long-term forces on the vote, 43, 80, 86; long-term component of short-term forces, 88–97. *See also* ideology, political; party identification; party loyalty in presidential voting

Los Angeles, 65

Louisiana, in the election of 1876, 177, 272n7, 273n10

low information rationality, 239n6. *See* information short-cuts

"Lust in my heart," 1976 campaign gaffe by Carter, 113

"L-word" in the 1984 campaign, 68

Luskin, Robert, 238–39n5

McAdoo, William G., 169

McCain, John, 71, 207, 233n1

McCarthy, Eugene J., 64, 65, 183

McClure, Robert D., xv, 233n2, 235n13

McGovern, George S., 65, 66, 86, 96, 148, 153, 157, 159, 160, 169, 256n6, 257–58n11, 261n24

McGovern-Fraser Delegate Selection Reform Commission, 126, 152, 246n21

McKenzie, G. Calvin, 125

McKinley, William Jr., 124, 169, 171, 255n1, 271n3, 277n10

MacKuen, Michael B., 253n23

macro-level analysis, xvi, xxi, 216

macropartisanship, 82, 83, 86, 224, 225, 249n4, 249n5, 277n1

mafia, in the 1960 election, 274n16

Mahar, Michael, 241n15

Making of the President, The, xxi; 1960, 123

mandate, presidential, 67, 262n29

manipulation of voters by the campaign, 4, 91

Mann, Thomas E., xvi

Marcus, George E., 253n23

Maryland, in the election of 1916, 272n5

Massachusetts, in the election of 1972, 66, 272n5

Mass Media Election, The, xv

Mean streak, perception of candidate having a, 122, 260n17

measurement error (in surveys), 234n6, 242n6, 244n12, 244–45n16, 246n27, 249n6, 251–52n15

media (press), role in campaign, xxii, 21, 25–27, 42–44, 50, 57, 61, 93, 97, 120, 126, 127, 139, 143, 146, 196, 198, 200, 215, 235n13, 241–42n1, 245n17, 252n19; adversarial role of, 44, 126

median voter, 30, 87, 114

Memphis, site of King assassination, 65

Miami, site of the 1968 Republican Party convention, 65

Michigan, in the election of 1960, 63, 64

micro-level analysis, xvi, xxi

midterm elections, 35, 258n14; of 1934, 245n20; of 1994, 70, 14; of 2006, 205, 206, 208

Miller, Warren E., 235n11, 267n5, 277–78n3

Miller, William E., 93

minimal effects conundrum, xx, 5, 10–12, 21, 26, 36, 37, 98, 189, 191, 192, 196, 197, 235n11, 235n13, 239n9; campaign message version of, 37; causal model of, 11. *See also* campaign effects, constraints on, and interest, political

minimum wage, as a campaign issue, 89

minority party, 10

Minnesota, in the 1984 election, 68, 169

Mirer, Thad W., 239n6

misery index, 92

Mississippi: in the election of 1868, 171

Missouri, in the election of 1916, 272n5

mobilizing effect of the campaign, xx, 4, 50, 51, 144, 184, 196–98, 249n4, 261n26; of nomination contest, 259n15

Pearl Harbor, 73
Peirce, Neal R., 271n4
Pentagon, The, and the 9/11 terrorist attack, 73
People's Choice, The, 5, 7, 197, 234n8, 275n1
performance of the incumbent. *See* approval of president's job performance; record, of the candidates
Perot, H. Ross, 69–71, 74, 83, 104, 122, 123, 164, 230, 243n8, 250n8, 260n18, 268n10, 268n11, 271n23
Persian Gulf War, 69, 73
personal finances of voters, 135, 141, 264n8
Pinckney, Charles, 277n10
Poland, and Ford gaffe in 1976 campaign, 113
Polarization of the electorate, 72, 73, 145, 180, 184, 206, 208, 209, 267n5
polarizing effect of campaign, 145, 267n5
political advertisements on television, 96, 123, 235n13
Political Control of the Economy, 128
political parties (the two major), 23, 50, 51, 79, 115, 202, 235n11, 253n21, 278n4; dependability (stability) of issue differences between, 13, 88, 89, 203, 252n19; issue differences between, 13, 30, 89, 184, 198, 202, 203, 211, 252n19; platforms of, 144, 266n2. *See also* internal party divisions; party identification; party loyalty in presidential voting
political science perception of campaign effects, xx, xxi, 189, 234n3
"politics as usual" (versus third-party politics), 122
polls, errors in, 31, 53, 59–61, 98, 147, 161, 216, 224, 233n1, 234n6, 242n5, 243n8, 243n9, 246n27. *See* correcting survey data
Polling Report.com, 233n1
Polsby, Nelson W., 233n2
Pomper, Gerald M., xxi, 67, 268n9, 268n10
Popkin, Samuel L., 30, 35, 91, 233n2, 239n6
Populist Party, 171, 271n1

populists, 169, 171
position issues, 252–53n20
positive carryover effect of a nomination contest, 259n15
positivity bias of voters, 39, 112, 113, 122, 127, 257n11
Potter, Clarkson N., 273n10
Potter Investigation (House) Committee into the 1876 presidential election, 273n10
poverty, as a campaign issue, 253n21
predictability of the national vote. *See* forecasting elections
pre-campaign context. *See* fundamentals of campaign context
preference (trial-heat) polls, xxi, 15–20, 22, 49, 52, 54, 58, 59, 67, 68, 70, 73, 75, 79, 80, 106, 130, 133, 135, 137, 141, 146, 150, 152, 154, 156, 157, 158, 161, 164, 180, 181, 183, 184, 187, 194, 200, 210, 233n1, 234n5, 237n1, 237n19, 239n19, 240n13, 241n17, 241–42n1, 242n5, 242n6, 242–43n7, 243n8, 243n10, 244n15, 245n18, 246n24, 246n27, 247n30, 248n31, 255n3, 263n5, 264n9, 265n10, 267n6, 268n8, 268n9, 268n11, 268n12, 268–69n13, 269n18, 269n19, 274–75n19, 275n20, 277n9; summer, 70, 147–50, 155, 157, 162, 210, 246n12, 268–69n13; fall, 154–57, 162, 268–69n13; temporary or lasting changes in, 23, 53, 150, 153, 154, 243n9, 244n12; volatility in, 53, 147, 150, 154, 157, 210, 235n12, 242n6, 243n10, 269n13. *See also* convention bumps, temporary or lasting effect; debate, effect of presidential, temporary or lasting effect
Presbyterian minister of 1884 campaign gaffe. *See* Burchard, Samuel D.
president as world leader, 114
Presidential Campaign 1976, The, 274–75n19
presidential coattails, 4, 250n11
presidential-congressional relations, 119
presidential primaries, 40, 46, 65, 66, 69, 70, 89, 93, 125, 126, 127, 202, 205, 246n21, 259n17, 269n14; vote in as indicator of party unity, 258n14

243n10, 270n21, 277n9. *See also* reinforcement effect of campaign, of partisanship

Restoration view of partisanship, 214, 215, 216

retrospective evaluations, 5, 13, 21, 26, 72, 92, 97, 102, 122, 124, 135, 136, 196, 236n15, 245n20, 253n24, 262n1, 264n8, 265n12

revisionist view of partisanship, 214, 215

revitalization of partisanship. *See* reinforcement effect of campaign, of partisanship; restoration of partisanship by the campaign

Ribicoff, Abraham I., 152

Rice, Tom W., xv, 236n17, 258n14, 266n3

Richards, Ann, 69

Richardson, William (Bill), 206

Rivers, Douglas, 242n1

Roberts, Brian E., 242n6

Robertson, Pat, 68

Rockefeller, Nelson A., 65

Rohde, David W., xxi, 156, 191, 215, 233n2, 253n24, 261n27, 268n10

Romney, Mitt, 207, 233n1

Roosevelt, Franklin D., xxi, 5, 6, 62, 67, 70, 109, 122, 124, 126, 169, 170, 234n6, 234n7, 237n20, 245n20, 255n1, 257n10, 260n20, 275n1, 277n10

Roosevelt, Theodore, 56, 67, 104, 168, 171, 172, 237n20, 246n22, 260n18, 272n6

Roper, Burns, 240n13

Roper Center for Public Opinion Research, 251n15

Roper Poll, 274n17

Rose Garden strategy, 24, 38, 120–21, 237n21

Rosenstone, Steven J., 266n3, 276n7

"Rum, Romanism, and Rebellion," 1884 campaign gaffe harming Blaine's candidacy, 179, 185, 187, 273n11, 274n12

Russell, Richard B., 63

Scammon, Richard M., 89, 123

scandals, 86, 101, 103, 140, 176, 177, 179, 181, 183, 206

second-term advantage, 104–10, 125

second chance nominations, 199

September 11, 2001 terrorist attack, 72, 100, 153, 184, 207

Seymour, Horatio, 171, 271n2

Shanks, J. Merrill, 267n5, 277–78n3

Shaw, Daron R., 52, 241n1, 242n6, 243n10, 244n11

Sherman, John, 178, 179

short-term forces on the vote, 9, 13, 43, 80, 81, 88, 225, 249n6, 277n1; long-term component of short-term forces, 88–97, 252n18. *See also* economic voting; issue voting

show-business techniques, use in campaigns of, 201, 202

Shriver, Robert Sargent Jr., 266–67n4

Sigelman, Lee, 236n17

Silbey, Joel H., 215

"Simple Act of Voting, The," 239n6

Smith, Al, 168, 169, 273n10

social issues, 88, 207

soft money (distinction of campaign finance regulations), 261n26

sophistication, of the electorate, 35, 87, 238n4

South Carolina, in the election of 1876, 177, 178, 272n7, 273n10

South Dakota, in the election of 1892, 271n1

Southern Democrats, 64, 65, 82, 182, 272n9, 276n7

spin doctors, 37, 98

stability (continuity) as a campaign theme, 39, 122–25, 262n30

stability in individual vote choice or intention, 5–7, 9–12, 21, 28, 30, 34, 59, 98, 112, 196, 197, 234n4, 234n5, 234n6, 235n11, 248n2, 254n28, 268n10, 270n20

stable context of campaigns, 27, 47, 78, 79–101, 102, 129, 232. *See also* early deciders of vote choice

"Stay the Course," 1988 Bush campaign slogan, 39, 124

Steeper, Frederick T., 261n24

stereotypes, use in campaigns, 239–40n9

Stevenson, Adlai E. II, xv, 51, 63, 93, 96, 137, 141, 157, 163, 168, 209, 246n26, 256n6, 258–59n14, 266n3, 277n10

Stimson, James A., 252n17, 269n17
Stokes, Donald E., 10, 235n11
Stone, Walter J., 259n15
stumping by candidates, 61, 272n6
style issues. *See* valence issues
substance of campaigns, xx, 12, 25, 37, 42, 56, 89, 200, 201. *See also* issues, public policy, in campaigns
successor candidates (of incumbent's party), 14, 15, 19, 34, 41, 118, 121, 124, 129, 140, 141, 154, 156, 173, 194, 209, 210, 236n16, 255n3, 257n8, 265–66n13, 268n12, 269n17
Sundquist, James L., 123
Super-Tuesday primaries, 69, 70, 71, 246n21
supply-side economics, 68
support for political institutions, 258n13
Survey of Current Business, 276n5
swing voters, 40, 72

Taft, Robert A., 62, 63
Taft, William Howard, 67, 109, 168, 170, 171, 237n20, 246n22, 272n6, 277n10
Taliban government in Afghanistan, 73
Tammany Hall, 177
tank ride, 1988 campaign gaffe by Dukakis, 57, 113, 165
targeting states, by candidate's campaign, 196
"tax-and-spend liberals," 68
tax policy, as a campaign issue, 13, 34, 40, 68, 69, 88, 89, 128
Teeter, Robert, 261n24
Television news, 235n13. *See also* media (press), role in campaign
terms, number of consecutive for the president's party, 13, 24, 38, 39, 62, 68, 71, 74, 104, 106–10, 118, 122–25, 208, 236n17, 255n2, 255n3, 256n4, 256n5, 263n6; link to presidential incumbency advantage, 24, 38, 118, 255n2; and party unity, 118, 208
terrorism, war on, 73, 100, 184, 207
Texas: in the election of 1868, 171; in the election of 1960, 181
Tetlock, Philip, 236n16

theory of the predictable campaign, xvi, xix, xx, xxi, 23, 25, 26–48, 59, 62, 75, 132, 136, 152, 162, 190, 197, 200, 202, 205, 207, 237n1, 245n17, 247n30
thermometer questions. *See* feeling thermometer survey questions
third-party (or independent) presidential candidates, 7, 9, 58, 65, 67, 70, 71, 74, 104, 109, 110, 122, 156, 158, 164, 170, 182, 183, 209, 210, 230, 232, 256n4, 260n18, votes for, 33, 58, 65, 70, 71, 230, 232, 250n8, 256–57n7, 271n23, 278n6; support for among late deciders, 230
third-term penalty, 15, 107, 108, 255n3, 255n4. *See also* terms, number of consecutive for the president's party; second-term advantage
Thompson, Fred, 207
Thurmond, James Strom, 62, 74, 170
Tien, Charles, 237n19
Tilden, Samuel J., 71, 177, 178, 273n10
time of vote decision, xix, 7–9, 21, 23, 25, 26, 28–31, 42, 43, 45, 48, 79, 80, 98, 99, 117, 157–62, 227–32, 234–35n9, 269n15, 270–71n22; and party loyalty, 230. *See also* early deciders of vote choice; late deciders of vote choice
time-series of polls, xxii, 52, 54, 233n1, 242–43n7, 243n9, 244n11, 244n14, 252n18, 269n17
tolerance of political differences, 258n13
trailing candidate (in preference polls), 27, 41, 43, 46, 143, 145, 150, 152, 154, 157, 158, 159, 160, 163, 199, 202, 210, 232, 233n1, 241n17, 274–75n1
trial-balloon proposals, 113
trial-heat and economy forecasting model, 19, 20, 106, 140, 173, 185, 187, 193, 236n16, 247n30, 255n3, 264n9, 275n20
trial-heat polls. *See* preference (trial-heat) polls
Troy, Gil, xxi, 5, 202, 233n2, 262n29, 272n6
Truman, Harry S., 15, 39, 61, 62, 74, 75, 157, 170, 183, 184, 187, 192, 246n25, 257n10, 277n10

OTHER BOOKS IN THE JOSEPH V. HUGHES JR. AND HOLLY O. HUGHES SERIES ON THE PRESIDENCY AND LEADERSHIP

ISBN-13: 978-1-58544-644-5
ISBN-10: 1-58544-644-0